BERKELEY
. INSIDE/OUT .

BERKELEY

. INSIDE/OUT .

A Guide to Restaurants, Entertainment,
People and Politics

Don Pitcher

History by Malcolm Margolin

HEYDAY BOOKS, BERKELEY

Cover design by Sarah Levin.

Interior design by Tracey Broderick, Kit Duane, Sarah Levin.

Published by Heyday Books, P.O. Box 9145, Berkeley, CA 94709.

ISBN: 0-930588-33-9

Printed in the United States of America.
10 9 8 7 6 5 4 3 2 1

Dedicated to Berkeley and Alaska,
two of the wildest places on this wonderful planet.

Acknowledgments

Mark Twain ended his *Huckleberry Finn* with the lament, "...if I'd a knowed what a trouble it was to make a book I wouldn't a tackled it and ain't agoing to no more. But I reckon I got to light out for the Territory ahead of the rest, because Aunt Sally she's going to adopt me and sivilize me and I can't stand it. I been there before."

There were many days during the writing of this guide when I felt the same way, and for the last several years friends of mine have watched this book grow from an exciting small project into "the book that ate Berkeley." After a while it seemed that each door I opened led into another new world of which I had no knowledge. Berkeley truly is an amazing city.

In researching this book I was helped by hundreds of people, but a few especially stand out. Malcolm Margolin, the publisher, author of the chapter on Berkeley's historical setting, pool shark, and computer novice, went far beyond the call of duty. When we first sat down to discuss the book, Malcolm warned that I would find him a bear to work with. He was right. He set high standards, forced major rewrites, and toned down my caustic remarks. But because of his guidance, *Berkeley Inside/Out* is vastly better than the 100-page romp across Berkeley that I had envisioned. I feel honored to have been able to work with someone who has such a thorough knowledge of this city and the world beyond, and who is also an accomplished writer and observer of the natural world.

This book would not exist without the generous creative assistance and financial backing of Holly Miner. She printed many of the photos in this book while eight months pregnant with twins!

The staff at Heyday Books spent far too much time on this manuscript. Kit Duane deserves special thanks for overseeing the enormous task of putting all the pieces into a coherent whole and doing the final edit. Tracey Broderick spent many days checking facts and offering feedback, as well as helping with the typesetting, editing, and design. She contributed particularly to the section on the University. Editor Sylvia Brownrig reworked my ramblings—cutting, slicing, and dicing so that the final volume wouldn't require built-in wheels. Sarah Levin brought her considerable design skills to play in both the book's cover and its interior layout. Thanks also go to Dan Duane, Dennis Dutton, Karen Gosling, Paul Strickberger, Lisa Tranter, Elizabeth Weiss, and Marianne Wyss for their help on various other aspects of this book, and to Canterbury Press for production advice and for bringing the book to its final form.

Beyond the small circle at Heyday Books, a number of people stand out for taking the time to assist me. The tolerant staff at the public library let me rifle through their extensive clipping files, and they spent many hours tracking down obscure bits of information. Anthony Bruce and Gayle Reynolds of the Berkeley Architectural Heritage Association and Ken Pettitt of the Berkeley Historical Society were of tremendous assistance in making sense of the city's rich and complex history and in supplying historical photos. Campus Archivist Bill Roberts opened the University's collection of old photographs to my eyes and allowed their publication. Becky White of the University's Community

Living Office and Mayor Loni Hancock skimmed relevant chapters of this book, offering helpful criticisms. Michael Rossman took the time to help me gather background information and stories from the 1960s. Thanks also go to two photographers—Alan Copeland (415-621-0230) and Harold Adler (415-530-1708)—who allowed use of their valuable images from that tumultous era in Berkeley's history.

I also owe a debt of thanks to the dozens of people who allowed me to take their photo ("just one more, but this time with your arms crossed..."), and to those friends—especially Holly Miner, Sheri Woo, Bill Trush, Glenn Ryburn, Marian Huber, and Dave Sutton—who offered encouragement on a project whose completion I always claimed was "just two weeks away." The historical introduction by Malcolm Margolin owes a debt of gratitude to Charles Wollenberg, Randy Milliken, Steve Sanfield, and Rina Margolin.

Despite the length of this guide and my best efforts to the contrary, there are undoubtedly certain aspects of this complex city that I have either missed or described inaccurately. In addition, places go out of business and new ones spring up all the time in Berkeley. If you have any additions, comments, complaints, or compliments about this guide, or would like to suggest changes for subsequent editions, please write me c/o Heyday Books, P.O. Box 9145, Berkeley, CA 94709.

Contents

Introduction 1

Berkeley in an Afternoon 3
Ten things to do in a brief visit.

Historical Introduction 6

Neighborhoods 40

The University 54

The People of Berkeley 86
Berkeley's population and Berkeley celebrities.

Economy and Business 102
Economic history and interesting local businesses.

Politics 117

City Government 126
Form of government, city council meetings, crime statistics
and prevention.

Touring Revolutionary Berkeley 136
Historical guide to Berkeley's 60s, with map keyed to
major events.

Religion 160

The Buildings of Berkeley 165
A Tour of Victorian Ocean View and Touring Maybeck Country,
tours of architecturally interesting buildings with keyed maps.

Arts and Entertainment 187
Museums, art galleries, theater, dance, music, movie
theaters, readings, and wall paintings.

City Parks 205

Marina 214
Adventure playground, yacht club, sailing club, parks, etc.

Regional Parks/Wildlands 222

Recreation 235
Bicycling, city recreation centers, games, gardening,
ice-skating, running, swimming, UC sports, YMCAs, and youth activities.

Restaurants and Cafes 252

Coffeehouses, Bakeries, and Sweetshops 280

Groceries and Markets 290

Nightclubs and Bars 297

Hotels and Motels 305

Community Services 313
Children's services, services for the disabled, finding work,
information services, libraries, local events, pets, radio stations,
recycling, schools, senior citizens.

Health Care 337

Finding Rental Housing 343

On the Street 347
Food, shelters, and support services.

Transportation 355
BART, buses, shuttles, railroads, and getting to and from
local airports.

Berkeley Trivia 364

Index 365

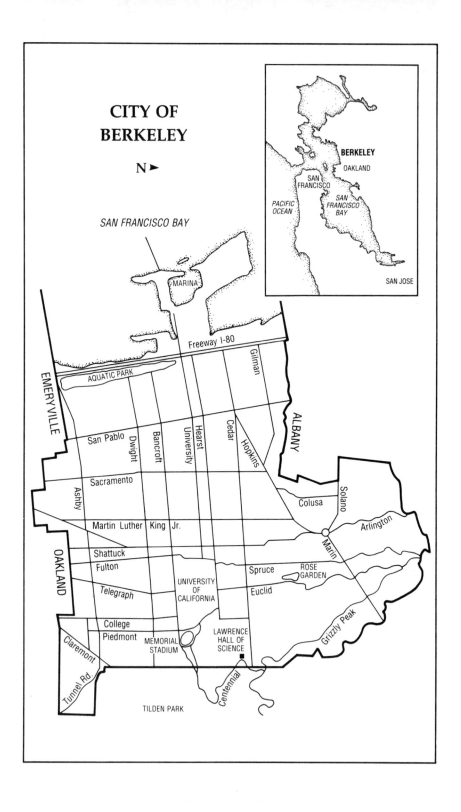

Introduction

What is this city called Berkeley? The news media view Berkeley ("Berzerkeley") with a bemused and condescending attitude. They snicker at the shenanigans of its politicians ("the only city with its own foreign policy"), rave over its restaurants ("Gourmet Ghetto"), and search out its inconsistencies. If your only knowledge of Berkeley came from the media, you might expect a city obsessed with radical ideas; its streets lined with psycho-babbling new age types; its stores stocked with nothing but sun-dried tomatoes; while Nobel Laureates wax eloquent on the extinction of the dinosaurs. The stereotypes of Berkeley do have a basis in reality, and the city does sometimes come perilously close to slipping off the edge of societal norms, but it is this proximity to chaos that keeps Berkeley so alive and creative.

Berkeley is a city of unexpected diversity. Saunter along the Berkeley pier on a fall afternoon and you'll meet Latino, Asian, white, and black families fishing for striped bass. Nearby, men dressed in deck shoes ease their sailboats from slips in the yacht harbor, and children fly kites in the Marina parks. Across the roaring freeway, factories bustle with activity and artisans build ceramic sculptures in nearby studios. Retired folks head for classes at the North Berkeley Senior Center, while teens race to make volleyball practice at Donahue Gym. From the University's Sproul Plaza floats the sound of bongo drums. On nearby Telegraph Ave., street vendors sell jewelry and tie-dyed shirts, while panhandlers look for the generous. Just north of the campus a graduate student is studying liberation theology over a caffe latte. High in hills crowded with sumptuous homes, a group of Japanese tourists stands outside Lawrence Hall of Science surveying one of the most magnificent views (and sunsets) in the world— San Francisco Bay has turned silver, the Golden Gate Bridge is bedecked with its necklace of lights, and the sun is setting in an apricot glow behind the summit of Mt. Tamalpais.

Berkeley's contributions to society have ranged from research that led to the creation of atomic weapons to culinary developments that revolutionized American cooking, from discoveries in genetic engineering and superconductivity to a radical activism that sets off political seismographs far beyond the city's borders. Berkeley's international reputation as an intellectual mecca and a dynamic social center continues to make it a magnet for inventive people and new ideas.

Growing up on the other side of the American continent during the 1960s, I learned about Berkeley from newspapers and television. The images were bizarre: dope-smoking hippies crowding city council chambers; confrontations between students and police over a place called People's Park; tear gas filling the air after an antiwar march; free love; and communes. From the sheltered perspective of Norridgewock, Maine, the city of Berkeley looked like another planet. I knew it was a place I had to see, but it was not until 1977 that the chance finally came. While considering graduate school at Berkeley, I dropped down from Davis for a visit. A friend who knew the city dragged me across campus and up Telegraph Avenue. We sat in Cafe Renaissance, drinking strange black goop from a tiny cup and looking out the window at an extraordinary blend of styles and races, street musicians, panhandlers, students, professors, and outrageous loonies. The scent of marijuana wafted through the air. In contrast to the quiet study halls of UC Davis, there were bookstores filled with poetry anthologies and restaurants that offered something called quiche. Street musicians competed with street preachers on Sproul Plaza; people talked about foreign language films. Here was a place where the man who fixed your car had a Ph.D., and where people hung out in bookstores, browsing until the owners sent them out the door at 11 pm. Berkeley is a city that inspires either love or hate; for me it was love at first sight. My second day here, I sent in my application to the University.

The city has changed drastically since I arrived more than a decade ago. Telegraph Ave., once a way station on the road to the future, has deteriorated into a last stop for many with nowhere else to go. Computer enterprises have replaced aging steel plants in West Berkeley. Nouvelle cuisine restaurants have moved into North Berkeley, drawing traffic jams of people. The Berkeley dump was transformed into a city park with rolling hills where children throw frisbees. Those on the Left have grown older, and now have children of their own. They've taken over the city government, and call themselves progres-

sives instead of radicals. Still, the essential characteristics remain: an intellectual heart that challenges; a concern for the world beyond the borders of Berkeley; a tolerance for people outside society's norms; and a contagious sense of energy.

In some ways, the words "Inside/Out" in the title of this book are a reflection of my own peculiar connection to this fascinating city. In recent years I have alternated between summers in Alaska and winters in Berkeley. Each move is a shock. Heading north to Alaska means leaving behind an educated cluster of friends, the coffeehouses and Thai restaurants, discussions of U.S. foreign policy, and the opportunity to dance to world beat bands. But when I return, the city doesn't look quite as wonderful. The people seem politically insular, trash blows down Telegraph Ave., the old conflicts between the University and the community drag on amid incessant bickering, and I am suddenly awakened by police sirens in the night. The quiet sounds of a canoe paddle splashing into a remote Alaskan lake or the sight of a bear catching fish from a stream are far, far away.

Yet still Berkeley draws me back.

Everyone in Berkeley has criticisms of the city. For the ideological leftist, it has become too enamored with middle-class consumerism. For people without a roof overhead, it seems like a bunch of liberals who brag about their concern for Central Americans, while averting their eyes from problems closer to home. To those raising families, crime seems rampant and the schools unevenly run. Neighbors of the University see a monster waiting to grab their property for another research facility. Yet when asked why they live here, most would answer that Berkeley's advantages, especially its rich intellectual and cultural life, far outweigh its problems; people stay because they are invigorated by the city and its people. Besides, criticizing the city is itself a Berkeley tradition.

This book is about the city of Berkeley and its people. It is meant for short-term visitors, for students, and for those who have spent many years in Berkeley and simply want to know more about their home. After several years in Berkeley I thought I knew the city well, but researching this guide has been a revelation. I've realized how wrapped in our own circles we become, and how complex Berkeley and its people really are. I hope this book helps open your own eyes to this city, as it indeed has opened mine.

BERKELEY IN AN AFTERNOON

Okay, so your cousin from Nebraska just called to say he is coming out for a few days to see this weird place on the left coast of America. How do you keep him amused? Or...you're a student at Fresno State thinking of applying to graduate school at Cal. What should you look at when you come for a visit? Or...you're a tourist from Germany staying in the San Francisco youth hostel and want to see the notorious "Berzerkeley."

Berkeley has much more to offer than Telegraph Ave. and Gourmet Ghetto. The following list of places to go in one afternoon is by no means

Musicians and students at Sproul Plaza. Photo by Don Pitcher.

all-inclusive, but is intended to provide a sampling of Berkeley's varied fare.

Telegraph Avenue

This is the best place to start. Here you can buy jewelry and other handicrafts, have your palm read, or drink espresso at any of a dozen coffeehouses. Telegraph Ave. is the heart of student Berkeley and is the city at its most intense.

Sproul Plaza and the UC Campus

Since you're in the area, be sure to spend some time on Sproul Plaza. The best time is noon on a warm spring day when political activists mingle with street preachers, young Republicans, frat jocks, and musicians. Continue through Sather Gate to explore the campus (see "Touring the Campus" in *The University*) and be sure to

The pier at the Berkeley Marina. Photo by Don Pitcher.

visit Doe Library, Hearst Mining Building, and the Campanile. An excellent place to spend a restful few hours is the comfortable Morrison Library on the lower floor of the main library.

Gourmet Ghetto

Head north up Shattuck Ave. from the corner of University Ave. until you pass Cedar Street. The cornerstone of Gourmet Ghetto is Chez Panisse, a famous restaurant in an unassuming building, where creative (and expensive) food has brought national acclaim to the restaurant's founder, Alice Waters. Even if you can't afford Chez Panisse, be sure to visit the other landmarks of this area: Peet's Coffee, Cocolat, and the Cheese Board.

Berkeley Marina

It takes many residents a long time to discover Berkeley's surprising shoreline. The half-mile-long pier provides magnificent views of San Francisco Bay, and you can fish without a license. You'll find fields for kite flying, a dynamic children's playground (with old forts, cans of paint, loose lumber, and a cable ride), and restaurants perched on the water's edge.

Tilden Park

Just a short drive uphill from hectic downtown Berkeley is Tilden Regional Park, a 2000-acre swath of green along the hills. Children of all ages will love the carousel, the little trains, and the botanical gardens.

Lawrence Hall of Science

While you're in the Berkeley hills, stop by the impressive museum on North Canyon Rd. named for Nobel Laureate E.O. Lawrence. Since the

Cody's Books on Telegraph Avenue. Photo by Don Pitcher.

museum offers everything from moving dinosaurs to a space shuttle cabin, you're guaranteed to find something of interest.

A Sunset

As dark approaches and lights gradually ornament the hills around the bay, you begin to realize how many people live here. Favorite places to view sunsets are the Berkeley Rose Garden in North Berkeley, Indian Rock, and Lawrence Hall of Science.

Thai Restaurants

Dinner at one of Berkeley's dozen or so Thai restaurants should give your cousin from Nebraska a few stories for the folks back at home. Everyone has a favorite place, but it's hard to go wrong at either Cha-Am or Plearn.

Hanging Out in a Bookstore

Only in Berkeley would this be a hip thing to do. Cody's, Moe's, or Black Oak have the most eclectic crowds. Together, the dozens of other bookstores offer one of the best selections of books in the United States. The bookstores are also great places to hear readings by well-known authors and poets.

Brennan's

The place that time forgot is a good place to end a day in Berkeley. Cheap American food, great Irish coffees, a tacky decor, and a cross-section of people—what more could you ask for?

Although others might disagree with my choices, these should give the Fresno student a taste of her future graduate life; the cousin and the German tourist an idea of what all the Berkeley rumors are about. For a more in-depth view of Berkeley, read on.

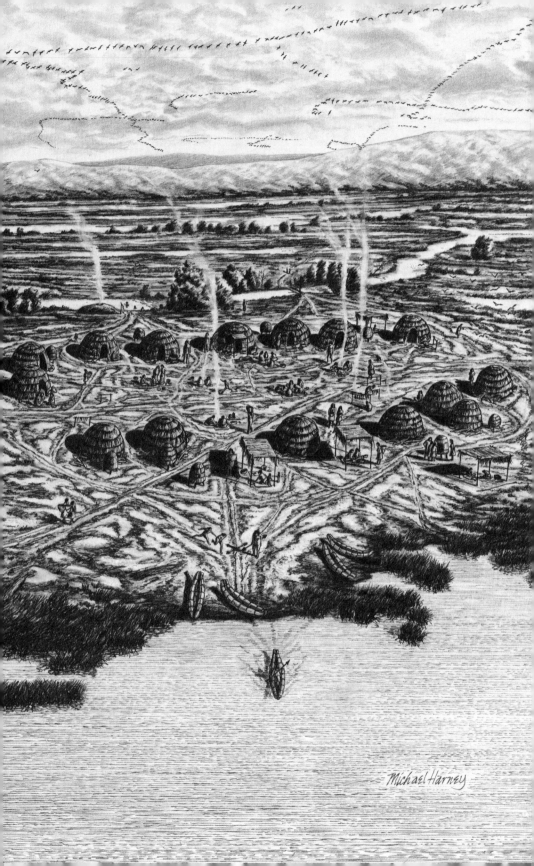

Historical Introduction

by Malcolm Margolin

In October 1769, the Spanish explorer, Gaspar de Portolá, was leading his "crew of skeletons," as he called them, along the western shores of the San Francisco Peninsula. On the afternoon of the 31st, after pulling the mules across several difficult ravines, the party reached the outskirts of Pruristac, an Indian village near present-day Pacifica. Exhausted from three months of marching through strange lands, afflicted with the onset of scurvy, and on the verge of starvation, the "crew of skeletons" collapsed.

It had been nearly three centuries since Christopher Columbus had set foot in the Western Hemisphere. The major cities of Mexico and South America had long been settled; the cathedrals that Cortez had built 250 years before out of the ruins of Aztec temples were already venerable, their stone steps worn smooth by the feet of generations of worshippers. Across the continent in Boston and Philadelphia, a self-confident and restless citizenry walked streets that would be quite familiar to us today. Yet so remote were these Pacific shores that this was the first land expedition any European power had launched this far north into California.

Portolá was charged with finding Monterey Bay, sighted from a Spanish ship 150 years earlier and roughly mapped, but he had passed by it several days before without recognizing it. Confused and at the edge of defeat, his party encamped at Pruristac to take navigational readings. The people of Pruristac brought seed cakes and other foods, Miguel Costansó, the expedition's engineer, set up his sextant, the muleteers pastured the animals and treated their wounds, and Portolá ordered Sergeant Ortega to hunt for deer. Gathering a few of the most able men, Ortega climbed higher and higher along the grassy slopes that rose to the east. When he reached the ridgetop, he stopped, scarcely able to believe his eyes.

Spread out beneath him, as in a vision, lay a great inland sea. The eastern shoreline of the sea was softened by vast, dark green marshes, cut by arabesques of sloughs and channels. Beyond the marshes a wide, grassy plain stretched eastward to a wall of hills. To the south, extending into the haze as far as the eye could see, was a great oak-dotted savannah. Streams, their courses marked by willows and cottonwoods, wound through the savannah or tumbled down the wall of hills and spread out across the plains. Ortega looked from north to south, south to north, then rushed back to the encampment. He had discovered, as Portolá wrote in his diary that day, *un imenso brazo del mar* — an immense arm of the sea— and, as Ortega told the commander, wherever he looked he saw smoke rising up from the countless villages of Indians who lived along its shores and within its valleys.

The Huchiun

San Francisco Bay—as the immense arm of the sea would later be called—

*Opposite: Indian village on the shore of San Francisco Bay. Illustration by Michael Harney, from **The Ohlone Way**.*

which was "discovered" by the Spaniards in 1769, had already been inhabited for several thousand years. The people whose villages rimmed the bay belonged to dozens of tribal groups, politically independent from each other but nonetheless culturally and economically linked. Those who lived in what is now the Berkeley/Oakland area were known as the Huchiun. They spoke Chochenyo, one of the eight Ohlone (or Costanoan) languages. To their south, near present-day Hayward, lived another Chochenyo-speaking group, the Yrgin. The Karkins, after whom the Carquinez Straits would be named, lived to the north and spoke another Ohlone language. East, in what is now Orinda and Lafayette, dwelled the Saclan (sometimes referred to as the Acalanes), who spoke a Miwok language. So it was throughout the Bay Area—one could scarcely travel a dozen miles without passing from the territory of one group into the territory of another, without leaving behind one language to hear the words of another.

The lives that the Huchiun and their neighbors led were perfectly adapted to what is probably the Bay Area's greatest ecological advantage—its extraordinary natural diversity. When the wheeling and diving of cormorants and other sea birds showed that the open waters of San Francisco Bay were alive with smelt and other schooling fish, the Huchiun ventured forth in fleets of reed boats to set their nets. The mudflats at the fringe of the Bay provided fertile beds of clams, oysters, and other shellfish, which the Huchiun pried out of the mud with sharp-pointed, fire-hardened digging tools. In the saltwater marshes that fringed the shoreline,

and in the freshwater marshes and ponds created by the creeks that spread out over the flatlands, the Huchiun fished, gathered plants, and hunted among flocks of geese and ducks that migrated into the area in such numbers that each fall they darkened the sky with their flight. Every winter, when silver salmon and steelhead trout fought their way up Strawberry Creek, Codornices Creek, and El Cerrito Creek to spawn, men with harpoons would be waiting for them, while women would cut basketry shoots from the willow trees along the creek banks, and children would gather firewood. In the plains that extended from the edges of the saltwater marshes eastward to the hills, ran herds of pronghorn antelope, tule elk, and deer; the Huchiun hunted them all with snares, bows and arrows, and in communal drives. The meadowlands also provided wild grains and other edible flower seeds, spring greens, bulbs for eating, and roots for basketry. The oak forests supplied deer, quail, and other game, as well as edible acorns, which were gathered each fall, dried, and stored in granaries for the rest of the year. Redwood forests, berry-rich brushlands, quarry sites, and sacred places were also each visited at appropriate times of the year.

The ripening of various crops and the seasonal availability of game and fish determined a pattern of life. At certain times the Huchiun gathered together in villages, at other times they spread out in smaller family groups. They came together for deer drives, dances, feasts, and religious observances, then separated once more for further gatherings and harvestings.

It is often said that the native

people of the Bay Area lived lightly upon the land, without altering it in any way. This is not quite true. They didn't destroy, but they did alter. Like native people throughout much of California they regularly burnt their meadowlands to clear the brush, create good game habitat, and encourage the growth of certain annual grasses and flowers from which they could more easily harvest grain and seed. They tended to confine their digging of bulbs and roots to certain areas, thus keeping the soil loosened in those areas and encouraging the growth of larger bulbs and straighter basketry roots. Their continual pruning of willow and hazel fostered the growth of long, straight shoots, ideal for basketmaking, and they planted tobacco along the margins of the streams. At the time the Spaniards arrived, in short, the Bay Area was not a "virgin wilderness" over which tribes of "wild" people roamed. The Bay Area was a deeply inhabited environment, and its landscape bore the cultural imprint of its people as surely as did the farmlands of Europe or New England.

What the Huchiun could not obtain from their own territory was available to them by networks of trade that extended far beyond their boundaries. Pinenuts, obsidian, and wood for bows came from the east, abalone from the west, cinnabar ore (used as paint) from the south. Just as the foot trails that radiated out from their villages were worn deeply into the earth from centuries of continuous use, patterns of life were worn deeply into their senses—patterns so successful that they looked not to social innovation or technological development for their betterment, but rather to the wisdom of the elders and the events of

the distant, mythic past. They kept their population in balance with what the environment could support, so they had no need for territorial expansion. The various tribal groups quarreled among themselves, but there was no real warfare. Neither their myths nor their memories bear any account of starvation.

It is often said that the Indians of the East Bay have disappeared without a trace, but this too is not quite true. The construction of a roadway, the digging of a foundation, or the laying of a pipe often unearths artifacts or burial remains of these early inhabitants. Much probably remains beneath the parking lot of Spenger's Restaurant at the foot of University Ave. where a major center was located: at the turn of the century, a mound of shells and other remains at this location measured some 300 feet across and over 20 feet deep, a witness to centuries of abundance. Mortar rocks, where the women pounded acorns and seeds, can still be found at Mortar Rock Park in the Berkeley hills, alongside Albany Hill near El Cerrito Creek, in Wildcat Creek, and elsewhere. An outcropping of hematite in Oakland shows the remains of their quarrying operations. The language they spoke, Chochenyo, was still being spoken in the present century, and there exist grammars, word lists, and even tapes of native speakers. Their descendants still live among us, often to this day retaining many of the attitudes, manners, and sensibilities of the original inhabitants. But because of historic circumstances—notably the complete failure of early Europeans to recognize the value of knowledge, religious practice, or social customs that differed from their own—the Huchiun have had little effect on the subsequent history or culture of Berkeley, and tragically, much of their knowledge has been lost.

The Spanish Conquest

That Europeans had anything to learn from the native people was an idea so outlandish that it never so much as crossed the Spanish mind. The Spanish government that had sent Portolá on his long, arduous journey was responding—reluctantly—to a political need to establish a presence in California lest it be occupied by other European powers. The church, desirous of converts, was at first a willing partner in this enterprise; in years to come, under the zealous leadership of Junipero Serra, it would become a driving force.

A mission and fort were established at Portolá's base camp in San Diego in 1769. The following year a second mission and fort were founded in Monterey as the headquarters for Alta (as opposed to Baja) California.

In 1772, Pedro Fages, governor of California, accompanied by a missionary, Juan Crespi, twelve soldiers, a muleteer, and an Indian servant originally from Baja California, set out from Monterey to further explore the San Francisco Bay. On March 27, they passed through present-day Berkeley, camping along the banks of either Strawberry Creek or El Cerrito Creek. Because the plains of the East Bay were marshy at that time of year and the party was much afflicted with mosquitoes, they kept to the edge of the hills, touching upon what is now the southwestern corner of the University campus, where a plaque has recently been placed to commemorate

their passing. They saw no Indians—had they fled?—but they killed a grizzly bear, and in his diary Father Crespi describes the plain as having "many lilies and an abundance of very leafy sweet marjoram."

On October 23, 1775, Juan Bautista de Anza set forth from Sonora, Mexico with a group of prospective colonists—238 men, women, and children from Mexico's impoverished northern provinces who had been recruited during the previous spring and summer, as well as a thousand head of livestock. After a fearful crossing of the Mojave Desert, they reached San Diego and headed north. Arriving at San Francisco on July 1, 1776, they founded Mission Dolores and established the San Francisco presidio, or military fort.

On October 22, 1780, Father Noriega penned an entry into the Mission Dolores register, announcing that two brothers, aged four and two, of the Huchiun tribe had been received, had accepted baptism, and had been given the Spanish names Ladislao Antonio and Miguel Jacobo. In the years that followed, other members of the Huchiun were drawn into the mission: five in 1791, 33 in 1792, none in 1793, 163 in 1794, seven in 1795, etc. Once they were baptized and took up residence at the mission, the Indians were generally kept by force. As conversion depleted the population still living independently, the family and trade linkages by which people supported themselves were broken, making it increasingly difficult to maintain traditional Indian life. European diseases, against which the native people had no immunity, raged within the crowded mission—over 300 Indians at Mission Dolores died in the measles epidemic of 1806 alone—

and spread throughout the surrounding countryside, killing hundreds and chasing the terrified and depressed remnants into the mission for help or, in many cases, last rites. On December 1, 1809, an entry in the register of Mission Dolores records that a sixteen-year-old Huchiun male named Aschupis, had been given the rites of baptism and received the Spanish name, Concordio. There is no further mention of the Huchiun in the baptismal record: a way of life that had existed for thousands of years came to an end.

Rancho San Antonio

For many years the lands of Berkeley remained depopulated, used only for grazing mission livestock. Then, in 1820, Luis Maria Peralta requested that the Spanish government grant him land in the Santa Clara Valley. Born in northern Mexico, Luis Maria had accompanied the de Anza expedition north at the age of seventeen, and since 1781 he had served in the Spanish army at Monterey, San Francisco, and at the *pueblo* of San José, eventually attaining the rank of sergeant. But land in the Santa Clara Valley was becoming scarce, and instead the government offered him some 46,800 acres (over 70 square miles) of otherwise unclaimed land that stretched along the eastern shores of the bay from San Leandro Creek in the south to El Cerrito Creek in the north. Spain, however, lost California in Mexico's rebellion the following year, and in 1824 the Mexican government, eager to maintain a population in its northernmost frontier, regranted the East Bay lands to Peralta. Luis Maria, a man of great piety, expressed thanks by naming his land Rancho San Antonio, after St. Anthony of Padua, patron saint of the Franciscan order. In 1826 he retired from the army after 45 years of service, taking up residence in San José, while leaving his East Bay lands to the care of his four sons.

One of the sons, Vicente, built an

The diseño, *or original land grant map, for Rancho San Antonio. Courtesy of the Bancroft Library.*

adobe house just to the south of the Berkeley border, at what is now Telegraph Ave. at about 56th St., an area later to be known as the Temescal section of Oakland. Vicente was described in later years by William Heath Davis, an early Anglo settler, as being "about six feet tall, finely proportioned, weighing about 225 pounds, hospitable, kind, and full of native dignity."

His [Vicente's] surroundings were in keeping with his appearance, manners, and tastes. I have ridden in company with him, going to the Feast of San José, when he was attired in a costly suit trimmed with gold and silver lace—sitting with ease and grace on his horse, which was equally well equipped, followed by two mounted and well-dressed *mosos* twenty feet in the rear, and his wife about two or three hundred yards distant with her splendid mounted cavalcade, the whole forming a picture worthy of admiration.

In 1841, another of Luis Maria's sons, José Domingo Peralta, married and with ten children, built an adobe along the banks of Codornices Creek. José Domingo, Berkeley's first resident of European descent, had been born at Mission Santa Clara in 1794. Short, stocky, and dark, he looked more like his father than his brother, Vicente. He was said to have had a courteous and friendly bearing and an impetuous nature. The first adobe he built measured 30 x 18 feet. It had a tile roof and a dirt floor, and it was located near what is now Albina St., not far from the corner of Hopkins and Sacramento Streets.

By 1842, José Domingo had settled

into his adobe in Berkeley, Vicente remained in Temescal, while the two other sons of Luis, Ygnacio and Antonio, had established themselves in houses further to the south. Ygnacio controlled that portion of Rancho San Antonio that lay between present-day San Leandro and Fruitvale, while Antonio held the area from Fruitvale to Lake Merritt, including Alameda.

The world in which José Domingo Peralta lived—like that of his neighbors, Francisco Castro, Felipe Briones, Ygnacio Martinez, and others—was one of contradiction. Retired soldiers, most of whom were unable to read and write, they had enlisted in the Spanish army out of poverty and hopelessness, but now sat high in the saddle and greeted each other as *Don*, an honorific to which their land holdings entitled them. Their wives became *Doñas*. Their land that stretched for miles, their cattle that dotted the meadowland in herds of thousands, their immense families and perhaps a few Indian servants, all conferred upon them an aristocratic, almost feudal air.

And for the most part they rose to the occasion, acting with a courtliness, a generosity, a "Spanish hospitality" that later visitors would long remember. They traveled to weddings, church holidays, and feasts in grand processions. Their *fiestas* and *fandangos* were legendary, as violins were drawn, and finely dressed, high-spirited young women and men danced. Often on the sidelines Yankee seamen or traders, on shore leave from their ships, watched. To them, brought up in a New England still chilled by its Puritan background, this Latin temperament—hot-blooded, elegant, and unabashedly sensual—was something of a revelation, and their romantic descriptions of this era echo strongly even to this day.

Yet while in some ways the lives of the Spanish settlers resembled those of feudal lords, in terms of their day-to-day living the Peraltas were little more than self-sufficient homesteaders. They raised almost all their own food from small gardens, they ground their own grain and baked their own bread, wove their own cloth and made their own clothing. Their land supplied them adobe for bricks and wood for framing, their cattle gave them meat and leather.

Herds of longhorn cattle were their one source of income—hides and tallow being the only commodities their land could raise for which there was a market. Each year the families of the East Bay would gather together for a great roundup and slaughtering. Although this was a time of feasting, dancing, and rodeos, in truth the daily business of slaughtering cattle, skinning them, preparing the hides, and rendering the tallow was hard work, and ugly too. The hides were piled near the shore, while arrangements were made with Yankee sea captains. When the money was counted out, it went for necessities such as tools, nails, ammunition, or thread, and perhaps if there was anything left over for some luxuries as well—a few yards of lace, a new dress for a daughter approaching marriageable age, or perhaps even a chair so that *Doña* would no longer have to greet guests while sitting on a mat on a bare earth floor.

The rancho era in the East Bay was short-lived. In 1846, only four years after José Domingo moved into his house on Codornices Creek, the United States declared war on Mexico. In 1848, the Treaty of Guadalupe

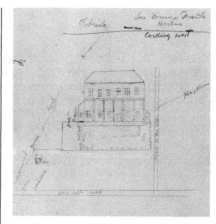

José Domingo Peralta's second house in Berkeley, drawn by his daughter, Virginia Peralta Osuna. Courtesy of the Bancroft Library.

Hidalgo ceded California to the United States, and in 1849 the Gold Rush brought tens of thousands of new settlers into the Bay Area.

Luis Maria Peralta, still living near San José, was now nearly ninety. He had arrived before the founding of Mission Dolores, and had witnessed the growth of the Spanish presence in the area, and now its passing. When gold was discovered he advised his sons:

My sons, God gave the gold to the Americans. If He had wanted the Spaniards to have it, He would have let them discover it before now. So, you had better not go after it, but let the Americans go. You can go to your ranch and raise grain, and that will be your best gold, because we all must eat while we live.

It was wise-sounding and philosophical advice that this old soldier gave to his children. But in the new world which was fast spreading about them, wisdom and philosophy counted for little, and Luis Maria Peralta could not give his sons what they needed most—money. In this new world, people without money were people without power. Rich in land, cattle, and children, the Peraltas lacked money with which to pay the property taxes that the new government levied. They lacked the money to pay the lawyers whom they needed to represent them before the Land Claims Commission, which was judging the validity of their claims in procedures that dragged on for 25 years. They lacked money to effect the eviction of newcomers who so arrogantly squatted on their land and stole their cattle. When José Domingo tried to take the law into his own hands and evicted some squatters, he was jailed and fined $700 for assault.

There was only one way that the Spanish ranch owners could raise money, only one thing that was saleable, and that was their land. From the time of statehood through the next decade, the history of the Peralta family, like the history of most of the other Spanish land grant families in California, is a story of lawyers, speculators, agents, and outright swindlers who cheated them; of forced land sales at often ridiculously low prices; of piling debts, mortgages, and increasing poverty. New Englanders and Southerners who had failed in their attempts to plunder the Sierra for gold, found another source of plunder along the shores of the East Bay.

Over the years the Peraltas' land slipped away from them. When José Domingo Peralta died in 1865, he was buried in an unmarked pauper's grave at St. Mary's Church in Oakland. In 1872, the Alameda County sheriff arrived at the family house to evict his wife and children. The last remnant of the estate was partitioned by 1878; the income derived from the final sale went to the lawyers and speculators who had filed claims against it.

Ocean View

In 1846 there were approximately 150 people living across the Bay in Yerba Buena, as San Francisco was then called. Soon a trickle of newer immigrants began to arrive, and with the Gold Rush of 1849 the trickle turned into a torrent. Every day ships entered the Golden Gate, and no sooner had the anchor been dropped than passengers and crew alike raced for the gold fields, leaving the ships abandoned in their moorings. Overnight, the small town of San Francisco exploded into a city of 20,000 people living in tents, shacks, shanties, and hastily thrown together houses. Property values soared, one lot in Portsmouth Square selling for $45,000.

The newcomers who returned from the gold fields, often disappointed, were tough, aggressive, and entrepreneurial. What brought them to California was a quest for wealth, and if they couldn't find it in the mines, perhaps they would find it elsewhere. The newcomers quickly changed the pace of life throughout the Bay Area, erasing almost instantly all traces of the leisurely Spanish style of living.

1849 was not very long ago—two moderately long human lifetimes would span the gap between then and now—and the people who began to settle in San Francisco and around the Bay were not very different from the people who live here today. The history of Berkeley after 1849 is the story of people very much like ourselves, who came to farm land, set up businesses, and, later, found a university.

By the mid-1850s a small community of settlers began to cluster near the shores of the Bay in what was then, and still is, an area of Berkeley called Ocean View. The great attraction of this *contra costa*—this other coast—was that while close to the booming market of San Francisco, land was still cheap and water, at least for the needs of the time, was plentiful.

Probably the first of the settlers was Captain James Jacobs. Born in Denmark, he set out for the gold fields while still in his early twenties. Although failing to become wealthy, he seems to have made enough to purchase a sloop in 1851 which he used to transport freight between San Francisco, other bayshore communities, and Sacramento. By 1853 he had taken

to mooring his boat at the outlet of Strawberry Creek, probably to take advantage of the fresh water and to avoid the high dockage fees in San Francisco. Here he built a small dock—Jacob's Landing, as it was known—and later a house.

At about the same time the county, hoping to encourage development, widened the trail that ran from Oakland north to the Castro Ranch in present-day San Pablo. Along this road—later called San Pablo Ave.—a stageline was established. In 1854 Captain William Bowen, originally from Massachusets, set up a way station and inn alongside the road, near the corner of what is now Delaware St., and in subsequent years he added a grocery.

Also in 1854, a German immigrant, John Everding, attracted not only by the open land and the free-flowing water, but especially by the transportation opportunities offered by Jacob's Landing, opened the Pioneer Starch

When San Pablo Avenue was a dirt road. Date unknown. Courtesy of the Bancroft Library.

On the Schmidt farm, Sacramento Street near Cedar, ca 1890. Courtesy of the Berkeley Historical Society.

and Grist Mill near what is now University Ave. and 2nd Street. It produced basic materials such as starch, chickenfeed, washing powder, and soap, and with its ten employees and their families the population of Berkeley was suddenly much expanded.

With a local market now developing, Zimri Brewer Heywood, born in Maine, opened a lumberyard in 1856 near the foot of what is now Delaware St., supplying the local residents with housing material. Heywood also helped Jacobs expand the wharf so that it could more easily accommodate the receiving of lumber and its transshipping to other developing communities.

At the same time this little town of business enterprises was growing up near the bayshore, farmers began to spread out into various parts of the Berkeley flatlands. Among those early farmers whose names are now commemorated in city street names, thus suggesting the locations of their farms, were William and Mark Ashby, Michael Curtis, Henry Carleton, James McGee, John Kelsey, Noah Webster, and Bradshaw Woolsey. These, and several others, such as Orrin Simmons and Napoleon Byrne, raised grain which they sold to the Pioneer Starch and Grist Mill, as well as truck-garden crops for San Francisco and the growing Oakland market.

To serve the expanding population, a one-room schoolhouse was built in 1856 on San Pablo Ave., just north of Bowen's Inn and Grocery. The location made it convenient for the school children to stop at the grocery for penny candy or a sack of flour before heading along the footpaths, cow trails, and dirt roads that led to their homes. Most of these children spoke English without a foreign accent. Not so their parents. Most of the residents of early Ocean View were foreign born. Many of them—like the Curtises, the McGees, and the Brennans (who opened a livery stable at what is now University Ave. and 2nd St.)— were refugees from the terrible potato famine of Ireland in 1846-47. They were hardworking people, and they hoped, and had every reason to expect, that here in Ocean View they would establish a new and good life for themselves and their children.

By 1860 the United States census showed Ocean View with a population of 69 people. With a new wharf, a road that led to Oakland, a lumberyard, grocery, inn, and school, and with land still cheap and plentiful, the stage was set for continued and rapid growth.

The University

The early history of Ocean View, while of interest to local residents, is not too different from the histories of dozens of other small communities that were then springing up around the Bay, founded by refugees from the Irish potato famine, the revolutions that plagued Europe in 1848, the failure of the gold mines to provide wealth for more than a few, the Taiping Rebellion that swept through China in 1850, and later the American Civil War that destroyed the South. Had Berkeley developed along the lines established by the pioneer settlers and farmers of Ocean View, the city of today would probably not be much different from Union City, Petaluma, Antioch, or the other communities of the 1850s that were then building wharfs, attracting industries, and establishing farms. Ocean View—like Fruitvale or Temescal—might very well have been eventually absorbed by the growth of its aggressive neighbor, Oakland.

What makes Berkeley so distinctive was the decision to found the University of California here. The roots of that decision go back even before the Gold Rush. When California became a state in 1848, the Protestant churches of New England saw it as a fertile ground for their missionary efforts. Of special concern was the fact that the Indians and earliest settlers had known only the Church of Rome, and that nowhere in this immense land was there a Protestant church to correct the theological backwardness of the past and provide guidance to the new settlers who would surely flock here. To ensure a Protestant presence in California, the eastern churches resolved to establish a California liberal arts college on the model of Harvard or Yale. Such a college would, they hoped, become the training ground for the lawyers, doctors, teachers, and civic leaders who would form the core of a properly educated commonwealth.

With that in mind, the Home Missionary Society dispatched Reverend Samuel Willey, a graduate of Dartmouth College and the Union Theological Seminary, who arrived in California in 1849. In 1853, he was joined by Reverend Henry Durant, a graduate of Yale College. Recruiting a distinguished board of trustees, in 1855 they chartered the College of California, a non-denominational Christian liberal arts college, for which they selected a site between 12th and 14th Streets in downtown Oakland.

But even as the land was being cleared for the new campus, Willey, Durant, and the board of trustees were having serious doubts about planting a college amidst the saloons, gambling dens, loose women, and other fixtures of life in this gritty frontier town. As the first campus buildings were being constructed, they were already looking for a new, more secluded site, eventually settling upon the area along the banks of Strawberry Creek in the slopes above Ocean View.

The site was dedicated on April 16, 1860, and by 1864 land purchases were completed. Setting aside an area for the future campus, the board of trustees created the College Homestead Association to subdivide the remaining land and resell it as building lots to future residents. Their reasons for doing so were twofold. On one hand they badly needed money to repay loans and to construct the new campus. On the other hand they hoped to forestall random development and create around the campus a community of solid citizens who would reflect the social values they wanted to impart to the students who would eventually enroll there.

The College Homestead Association subdivision lay to the west and to the south of the campus. Streets were laid out in a grid. Those running north to south were named alphabetically after prominent men of science: Audubon (later College Ave.), Bowditch, Choate (later Telegraph Ave.), Dana, Ellsworth, Fulton, etc. Those running east to west were named after men of letters: Allston, Bancroft, Channing, Dwight, etc. Within this grid of literary and scientific names, 125 one-acre lots were surveyed. An early map of this subdivision shows a pattern of streets and lots that differs little from the area we know today.

But selling relatively expensive lots in an undeveloped and somewhat remote part of the East Bay was not an easy task. In its early promotional literature the College Homestead Association presented its lands as an ideal site for what would later be called a "bedroom" community for those who worked in San Francisco. The climate here was moderate, a ferry had been established between Oakland and San Francisco, and from here the fantasy developed:

The man of business comes aboard the boat at San Francisco after business hours and sits down comfortably and at rest in a clean, airy saloon to read his evening paper. By the time it is read he is across the bay, ready to enjoy socially the home: and he finds this home not like the place he has left, exposed to the chill, and wind, and fog, but in a warm summer air, in which he can linger in comfort and safety with his children till nightfall. In the morning, at such an hour as he chooses, he takes his seat in the cars or on board the boat, and no sooner is he possessed of the morning's news than he is at the city landing, and finds himself at business as early as his neighbors.

Conveniently absent from this picture was the means by which the man of business could get from the pier to his home, for there was as yet no public transportation between the College Homestead Association sites and downtown Oakland.

By 1866 it was clear that a name was needed for the new community. Frederick Law Olmsted, the landscape architect who had been advising the trustees on the design of the campus, suggested that it be called Peralta. The trustees chose instead to name it after George Berkeley, the English Bishop of Cloyne. Although Bishop Berkeley had never visited California (he died in 1753), he had nevertheless predicted in an often quoted poem that "Westward the course of empire takes its way." In this poem, he decried the decay of Europe with its "pedantry of courts and schools," and predicted that in a westward land, "Where nature guides and virtue rules," there would be a renaissance of learning "Such as [Europe] bred when fresh and young/ When heavenly flame did animate her clay."

Although all the lots of the College Homestead Association had been sold by 1867, there were few houses under construction and no building activity on the campus site. The College of

California still held classes in Oakland, but it scarcely had the money to support its distinguished faculty and small but enthusiastic student body, let alone expand to Berkeley.

At the same time, it was becoming desirable for the State of California to open a state university. The state constitution of 1849 had provided for one, and in 1862 the U.S. Congress passed the Morrill Land Grant Act which would bestow on any state that opened a college an immense acreage of federal land for its support. In 1867 Governor Frederick Low attended the College of California commencement exercises in Oakland, where he was said to have remarked to Samuel Willey, "You have here, in your college, scholarship, organization, enthusiasm, and reputation, but not money. We, in undertaking the state institution, have none of these things, but we have money. What a pity they could not be joined together." That very year the board of trustees of the College of California approached the state officials with an offer to turn their holdings over to the state. The offer was accepted in 1868, and by 1870 construction of North Hall and South Hall on the new campus land had begun. In 1873, a year after the Alameda County sheriff had evicted the widow Peralta from her home, caravans of carriages brought books, desks, students, and faculty members from Oakland to Berkeley, and the newly founded University of California opened its doors. A thousand people from San Francisco, Oakland, and the surrounding area gathered at the first commencement to hear President Daniel Gilman declare, "Although the sound of the hammer is still heard upon the walls, and the grounds are not yet graded, we have come up hither to this house of our expectations."

In 1875, two years after the opening of the University, Reverend Henry Durant died. In a memorial service held in his honor, John B. Felton, a University Regent, recounted how, many years before, Reverend Durant came to choose the Berkeley site:

He passed in review many of the most beautiful valleys of our state, so rich in landscapes that delight the eye and gladden the heart. One by one he rejected sites full of beauty, for in his mind there was an ideal spot where nature would present herself in her loveliest form to the young student and lead him by her display of outward beauty to an appreciation of all that is good and beautiful in the inner world of the heart and the mind. One morning in spring, when the air, purified by the rains of winter, brought out in clear relief the lines of ocean, valley, hill and mountain...he passed through fields unbroken by road, untrodden by man, and came to the present site of Berkeley. "Eureka!" he exclaimed. "Eureka! I have found it. I have found it."

Perhaps, like the founding of Rome, the discovery of the Berkeley campus site had, even as early as 1875, already passed into myth. There is evidence that the decision to locate the College of California here was not so much a flash of inspiration as a reasoned choice, with much wavering over the desirability of other sites, an engineer's report on whether ample water could be developed, and preliminary negotiations with landowners over the price of the land. Yet even if it is part myth, it contains, like all myths, a fundamental truth. The founders of the University were not just looking for a suitable site, but for an "ideal" site. What they saw along the banks of Strawberry Creek was a landscape of great natural beauty, to their eyes devoid of the history of those who had come before, upon which to build an ideal University and an ideal community around it.

It was a utopian vision, but the word "utopia" would not have been to their liking. The phrase they did use to describe their vision of an ideal university was "Athens of the Pacific." The image of Athens haunted and inspired them. "I do believe," remarked Henry Durant, "the second Greece, a greater Greece, will come to the world here." In the eyes of the founders, the physical similarities between Berkeley and Athens were astounding, almost mystical. Both were surrounded by hills to the east and a plain that sloped to the west and ended at a seaport. There were serious suggestions that Strawberry Creek be renamed "Ilissus," and that the peaks of the Berkeley hills be named for those that towered over Athens.

It was not, of course, the real Athens that Reverend Durant, Reverend Willey, and the early founders sought to duplicate. The flesh-and-blood Athens of Socrates, with its sexual mores, its social institutions, and its pagan beliefs and practices would have appalled them. Rather, it was in part the Athens they saw through the writings of Aristotle and Plato, the Athens of Pericles that had been filtered and cleaned through two thousand years of European interpretation and history. It was also in part an Athens of their own imagining that

they sought, one in which chaste students would stroll through meadows and groves with their wise professors, and by discussing philosophy, theology, literature, the sciences, and art, thereby prepare themselves for responsible careers in business or in civic leadership. It was an Athens in which a vigorous, independent, and industrious citizenry would read the daily newspaper on their way to work each morning. The "Athens of the Pacific" which they envisioned was, in short, a distinctly 19th century, very American, and very Protestant, Athens.

While the idealistic vision of the University founders might not have aged very well, it was deeply felt, and the best of it may still be with us. The sense that Berkeley could become a truly great University surrounded by a just, prosperous, and enlightened community of citizens is one that has remained—not in the specific content of the University founders' vision, but in a thrust toward utopianism and idealism that has, even as it has changed, been worked deeply into the politics and consciousness of the city.

The idealism of the University's founders also contrasts with the motivation of those in the working-class town of Ocean View. Ocean View had not been settled by people who came to Berkeley to establish the "Athens of the Pacific," but by those who hoped to beat high rents, set up serviceable inns, grist mills, and lumber yards, and establish farms on cheap land with adequate water and ready access to a marketplace. This contrast between an idealistic and literary University, in which faculty and students alike would draw financial support from Sacramento or from parents, and the necessarily self-sufficient, work-

The horse-drawn trolley that ran from Oakland to the University campus, 1873. Courtesy of the Bancroft Library.

ing-class, largely immigrant community to the west would also abide for many decades. It would become a source of tension, sometimes destructive, often creative—a tension that would be a dominant force in the shaping of Berkeley, and one which can still be felt to this day.

The Bucolic Age

In 1873-74 the University had 191 students, 22 of them women, and to serve them a horse-drawn trolley line was established to run from Oakland to the University. The trolley ran down Choate St. (now Telegraph Ave.) and stopped between Bancroft Way and Allston Way, where Sproul Plaza is today. At this terminus a cluster of enterprises quickly sprang up: a rooming house capable of accommodating twenty people; a French restaurant (an Oakland newspaper claimed that it was so expensive that it would bankrupt the students); and the University Parlor and Coffee Shop, which advertised late hours—it would serve coffee until 10 pm. These were soon followed by a meat market,

a grocery which opened in 1874, a second hotel with a dining capacity of 200, and a Chinese laundry.

For a while it seemed that the area around Telegraph Ave. and Bancroft Way would become Berkeley's main business district, but in 1876 Francis Shattuck and J. L. Barker, owners of property to the west of campus, convinced the Central Pacific Railroad Company to run a train down what is now Shattuck Avenue. At its terminus, between Center St. and University Ave., another cluster of shops and enterprises grew.

Ocean View, too, was experiencing a significant building boom. In 1874 a ferry service was launched between San Francisco and Jacob's Landing. It turned out to be short-lived, but within three weeks after the first boat docked, over 200 lots were sold at prices ranging from $175 to $465.

Throughout the 1870s, many more factories were established in Ocean View. The Niehaus and Schuster Planing Mill opened in 1874 and began turning out the moldings, scrollwork, and other extravagances that would adorn the Victorian houses of Berkeley and the Bay Area. The Cali-

Trail along northern edge of campus, that later became Hearst Avenue, 1895.
Courtesy of the Bancroft Library.

fornia Watch Company moved here in 1876, and in 1877 the Standard Soap Company erected a four-story factory, the largest of its kind in the nation. The same year the Griffin Glove Factory arrived, and to ingratiate itself with the local community advertised that of the 150 workers it intended to hire, not one would be Chinese. In 1878, the Wentworth Boot and Shoe Company was established, and two years later Berkeley had a refinery that processed oil from Ventura County into kerosene and other petroleum products.

In 1877 a newspaper, the *Advocate*, began printing in Berkeley, and that year it described the building boom that was taking place:

In every direction new houses are springing up, new people are coming, and are making their

homes....The time is not far distant when from Oakland to the northern line of Berkeley the whole space will be lined with the elegant mansions of our wealthiest citizens.

Buildings were going up everywhere. Each morning the horse-drawn trolley on Telegraph Ave. and the steam train on Shattuck Ave. would bring crews of carpenters, plumbers, and masons. All day the dirt roads of Berkeley were plied by carriages hauling building materials from the lumberyards along the bayshore, and everywhere one went one could hear the pounding of hammers and the rasping of hand saws.

Yet despite the rapid development there was still plenty of space, and Berkeley still retained its rural nature. In later years, in fact, the 1870s would be known as the "Bucolic Age of Berkeley." In 1898 Reverend Edward

Payne would remember that Berkeley was then "for the most part as God and nature and the plowshares of a few ranchmen had made it."

By far the larger part had the appearance of an open common. The streets were few, but numerous footpaths ran in all directions and led straight across fields to everybody's door. There was hardly a right-angled corner to turn in all the eastern portion of the town.... Detached patches of grain and hay ripened under the July sunshine.... The hills eastward held out as today their irresistible invitation to the stroller, but wore the grace of a more perfect solitude than now. One might wander there all day and be utterly alone except for the browsing kine and the inquisitive ground squirrel.

In the 1930s, longtime resident Otto Putzker reminisced that Berkeley of the 1870s resembled a big ranch.

From our house on Telegraph Ave. we could see tall grain fields in all directions....From Shattuck down to the water there were truck gardens and swamps. At Ashby, around Shattuck, Adeline, and Grove [now Martin Luther King, Jr., Way], I had a rowboat and used to go duck hunting. Then there were lots of cattle driving through this town. I've seen cowboys, the real thing, driving steers by the thousands right over the hills."

Incorporation

If there was a contradiction in Berkeley's love of its bucolic setting and its enthusiasm for urban development, no one seemed to notice. Fields of grain, gnarled oaks along running streams, marshes into which migrating ducks settled, and footpaths throughout the hills were all obviously desirable. So too were the promises of rows of expensive houses, paved streets, factories, and business enterprises. The 1870s were optimistic times in California history. Open land stretched for miles in every direction, technology and development offered limitless hope for comfort and improvement; and perhaps, without thinking about it too deeply, people assumed that all the good things of the world—a great city and a lovely, productive countryside—could exist at the same time and in the same place.

As Berkeley and Ocean View continued their development, the need for local control became apparent. An area with a rapidly growing population needed sewer lines, better streets, schools, police, libraries, a jail, and regulations governing the licensing of saloons, the disposal of garbage, and the pasturing of animals. In the face of such needs, the citizens of Berkeley and Ocean View, and those who lived in the scattering of houses and farms between them, found themselves powerless. The entire area was part of the large, unincorporated county lands, governed—and generally neglected—by the Alameda County Board of Supervisors. The only way to assume local authority was to incorporate as a township.

An early attempt at incorporation was initiated by Henry Durant, who in 1874 called a meeting of the citizens of Berkeley and Ocean View. Not only was it inherently desirable to incorporate, Durant argued, but, as Judge

John Dwinelle pointed out, it was an urgent necessity if the area was to be kept "out of the jaws of Oakland." A spirited debate followed, but in the end a motion to incorporate was defeated, largely because of the power of the farmers who feared, and rightly so, that incorporation would bring an increase in land values, property taxes, and regulations that would soon drive them out.

In the following years, however, a serious threat emerged. A move was afoot in Oakland to divide Alameda County, creating the City and County of Oakland, which—according to the proposal—would have included Berkeley and Ocean View. The possibility loomed that if the entire county voted for such a proposal, Berkeley and Ocean View would have become part of the City and County of Oakland, whether they wanted to or not. Not only would this have destroyed any hope of local control, but it would have linked them with the financially overextended Oakland, making Berkeley and Ocean View responsible for Oakland's debts and, in the eyes of many, its chronic overspending. Although nothing came of the threat, the citizens of Berkeley and Ocean View were shocked into a rec-

ognition of their vulnerability, and another vote for incorporation was held in 1878. By this time a building boom had been long underway, and—with a population approaching 2000—homeowners, factory workers, and businessmen now greatly outnumbered the farmers. Ninety percent of those who cast ballots opted for incorporation, and a petition to that effect was submitted to the state legislature. On April 1, 1878, the governor signed the Act of Incorporation which for the first time merged Berkeley with Ocean View into a single political entity.

It seems, on the surface, rather odd that Berkeley and Ocean View should have joined together. Given their antagonistic values and different class structures, as well as their mutual distrust for each other, it seems that they would have done everything possible to stay apart—the further the better. But geographically they were rather close, and increasing development had brought them even closer. The University officials watched with alarm as taverns spread throughout Ocean View, just beyond the one-mile alcohol-free limit imposed by the state legislature to protect college students, and these taverns began to attract an

View from Charter Hill, 1884. Hillegass Tract to the left. Campus buildings from left to right are Harmon Gymnasium (in the trees), South Hall, Library Building, North Hall, Mechanic Arts Building. Courtesy of the Bancroft Library.

increasing number of students. Ocean View watched with equal alarm as upslope homes and businesses began to pollute the streams that flowed into the flatlands. Berkeley and Ocean View were, like it or not, mutually interdependent, and the only way one party could exert any control over the other was if they were part of the same political body. Thus, at least in some respects, it was not so much mutual interest as mutual antagonism that brought these two divergent communities together. In later years the antagonism and competition between them would manifest itself in struggles over political power, over regulation, over the placement of the town hall, schools, libraries, post offices, fire stations, roadways, and other civic services—a competition which, for the most part, was won again and again by the uptown interests.

Early Growth

In the two decades after incorporation, there were spurts and lulls in Berkeley's growth, but the overall trend is clearly indicated by the census figures: 2000 people in 1880; 5000 in 1890; and 13,000 at the turn of the century. Gas mains were laid from Oakland to Ocean View as early as 1877 to serve the factories, and over the next several years branch lines spread to other parts of the city. By 1882, Berkeley had its first telephone exchange. 1881 also saw the first volunteer fire company; by 1894 there were six such companies, and by 1904 a professional fire department. Electricity came in 1890, and the first bank, opened by Francis Shattuck, followed two years later. In 1895 the

Berkeley Way (foreground) intersecting with Oxford Street, ca 1902. Courtesy of Berkeley Historical Society.

post office initiated home delivery of the mail, which meant that Berkeley residents had to number their houses for the first time. Factories continued to find Ocean View, now often called West Berkeley, to their liking, and home construction never ceased. Berkeley High School, founded in 1882, had 31 students in 1883, 270 in 1895, and 330 the year after. In 1895 the *Advocate* remarked:

> In all available parts of the city the busy carpenters, lathers, and plasterers are converting great chaotic piles of lumber and sand heaps into neat Queen Anne cottages, modern flats, and houses combining the latest improvements with the picturesqueness of antiquity.

The University, too, was growing steadily. By 1887 it had, in addition to North Hall and South Hall, the Mechanic Arts Building, the Bacon Art

Shattuck Avenue looking south from corner of University Avenue, ca 1892. Courtesy of the Berkeley Historical Society.

and Library Building with 33,000 books, and the Harmon Gymnasium. Daniel Gilman, an early University president, revisiting the campus in 1887 after a twelve-year absence, exclaimed, "This University seems to have grown like one of your eucalyptus trees."

Yet despite the University's growth, its grounds still retained a pastoral air. At about the time of Gilman's visit, the poet Joaquin Miller wrote an article describing the campus:

> It sits in the lap of huge emerald hills, and in the heart of a young forest, with little mountain streams bowling and tumbling about; wild oats up to your waist in the playgrounds and walks, and a sense of largeness and liberty and strength and grandeur that I have never felt in and about any university before.

As the rest of Berkeley was rapidly building, the University campus would in the years to come—despite a prodigious building spurt of its own—take on the role almost of an urban park, a low-key version of Golden Gate Park in San Francisco or Central Park in New York, an oasis in the heart of the city.

As Berkeley grew, a number of factors served to shape its development and give the city its character. Especially important were the economic inclinations and aesthetic tastes of its real estate developers, preeminently those of Joseph Mason and Duncan McDuffie. The London-born Mason opened a real estate and insurance business in a small wooden storefront at the corner of Shattuck Ave. and Dwight Way in 1887, and soon began buying parcels of land and subdividing them. Following the quick-build practices of the day, he laid out the streets in a grid pattern without regard for the preservation of open space and with only the most grudging concessions to topography. Among his developments are Fairview Park, at the southern edge of Berkeley above Telegraph Ave. at about Alcatraz St., and Kellogg Ranch, north of the campus from Hearst Ave. to Cedar St., between Oxford and Arch Streets.

By the time Duncan McDuffie joined Mason as a partner in Mason-McDuffie in 1905, much of the flatlands had been built up, and the only large lots still easily available were those closer to the hills. Engaging the services of the landscape architect, Frederick Law Olmsted, McDuffie planned his tracts with larger, often odd-shaped lots and streets that curled about the contours of the land. Typical of these developments is the 120-acre Claremont Park, north of Ashby Ave., with its contoured roads, planted street trees, and luxurious lots. It is partly because of the success of these subdivisions that the grid pattern of streets never extended into the hills, as happened in San Francisco and elsewhere in the East Bay.

The other important factor that shaped Berkeley's growth was the placement of its train and trolley lines. The first commercial district, as already mentioned, arose at the terminus of the horse-drawn streetcar line at what is now Telegraph Ave. and Bancroft Way. Other clusters of shops and business enterprises sprang up at the various stops of the Central Pacific Railroad: Lorin Station (at Adeline and Alcatraz), Newbury Station (at Adeline and Ashby), Dwight Station (at Dwight and Shattuck), Berkeley Station (at Center and Shattuck), and later Berryman Station (at Rose and Shattuck). Likewise, businesses formed at various points along San Pablo Ave., at first because of the stageline that ran along it, and after 1901 because of an electric trolley line that connected Ocean View with Emeryville and downtown Oakland. Another electric line established along Grove St. (now Martin Luther King, Jr. Way) in 1891, the first such line in the Bay Area, led to some business development here.

The earliest public transportation in and out of Berkeley was north-south toward the Oakland ferry, with the major routes along Telegraph Ave., Shattuck Ave., Martin Luther King, Jr. Way, and San Pablo Ave., all more or less converging at a point in downtown Oakland. When the Emeryville ferry started operating from what is now the foot of the Bay Bridge, some of the lines bent to connect to it. The east-west lines, however, were late in coming, leading to the continued isolation of Ocean View. It was not until 1891 that the first horse-drawn streetcars ran more or less along University Avenue. In 1923, a ferry line was re-established between the Berkeley pier and San Francisco, carrying not only passengers but automobiles as well, making University Ave. the major east-west arterial for automobile traffic in and out of Berkeley.

Berkeley wharf, 1888. Courtesy of the Bancroft Library.

The effects of this development along transit routes has been far-reaching. Because of it, Berkeley, unlike other cities, has no strong commercial center from which roads radiate out, but rather many smaller, neighborhood shopping districts, each with its distinctive history and personality. This gives Berkeley the aspect of a collection of villages, which indeed it is, and it has led to the situation today wherein Berkeley is composed of many distinctive neighborhoods, each with its own commercial center.

As railroad service spread within Berkeley and throughout California, the city lost its status as an agricultural region. Land had gotten more expensive, taxes higher, water increasingly scarce, and Berkeley's major advantage—its proximity to San Francisco—no longer counted for much. Crops raised in other areas, notably the Central Valley, the Delta, and for a time the Santa Clara Valley—all areas with more sunshine, more water, and cheaper land—quickly came to dominate food production and render Berkeley's agriculture obsolete.

At the same time railroads and trolleys were making Berkeley's homesites increasingly accessible to San Franciscans and bringing about rapid development, they also made the businesses and cultural opportunities of Oakland and San Francisco readily accessible to Berkeley. Unlike other communities, Berkeley did not have to develop or do without great urban theaters, nor did it have to develop or do without a major financial center. These were available nearby. In short, Berkeley never really had to become culturally or economically self-sufficient. So even as it was growing quickly in size, it seemed to remain in the lee of the larger cities, retaining something of a sheltered, small town, collegiate aspect, a taste of which remains to this day.

In 1899 Benjamin Ide Wheeler was appointed University president, and in his first address to the student body he said:

> I want you to find in me a personal friend. I want you to come to me, and come as persons. Tell me your names. Please, do not be afraid to come about petty matters, little matters. What interests you will interest me. And I hope I am going to have time enough to know about your petty affairs.

The University had by then some 2000 students and 150 faculty members, so perhaps the offer was by then already a nostalgic tribute to the ideals of a previous age. But the sense of community and neighborliness was strong, and in the twenty years of his presidency Wheeler would be a familiar figure, riding his horse through the campus, stopping now and then to chat with students.

A Model City

Beginning in 1903, Berkeley underwent a growth spurt that would dwarf all others. It came about, once again, because of an improvement in transportation. A network of electric trains, known as the Key Line, spread over Berkeley and whisked riders to waiting ferries in Emeryville, reducing the commute time between Berkeley and San Francisco to a mere 36 minutes.

The Key Line was already causing a

building frenzy in Berkeley when the 1906 earthquake and fire devastated much of San Francisco. Between ten and twenty thousand San Franciscans fled to the East Bay. They were hungry, half-dressed, bereft of house and all their possessions, and they arrived in a state of shock. Churches, fraternal associations, city buildings, campus halls, and private homes threw open their doors, and ad hoc relief committees instantly formed. Bakeries baked thousands of extra loaves of bread, and townspeople contributed whatever food, blankets, bandages, and medicine they could spare. Many of those who fled to Berkeley stayed, rebuilding their homes (and their lives), reestablishing their shops and factories here. The population that had numbered 13,000 in the 1900 census reached 40,000 by 1910, and only two years later it topped 50,000.

Berkeley not only grew in numbers but in area, as it stretched out to embrace the communities and subdivisions that were springing up outside it. Lorin and Newbury, in South Berkeley, had already been annexed in 1891 and 1892 respectively; Claremont was annexed in 1906; Northbrae in 1908; and the North Berkeley Hills/ Thousand Oaks area in 1920.

Public utilities and municipal services struggled to keep pace. No sooner was a school budgeted, land acquired, schoolhouse built, teachers hired, and the doors opened, than it was already horrendously overcrowded and yet another school house had to be built. Public libraries never seemed to have enough books, post offices expanded and opened branches, and the fire department bought more engines and opened substations. No longer a rural area, pavement began to cover the streets and cement replaced wood on the sidewalks of Shattuck Avenue.

Water was chronically scarce, as the population quickly outgrew what local streams and wells could provide; and over several decades a parade of privately-owned water companies concocted schemes for damming creeks, building reservoirs, and drilling tunnels through the hills to tap into Wildcat Creek and the other streams to the east. But the needs of the city continually outstripped any solution that was proposed, and water was a problem for Berkeley until 1929, when the newly formed East Bay Municipal Utility District created Pardee Reservoir by damming the Mokelumne River in the Sierra foothills and running pipelines into Berkeley and other East Bay cities.

As Berkeley evolved from a collection of villages into a city, the form of government changed too. In 1909, a new charter provided for initiatives, referendums, and recalls, and stipulated that those running for city office could not list their party affiliations. Another charter, adopted in 1923, inaugurated the city manager form of government, in which the elected officials appointed a professional city manager to administer the workings of municipal government. At a time when other American cities had fallen under the dominance of political bosses and corrupt, or at least self-serving party machines, Berkeley's politics were widely hailed as the height of reform.

In 1896 Phoebe Apperson Hearst— widow of George Hearst, mother of William Randolph Hearst, and a University Regent—contributed funds for an international competition among architects for the design of an enlarged campus. The goal of the design

Huston's Shoes, 2216 Shattuck Avenue, 1926. Courtesy of the Berkeley Historical Society.

was "to treat the grounds and the buildings together, landscape gardening and architecture forming one composition . . . in which there is to be no sordid or inharmonious feature." This design would be "so in harmony with the universal principles of architectural art, that there will be no more necessity of remodeling its broad outlines a thousand years hence than there would be of remodeling the Parthenon."

Something of the same visionary idealism also inspired the citizens of Berkeley. They desired a beautiful, harmonious, perhaps even eternal city. Their desire for the good life was reflected in a push toward social reform. In 1909 they voted to extend prohibition to the entire city. In 1911 they voted heavily in favor of women's suffrage, even though it was defeated in the rest of Alameda County, and in what turned out to be a brief swing to the left, elected a socialist mayor.

The spirit of reform and utopianism manifested itself in almost every aspect of municipal government. In 1916, Berkeley became the second city in California to form a planning commission and institute zoning regulations that would govern growth. It was the first city in the nation to develop a public health department, offering prenatal care, among other services, and employing public health nurses, who by the end of the 1930s would number thirteen. Its death rate and infant mortality rate were among the lowest in the nation. Its crime rate was also low, and while its police force under August Vollmer was considered the most advanced in the nation, its per capita expenditure for police protection was well below the national average. Its fire department was so highly regarded that the National Fire Protective Association rated Berkeley one of the country's twelve safest cities. In 1929 a study of city governments by Jerome Kern named Berkeley one of the two best governed cities in America. In 1934 another study, by Howard P. Jones, singled out Berkeley as the best governed of all medium-sized communities in the nation.

It seemed that nothing could ever affect Berkeley's preeminence as an enlightened, well-governed, prosperous city—not even natural calamity. In 1923 a brush fire that started in the hills north of campus went out of control, and shifting winds brought it raging toward Berkeley, destroying houses, hotels, schools, sororities, and libraries, until another shift of wind stopped it at the very edge of campus. Six hundred building were destroyed in the fire, including many palatial homes, and 4000 people were left homeless. Yet, as with the San Francisco earthquake, citizens rallied around the victims. And, while the memories of the fire would survive for decades, within a few years elegant homes once again appeared throughout the hills.

These were good years at the University as well. In 1934 the American Council of Education declared it the equal of Harvard in the total number of excellent or adequate fields of instruction. With its reputation as a center of liberal arts education well established, it now began to forge into a position of world prominence in the sciences, especially in the new, exciting, and (in those more innocent times) promising field of atomic and subatomic research. As for the students, while taking advantage of re-

nowned teachers, a world-class library, and well-equipped labs, they would best remember this era as one of fraternities, sororities, school spirit, football games, and parties that lasted far into the night.

Ocean View also prospered, with nearly 200 factories in operation by 1930. Included among them were what was generally regarded as the finest machine shop in the nation, and other factories that made laboratory equipment, gears, electrical appliances, thermostats, oil-well drills, railroad cars, motorboats, musical instruments, chemicals, furniture, mineral and vegetable oils (the nation's largest producer of coconut oil was located here), furnaces, inks, and more. Berkeley even had an airplane manufacturer!

Although by the 1920s and 1930s, second-generation Americans out-

Berkeley fire, 1923. Courtesy of the Bancroft Library.

Key Line Train on Shattuck Avenue, 1942. Courtesy of the Berkeley Historical Society.

numbered immigrants in Ocean View, a large number of people were still foreign born. In addition to those from England and Canada, there were sizable populations of Germans, Italians, Swedes, and Finns. The 1930 census also listed 2177 blacks and 1653 people of Asian origin.

By 1930, when the Great Depression settled over America, Berkeley had reached a population of 82,000, and it was the seventh largest city in California. While there are memories of bankruptcies, unemployment, people selling apples on street corners, and a continual scrimping on the part of many to make ends meet, Berkeley seemed to have suffered less during the Depression than the rest of the country. The University, by far the city's largest employer, continued to expand under the dynamic presidency of Robert Sproul. Although the construction rate of private homes fell, several large private and public

buildings were erected during this era: the University Christian Church in 1931, an addition to the YMCA, the United Artists Theater in 1932, and a major addition to the post office. The City of Berkeley was in sound financial shape from years of excellent management, and in 1931 alone was able to spend $300,000 on improvements. Federal aid, in the form of WPA projects, resulted in the construction of a yacht harbor, the Rose Garden, and Aquatic Park. Even in the Depression, Berkeleyans were optimistic; in 1934 they voted along with other East Bay cities to increase their taxes and found the East Bay Regional Park District in order to protect the lands to the east of them and develop what is now Tilden Park.

It might be taken as an indication of people's contentment that in 1932, generally regarded as the worst year of the Depression, there were 31,000 Republicans in Berkeley and fewer than 11,000 Democrats. Although there was an increase in Union activity in West Berkeley, and some radical agitators among faculty and students on the campus, nevertheless, in the landslide election of Franklin Roosevelt in 1932, Berkeley stood out from most of the rest of the nation by voting solidly for Hoover. This suggests that while they didn't enjoy the Depression, Berkeleyans had not been hurt enough to want to change the status quo; the vast majority of them liked things the way they were.

In 1939 Edward Thorndike of Columbia University examined 310 American cities with populations of 30,000 or more, and ranked them for "goodness of life" according to some 150 criteria, such as infant mortality, deaths from homicide, per capita expenditure for education, teachers' salaries, etc. Berkeley was ranked among the top five cities in the nation.

By the onset of World War II, Berkeley had—in its own eyes and in the eyes of the world—achieved something enviable. It had long since outgrown the dream of a bucolic small town, but it seemed to have realized another dream—that of a prosperous, well-managed, self-satisfied city. Berkeley was certainly not perfect, especially to the blacks, Japanese, Chinese, and many other working-class families living in the flatlands who were marginal to, or even excluded from, the "goodness of life." But whatever its failings, most of Berkeley was proud of its achievements, content in its daily life, and optimistic that the future had even greater blessings in store.

In 1911 then-mayor J. Stitt Wilson said, "Any kind of a day in Berkeley seems sweeter than the best day anywhere else." In 1940 a majority of

Children at the American Trust Co., now Wells Fargo, late 1920s. Courtesy of the Berkeley Historical Society.

Berkeley's residents would have echoed that sentiment. They were in love with their city, and in love with themselves for living in it.

Change and Conflict

In 1950 Berkeley's population reached 114,000, and the city was showing signs of overcrowding and (at least by California standards) even old age. Houses that had been built during the construction booms of the 1890s and the early 1900s were now some fifty years old. Many were being torn down, while many others fell into disrepair. In their place developers were putting up multi-unit dwellings and apartment complexes, often in great haste, without attention to architectural style or even decent building materials.

The decay of older houses and the spread of shoddy, multi-unit dwellings conspired with other factors to hasten the flight of many middle-class people from Berkeley, especially from the flatlands. The completion of the Bay Bridge in 1936, the construction of the Caldecott Tunnel through the Berkeley hills in 1939, and the development of a freeway system throughout the East Bay put the cattle-grazing lands to the north and east of Berkeley within easy reach of a new, automobile-owning citizenry and offered the premium of almost instant connection with San Francisco. Walnut Creek, a village of 1,500 in 1940, grew to 40,000 in 1970. Concord grew from 1,400 to 85,000 in the same period.

As Berkeley's middle class deserted the Queen Anne cottages on trolley lines to pursue the new American dream—a split-level ranch house with a green lawn, a two-car garage, and a swimming pool—newer settlers moved into the houses they had left behind and into the multi-unit dwellings. Foremost among them were blacks. In the early 1940s, some 75,000 blacks were among the half-million people who migrated into the Bay Area, attracted by job offers in wartime industries, especially at Kaiser Shipyard in Richmond, which employed 100,000 people. When the war was over, rather than return to the cotton fields or Midwestern cities from which they had fled, many stayed. Berkeley's black population, which was 4% of the total in 1940, rose to 12% in 1950; 20% in 1960; and 24% in 1970.

Berkeley already had a small black community before the war. Its roots went back to the late 19th century, when the Pullman Company, the nation's largest employer of blacks, selected the Southern Pacific Railroad's Oakland terminus as its base for changing crews of porters. Many of the porters brought their families and settled in the neighborhood around the railroad yards. Spreading out from there, the community inched into south Berkeley in the 1920s and slowly expanded.

The settlement of blacks in Berkeley exposed what had perhaps been the weakest part of the city's social vision, namely its repeated failure to include racial minorities or widely divergent ethnic groups in its dream of the ideal city. The very founders of the city were quick to obliterate the Spanish presence here, as were the Spanish quick to obliterate the Indians traces. Strong anti-Chinese sentiment prevailed throughout the 19th century, leading to anti-Asian riots in Ocean View in 1903. And in 1942, while many Berkeley citizens were admit-

tedly distressed, the U.S. government rounded up 1200 Japanese residents of Berkeley and sent them to internment camps. It is not that Berkeley treated racial minorities any worse than the rest of America did; far from it. But it is fair to say that in its attempt to create a model city, Berkeley did not rise very much above the rest of America either. As late as 1940, merchants along San Pablo Ave. were posting signs that read, "No Negro Trade Solicited." Although black women were admitted into many of the area's nursing schools, they were not allowed to live in the hospital dorms or use the rooms set aside for students. In 1956, the only black employee in all downtown Berkeley was one woman who worked at Hink's Department Store—as a maid. The downtown business interests in effect boycotted black workers because they were afraid that they would attract black shoppers who would chase the wealthier white shoppers toward the suburban malls. In 1959 only two out of 88 large companies in Berkeley had as much as a single black sales representative. As late as 1961, there was no black policeman on the Berkeley police force, only one black fireman, and Berkeley voters defeated a "Fair Housing" ordinance that was put on the ballot.

At the beginning of the 1960s, the white citizens of Berkeley suddenly woke up to the fact that the city had a substantial black population, nearly one fifth of the city's total, and that it was almost totally unintegrated into the social, cultural, economic, or political life of the community. The Civil Rights Movement that was then sweeping America served to make people aware of how deep, shameful, and urgent the problem was, and it is

Sacramento Street, 1939. Photo by John Eskridge. Courtesy of the Berkeley Historical Society.

to Berkeley's credit that a number of remarkable actions were taken to remedy the situation. The liberal Democrats, despairing of ever wresting control from the conservatives who dominated city government, and moved by a sense of social justice as well, saw the black community as a natural ally. Slates of white and black liberal Democrats were formed, and in 1961 Berkeley elected its first black school-board member and its first black city councilmember, Wilmont Sweeney. In the early 60s, students and other Berkeley residents picketed and threatened to boycott various downtown Berkeley businesses that hadn't hired blacks, and Berkeley instituted affirmative action programs in the police, fire, school, and other city departments and agencies. In 1964, Berkeley became the first school district in the nation to desegregate its schools, and a few years later it became the only school district to cross-bus its students without a court order. By 1971, Berkeley had a black mayor, Warren Widener.

The 1960s were heady, hopeful, and exciting times for Berkeley's black community. The two slogans of the time—"Black Power" and "Black Is Beautiful"—were not just pious wishes, but words to live by. Women wore vibrant Afros, and men strode proudly and aggressively down the streets of Berkeley. Soul food restaurants sprang up, and the Black Panther Party was formed just over the border in Oakland. There were courses in black history and black literature being called for in local colleges and high schools, a pride in black struggle and accomplishment, and anger at generations of injustice.

The black community was flexing its muscles, and by the mid-1960s, Berkeley found itself confronted with an aroused, angry, and politically active group which, although it now had a foot in the door, nevertheless felt itself to be by and large politically and economically outside the power structure, alienated from the society at large, and demanding not just an equal voice in city affairs, but a more-

Congress of Racial Equality picketing on Shattuck Avenue, Christmas season, 1963. Courtesy of the Berkeley Historical Society.

than-equal voice to compensate for the generations of enforced silence. And while many white citizens resented the intrusion of this group into the politics and even more into the consciousness of the "model" city, nevertheless there was something in the justice of the black cause that served to challenge the legitimacy of anyone in Berkeley who even remotely looked like "the Establishment."

The University also underwent a substantial change of character. Earlier in Berkeley's history it was deeply involved with local affairs, shaping the urban development around it and leading the move to incorporate the city. Its faculty were prominent citizens of Berkeley, serving on civic boards and agencies, active in planning and administering city affairs. But as its buildings and enrollment increased, it seemed to outgrow its interest in the city and even to lose the sense of its original mission—to train the character and improve the morals of local people who would form a core of enlightened California citizenry. As telephones, trains, and airplanes linked it ever more closely with the rest of the nation, it seemed to see itself in competition with and at the same time linked to the great universities of the east, and increasingly it would take its cues not so much from Berkeley, or even Sacramento, but from the East Coast and especially Washington. The story of the 30s, 40s, and 50s is that of a university casting off its local ties and turning for its identity to a distant community of scholars, and for its money to a distant government. This trend would most clearly manifest itself in a history department that no longer taught California studies, an anthropology department that was, after the great days of Alfred Kroeber, increasingly embarrassed to be studying California Indians, and ultimately a move toward military research and those sciences which offered the greatest international prestige, and not incidentally, the greatest source of federal funds.

The image of Athens would continue to be used, and commencement addresses would still pay homage to the idea that the mission of the University was to form character in its students. But another metaphor came into being as early as the turn of the century: "A City of Learning." It was an apt metaphor, for by 1950 the University shared many of the characteristics of a city: a proliferation of imposing buildings and expensive facilities, a high level of creative intensity, overcrowding, and the concomitant of overcrowding, alienation.

The University underwent a prodigious growth spurt in the early 1960s, expanding in part because of some internal compulsion, in part because the children of the post-war baby boom had reached college age. Between 1960 and 1964 enrollment grew from 18,700 to over 25,000 students. By now, even the metaphor of the "City of Learning" was inadequate. The University, in an image introduced by University President, Clark Kerr, was now a "multiversity" run along the lines of a major corporation, with many campuses, scores of independent research programs, and facilities in other states, managed not by its faculty, but by highly trained administrative professionals.

The students who were pouring into Berkeley in the early 1960s were quite unlike those of the previous decades. In the age of the "multiversity," school spirit seemed foolish and embarrassing. A national shift of values had likewise made fraternities and sororities seem hopelessly conservative, racist, and bound in silly rituals, so that in 1964 only 350 women students "rushed" the sororities. With dormitory construction lagging far behind the enrollment spurt, a large proportion of the 25,000 students at the University in 1964 were renting off-campus apartments. If these students no longer felt a strong identification with the University, neither were they part of the social fabric of the city. With the Vietnam War, the generation gap had widened into a chasm, and many students were hostile to what they felt were the values of the country as a whole. Thus, in the early 1960s Berkeley found itself with two huge groups of people living in its midst—blacks and students—who felt themselves cut off from political power, embittered, frustrated, impatient, and not at all part of the social and cultural history of the city.

In addition to blacks and students, yet another group of settlers who felt themselves outside the power structure found their way to Berkeley, and they, too, came in great numbers. In the 1950s they were sometimes called beatniks, and later hippies, but neither term does justice to the complex nature of these new settlers. Many were artists, writers, craftspeople, and others who, after graduating from college, as many of them did, found no place in American society and headed west—like many before them—to create a society of their own. Willing to experiment with their lives, they often used drugs, were prone to novel living arrangements, and avoided the clothing, work habits, and dwelling standards of "the Establishment." Like the immigrant groups who preceded them, many were first attracted to the Bay Area by San Francisco, settling in Berkeley because of its more congenial atmosphere and lower rents. Although unconnected to the University, they liked living in its shadow, taking advantage of the bookstores, movie houses, music, and other advantages the University offered. The popular image of Berkeley during the 1960s and 70s—of men with long hair, women wearing ankle-length, cotton-print dresses, of "be-ins" and music festivals, of the streets lined with old cars painted in psychedelic designs— is less that of the student population than of these de-institutionalized nomads and experimenters.

Long before the migrations of the 60s, Berkeley had played host to a class of artists and writers. In the early part of the century, the poet Charles Keeler and the painter William Keith were among those whose presence invited visits from John Muir, Joaquin Miller, Jack London, and others. In the 1920s and 30s the home of the eccentric and charismatic linguist, Jaime de Angulo, was a major center of Berkeley's bohemian community. In the late 1940s and 50s, poets like Robert Duncan and Jack Spicer lived in Berkeley, as did Allen Ginsberg and Gary Snyder. But while the way had been paved for the newcomers of the 60s, there was nothing to prepare Berkeley for the vast numbers of drop-outs who arrived in Volkswagon buses, who hitchhiked into town, or who (unlike previous generations) remained after graduation from the University to take up residence in the low-rent and deteriorating older homes of the flatlands.

This group was part of what was once called the international "youth culture," or "counterculture," and Berkeley in the 60s was, perhaps, along with Amsterdam, its capital. But, of course, in subsequent years the inevitable happened—the youth culture aged. In the 1970s many of its members moved out of Berkeley to continue the "revolution" in the hinterlands of Mendocino and Humboldt counties. Many of those who stayed began buying and remodeling homes, and raising children. Some became successful artists, others established automobile repair shops, returned to college to get degrees in psychology, or entered politics. In the 1970s and 80s their boutiques, woodworking shops, typesetting enterprises, and art studios spread through the aging industrial area of town and revitalized it. They helped found Berkeley's three

current growth industries: outdoor equipment, publishing, and gourmet foods. Paradoxically, many of these newcomers—whom the older residents of Berkeley saw in the 60s as being so disruptive and lawless—have gradually over the years trimmed their hair, stopped their stone-throwing, and moved into positions of cultural, economic, and political leadership in the city.

By 1960 Berkeley was no longer a model city. The middle class, which paid high taxes and demanded relatively few services, had fled to the suburbs, replaced by people who were poorer and in greater need of health, housing, recreation, schooling, and other city services. The era when sewage could be dumped in the Bay and garbage piled along the shore also ended, involving municipal government in greater expenses. The shopping centers suffered in competition with suburban malls, and industry was being drawn toward the industrial "parks" of the suburbs as well. With the University expanding and BART being built, both of which involved the demolition of houses that had once paid property taxes, Berkeley's budget was under the double strain of increased expenses and diminished income.

But if Berkeley in 1960 was no longer a model city, it had become a far more interesting city than it had been twenty years before. The contrasts were staggering. Within a half-hour walk from the middle of town one could visit a steel foundry, a world-class library, a run-down tenement, a palatial Maybeck home, a meadow where deer were browsing, a bayshore where sea birds were wheeling, or a pool hall where it seemed that half the players had been in prison within the last six months. Those with the greatest intellectual attainments lived blocks from others with scarcely a sixth grade education. It was an environment that many found frightening, others stimulating, and by the 1960s Berkeley had become a place where the contrasts and contradictions of America could be seen and felt most keenly.

The "revolution" of the 60s is covered elsewhere in this book (see *Touring Revolutionary Berkeley*), and with the 1970s and 80s we move out of history and into current affairs.

When Sergeant Ortega of the Portolá Expedition first viewed the bayshore from the ridgetops of the San Francisco Peninsula in 1769, this was one of the most remote areas of the world; it would be nearly a year before news of the momentous discovery would make its way to Spain, and many more months before it would become known in other European courts. Today, an event in Berkeley can be broadcast instantly throughout the world, and events in Europe, South America, and Asia are as close as a fax machine, the nightly news, or the morning paper. Berkeley's isolation ended long ago, and its citizens, beyond local loyalties, are first and foremost citizens not of Berkeley but of the world. Although proud of local artistic culture, they are far more affected by movies produced in Hollywood than plays performed in local theaters, more influenced by national bestsellers than by poets reading in the local bookstores. Many of today's Berkeley residents have the daily *New York Times* delivered to their doors, and are often more aware of what is going on in Central America than in their own hometown.

Yet even as Berkeley has become more international in outlook, it is clearly different from any other city in the world. The local flavor is still strong, civic passions run hot, and the neighborhoods are a real force in defining people and binding them together. The contrasts of Berkeley— while at times bothersome and even bitter—are nonetheless energizing. Berkeley has a dramatic mix of educated and uneducated, rich and poor, homeowners, renters, and homeless, abled and disabled, transient students and long-term residents, and people from a variety of distinct ethnic and racial backgrounds. The beauty of the hills and the bay contrasts with the congestion of some of its neighborhoods, BMWs compete with bicycles for space on the streets, and it is only a five minute walk from McDonald's at the corner of University and Shattuck to Chez Panisse in the heart of Gourmet Ghetto.

Despite the glib characterizations of the national media, there is no such thing as a typical Berkeley resident. There is no single symbol that can be used to represent all of Berkeley. There is not even a single duality— town-gown, black-white, hills-flatlands, left-right, etc.—that adequately defines the city. Berkeley has become a city of diverse neighborhoods and even more diverse constituencies, bound together not by common beliefs and values but by the gifts of its historic past—its semi-independent neighborhoods, its political activism, its architectural distinctiveness, its artistic vitality, and more than anything else, a thrust toward idealism and utopianism that is still woven strongly into the civic fabric and the daily life of those who live here.

Neighborhoods

From the air, Berkeley's topographical features are obvious—San Francisco Bay to the west, the sharply rising hills to the east, and a gently-sloping plain in between. Its urban geography, however, shows the city to be a complex of many neighborhoods. These neighborhoods have diverse historical roots: West Berkeley began as the separate industrial town of Ocean View, and joined with the University settlement to form Berkeley in 1878; other commercial districts such as South Berkeley or downtown developed around the train stations.

In many ways, Berkeley's neighborhoods follow patterns common elsewhere in America—the hills tend to be home to wealthy professionals, while blue-collar and low-income families occupy the flatlands. This situation is complicated, however, by the astronomical cost of housing in the city as well as the diversity of housing in every neighborhood—you'll find shabby bungalows in the hills and manicured Victorians in the flatlands.

The people of Berkeley identify themselves with their neighborhoods. Those who live in the hills are proud of their large homes and majestic views; Southside residents find their area more invigorating; Westbrae families enjoy the quiet suburbs.

While in other American cities neighborhoods tend to lose their distinctive character, several developments have helped preserve the integrity of Berkeley's neighborhoods. The Neighborhood Preservation Ordinance, passed by the voters in 1973, provided strict regulation of demolitions, halted the construction of new apartments to replace older homes, and encouraged building rehabilitation. Traffic diverters in side streets keep motor vehicles on the main thoroughfares and allow residential areas to preserve their individual characters. In addition, a 1986 vote to return (after 77 years) to district elections for the city council has led to an increasing focus on neighborhood issues, as councilmembers must now answer to a local constituency.

There are now 67 neighborhood groups listed by the City Planning Department, including some with large and active memberships and others that are really only one-person soapboxes. The oldest, Park Hills Homeowner's Association, dates back to 1939. (This group succeeded in annexing their neighborhood, originally part of Contra Costa County, to Berkeley in 1957 in order to gain better city services.)

A coalition of neighborhood groups known as the Council of Neighborhood Associations (CNA), established in 1974, attempts to coordinate neighborhood participation. In addition to monthly meetings, CNA produces a newsletter ($10/yr, P.O. Box 1217, Berkeley, 94701) "to let the neighborhoods know what's coming down before it lands on them."

Opposite: North Berkeley hills from Indian Rock. Photo by Don Pitcher.

North Berkeley Hills

This neighborhood climbs steeply above the city, its wide main streets lined with large sycamore trees. On the narrow, winding side-streets, cars park half on the sidewalk and overhanging vines drape the dozens of shaded paths connecting the byways. The cars are newer and fancier than those on the flatlands and boast fewer political bumper stickers than one expects in Berkeley.

The North Berkeley Hills neighborhood was one of the last to develop. In 1907, just after San Francisco's devastating earthquake and fire, developers Louis Titus and Duncan McDuffie proposed that the state capital be moved from Sacramento to Berkeley, and offered to donate 40 of the 1000 acres they owned in the area for the site. They began their development with a hub-and-spokes street arrangement as an entrance to the capitol site: John Galen Howard designed the Arlington Circle (the "hub") and its elaborate centerpiece fountain as part of a "City Beautiful Plan for Berkeley." (The fountain was later destroyed by a runaway truck.) The streets were named for California's counties. Hillside rock outcroppings with outstanding vistas, such as Indian Rock and Cragmont, were set aside for city parks. Although supported by Bay Area voters, the measure to move the capitol lost heavily in the statewide count in 1908, and North Berkeley Hills was left to development for Berkeley's wealthier residents. The Northbrae, Cragmont, and North Cragmont sections were opened over subsequent years. Even today the rose-pink sidewalks (Berkeley's first concrete walkways) and rustic stone corner pillars are evidence of the developers' appreciation for detail.

Although it might be hard to envision today, a fire in 1923 destroyed nearly 600 houses in the hills north of campus. While many historically important houses were destroyed by the fire, roads in North Berkeley Hills still switchback past structures designed by Henry Gutterson, John Galen Howard, Bernard Maybeck, Julia Morgan, and John Hudson Thomas (see "A Tour of Maybeck Country" in *The Buildings of Berkeley*). Today, professors and professionals live in houses that are among the most substantial and expensive in Berkeley. More than 75% of the homes are owner-occupied, which is twice the city-wide average. North Berkeley Hills is also the only neighborhood in Berkeley without a shopping district; and the crime rate is the lowest in the city.

Claremont

Berkeley's most exclusive setting takes its name from the majestic hotel that graces its southeast corner. The real estate firm of Mason-McDuffie created the Claremont in 1905 as a bucolic alternative to San Francisco. Duncan McDuffie, an early member of the Sierra Club, developed the "private residence park" design, which provided a radical change from the traditional grid pattern of streets and served as a model for subsequent housing developments in North Berkeley Hills.

Today, two small shopping areas near Claremont and Ashby Aves. offer gourmet food and wine. The intersection is a nightmare—40,000 cars enter or leave suburbia via Tunnel

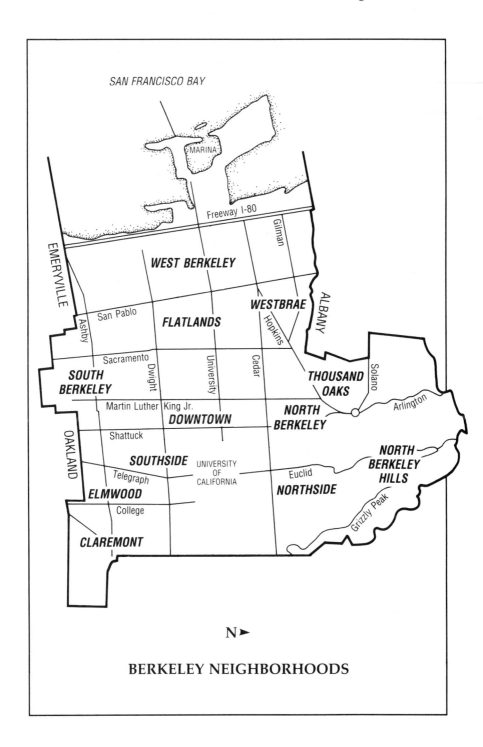

BERKELEY NEIGHBORHOODS

Claremont neighborhood view. Photo by Kit Duane.

Rd.—but once you enter the adjacent residential streets, all is quiet. Many of the magnificent houses on the tree-lined avenues offer spectacular views of the Bay.

Elmwood

The Elmwood has managed to keep its neighborhood character in spite of its hectic location. The name comes from Elmwood Park, a tract of land developed in 1905, and from the century-old elms still lining the streets. The last Elmwood hay harvest is depicted in Alfred Deakins's landscape painting *College and Ashby, 1898*, now hanging in the Oakland Museum. By the 1920s, commercial and residential developments had sprung up around the intersection.

Unlike the rest of Berkeley, Elmwood has held onto its small-town charm, with a hardware store, the nicest library in town, a movie theater, a shoe repair shop, and an old-fashioned donut shop. Recently, however, this status quo was endangered by the same forces that transformed North Berkeley into Gourmet Ghetto. For 30 years, Ozzie Osborne (not the rock star) operated his Norman Rockwell-like soda fountain within the Elmwood Pharmacy, becoming a community leader and minor folk hero. In 1981, new landlords attempted to quadruple rents, but they had not counted on the peculiar Berkeley amalgamation of a desire to preserve history and an openness to radical planning concepts. (For more about the Elmwood Pharmacy, see "American Restaurants" in *Restaurants and Cafes*.)

Beyond congested College and Ashby Aves., the Elmwood neighborhood remains a quiet place, with lovely old brown-shingle homes designed by Julia Morgan and other well-known architects. Home prices and rents are high.

Southside
(Telegraph Avenue)

Telegraph Ave., established in 1873, is for many people synonymous with Berkeley, because it still has much of the character for which Berkeley was famous during the Free Speech and anti-Vietnam War movements of the 60s. The jostling crowds, people begging for change, Tarot card readers, loonies muttering to themselves, snatches of music from street musicians, and over it all the aroma of espresso—this is the Berkeley that frightens our proverbial cousin from Nebraska. And this is the Berkeley that has proven such a strong draw to young people.

Unlike other commercial areas in Berkeley, Southside businesses are almost entirely devoted to the student population. As a result, stores tend to change with the arrival of new trends, although a few staples—coffeehouses, fast-food places, and bookstores—remain. Attempts to preserve some of the older and less fashionable establishments have generally failed, and some fear the Avenue will soon resemble a suburban shopping mall.

Ten high-rise dorms, the International House, the Rochdale student apartment complex, and dozens of fraternity and sorority houses make the area bordering campus one of the most crowded in North America (over 26,000 people/square mile—New York City averages 23,500 people/square mile). South of Dwight Way the population thins out, and older brown-shingle and Victorian homes grace the streets. Telegraph Ave. has suffered serious robbery problems in recent years, due in part to the numbers of drug dealers and people who prey on the vulnerable. Residents, largely students, tend to move quickly on to other places—in some parts of Southside only 5% have kept the same address for five years or longer!

Southside (Telegraph Avenue) scene. Photo by Don Pitcher.

Northside

Just north of campus, one of Berkeley's smallest shopping districts contrasts sharply with Southside's rowdy exuberance. In the hilly Northside cafes you are more likely to hear theological discussions than political ones. Northside is home to "Holy Hill," a collection of religious institutions brought together in the Graduate Theological Union. Recent expansion by both the GTU (the new library) and the University (planned student housing) has created conflicts with local residents. Traffic is heavy on both Hearst and Euclid Aves., but surrounding streets are quiet and scenic. Northside's numerous apartments gradually thin out as you head uphill into the more substantial homes in North Berkeley Hills.

North Berkeley

This neighborhood's commercial district follows Shattuck Ave. for several blocks near its intersection with Cedar Street. The surrounding middle-class neighborhood is considered one of Berkeley's most desirable places to live and raise a family. The homes are a mixture of brown-shingles, old Victorians, and bungalows, laid out on quiet streets, with a gentle westerly slope.

North Berkeley had its origins in the 1878 extension of the steam railroad from downtown to a new terminus at Shattuck and Vine. Railroad men and their families settled there, and soon a number of retail businesses crowded the intersection, gradually spreading out along Vine Street. For many years North Berkeley

remained an ordinary section of Berkeley. The transformation into today's upscale shopping district began in 1966 with the arrival of Peet's Coffee. The Cheese Board followed (see *Economy and Business*), and the area soon attracted others whose roots were in the counterculture, including the Juice Bar Collective and a number of alternative educational establishments such as the Synergy Power Institute, Jungian Dreamwork Institute, and Acupressure Workshop. Gourmet restaurants and shops such as Cocolat, Pig by the Tail (R.I.P.) and especially Chez Panisse, helped to establish the area's national reputation for fine food, but if you ask a local, Peet's, the Cheese Board, and Black Oak Books—three of Berkeley's landmark institutions—would be the main attractions. "Gourmet Ghetto," as it's popularly known, suffers somewhat from its own popularity. This is the only major shopping area in Berkeley without a city parking lot, and traffic congestion is severe. Once you head away from the main thoroughfares, however, you'll find the quiet middle-class surroundings a wonderful place to live.

Thousand Oaks (Solano Avenue)

As a remote outpost of Berkeley's hip culture, Solano Ave. is schizophrenic, lying partly in Berkeley and partly in sedate Albany. This curious city division (right down the middle of the street for four blocks) dates back to an instance of gerrymandering in the 1900s.

John Hopkins Spring, a large landowner, developed Thousand Oaks and the shopping district along Solano Ave. shortly after the San Francisco earthquake and fire of 1906. For years Berkeley garbage wagons had been dumping their loads at Albany Hill, much to the neighbors' chagrin. To stop this, an army of indignant local housewives held off the wagons with two shotguns and a rifle, and then hired lawyers to prepare incorporation papers for their turf. There was only one problem. Workers at the Spring Construction Camp—based on what is now upper Solano Ave.—were opposed to the creation of a new town. A grandiose dream of moving the state capitol to North Berkeley was then being debated and the construction workers stood to gain by remaining in Berkeley. To prevent the workers from defeating the move for incorporation, the new Ocean View (now Albany) city boundaries were gerrymandered to exclude the workers. The result was the dual identity—half Berkeley, half Albany—of Solano Ave. today. The first act of the new Ocean View city attorney was to prohibit outside garbage from being dumped in the town.

While the Thousand Oaks has grown rapidly in recent years and traffic now overflows into neighborhood parking places, the combination of simple bungalows and cottages along with grander homes makes the neighborhood an attractive place to live. In addition to a typical Berkeley collection of coffee shops and bookstores, Thousand Oaks offers visitors longtime favorites such as McCallum's Ice Cream Parlor, as well as an excellent selection of Chinese and Japanese restaurants.

Westbrae

On the border with Albany, bucolic Westbrae is a well-kept neighborhood peopled with middle-class families. Traffic is heavy on Gilman St. and Hopkins Ave., but the side streets are quiet. Locals crowd the benches in front of the popular Toots Sweets and Brothers' Bagels on weekend mornings, reading newspapers purchased from the only real live street vendor left in town. Nearby, the Monterey Market sells an abundance of fresh produce. Westbrae's mix of the old and the new covers the spectrum from a nursery founded in 1922 to a new-age shop selling crystals and books on astrology. Unfortunately, the BART tracks slice through the center of this commercial district, rising out of the ground near Cedar St. and heading north.

Westbrae was the first part of Berkeley to be settled by Europeans. José Domingo Peralta built an adobe dwelling on the south side of Codornices Creek in 1841 and later added a wood-frame home just north of the present 1521 Hopkins Street. A plaque at 552 Vicente Ave. commemorates his tenure. The odd triangular intersections in Westbrae demarcate the Peralta homestead's boundaries.

Downtown/The Flatlands

In 1876 businessman F. K. Shattuck convinced the Central Pacific Railroad to run a spur line from Oakland through his property along the west side of the University campus, with a terminus at Shattuck and University Avenues. The area gradually grew into Berkeley's official downtown.

Laundry and roses in Berkeley flatlands. Photo by Kit Duane.

(The peculiar split of Shattuck Ave. at Center St. allowed the electric trolleys to go around the station.) The real boom in growth followed the 1906 San Francisco earthquake and fire. By the 1920s most of the buildings that make up downtown today had been completed.

Although its importance has been somewhat eclipsed by other neighborhood shopping districts, particularly those in North Berkeley and on Telegraph Ave., Berkeley's downtown is still healthy with a mixture of commercial and government buildings. At its center is the brick plaza that squats above the BART station. There, high school kids smoke cigarettes, buttondown businessmen hurry off to the office, university students stop for a doughnut and coffee, and panhandlers eye the commuters heading down the escalator to catch a BART train to San Francisco. This is the tran-

sit hub of Berkeley, where commuters catch BART or AC Transit, shoppers park in the many garages, and students hop on the UC Berkeley shuttle up to campus. In the evening, downtown Berkeley's cinemas and theaters attract crowds of people, who head off after the show for coffee at Au Coquelet or a drink at Triple Rock Brewery.

The construction of BART in the 1960s destroyed over 200 homes in the flatlands of Berkeley, leaving behind a strip of land that became Ohlone Park. Today the park is a popular place for volleyball, basketball, jogging, and walking with the family canine. This is the heart of Berkeley Citizens' Action country: it seems that every second stop sign has been altered in some way (Stop Contra aid, Stop war, Stop veal farming...). There are probably more old VW vans here than anywhere else in the city. With its air of gone-to-seed rusticity, this central portion of the city might be considered "just right": not too wealthy but not too poor; unpretentious, but also not without a sense of self-esteem. The racially mixed community resides in apartment buildings and modest homes, restored Victorian houses, and bungalows from the 20s and 30s.

South Berkeley

For many years South Berkeley was little more than open ranch land, with orchards, a duck and chicken farm, and a few scattered houses. Construction of the Berkeley Branch railroad in 1876 led to rapid development of the area. Businesses clustered around two of the stops—one at Adeline and Alcatraz Aves., the other at Shattuck and Ashby Aves.—and the excellent public transportation system attracted settlers, who turned the ranch land into sites for apartment houses, bungalows, simple cottages, and large colonial revival homes. Many of the area's predominantly black population (over 75% in the 1980 census) arrived during World War II to work in the shipyards and other wartime industries. A number of these older residents have remained in the homes they bought then—neat, modest houses with brightly painted sidewalks. South Berkeley has one of the lowest turnover rates of any part of the city.

Unfortunately, other South Berkeley homes and apartments reflect the poverty, drugs, and crime that impact the area (see "Law and Disorder" in *City Government*). This is Berkeley's poorest neighborhood. Lat-

ticework iron bars guard corner stores against burglary, and reports of drug-related violence are all too frequent. In spite of these problems, South Berkeley has its advantages. Lower commercial rents here make it possible for small businesses that might not make it elsewhere to survive, and those looking to buy or rent a house appreciate the affordable prices. While there are few grocers or general merchandise retailers in the commercial sections, an area is developing near the Ashby BART station with a collection of antique shops, the popular Brick Hut restaurant, and a number of newer shops and restaurants. In addition, the influential Black Repertory Group has found a new home on Adeline St. (see *Arts and Entertainment*).

West Berkeley

Also known as Ocean View, West Berkeley is an odd amalgamation of industry, retail businesses, and working-class neighborhoods that differ markedly from the rest of the city. Since its beginnings in the 1850s, the area has been home to many minority settlers, originally German, Irish, French, Chinese, and Finns. Today, over 50% of the residents of West Berkeley are black and 14% are Hispanic.

Residents of West Berkeley live in lovingly restored Victorians from the Ocean View era, in dilapidated wooden cottages strewn with litter, in well-maintained small bungalows, and in aging buses on the back streets. The Delaware Street Historic District (Delaware and 5th Sts.) includes fourteen renovated Victorian buildings (see "A Tour of Victorian Ocean View" in *The Buildings of Berkeley*). West Berkeley is still Berkeley's manufacturing center: Cutter Labs and North Face are two of the largest employers in the area, and dozens of smaller companies produce everything from rubber stamps to scaffolds.

While San Pablo Ave.'s auto shops and fast-food joints have mostly set the commercial tone for the area, shops selling saris and Indian food are turning the lower stretch of University Ave. into a "Little India," and upscale shops and cafes are moving in. Several successful restaurants (Spenger's, Juan's, and Brennan's) have always attracted visitors to West Berkeley, but recently, artists and small businesses have taken over abandoned warehouses, and the gentrification process has begun in earnest. The area still has some of the lowest rents in Berkeley, but rates are increasing and forcing out some residents with lower incomes.

Street Names

Though it isn't obvious today, there was once a method to the madness of Berkeley's street names. As the streets were plotted in 1866, all north to south streets were named after American scientists and arranged alphabetically: Audubon, Bowditch, Choate, Dana, Ellsworth, Fulton, Guyot, Henry, Inman, John Jay, Kent, Lieber, and Mitchell. The names of American literary figures were given to the east to west streets, which were designated as "ways": Allston, Bancroft, Channing, Dwight, Everett, Fulton, Goodridge, Hawthorne, Irving, Jarvis, Knapp, Lowell, and Motley. Only a few of these street names survive today, and the alphabetical arrangement has long been obscured as new streets have been sandwiched between the older ones. Certainly the most unfortunate of these changes was that involving Audubon Street. Named for the famous naturalist John J. Audubon, it was prosaically renamed College Avenue. Telegraph Ave., named for a line of telegraph poles that continued on over the hills to the East Coast, was originally called Choate St., after New England physician Dr. George Choate. Shattuck Ave. was originally Guyot Ave., after American geographer Arnold Guyot. Others of these "famous scientist" names survive: Bowditch (America's first philosopher and expert on celestial ship navigation), Dana (professor of natural history at Yale), Ellsworth (first U.S. Commissioner of Patents), and Fulton (for the inventor of the steamboat). Robert Fulton's steamboat, the Claremont, also was used as a street name.

The surviving names of Berkeley's east-west ways included Allston (painter and poet), Bancroft (historian and Secretary of the Navy during the Bear Flag Rebellion), Channing (Unitarian minister), and Dwight (first President of Yale).

Berkeley's oldest street is San Pablo Ave. in West Berkeley. The route began as a cow trail and bridle path connecting East Bay ranches belonging to the Peraltas and General Castro. In 1852, as the Spanish land grants were disintegrating under the onslaught of American squatters, a public highway was laid out from Oakland to the old Spanish settlement of San Pablo. By the following year stagecoaches were stopping on the route at Bowen's Inn in Ocean View.

In the North Berkeley hills, several streets were named for famous California writers: Bret Harte, Charles Keeler (Berkeley's "Poet Laureate"), Joaquin Miller, John Muir, George Sterling, Robert Louis Stevenson, Charles Warren Stoddard, and Mark Twain. Many other North Berkeley street names come from a 1908 effort to move the state capitol to Berkeley. Arlington Circle was planned as the entrance for the new capital building and the surrounding land was divided into streets named for 30 of the state's counties. These include: Alameda, Amador, Colusa, Contra Costa, Del Norte, El Dorado, Fresno, Lassen, Los Angeles, Madera, Marin, Mariposa, Mendocino, Merced, Modoc, Monterey, Napa, Sacramento, San Benito, San Diego, San Mateo, Santa Barbara, Santa Clara, Shasta, Sierra, Solano, Sonoma, Sutter, Tulare, and Yolo. Interestingly, there is no San Francisco, though Berkeley does have a Francisco Street.

Ten states were used as Berkeley street names: California, Colorado, Delaware, Maryland, Michigan, Idaho, Oregon, Nevada, Virginia, and Vermont. Berkeley also fell victim to another cliché in street naming, the presidents—Grant, Harding, Harrison, Jefferson, Lincoln, McKinley, Roosevelt, Tyler, and Wilson. Surprisingly, there is no Washington Street. (Nearby Albany is filled with presidential street names.)

Many Berkeley streets were named after early local settlers and business leaders. José Domingo Peralta and his brother Vicente owned the Spanish title to all of Oakland, Berkeley, and Albany, but were overrun by American squatters in 1852. From this family came the names Peralta Ave., Vicente Road, and Domingo Avenue. Hopkins St. was named for John Hopkins Spring, a turn-of-the-century developer of North Berkeley. Warring St. (originally Asylum St.) was named for the first superintendent of the State School for the Deaf, Dumb, and Blind, Warring Wilkinson.

William Hillegass, James Leonard, Francis Kittredge Shattuck, and his brother-in-law, George M. Blake, were the first property owners of what became downtown Berkeley. In the early 1850s they had arrived in California hoping to strike it rich in the gold mines. Unsuccessful, they settled in the Bay Area. Leonard used his land for ranching, but the other three partners were more interested in politics and business. Blake went on to serve as a district attorney, city council member, mayor, and judge in Oakland. Hillegass and Shattuck jointly operated a livery stable business, invested in a Mt. Diablo coal mine, and helped form a stage line to Berkeley. Shattuck was a leading figure in the development of both Berkeley and Oakland, founding the first bank in Berkeley (later to become American Trust Co.) and serving as mayor of Oakland. Blake, Hillegass, and Shattuck all had Berkeley streets named for them, and even Shattuck's middle name (Kittredge) was given to a street. Leonard stayed out of the limelight, preferring the simple farming life. Although it was once suggested that Telegraph Ave. be named for him, his wife would have none of it.

Durant Ave. is named for Reverend Henry Durant, first president of the University and onetime mayor of Oakland. University president Daniel Coit Gilman, two professors named Le Conte, and professor Hilgard were all memorialized in Berkeley street names. The name Hearst Ave. comes from Phoebe Apperson Hearst, a part-time Northside resident, heir to the Hearst fortune, and a major benefactor of the University.

Many other Berkeley streets are named for pioneers and early businessmen. These include the early ranchers Mark and William Ashby, Amasa Drake Colby, John Garber, and J. B. Woolsey, responsible for linking Berkeley with Oakland via a Telegraph Ave. railroad. Other street names come from pioneers Thomas Addison, H. B. Berryman, Charles Erskine Carleton, Milvia Chappllett, Michael Curtis, Cyrus T. Hopkins, and George F. Parker. One of the most unusual name origins is that of Prince St., named for a horse belonging to J. B. Woolsey. Gayley Rd. was named for UC English professor Charles Gayley, who wrote the first University song, "Our Golden Bear." He was moved to compose the anthem after the track team of 1895 returned from a victorious tour of eastern universities. The gold embroidered grizzly bear on the track team's banner became the University's symbol.

Berkeley's numbered streets are convoluted. Highway 80 lies over the old 1st, and the railroad tracks sit atop 3rd; so numbering starts at 2nd, skips to 4th, and then continues through 10th. In South Berkeley, several of Oakland's street numbers creep across the border (62nd through 67th), although the house numbers continue with the Berkeley numbering system.

Two Berkeley streets, Posen and Albina, received their names from one of the most controversial and colorful characters of the late 19th century—Maurice B. Strellinger, alias M.B. Curtis. Strellinger was an actor who achieved a national reputation for his comic role in the play "Sam'l of Posen." This fame brought wealth with which he purchased large tracts in Berkeley, headed the new electric utility firm, and built the magnificent Peralta Park Hotel near the present St. Mary's High School (the hotel burned in 1946 and was eventually torn down). Strellinger's reputation came crashing down when he was charged with murdering a San Francisco police officer in 1891. After four sensational trials, a jury finally acquitted him, but his reputation was destroyed. He died a pauper in Los Angeles. Berkeley still has Posen St., named for the character he played; and Albina St., named for his wife.

The University

Established in 1898 as the first University of California campus, Cal is Berkeley's reason for existence and the city's intellectual center. As with the community that surrounds it, the University is filled with contrasts. Included within the 1232-acre campus are quiet wooded groves along Strawberry Creek where you can imagine yourself far away from the city. There are broad grassy lawns, perfect places to study or nap on a sunny day. There are also more than a hundred buildings of all designs—modern concrete monstrosities, sumptuous Beaux Arts masterworks of carved granite, and hidden rustic redwood structures from a simpler era. There are classrooms packed with 500 students furi-

Eucalyptus grove. Photo by Don Pitcher.

ously taking notes and hoping they make it past the next exam, but there are also graduate seminars where students discuss agro-forestry practices in Indonesia or design an architectural model for a new theater. Packed library study halls buzz with the voices of Chinese, French, Mexican, and American students, while the dimly-lit back corridors hide cubicles where others study quietly, their desks piled high with books. And each hour, as the bells of the Campanile toll, hordes of students pour out the doors and up the hills to their next class.

But when break time comes, the real focus of student life becomes apparent. Sproul Plaza, an open asphalt and brick space on the southern edge of campus, is the clash point between the intellectual forces of the University and the economic and social forces of hectic Telegraph Avenue. The Plaza epitomizes the diversity and intensity of the University, with its intermingling of students and city people, of professors and performers, of intellectual ferment and plain old people-watching. Students crowd past card tables piled high with Marxist literature, student poetry books, petitions for new ballot initiatives, religious pamphlets, and pleas for University divestment from South Africa. Bulletin boards are plastered with notices upon notices, as if they were the growth rings of a tree. Behind all this, the monolithic columns of the administrative building, Sproul Hall, cast disdainful shadows of power and

Opposite: Pet pig on campus, 1989. Photo by Don Pitcher

Students at Sproul Plaza. Photo by Don Pitcher.

bureaucracy on the chaos below.

Take the time to sit along Sproul for a while and watch the crowds. There are students, over 30,000 of them (21,000 undergraduates and 9000 graduates), garbed in clothes that run the gamut from straight-laced preppie to techno-punk. While 85% of the undergrads and 50% of the grads are from California, students come to Berkeley from every state, and foreign students represent more than 100 different nations. Over half are from minority groups.

A cross-section of Berkeley passes through Sproul Plaza during each day: boisterous frat house jocks, students in speeding electric wheelchairs, panhandlers, nattily-dressed faculty members, skate-boarding high schoolers, street preachers, folk musicians, Maoist revolutionaries, right-wing Moonies, and just about every other imaginable member of society.

Sitting on the steps facing Sproul Plaza is like watching performance art.

One spring afternoon I walked through the Plaza and noticed two characters drawing laughter from the passers-by. One was a street preacher silently carrying a large cross with the word "JESUS" in bold letters. Following him was one of the perennial campus denizens, a bearded man wearing a women's dress opened to reveal a bra, walking on unmatched high-heeled shoes. He was holding a small hand-lettered sign that said "SUSEJ." No explanation was needed for his reversal of the letters or his choice of this preacher to parody. It was simply another slice of life on Sproul Plaza.

Rick Starr stands on the corner, crooning dreadful, off-pitch versions of Perry Como and Frank Sinatra classics into a toy microphone. After each song there is a smattering of applause and catcalls from the lunch hour crowd. He takes a bow and then pointedly directs his next song to an embarrassed student as she quickly hurries away.

As the students rush across the plaza in front of Dwinelle Hall, the "dot man," whose clothes are covered in bright polka-dots, waves his arms, turns quickly and points in various directions, as if he were a traffic cop at a busy intersection. Most students smile, but don't catch the subtle jab, simply thinking him an odd but familiar part of the scene. At other times he climbs into one of the giant urns near Sather Gate, dangling a piece of paper from a fishing pole, as if he were fishing in a school of people.

Why is the Berkeley campus so alive? Although the benign weather and the compact layout of the campus may have something to do with it, much of the credit must go to the kinds of people who are attracted to the University and the city. Berkeley began as an idealistic University, a place envisioned by its founders as "The Athens of the West." The flush of money from those who struck it rich in the Gold Rush helped the new University attract and maintain topnotch researchers, but once freed from the social constraints of East Coast society, students at Berkeley were encouraged to head in new directions. Eventually this freedom to question led to open revolt on the issues of free speech, civil rights, University research policies, and the Vietnam War. The battles have simmered down since the late 60s, but Berkeley still attracts students who share idealistic ideas, and who are willing to organize protests, most recently over the University's investments in South Africa. Although those who remember the 60s decry the "conservatism" and "complacency" of today's students, Cal students consistently vote to the left of the rest of the nation, and more Peace Corps workers come from Berkeley than any other institution in the country.

ETHNIC MAKEUP OF THE UNIVERSITY IN 1988-89

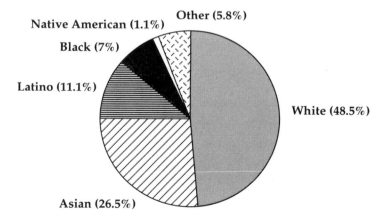

Native American (1.1%)
Other (5.8%)
Black (7%)
Latino (11.1%)
White (48.5%)
Asian (26.5%)

Attending the University

Berkeley is a highly competitive school at both the undergraduate and graduate levels. Only a third of all undergraduate applications are accepted and many students attend other colleges first, hoping to transfer to Berkeley in their junior year when their chances of getting in and doing well are better. At the graduate level the acceptance level is higher, but so is the caliber of the applicants. The racial mix of Cal has changed greatly in recent years. In 1970, 80% of the students were white, but by 1988 they were slightly in the minority. The Asian student population doubled over that same time period.

The Berkeley campus includes fourteen colleges and schools, each with its own degree requirements. Students choose from more than 100 different fields, and if none fill the bill they can create their own major. The *General Catalog* (available from the campus textbook store, 642-0770) provides a good overview of the University and the various degree programs.

Physical sciences lecture hall. Photo by Don Pitcher.

The Negatives

New students arriving in Berkeley often find it overwhelming. While some thrive on the anonymity such a large school offers, others find it bewildering. The classes are rigorous, and finding a place to live presents a serious challenge. Students have to struggle with inadequate study facilities, overcrowded libraries, and the daunting prospect of making course selections without adequate counselling. Other complaints include the narrow focus of some programs, particularly business and engineering, where the abundance of required technical classes leaves room for just a few liberal arts electives. And despite pressure in the more popular fields to push students through in four years so that others can take their place, simply getting into a popular or required class may require standing many hours in lines. Hundreds of students are regularly turned away from such basics as English 1A. Faced with these and a myriad of other problems, many students, especially minorities, drop out or transfer to other schools.

The Positives

Many of the problems at Cal occur in other large universities as well, so most students quickly look beyond its negative attributes to the features that make Berkeley such a great place to get an education. The energy, diversity, and activism that thrive in the city draw some students, while the school's international reputation for excellence draws others. With a plethora of daily events—concerts, lectures, films, readings, rallies, exhibitions, and plays—it is practically impossible to be bored as a student at Cal. Add the dozens of student organizations, intramural sports teams, and other activities, plus the many off-campus goings-on, and it becomes obvious why Berkeley is such a popular place.

As a public institution, UC Berkeley has earned an unparalleled reputation. In 1988 *U.S. News and World Report* ranked the reputation of Berkeley's undergraduate education sixth in the nation and first among public institutions. In a recent national survey, Berkeley was rated the best overall graduate institution in the U.S., with 30 of 32 graduate departments ranked within the top ten in the

UNIVERSITY FUNDING SOURCES (1988)

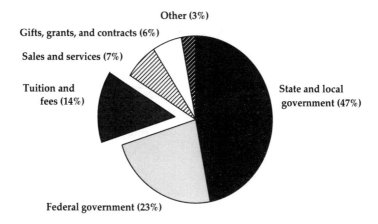

Other (3%)

Gifts, grants, and contracts (6%)

Sales and services (7%)

Tuition and fees (14%)

State and local government (47%)

Federal government (23%)

UNIVERSITY SPENDING (1988)

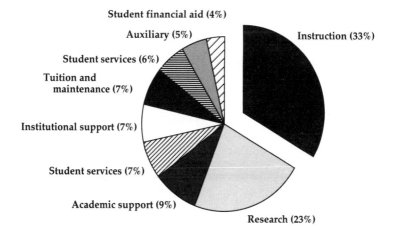

Student financial aid (4%)

Auxiliary (5%)

Student services (6%)

Tuition and maintenance (7%)

Institutional support (7%)

Student services (7%)

Academic support (9%)

Instruction (33%)

Research (23%)

nation. Its faculty ranks as the best in the nation in the fields of anthropology, chemistry, civil engineering, history, music, and statistics. University officials like to point to a number of other statistics:

- The current faculty includes ten Nobel laureates, 95 members of the National Academy of Sciences, and 56 members of the National Academy of Engineering.
- The faculty includes more Guggenheim Fellows and Presidential Young Investigators awards than any other university.
- More undergraduates from Berkeley go on to complete doctorates than from any other university in the nation.
- The University library, with nearly seven-million volumes, is the largest in the western United States.
- Twenty-one UC students have been Rhodes scholars and eleven have been Marshall scholars.
- Thirteen Berkeley faculty members have been awarded the prestigious "genius grants" from the McArthur Foundation.
- Four faculty members have received Pulitzer Prizes, the most recent being Walter McDougall (1986) in history.

Getting In

Pick up undergraduate application forms at the Office of Admissions and Records, 120 Sproul Hall (642-0200). Berkeley operates on the semester system, with the priority filing period in November for the following fall semester. Those interested in graduate school will need to contact the department they are considering, since departments differ in deadlines and application procedures. See the

Sather Gate. Photo by Don Pitcher.

General Catalog for more information. The Graduate Admissions Office (California Hall, 642-7405) produces a free handbook for incoming grad students.

Costs

University fees for both graduates and undergraduates are approximately $1500/yr for Californians and $6000/yr for non-residents. Compare this price with the soaring tuition at Ivy League and private schools, and it becomes obvious that Cal is one of the best educational deals available. In addition, nearly half the students at Berkeley receive financial aid to help them through school.

Learning the Ropes

New students should be sure to get a copy of *Resource* (free), a helpful publication that provides brief descriptions of the available student services and directs you to other places for more information. Pick one up from **Student Activities and Services** (102 Sproul Hall, 642-5171). **Calso** (102 Sproul Hall, 642-4970) conducts undergraduate summer programs for freshmen or transfer students and their parents. For additional student housing and employment information, see *Community Services* and *Finding Rental Housing*. The University also offers childcare services for student families. Contact **Child Care Services** (2537 Haste St., 642-1827).

Student Government

The **Associated Students of the University of California** (ASUC offices are in Eshleman Hall) is the official student voice on campus. The ASUC oversees a $15-million operating budget that employs over 500 students in a variety of stores (books, gifts, electronics), cafes, a pub, a bowling alley, and more than 150 student groups. They are also involved in peer counseling, lobbying, organizing concerts and movies, running a student advocate's office and various magazines, and many other areas of student services. These include a Box Office, a Travel Center, a ski lodge, and the ASUC Studio. The ASUC is run by students elected each semester. The Graduate Assembly (Anthony Hall, 642-2175) represents graduate students on campus.

Daily Californian

Established in 1874, the free *Daily Californian* (2150 Dwight Way, 548-8080) primarily covers University and city issues and events. The paper is unique among student papers in its independence from the University, a hard-won result of the 60s Free Speech Movement. Check the classifieds for apartment rentals, cheap cars, and part-time job opportunities.

Students voting for ASUC candidates. Photo by Don Pitcher.

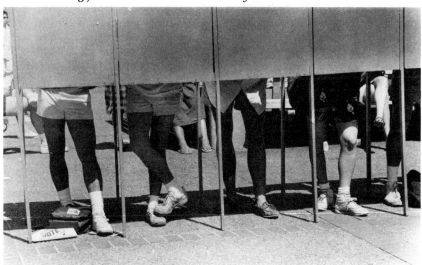

From the Inside:
A Student's View

"I go to Cal"—this simple statement stirs both love and hate within me. Outside campus boundaries, I bask in the glory of my dignified and reputable institution. Yet when that same institution laughs at my petty requests for books, money, or classes, I grow to despise Cal—the distant demi-god that looms threateningly over my education.

Undergraduate Tracey Broderick, senior majoring in English and Mass Communications. Photo by Don Pitcher.

I remember the night campus police armed with billy clubs threw 30 students out of a campus building. Since we were waiting to enroll in required English courses, we had to sleep overnight on the steps in the cold January rain. Such atrocities stem from the overcrowding and underfunding that also create the dreaded large lecture courses. In these anonymous classes the professor becomes just a grade-giver, the student becomes just a grade, and interaction seldom occurs.

Cal's most positive quality is an overwhelming excellence. You find that your freshman chemistry professor wrote your nationally applauded chemistry textbook between Nobel Prize-winning research sessions, and your roommate got perfect scores twice on the college entrance exam. With such participants, classroom discussions can become exchanges of wisdom that compensate for any bureaucratic hassle.

In the end, a feeling of intellectual fulfillment will never march up to you with a welcoming smile at Cal—you must chase and catch it yourself. This chase to learn devastates some students who drop out or transfer. Yet I believe I speak for the majority of Cal undergraduates when I say that despite our premature gray hairs and subconscious yearnings for the organized ease of Ivy League schools, we are glad to be here. It is quite an experience.

—Tracey Broderick

Nobel Laureates at Berkeley

Berkeley fundraisers like to point out that present or past faculty members at Cal have won as many Nobel Prizes as the entire Soviet Union—fifteen each. Those listed below are past or present University faculty members.

Ernest O. Lawrence, *1901-1958,* received the Nobel Prize in Physics in 1939 for his invention of the cyclotron while he was teaching at Berkeley. A brilliant young physicist, he attracted many others to the University (including seven other Nobel winners), establishing what later became Lawrence Berkeley Laboratory (LBL). Lawrence was a major player in the development of the first nuclear bomb, a legacy that is carried on today at Lawrence Livermore Lab, where the nation's nuclear arsenal is created.

John H. Northrop, *1891-1987,* was co-winner of the 1946 Nobel Prize in Chemistry for his work with pepsin, a digestive enzyme that proved vital in the development of new drugs.

William M. Stanley, *1904-1971,* was co-winner (with John Northrop and J. B. Sumner) of the 1946 Nobel Prize in Chemistry. His award was based upon the isolation and crystallization of the first virus ever purified, the tobacco mosaic virus.

William F. Giauque, *1895-1982,* was awarded a Nobel Prize in Chemistry in 1949 for his work on a crucial experiment that brought materials to $-459.688°$F, close to absolute zero. Giauque Hall, home of one of the most powerful continuously operating electromagnets on earth, was named for him in 1966.

Edwin M. McMillan, *1907- ,* came to UC Berkeley in 1932 to work with E. O. Lawrence and his cyclotron. With Philip Abelson he discovered Neptunium (Element 93), the first element found to be heavier than uranium. He went on to help develop radar and sonar, and worked on the uranium and plutonium bombs. He and Glenn Seaborg were awarded the Nobel Prize in Chemistry in 1951 for their "discoveries in the chemistry of transuranium elements."

Glenn T. Seaborg, *1912- ,* who holds title to the longest entry of any person in *Who's Who in America*, was co-discover of elements 94-102 and 106. He helped develop the plutonium bomb and served as head of the Atomic Energy Commission for a decade. Sea-

Nobel Laureate Glenn T. Seaborg before the Lawrence Hall of Science. Photo by Don Pitcher.

borg shared with Edwin M. McMillan the 1951 Nobel Prize in Chemistry. He served as Berkeley Chancellor from 1958-61 and is presently director of Lawrence Hall of Science.

Owen Chamberlain, *1920-* , another of E. O. Lawrence's protégés, was involved in the firing of the first atomic bomb in 1945 (although he lost a $5 bet that it wouldn't work). Working with Emilio Segrè, Chamberlain later used the Berkeley Bevatron to create anti-protons, which were the first indication that all atomic particles have twins with opposite polarities. For this work they shared the 1959 Nobel Prize in Physics. Chamberlain is active today in the anti-nuclear movement.

Emilio Segrè, *1905-* , the first Ph.D. student under Enrico Fermi, fled the fascism of his native Italy and came to Berkeley in 1938 to work at the Radiation Lab. He was involved in development of the atomic bomb and shared the 1959 Nobel Prize in physics with Owen Chamberlain.

Donald A. Glaser, *1926-* , was only 34 years old when he was awarded the 1960 Nobel Prize in Physics for his development of the bubble chamber. Bubble chambers are used to detect the fleeting presence of atomic particles and have proven essential to understanding atomic structure. (The idea came to him while he was watching a stream of beer bubbles rise in a glass at a Michigan bar.)

Melvin Calvin, *1911-* , attracted to Berkeley by E. O. Lawrence's Radiation Lab, discovered that Carbon-14, a product of the Lab's cyclotron, could be used as a tracer in many biological experiments. Calvin's use of C-14 to trace the carbon cycle in photosynthesis led to his 1961 Nobel Prize in Chemistry.

Charles H. Townes, *1915-* , was awarded the 1964 Nobel Prize in Physics for his work on masers (microwave amplification by stimulated emission of radiation). Working with his brother-in-law, A. L. Schawlow of Stanford, Townes later went on to develop the more practical laser, a product that has revolutionized everything from eye surgery to nuclear warfare.

Luis W. Alvarez, *1911-1988*, perhaps the greatest experimental physicist of this century, Alvarez's varied career spanned the development of the detonator for the atomic bomb; the patents for more than 30 inventions; the discovery of many nuclear particles; and the proposal that an asteroid caused the mass destruction of the dinosaurs. Like many others, Alvarez began his career as one of E. O. Lawrence's "Rad Lab boys." A vital member of the Manhattan Project, Alvarez was a scientific observer aboard the aircraft following the plane that dropped the first atomic bomb on Hiroshima. He was awarded the Nobel Prize in Physics in 1968 for his development of the hydrogen bubble chamber and his discovery of numerous nuclear particles.

Czeslaw Milosz, *1911-* , a Lithuanian-born poet and novelist, was a cultural attaché for the Polish government from 1946-1950 before defecting to the West. Milosz joined the Department of Slavic Languages and Literatures at Berkeley in 1960 and was awarded the 1980 Nobel Prize in Literature for his

Nobel Laureate Yuan T. Lee. Courtesy of the University of California, Berkeley.

highly acclaimed book of poetry *Bells in Winter.*

Gerard Debreu, *1921- ,* received the 1983 Nobel Prize in Economics. The French-born Debreu applied mathematics to the study of economics, showing that under certain conditions the free-market system could reach an equilibrium (as predicted in 1776 by Adam Smith). His theoretical models of consumer behavior are used extensively in economic forecasting.

Yuan Tseh Lee, *1936- ,* shared the 1986 Nobel Prize in Chemistry with Dudley Hershbach (Harvard) and John Polanyi (Toronto) for the study of chemical reactions using the technology of particle physics. A native of Taiwan, Lee received his Ph.D. from Berkeley and conducts research at LBL.

Prominent Former Students

In addition to the plethora of Nobel Laureates, the University has also produced a large number of national (and international) figures in the areas of politics, business, athletics, entertainment, and literature. The following list includes some of the better-known individuals. Only degrees or attendance at Cal are listed, though many of the people also received additional degrees from other universities.

Stephen D. Bechtel, Sr., *1899- 1989,* was Senior Director of the Bechtel Co. and UC Alumnus of the Year in 1952. Bechtel attended Cal from 1919 to 1921.

Zulfikar Ali Bhutto, *1928-1979,* was awarded a B.A. in Political Science in 1950. He served as President of Pakistan for several years, but was ousted in a coup, accused of murdering a political opponent, and hanged by his successor. His daughter, Benazir Bhutto, was elected president of Pakistan in 1989.

Matt Biondi, *1965- ,* was a gold medal winner in the 1984 Los Angeles Olympic Games and top swimmer and water polo player in the nation from 1985 to 1987. Biondi picked up seven medals (four gold) at the 1988 Seoul Olympics. He received a 1988 B.A. in Political Economics of Industrial Societies.

Edmund G. (Jerry) Brown, Jr., *1938- ,* has been California Secretary of State 1970-74, Governor of California 1975-1982, and Chair of the California Democratic Party. Jerry Brown graduated from Cal in 1961 with a B.A. in Classics.

Joan Didion, *1934- ,* has written *Slouching Towards Bethlehem , The*

White Album, and *Miami*. She graduated with a B.A. in English in 1956.

March Fong Eu, *1922- ,* has been California Secretary of State since 1975. She received her B.S. in Agriculture in 1943.

John Kenneth Galbraith, *1908- ,* was a professor of economics at Harvard and is the author of many influential books on economics and social policy including: *American Capitalism, Economics and the Public Purpose,* and *The Anatomy of Power.* Galbraith graduated with an M.A. (1932) and a Ph.D. (1934) in Economics.

Lillian Moler Gilbreth, *1878-1972,* was a brilliant engineer and author of *Cheaper by the Dozen* who graduated in 1900 in engineering.

Rube Goldberg, *1883-1970,* was an artist and cartoonist famous for his wildly absurd mechanical contraptions that turned his name into a household word. Goldberg received an engineering degree in 1904.

Walter Haas, Jr., *1916- ,* is the retired chairman of Levi Strauss and owner of the Oakland A's. Haas holds a 1940 B.A. in Economics. He was Alumnus of the Year in 1984.

Philip Habib, *1920- ,* acted as President Reagan's Special Representative to the Middle East from 1981 to 1983. Habib received a 1952 Ph.D. in Agricultural Economics.

William Randolph Hearst, Jr., *1908- ,* Hearst Corporation president and grandson of Phoebe Apperson Hearst, attended Cal in 1926, but did not graduate.

Abbie Hoffman, *1936-1989,* was one of the most flamboyant members of the counterculture. Hoffman was a member of the Chicago Seven, founded the "Yippies" (Youth International Party) with Jerry Rubin, and otherwise raised hell. He received an M.A. in Psychology from Cal in 1960.

Bill Honig, *1937- ,* has been California Superintendent of Public Instruction since 1983. Honig holds a 1958 J.D. from Boalt Hall.

Stacy Keach, *1941- ,* once a fraternity boy, has been an actor, director, producer, and writer for numerous films, television programs, and Broadway shows. Keach received B.A.'s in English and Dramatic Art in 1963.

Stephen T. Mather, *1867-1930,* was the first National Park Service super-

A Rube Goldberg cartoon.

intendent and a highly influential environmental leader. Mather was an 1887 graduate in agriculture from Cal.

Robert S. McNamara, *1916- ,* acted as U.S. Secretary of Defense 1961-1968 and President of World Bank 1968-1981. He graduated with a B.A. in Economics in 1937.

Edwin Meese III, *1931- ,* was the controversial Deputy District Attorney of Alameda County in 1959-1967 and U.S. Attorney General 1985-1988. Meese received a J.D. from Boalt Hall in 1958.

Robert Misrach, *1949- ,* graduated in 1971 with a B.A. in Psychology, and is one of the nation's leading fine arts photographers.

Craig Morton, *1943- ,* was All-American quarterback at Cal and later for the Dallas Cowboys. Morton received a B.A. in Rhetoric in 1965. While a student, he was a strong opponent of FSM activists, attempting to break up protest rallies.

Gregory Peck, *1916- ,* acted in numerous films including *To Kill a Mockingbird* (Oscar in 1962 for best actor), *Twelve O'Clock High* and *Guns of Navarone.* Peck received a B.A. in English in 1942.

Dean Rusk, *1909- ,* has been a Rhodes Scholar, U.S. Secretary of State from 1961-1969, and Professor of International Law at the University of Georgia since 1970. Rusk received his J.D. from Boalt Hall in 1940.

Mario Savio, *1944- ,* was the celebrated spokesman for the Free Speech Movement while a student at Cal in 1964. Savio studied biology but did not graduate from Berkeley. He finally received his B.S. in Physics in 1984 from San Francisco State.

Irving Stone, *1903-1989,* authored many biographies, including *Lust for Life* (Van Gogh), *The Origin* (Charles Darwin), and *The Agony and the Ecstasy* (Michelangelo). Stone received his B.A. in Political Science in 1923.

Earl Warren, *1891-1974,* acted as district attorney for Alameda County from 1939-1943, governor from 1943-1953, and Republican candidate for vice president in 1948. He became chief justice of the U.S. Supreme Court in 1953 and served until 1969, during which time he headed the investigation into John Kennedy's assassination. Warren received a B.A. from Berkeley in 1912, followed by a J.D. in 1914 from Boalt Hall.

Robert Penn Warren, *1905-1989,* became the first U.S. Poet Laureate in 1986. He won the 1947 Pulitzer Prize for fiction for *All the Kings Men* and the 1958 Pulitzer Prize for poetry for *Promises: Poems 1954-1956.* Warren received his M.A. in English in 1927.

Pete Wilson, *1933- ,* has been U.S. Senator from California since 1983, acted as a California state legislator from 1966 to 1971, and mayor of San Diego from 1971 to 1983. Wilson received a J.D. from Boalt Hall in 1962.

Steve Wozniak, *1951- ,* was co-founder of Apple Computers with Steve Jobs. Wozniak received his B.S. in Electrical Engineering in 1986.

Building the Campus

Although it may be hard to envision today, the Berkeley campus was once planned on the "universal architectural principles" of formal axes, bilateral symmetry, classic architectural style, and a monumental scale. Originally designed to hold just 5000 students, the University now is home to 30,000. Fitting classrooms, research facilities, and administrative offices onto such a small plot of ground has strained relations with the city of Berkeley and has resulted in a hodgepodge of building styles. Today one finds graceful old buildings jammed against utilitarian concrete structures, and quiet brookside benches not far from crowded, hectic plazas.

In 1864, trustees of the fledgling College of California (later to become the University of California) hired the noted landscape architect Frederick Law Olmsted to develop a plan for the new Berkeley campus. Olmsted's plan departed radically from traditional college designs. In it he proposed a college that would be an integral part of the community and would blend with the surrounding natural environment of rolling grasslands and tree-lined creeks. His park-like plan eschewed dormitories ("large barracks"); instead students were to be housed in small cottages. With a grand view of the Golden Gate, the campus would consist of only two buildings, one for an assembly hall, faculty offices, and classrooms, and the other for the library, records, and scientific collections.

Olmsted's plan had little impact on the eventual campus, however, and a second plan proposed by San Francisco architect David Farquharson was adopted by the University Regents in 1870. It included six buildings

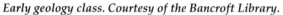

Early geology class. Courtesy of the Bancroft Library.

while maintaining Olmsted's general campus outline. When the first classes began at Berkeley in 1873 only two buildings existed, North and South Halls. Over the next two decades the University grew haphazardly, with wood-framed buildings erected wherever flat land could be found.

In 1896, Bernard Maybeck, then a lecturer in architectural drawing, proposed an architectural competition to design a new campus. With a $200,000 contribution from Phoebe Apperson Hearst, Maybeck travelled to Europe to organize the competition and to generate enthusiasm for it. The architects were given free rein to create a utopian "City of Learning" with "no definite limitations of cost, materials or style." According to the contest prospectus issued to the participants and the press, it was to be such a masterpiece of architectural design that "there will be no more necessity of remodeling its broad outlines a thousand years hence than there would be of remodeling the Parthenon."

The Hearst competition attracted both American and European aspirants, many of whom followed the grandiose principles of the Ecole des Beaux Arts in Paris, then the pre-eminent school of architecture. The winning architect, Henri Jean Emile Bénard, arranged his buildings along axial boulevards and city squares. After receiving his $10,000 prize, however, Bénard refused to supervise the project, returning to Paris in 1900. Maybeck did not want the enormous project himself and supported John Galen Howard (the fourth place finisher in the competition) as Bénard's replacement. When Howard arrived to become supervising architect, Maybeck resigned his lectureship and turned to his real love, designing buildings (see *The Buildings of Berkeley*).

George Kellham followed Howard as supervising architect, overseeing a major expansion of the campus along the southern edge. He was also responsible for the monstrous three-acre Life Sciences Building, then the largest academic building in the nation. Arthur Brown, Jr. became supervising architect in 1938 and was responsible for construction of Sproul Hall, Minor Hall, Donner Laboratory, and Stern Hall. He also proposed a new plan that prevented the construction of tall buildings, but allowed for a series of long structures around the campus perimeter. Most of these were not built. With the sudden influx of students after World War II, however, many temporary buildings were moved to the campus from old Navy camps; six of these aging wooden "T-buildings" are still standing.

When Brown left the post as supervising architect in 1948, he was replaced by a committee that proposed removing 28 older buildings and replacing them with modern structures. Many of these replacements were made, but the replacements looked like the work of a committee: modern office-style buildings began to spring up around the campus. The structures reflected Chancellor Clark Kerr's dehumanized ideas of the campus as a "multiversity," a place one critic described as, "more a mechanism—a series of processes producing a series of results—a mechanism held together by administrative rules and powered by money." One of the largest expansions occurred in the early 1960s when the University took over a portion of Telegraph Ave. and developed Zellerbach Hall and the complex of buildings around Sproul Plaza. This

John Galen Howard

Born in 1864, John Galen Howard received an education in architecture at both the Massachusetts Institute of Technology and the prestigious Ecole des Beaux-Arts in Paris, although he did not graduate from either school. Howard, the University's supervising architect for nearly a quarter century, designed twenty campus buildings. The first and perhaps the finest was the Hearst Mining Building, a lovely Beaux Arts masterwork. Others include Doe Library, Wellman Hall, Hearst Greek Theatre, Sather Gate, Memorial Stadium, and the Campanile. Howard viewed these buildings as part of the attempt to create a new Athens of the West: "It is the University's bounden duty to cultivate artistic ideals just as distinctly and indisputably as it is its duty to teach the beauties of literature and the wonders of science. The University fulfills only a part of its mission when it teaches the theory of beauty without its practice. Its duty is to inspire, to cultivate, to edify. And to do that completely it must have fine buildings."

Howard served as the first Professor of Architecture, greatly influencing such famed designers as Julia Morgan, John Hudson Thomas, and William Wurster. He lost his position as supervising architect in 1924 after a series of battles with the University Regents over campus development.

was followed by the razing of several more blocks to make way for twelve high-rise dorms on Southside and parking structures on both the northern and southern sides of campus. These and other projects led to a doubling of built-up space and public pressure to halt the destruction of surrounding neighborhoods. The issue came to a head in the People's Park riots of 1969 (see *Touring Revolutionary Berkeley*). Some of the buildings built during this era are quite attractive and humane (Zellerbach Hall and Moffitt Library), while others became monumental eyesores. The worst offenders are Evans Hall, Wurster Hall, and the series of highrise dorms just south of campus, all ugly, hurriedly-built concrete monstrosities.

The number of students continued to increase after this tumultuous time, but campus construction slowed temporarily. Recent years have brought another growth spurt with construction of the giant Recreational Sports Facility (1984), a four-story addition to the Life Sciences Building (1987), and a new 175,000 square foot Genetics and Plant Biology Building (1989). Up to 40 additional projects are in the planning stages, including several giant housing complexes, a new business school, a new hospital, and a controversial animal research facility. The end result may well be the "Manhattanization" of Berkeley. John Galen Howard must be spinning in his grave. Even historic People's Park is threatened by this onslaught of University development.

The people of Berkeley view these

developments as both a boon and a threat. New student housing will help to alleviate one of the city's most severe problems, the competition for scarce rental units. Many residents also work for the city's largest employer, the University, and stand to benefit from newer and more modern facilities and from new job openings. At the same time, however, they watch apprehensively as the University's continued expansion threatens surrounding neighborhoods. A "town-gown" conflict has always existed in Berkeley, but as land becomes increasing scarce it will certainly intensify. In many ways the city is trapped in a Catch-22 situation—it can shut down growth and thereby threaten the vitality and pre-eminence of one of the world's great universities; or it can allow new construction projects that would gradually devour the aspects of life in Berkeley that make it such an interesting and liveable city. Negotiating between these alternatives will be extremely difficult.

Lawrence Berkeley Laboratory
Lawrence Berkeley Lab (LBL) is the oldest national laboratory in the United States and the only one adjacent to a major university. Researchers here have discovered numerous subatomic particles and fourteen different elements. One of these, the highly radioactive Berkelium (Element 97), discovered by Glenn Seaborg and others, was even named for the city of Berkeley. LBL was also the home of J. Robert Oppenheimer, "Father of the Bomb," and many other nuclear researchers involved in creating the first nuclear weapons.

LBL originated when a hot young

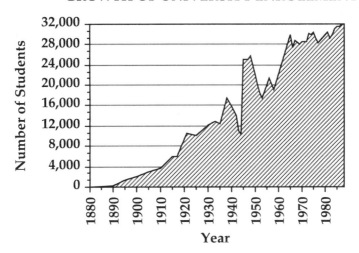

GROWTH OF UNIVERSITY ENROLLMENT

physics professor, Ernest O. Lawrence, left Yale for Berkeley, anxious to continue his work on photoelectricity. He soon attracted some of the nation's top graduate students with his rapid progress in nuclear physics. He and Ph.D. student M. Stanley Livingston developed the first cyclotron, a hand-sized device that used a magnetic field to accelerate hydrogen ions around a circular pathway. Realizing the tremendous potential of this work, the University established the Radiation Laboratory (Rad Lab) in 1931 and agreed to house and finance larger cyclotrons. Lawrence received a Nobel Prize in 1939 for developing the cyclotron, the first of nine Nobel Prizes awarded to those working at the Lab. This development opened a new era of "Big Science" research requiring dozens of interdisciplinary researchers working towards the same goals. The Rad Lab grew rapidly, and as World War II arrived it became a center for the development of methods to produce the first atomic bombs. Lawrence watched the first explosion of the plutonium bomb in the New Mexican desert without guilt, and although he opposed its use at first, he concluded that it would end the war with Japan more quickly. A few weeks later atomic bombs were dropped on Hiroshima and Nagasaki.

After World War II, the Rad Lab turned towards a mixture of military and peaceful nuclear research. The Lab continued to grow with development of four major accelerators—the 88-inch cyclotron, the 184-inch syncrocyclotron, the Bevatron, and the superHILAC. In 1952, the Livermore Naval Air Station, 45 miles east of Berkeley, became home to all of the Lab's military research work. It was renamed the Lawrence Livermore Nuclear Weapons Laboratory and is now deeply involved in all aspects of nuclear weapons and Strategic Defense Initiative, or "star wars," research. In 1983, Lawrence's wife tried in vain to have her deceased husband's name removed from the Livermore lab, saying, "The greater part of the research at the Livermore Lab not only dishonors Ernest Lawrence's name, it also dishonors a great University." University Regents refused the request, noting that only Congress could alter the name.

Ernest O. Lawrence died in 1958 and since that time the Lawrence Berkeley Laboratory has become much more diversified. Although its $170-million annual funding now comes almost entirely from the U.S. Department of Energy, it is managed by the University. Over 170 UC faculty members play leadership roles in LBL research and approximately 770 UC students participate in this research. The Lab employs more than 3000 people, conducting research in an incredible range of fields—electron microscopy, nuclear medicine, groundwater contamination, indoor air pollution, solar energy, artificial sky simulations, high-energy physics, and more.

Public access to Lawrence Berkeley Laboratory is restricted to prevent damage to its scientific equipment and visitors need to have either a specific reason for coming or a pre-arranged appointment with an LBL tour guide. A free shuttle bus transports employees and visitors from various points around the campus to the Lab on weekdays (see *Transportation*).

Telegraph Avenue entrance to campus, 1880. Courtesy of the Bancroft Library.

Sather Gate/Telegraph Avenue, 1911. Courtesy of the Bancroft Library.

TOURING THE CAMPUS

Even those who have lived in Berkeley for many years and attended the University will discover something new in an exploration of the campus. Free campus tours are given Mon-Fri at 1 pm, or Sat by special request, starting at the Visitor Center in the Student Union (642-5215). The hour-long tours cover many of the University's most interesting buildings. My own path covers similar ground. See keyed map in this chapter to follow this tour.

1 Sproul Plaza, the open area in front of the Student Union that is lined by London plane trees, their gnarled branches pruned back severely each winter, is bordered on one end by Bancroft Way and at the other end by Sather Gate (see below). Sproul Hall, built in 1941, is home to the Undergraduate Admissions Office, Campus Police, and a variety of other University administrative offices. Inside you may want to check out the old photos lining the first floor wall. Robert Gordon Sproul (1891-1975), one of the most influential University presidents, served from 1930 to 1958. During his tenure Cal experienced rapid expansion, an increasing focus on research, and growing international acclaim.

The domineering facade of Sproul Hall seems to epitomize the power of the University, a power that makes it a frequent target for critics. Sproul Plaza is famous as the site of hundreds of protest actions, which reached a peak with the Free Speech Movement of 1964 and the antiwar protests of the 60s. Recently, protests against University policy on South Africa and People's Park have re-ignited some of the powerful emotions of that period.

Sproul is a great place to just hang out—in fine weather it's packed with students and others listening to loony street preachers, watching jugglers and puppeteers, or checking out the latest Bob Dylan clone singing on the corner. Unbeknownst to most students, the nondescript fountain in Sproul Plaza is officially titled Ludwig's Fountain, after a German short-hair pointer ("Ludwig von Schwarenberg") that made his home there during the early 60s. Ludwig joined many a sit-in but preferred to stand in the fountain, stealing bites from sandwiches and dropping his wet ball in people's laps in the hopes they'd throw it for him.

2 Lower Sproul Plaza (just west and down the steps from the main plaza) is popular with the frisbee and hackey-sack crowd. On Wednesdays and Fridays during the school year you'll hear noon-hour concerts—past performers include Talking Heads, The Ramones, Eddie Money, and Devo. On weekends it's also a great place to listen to some of the hottest bongo rhythms anywhere. If you're looking for a meal, there are many choices in the Lower Sproul.

The "golden bear" sitting high atop a pedestal in the plaza was erected by alumni from the Class of 1929. There is considerable debate as to whether the critter more resembles a sick wolverine or a rabid raccoon. Some feel it unfortunate that the sculpture repels paint and is positioned in such a way that makes defacement very difficult. Emmy Lou Packard, a student of famed Mexican muralist Diego

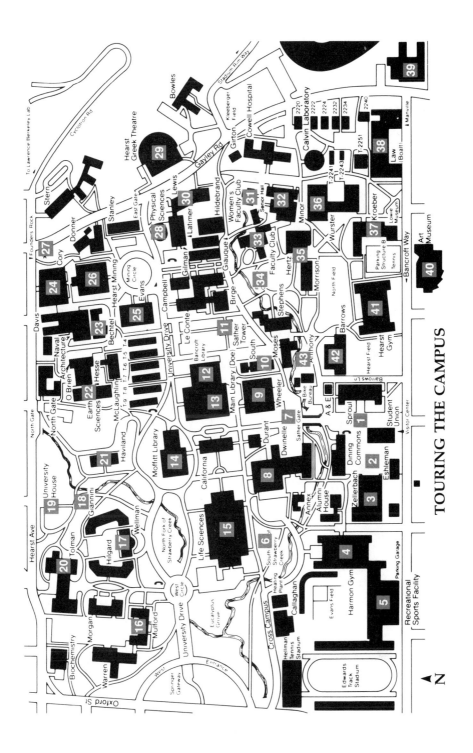

TOURING THE CAMPUS

Rivera, created the frieze on Lower Sproul, using potatoes, onions, radishes, and dry cereal to create images that represent California landscapes.

From Lower Sproul head down the steps just north of **3** **Zellerbach Hall** (1969), the University's outstanding performing arts center. Turn left in front of **4** **Harmon Gym** (1933), headquarters of men's athletics, and then right on Bancroft Way to the **5** **Recreational Sports Facility,** (see *Recreation*). Completed in 1984, this spacious and attractive building houses an array of facilities for students and the community. Ask at the desk to take a quick look inside. From RSF, retrace your steps back to Harmon and continue to the south fork of **6** **Strawberry Creek.** The creek once had resident trout and seasonal runs of steelhead, but culverting has destroyed the lower reaches through the city of Berkeley. The beautiful redwood trees were planted here in the 1930s. Follow the path alongside Strawberry Creek uphill to **7** **Sather Gate.**

Sather Gate, designed by John Galen Howard in 1910,

Stoney Burke.

is one of the primary symbols of the University (the other being the Campanile). It was built with funds from Jane K. Sather in memory of her husband, who was one of early California's wealthiest bankers. For many years Sather Gate served as the main entrance to the campus: it was the end of the line on the trolley car. (The circular concrete area in front of the gate marks the location of the trolley turntable.) The plaques that decorate Sather Gate were recently replaced after being in storage for decades— apparently the idea of a nude male figure with the words "erected by Jane K. Sather" was viewed as a bit too risqué. Just beyond the gate is a bridge over Strawberry Creek and another plaza in front of **8** **Dwinelle Hall** (1952), home to a great variety of humanities departments including history, French, German, and linguistics. John W. Dwinelle was an astounding man who graduated from college at age eighteen, passed his New York State Bar Exam at age 21 (while serving as editor of the *New York Daily Gazette*), and then left for California. Once here, he helped clear up the Spanish and Mexican land claims, was elected mayor of Oakland, served on the Board of Trustees of the College of California and in the state legislature. In 1868, he introduced a bill to establish the University of California, and he later served as one of the first members its new Board of Regents.

Dwinelle Hall is worth a visit for its mind-dulling, maze-like interior and the room numbers which appear to have been assigned entirely at random. Folklore has it that the rambling building was designed by two architect brothers who, after a fight, worked on separate halves while refusing to speak to each other. Stoney Burke, excoriator of the University and everything conservative, often holds court in crowded Dwinelle Plaza over the noon hour; gray-suited businessmen, beware!

Now head up the hill past the English department's abode, **9 Wheeler Hall** (1917), named for long-time President of the University, Benjamin Ide Wheeler. A former professor of philology and Greek at Cornell, Wheeler came to Berkeley only on the condition that he be given absolute control over faculty appointments and salary. He used this power to bring in top professors from the east—Henry Morse Stephens (history), Joseph Grinnell (zoology), Joel Hildebrand (chemistry), and Alfred Kroeber (anthropology), among others—making it a brilliant era for undergraduate education. (Most of these men now have campus buildings named in their honor.) Wheeler, impeccably dressed and riding a dark mare about campus, brought an aristocratic air to the campus. If his attitude toward students was paternalistic, he was still popular for his even-handed treatment and integrity. According to Wheeler the University should stand "for the purest things and the cleanest, loftiest ideals." His strict regulations and rah-rah boosterism transformed the University from a rough-and-tumble place with a reputation for heavy student drinking and all-out brawls into a place where tolerance and equality were the standards for behavior. During his twenty-year reign (he was forced to retire in 1919) the University at Berkeley grew from 2000 to over 11,000 students, even while new UC campuses opened in Los Angeles, San Francisco, Davis, Riverside, and San Diego. After

Wheeler retired, a faculty revolt returned control of appointments to the Academic Senate, which remains one of the most independent such groups in any American institution.

10 South Hall (1873), designed by the University's first official architect, David Farquharson, is the next stop. This old ivy-covered brick structure was one of the first two buildings on campus. (Its twin, North Hall, was torn down after being declared a fire hazard.) Interesting features include iron cresting along the roof, gargoyles on the downspouts, and a French Mansard-style roof. South Hall originally housed the University President's office, but is now home to the School of Library and Information Studies.

Just up from South Hall is the **11 Campanile**. For a quarter you can take the elevator up and then climb the last flight of stairs to the top, where there are spectacular views in all directions. Look up into the hills to see the **Big C** (as in Cal). Prior to Benjamin Ide Wheeler's administration, each fall had brought the "Rush," an all-out war between freshmen and sophomores. The classes met on an open field and wrestled each other until one class ended up on the ground, their hands and feet tied. After several serious injuries, the Rush was finally stopped in 1905 when Wheeler persuaded the students to put their energy into building a giant concrete C. A plaque on the C reads, "In memory of the rush buried by the class of 1907 and 1908, March 23, 1905. *Requiscat in pace.*" The Big C has become a yearly target of Stanford Big Game pranksters intent upon painting Berkeley cardinal red.

After leaving the Campanile, stroll across the beautifully landscaped

The Campanile

It's everywhere—on bookcovers, T-shirts, postcards, posters, and University catalogues. It is the Berkeley equivalent of the Golden Gate bridge, a symbol of the city and the University. Designed by John Galen Howard to resemble the campanile of Saint Mark's Plaza in Venice ("campanile" means bell tower in Italian), it was completed in 1915. At 307 feet it is the tallest structure on campus. Officially it is Sather Tower, named in memory of the wealthy donor who gave $144,000 to construct a monument to herself. (Jane K. Sather died four years before it was completed.) Inside the tower and unseen by most visitors is a huge collection of human, dinosaur, and other animal bones, primarily collected from the La Brea Tar Pits. The 50 tons of bones cover six floors of the tower.

The Campanile. Photo by Don Pitcher.

More bells were added to the original twelve in 1978 and 1983, bringing the total to 61 which cover a tonal range of four octaves. They are played by a keyboard of Brazilian hardwood linked to the clappers by cables; the carillonneur (someone is hired specifically for this rather obscure position) needs both strength and agility to strike the keys with a fist while simultaneously using the pedals for other bells. In addition to an hourly chiming, there are ten-minute programs three times a day—at 7:50 am, noon, and 6 pm. Sunday recitals start at 2 pm and last for approximately 45 minutes. Every year since 1930, on the last day of classes, the carillonneur plays a mournful old Irish folk song about a criminal named Danny Deever who is to be hanged the next morning. The bells are not played during exam week to keep students from taking this too seriously. In 1939, Francis W. Reid published *Chimes of the Campanile* with tunes such as this gem, *Hurrah for Berkeley*, sung to the tune of *Yankee Doodle:*

> "O Campanile, clang your bells,
> Raise a rough-neck row-row,
> Chant that best of UC yells—
> Old "Osky wisky wow-wow!"
>
> Peal a Paen from the skies,
> Shout song of frisky glee-glee,
> Sound that best of battle cries—
> Osky wow-wow, Wisky wee-wee!..."

plaza just north of the tower and then head down the steps towards the **12 Bancroft Library** (1949) (see "Libraries" under *Community Services*). Inside you can request items from a magnificent collection of historical documents or take a look at old paintings of wagon trains loaded with pioneers heading west. Back outside, turn right and go up a set of stairs into the **13 Main (Doe) Library** (1911), one of John Galen Howard's masterpieces of design. The particular interest is the Reference Room, with its high-arched ceiling, large windows, and hundreds of students hunched over the study tables. From there head down the stairs to the Morrison Library, a place for relaxing. Directly across the hall is the Map Room, which contains an extraordinary collection of maps from around the world.

From the library, head downhill, passing the **14 Moffitt Undergraduate Library** (1968) and the gigantic **15 Life Sciences Building (LSB)**, built in 1930 and for many years the largest building on any university campus in the world. LSB Annex, a major addition (completely different in design) was completed in 1987. The blue gum eucalyptus grove near West Circle is said to contain the tallest stand of hardwood trees in the Northern Hemisphere. They were planted in 1877. The grove makes a pleasant place to sit and escape the crush of people. **16 Mulford Hall** (1948), just to the north, is home to the Department of Forestry, and its hallways are lined with an interesting collection of woods from all over the world. (For a description of the more than 300 species of trees on the campus, see *Trees of the Berkeley Campus*, published by the University of California Division of Agricultural

Sciences and available at the ASUC bookstore in the Student Union Building.)

17 Wellman Hall (1912), another of John Galen Howard's works, is just up the hill from Mulford. It houses the Entomology Department and a small collection of colorful butterflies and other insects from around the world. Walk around the front of Wellman and past the beautiful large ginkgo tree beside **18 Giannini Hall** (1930), home to the College of Natural Resources. (Ginkgo trees are sometimes called "living fossils" because their leaves have been found in 200 million year old sediments.) A path leads behind Giannini to **19 University House**, the only structure built following the Bénard campus plan. Built to resemble an Italian Renaissance mansion, its splendid landscap-

Students studying at Moffitt Undergraduate Library. Photo by Don Pitcher.

ing incorporates Italian stone pines cabled together to keep them from falling over and a Paul Bunyan-sized floral clock donated in 1967 by the government of Switzerland. Begun in 1902, the building took nine years to complete at a cost of $215,000, unheard-of at the time. President Theodore Roosevelt once slept in the southeast bedroom, and the house has also seen visits by Presidents Truman and Kennedy. University House is today the official residence of the Berkeley chancellor and his family, although it is also still used for University receptions. It is not open to the public, but if you call in advance (642-1861), pleading and begging, they may let you in to see the large painting of Bishop Berkeley in the hallway. Peak behind the mansion to see the extensive lawns and exotic plantings.

Next to University House is one of the forgettable early 60s structures, **20 Tolman Hall**, named for an unforgettable psychology professor, Edward Chace Tolman. Tolman gained fame both for his work in psychology and for his 1950 refusal to sign the loyalty oath that the UC Regents insisted upon during the Cold War hysterics. Although the University fired Tolman, he was reinstated three years later. After his death in 1959, the University gave in to pressure and named the psychology building for him.

Now cross the bridge over the north fork of Strawberry Creek in one of the more secluded areas of campus. Redwood trees, some planted here before 1870, line the banks of the creek. (Redwood trees did not naturally occur on campus, though they were found in the Oakland hills.) Follow the path uphill past **21 Haviland Hall** (1924), home to the School

of Social Welfare, and on to the **22 Earth Sciences Building** (1961), a five-story box that looks like an office building. Inside, the Museum of Paleontology offers hallway exhibits of fossils and minerals. Be sure to check out the two seismographs and the panoramic view from the fifth floor patio. Exit Earth Sciences through the basement and check out the sabertooth tiger sculpture beside the building. Just to the south are six wooden two-story buildings (originally Navy barracks), brought to the campus as "temporary" structures (T-Buildings) during the post-World War II boom in students. For some reason they still remain as homes for smaller departments such as Peace and Conflicts studies and a variety of student services including career and course advising. Their demolition is planned for 1990, when they will be replaced by a new academic advising complex. For a comfortable break, stop at **23 Bechtel Engineering Center** (1980), where there is a Terrace Cafe upstairs and couches for relaxed study downstairs. **24 Cory Hall** (1950), home to

The Hearst Memorial Mining Building. Photo by Don Pitcher.

the Computer Sciences and Electrical Engineering Department, is just up the hill to the north. On the exterior walls of the top floor (added in 1985) are large raised-relief designs of integrated circuit microchips, painted in pastel colors—an odd combination of high technology with art deco design.

From Bechtel Engineering Center walk past the ugly ten-story **25** **Evans Hall** (1971). Architects call this style of design "neo-brutalism." Although it may be hard to believe, the interior of Evans is even worse, with concrete-walled cubicles more claustrophobic than cells in San Quentin. For contrast, visit the **26** **Hearst Memorial Mining Building** (1907), next door, John Galen Howard's Beaux Arts masterpiece. The building was funded by Phoebe Apperson Hearst, the first woman named a UC Regent. Inside you can admire the ceiling that curves upwards into three arched skylights, or take a look at the aging models of underground mining operations and the mineral collection. Just east of the Hearst Mining Building is a 200-foot mining shaft once used by geology students and now covered with an iron grill. Originally dug in 1916 to show mining methods, it is now closed to the public except on special occasions (such as Engineering Week). You can look through the iron grate into the tunnel. Next to the shaft is a small tin shack housing ventilation fans.

Die-hard Berkeley history fanatics may want to visit next the **27** **Founders Rock** just behind and up the hill from the Hearst Mining Building. From this rock with its then-impressive vistas of the entire Bay Area, Frederick Billings (after whom Billings, Montana was later named) was moved to think of Bishop George Berkeley's poem that concludes, "Westward the course of empire takes its way...." This inspiration led him to suggest that the new town be named for the bishop. The rock is no great shakes—today's vista consists of Cory Hall to the west and heavy automobile traffic to the north and east—so you'll have to use your imagination to recapture the atmosphere around the rock when it was a source of inspiration.

For a dose of hectic student life, head next to **28** **Physical Sciences Lecture Hall (PSL),** a large circular building with a 550-seat classroom where freshman and sophomores fend off boredom and conformity in giant introductory classes. Inside are TV monitors, giant blackboards, and a three-part lecture platform that allows lab demonstrations to be set up in advance and then rotated around to face the classroom.

For a very different sort of gathering place, walk straight uphill behind the Lecture Hall to the **29** **Hearst Greek Theatre** (1903), designed by America's most successful woman architect, Julia Morgan (see *The People of Berkeley*), and modeled after the one in Epidaurus, Greece. Before the theater was built, the site was found to be ideal for meetings, and was known as Ben Weed's ampitheater. The Greek Theatre has been the site of speeches by numerous world leaders, including Theodore Roosevelt, Woodrow Wilson, Nehru, and more recently, Philippine President Corazon Aquino. Check for an open gate and you may be able to wander about among the concrete pillars and rows of benches rising in a semicircle from the stage. It may seem a bit silly and pompous today, but the theater's capacity of 10,000 still makes it a great place for

Phoebe Apperson Hearst

Perhaps more than any other person, Phoebe Apperson Hearst (1842-1919) was responsible for development of the Berkeley campus. Born into a Missouri farming family, she longed to visit far-off places such as St. Louis. She exceeded her ambitions somewhat after meeting a cousin's cousin named George Hearst, a man 22 years her senior who had already attained considerable wealth by developing the incredibly rich mineral deposits of the Ophir Mine (Nevada), Ontario Mine (Utah), Homestake Mine (South Dakota), and Anaconda Mine (Montana). In 1862 Hearst acquired the *San Francisco Examiner* and eventually won a seat for the U.S. Senate. (Their son, William Randolph Hearst, was the powerful newspaper magnate after whom *Citizen Kane* was patterned.)

Regent Phoebe A. Hearst with President Benjamin Ide Wheeler leading the academic procession on commencement day, 1913. Courtesy of the Bancroft Library.

In the early years, Phoebe organized kindergartens and funded the Cathedral School for Girls in Washington, D.C., but after her husband's death in 1891, she started managing the many businesses in which he had been involved, and began to give away vast sums of money for philanthropic causes ranging from the women's suffrage movement to archaeological expeditions. For 22 years she served as an influential University Regent, the first woman to hold such a post. The University of California eventually received today's equivalent of more than $15 million from her. One of her first acts was to provide $200,000 to fund an international competition to design the new University campus. She wrote the Regents:

"I am deeply impressed with the proposition now before the Board of Regents, to determine upon a comprehensive and permanent plan for the buildings and grounds of the University of California on the site at Berkeley, and I heartily approve of the idea. I feel so imbued with the importance to the University and to the State of having such a plan, that I should be glad to aid in its complete and speedy realization. I may also say that I am the more anxious for this as I have in contemplation the erection on the University grounds of two buildings, one of them to be a memorial which shall testify to Mr. Hearst's love for and interest in this State. I would therefore suggest that I be permitted to contribute the funds necessary to obtain, by international competition, plans for the fitting architectural improvement of the University grounds at Berkeley; and I desire to say that the success of this enterprise shall not be hampered in any way by a money consideration."

Her support and the international attention it attracted led the state legislature to greatly increase funding for the University and brought topflight professors to the new school. Phoebe Hearst later funded construction of the Hearst Mining Building, the Hearst Greek Theatre, and Hearst Hall (later replaced by Hearst Gym for Women). She established 55 student scholarships for women (still operating), and often stepped in to help the University keep its brightest professors by providing funds for bigger salaries. She even moved closer to the University, living for a time in a house on the north side of campus (near Hearst Avenue, of course). Here she often met with students who viewed her as something of a fairy godmother. Every spring, the entire senior class was transported by train to her Pleasanton home for a picnic day. Phoebe Hearst died in 1919 at the age of 76.

festivals, Big Game rallies, Berkeley High School's wonderfully emotional red and gold graduations, or sitting under a full moon listening to the Grateful Dead.

From the Greek Theater follow Gayley Rd. past **30 Lewis Hall** (1947), where the College of Chemistry is housed, and turn off to pass three of the most unexpected buildings on campus, all of which echo the rusticity of many turn-of-the-century Berkeley brown shingle homes. The **31 Women's Faculty Club** was designed by John Galen Howard. Completed just before the disastrous 1923 Berkeley fire, it became a home for several families until they could rebuild their homes. **32 Senior Men's Hall** (1906), also by John Galen Howard, was built with massive redwood logs and served for many years as the home of the Student Union. Behind a secret door, the building also housed the Order of the Golden Bear, an all-male secret society (now open to all). Next door is the **33 Faculty Club,** my favorite campus building, designed by Bernard Maybeck and built between 1903 and 1914. Once exclusively for men, it is now co-ed and used for faculty parties, lodging for special campus guests, and a variety of other University functions. Its giant fireplace and exposed redwood beams give it a warm, hunting-lodge feeling.

Just west of the Faculty Club is **34 Faculty Glade**, a bucolic garden in the midst of the hubbub of campus which offers one of the best views of the Campanile. Turn up the hill and pass between the **35 Morrison** and **Hertz music buildings** (1958). Free noon concerts are given in the Hertz Music Hall every Friday during the school

University Art Museum. Photo by Don Pitcher.

year. The building also houses an amazing collection of antique organs that may be seen by appointment (642-2678).

36 **Wurster Hall** (1964) resembles a 10-story dragon and is home to the College of Environmental Design. From the outside, it makes your heart sink, and critics compare it to a factory, calling it "devoid of comfort or grace." Admirers enjoy the balcony, the small cafe, and the open airy feeling inspired by deliberately-exposed pipes and barren concrete walls. There are displays of student architectural projects and drawings, and on the inside stairwell paintings covered over by the sloppy spray-painted signatures of local graffiti terrorists.

Just east is **37** **Kroeber Hall** (1959) which houses the Lowie Museum of Anthropology and the Worth Ryder Art Gallery (see "Museums" in *Arts and Entertainment*). **38** **Boalt Hall School of Law** is on the other side of

the fountain. Take a look up Bancroft Way to the Spanish colonial-style **39** **International House** (1930) that faces the street. Berkeley has long been a leader in educating foreign students— in 1927 10% of all foreign students in the U.S. were attending Berkeley. I-House was established with John D. Rockefeller, Jr.'s money "to foster closer relations between students of American birth and those coming from foreign countries." Today half its residents are foreign students. The nine-story domed tower and interior courtyard make this one of the loveliest buildings in the city. Across Bancroft Way and a short walk down is the impressive **40** **University Art Museum** (1972), the largest university art museum in the country. Built of unsurfaced concrete, it has an enjoyable, airy feeling inside and is well worth a visit (see "Museums" in *Arts and Entertainment*).

Back on the other side of the street

is the **41 Hearst Gymnasium for Women** (1927), designed by Bernard Maybeck and Julia Morgan. The neo-classic building, funded by William Randolph Hearst in memory of Phoebe Apperson Hearst, was built to replace the old Hearst Gym that burned in 1924. The structure was once the largest and most modern gymnasium in the country. The striking black marble-lined swimming pool is still one of the finest places in Berkeley to swim and sunbathe.

Beyond Hearst Gym, follow the sidewalk past **42 Barrows Hall** (1964), the eight-story home of the Sociology Department and the School of Business Administration. Barrows bears a strong resemblance to the office buildings that some of its students will later inhabit. On the right, **43 Anthony Hall** (also known as the Pelican Building), was built for the student humor magazine, *The Pelican*, in 1957. Today it houses the Graduate Assembly Office. Out front is a bronze statue of a Pelican. The name Pelican originated in reference to the starched white blouses of early day coeds— apparently the male students thought it made the women look like pelicans. Next door is the old Powerhouse with two WPA murals from 1936 on the exterior walls and guarded by giant Chinese dogs. Sproul Plaza, where this walk began, is directly ahead.

The People of Berkeley

Many people in Berkeley cocoon themselves in their own tight world—be it academia, their neighborhoods, the streets, or the work-a-day job—and rarely go beyond cursory conversations with those outside their own social cliques. As a result, even residents who have lived here for 30 years still wonder about the characters they see every day. Is the waitress in the corner cafe also a painter or an actress? Is your neighbor down the street the same man whose name graced that award-winning documentary film? What does it mean to grow up a punk in Berkeley? Why does that middle-aged woman wear a dress made from an American flag? Is that disheveled man talking loudly to himself really a former mathematics professor? In Berkeley, appearances can be deceiving, but they can also be intriguing—the city is a people-watcher's paradise.

New York conjures up images of skyscrapers; Denver the magnificent backdrop of the Rockies; Los Angeles its web of smog-choked freeways. But Berkeley is not characterized so much by its setting as by its people. After more than a decade in Berkeley, I am still constantly amazed by the number of remarkable people who live here, not simply the intellectuals who dominate the University environs, but the social activists, the outstanding artists, chefs, writers, computer innovators, and entrepreneurs.

With a 1988 population of 106,900 people (10,019 people per square mile), Berkeley is America's tenth most densely populated city and California's second (after San Francisco). It is California's nineteenth largest in

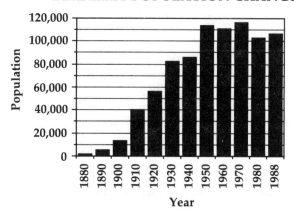

BERKELEY POPULATION CHANGES

Opposite: Street scene. Photo by Mark Sarfati.

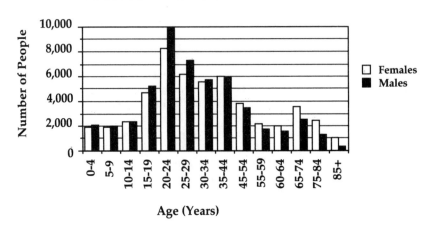

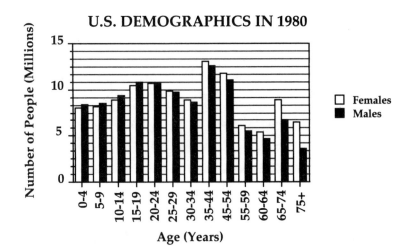

terms of population. In its early years as a city, Berkeley grew rapidly, reaching 40,000 by 1910 and 82,000 by 1930. Since 1950, however, the population has been relatively stable, due primarily to the lack of undeveloped land. The population of Berkeley is youthful, and this is reflected by the city's abundance of student-oriented fast-food joints, record shops, coffeehouses, hair salons, and copy places.

Berkeley is also diverse. The abundance of fine Chinese, Thai, Japanese, and Ethiopian restaurants; the fervent political activity; and the intellectual inquisitiveness that is Berkeley's hallmark could not have arisen without its cultural diversity. Although whites comprise two-thirds of the population and blacks another fifth, recent years have seen both blacks and whites decrease while the Asian population has

BERKELEY'S ETHNIC MAKEUP IN 1980

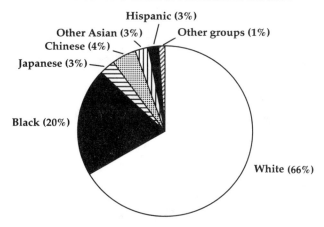

Hispanic (3%)

Other Asian (3%)
Chinese (4%)
Japanese (3%)

Other groups (1%)

Black (20%)

White (66%)

increased rapidly. In 1980 there were 6650 fewer blacks in Berkeley than a decade earlier, a decrease due both to the gentrification process that has forced lower income people out of Berkeley, and to the increasing proportion of elderly blacks whose homes are often sold to non-family members. (In the population as a whole, Berkeley's elderly decreased by 16% from 1970 to 1980, while the number of blacks over 65 rose by 52%.)

Berkeley Celebrities

The city of Berkeley is home to more than its share of nationally recognized individuals. A sampling of these local celebrities are described below; more can be found in the *University* chapter.

David Brower *1912-*
Probably the best-known national figure in the environmental movement, David Brower has a long and checkered history of activism. For many

years he headed the Sierra Club and led it into numerous political battles, including that which prevented the damming of the Grand Canyon. Although Brower was twice nominated for a Nobel Peace Prize, his forceful

David Brower. Photo by Don Pitcher.

GET THESE MEN

On The Ballot

ELDRIDGE CLEAVER

Ex-convict, author of Soul on Ice,
Minister of Information of the
Black Panther Party, victim of
recent gun battle with Oakland Cops.

PRESIDENTIAL CANDIDATE
N.Y. PEACE AND FREEDOM PARTY

Needed Now:
- PETITION WORKERS
- OFFICE VOLUNTEERS
- UPSTATE ORGANIZERS
- MONEY URGENTLY NEEDED.
  SEND TO:

DAVID McREYNOLDS

Draft card burner, field secretary
for the War Resisters League,
imprisoned eight times,
state-wide organizer PFP.

19th CONGRESSIONAL CANDIDATE
PEACE AND FREEDOM PARTY

PFP Platform-
- IMMEDIATE WITHDRAWAL
  FROM VIETNAM
- BLACK LIBERATION
- LOCAL DEMOCRATIC CONTROL
- ECONOMIC JUSTICE

Peace & Freedom Party

Poster for Peace and Freedom Party.

character and inability to control budgetary problems alienated the Sierra Club board of directors and led to his firing in 1969. Brower responded by founding Friends of the Earth that same year, but was ejected by its directors in 1986 for similar reasons. In spite of these setbacks, his accomplishments have been extraordinary, and he has achieved an almost mythical status among environmentalists. Brower's latest group is Earth Island Institute of San Francisco, an organization concerned with global environmental issues. His son, Kenneth Brower, is author of *The Starship and the Canoe.*

Don Budge *1915-*
In the 1930s the Berkeley Tennis Club became home to three Wimbledon champions: Helen Wills Moody, Helen Jacobs, and Don Budge. A gangling redhead, Budge grew up in East Oakland and attended Cal for a year before dropping out to join the U.S. Davis Cup auxiliary team. Not only did Budge win the Wimbledon in 1937 and 1938, he also became the first tennis player to achieve a Grand Slam—victories in the Australian, French, and U.S. championships as well as at Wimbledon.

Eldridge Cleaver *1935-*
Former Black Panther Eldridge Cleaver began life with a long series of run-ins with the law. He bounced from reform school into Soledad prison, first for selling marijuana and

later for rape. While in prison he completed the controversial and fiery autobiography, *Soul on Ice*, a book that brought him national attention. Paroled in 1966, Cleaver became Minister of Information for Huey Newton and Bobby Seale's paramilitary Black Panther party. Gun battles with the police were common for party members, and after a shootout two years later, Cleaver was arrested and charged with attempted murder. The arrest created a surge of support that led to his nomination as the Peace and Freedom Party's presidential candidate in 1968. This nomination in turn created a major controversy over his request to lecture at the Berkeley campus. In a rally on Sproul Plaza, Cleaver told a crowd of 5000: "They say we should follow in the footsteps of Martin Luther King, but when you turn your cheek, you get your head blown off your shoulders by a bullet." He went on to call Governor Reagan a "punk, sissy, and coward," before leading the crowd in a chant of "Fuck Reagan." While his attempted murder case was on appeal, Cleaver fled to Cuba, then to Algeria, and eventually to France and the Soviet Union. By the time he voluntarily returned to the U.S. in 1975, he had abandoned black militancy and become a born-again Christian. Cleaver now lives in Berkeley, remaining active in a variety of fields, including Republican politics.

Fred Cody *1916-1983*
In many people's minds, Fred Cody epitomized Berkeley's energetic creativity. In 1956 he and his wife Pat set up a small bookshop on Euclid Avenue. With a masters degree from the University of Mexico and a Ph.D. from the University of London, Cody saw bookselling as more of a cultural contribution than a financial endeavor. He was responsible for bringing the writings of Carlos Castaneda and many others into public view, and when Allen Ginsberg's poetry volume *Howl* caused the arrest of a San Francisco bookseller on obscenity charges, Cody protested by papering his windows with copies. Cody's Books headed south to a new store on Telegraph Ave. in the mid-60s, just as Berkeley turned into a tinderbox of political emotions. As plywood replaced broken windows all along the Ave., Cody's Books was never attacked, in part because of the Codys' ardent support for left wing and liberal causes. Cody allowed vendors to use the sidewalk in front of the store, and he helped found the Berkeley Free Clinic, the Emergency Food Project, and Camps, Inc. The store was sold to current owner Andy Ross in 1977.

Ron Dellums *1935-*
Berkeley's congressional representative Ron Dellums is considered one of the nation's most left-wing political figures. An ex-Marine who went on to receive an M.A. in Social Work from Cal, Dellums served on the Berkeley City Council in the late 60s before defeating liberal Democrat Jeffrey Cohelan for the congressional seat in 1970. (Arch-conservative Vice President Spiro Agnew fueled the fight by labeling Dellums a "radical extremist" who was out to "bring the walls down.") When he first arrived in Washington, Dellums painted his congressional office walls in psychedelic colors and plastered them with anti-war photos, but he has mellowed over the years. A founding member of the Congressional Black Caucus, he has

chaired the House Armed Services Subcommittee since 1983, drawing praise from both Democrats and Republicans for his fairness and careful preparation. He remains something of a lone voice on many issues—normalizing relations with Cuba, slashing defense spending, and nationalizing health care—but on some issues, such as divestment from South Africa, others have come to agree with Dellums.

Harry Edwards *1942-*

One of the most influential figures in American sports, Harry Edwards cuts a wide swath. Students jam his classes at the University, impressed both by his Paul Bunyan frame and shaved head, and by his no-holds-barred criticisms of racism in the sports world. Born into a St. Louis ghetto family, he was a star athlete in high school, but became disillusioned by

Harry Edwards in his UC Berkeley office. Photo by Don Pitcher.

inequalities and quit the college track team to pursue his studies. After getting an M.A. in sociology from Cornell University (where he studied the Black Muslim family), he headed to San Jose State University to teach. Angered by conditions for blacks on campus, he threatened to prevent the season's first football game. Despite Governor Reagan's warnings that he would call out the National Guard, the administration cancelled the game—the only time racial tensions ever forced such a cancellation. Suddenly in the limelight, Edwards next organized a black boycott of the 1968 Olympics. Although not entirely successful, the raised black power fists of two American track stars helped push race issues to the forefront. As a result, Edwards received more than 200 death threats, his dogs were killed, and he became the target of extensive FBI surveillance. He went on to get a Ph.D. in 1972 from Cornell and his thesis became a groundbreaking textbook, *Sociology of Sport*. After being offered a teaching position at UC Berkeley (an angry Governor Reagan said the hiring would be "a prime topic...at the next Regent's meeting"), Edward's classes became some of the most popular on campus. When he was denied tenure in 1977, massive protests and even pressure from President Carter forced the University to relent. Today Edwards fills a variety of roles—teacher, lecturer, consultant to the San Francisco Forty Niners and the Golden State Warriors, and special assistant to the Commissioner of Baseball.

David Lance Goines *1945-*

Artist and printer David Goines has created a unique reputation for himself by producing posters that work as

David Goines at St. Heironymous Press. Photo by Don Pitcher.

both art and advertising. Goines came to Berkeley in 1963 and stayed in the University long enough to be expelled for his Free Speech Movement activities ("disturbing the peace"). In 1970, after working as an apprentice at a small print shop, he bought the shop and renamed it St. Heironymous (sic) Press. Goines's distinctive designs and his use of earthy tones seem, for many, to embody the Berkeley aesthetic. He has produced more than 130 different posters, each of which he prints himself. His signed works sell for upwards of $3000 apiece. Many of Berkeley's businesses—Chez Panisse, Velosport, North Face, Berkeley Repertory Theater, Pacific Film Archives, and the Berkeley Public Library— have employed Goines to produce soft-sell poster-ads that quickly become collectors' items.

Whoopi Goldberg 1955-

Star of *The Color Purple* and other recent box office hits, Whoopi Goldberg has been a performer since she was eight. A founding member of the San Diego Repertory Theatre, she later joined Berkeley's Blake Street Hawkeyes. Her *Spook Show*, a series of outrageously funny character sketches, became an off-Broadway hit in 1984-85 and attracted Hollywood's attention. Her other films have included *Jumpin' Jack Flash* and *Clara's Heart*, as well as the *Star Trek* television program. Whoopi also helped organize a series of comedy benefits in 1988 to aid homeless people.

Wavy Gravy 1936-

Unofficial jester for Ken Kesey's Merry Pranksters, Wavy Gravy (a.k.a. Hugh Romney) has been called the clown-prince of the hippie generation. He helped run Woodstock, operating the "trip tent" for freaked-out freaks, running the free kitchen, and maintaining security by threatening to use cream pies and seltzer water for "riot

Whoopi Goldberg. Photo by Mark Sarfati.

Wavy Gravy. Photo by Don Pitcher.

control." Wavy and others from the Merry Pranksters later roamed the world, spending several years in ancient buses and on the New Mexico Hog Farm Commune. He landed in Berkeley in 1973 and now lives in a second Hog Farm Commune in North Berkeley. In 1968, Wavy was campaign manager for Pigasus Pig, the "first female black and white candidate for president." In 1972, he named a rock as a candidate for president along with a roll for vice president (kaiser rolls, jelly rolls, or whatever was on hand), noting that it would become the first vice president you could eat. When he spaced out and left the rock in a New York taxicab, Wavy decided to run "nobody for president." The slogans were easy to come by—"nobody's perfect," "nobody should have that much power," etc. Despite such flippancy, Wavy is today involved in a variety of serious ventures. He acts as a "FUNd" raiser for Seva, the preventable blindness organization, and manages the popular Camp Winnarainbow in Mendocino County, attracting an odd amalgamation of kids from wealthy new age or entertainment families, second generation hippie offspring, homeless and ghetto youngsters.

Ken Kragen *1938-*
Berkeley-born Ken Kragen is best known as the president of USA for Africa and producer of the "We are the World" song, but he also organized the "Hands across America" project in 1986 to raise funds for the homeless in this country. A 1958 graduate from Berkeley, he was Cal's "Alumnus of the Year" in 1986. Kragen has also managed performers, including the Smothers Brothers, Kenny Rogers, and Lionel Richie.

Jack LaLanne *1914-*

Best known for his long-running (1956-70) TV exercise program that demonstrated "Trimnastics" to housewives, Jack LaLanne was a 1934 graduate of Berkeley High. Fellow Berkeley students from that era recall his one-arm chin-ups and his raw vegetable lunches. The elderly LaLanne remains active. For his 65th birthday in 1979 he swam a mile across Lake Ashinoko at the foot of Mt. Fuji in Japan. No mean feat, especially since he was both handcuffed and shackled while towing 65 rowboats, each loaded with a ton of wood pulp!

Dorothea Lange *1895-1965*

Perhaps the most famous photographer to record the Depression Era, Dorothea Lange's haunting photos of migrant workers pierced the American conscience. In 1918 Lange arrived in San Francisco, where her portrait work soon gained a wide reputation among a wealthy clientele. The sudden devastation brought by the Depression sent her to the streets, to record the breadlines and desperation. With her husband Paul Taylor, a UC professor and photographer, she documented the plight of migrant workers and later went on to photograph the forced relocation of Japanese citizens during World War II.

Frances Moore Lappé *1944-*

The "Julia Child of the soybean circuit," Frances Moore Lappé mixes politics and food to fight world hunger. She is best known as author of *Diet for a Small Planet* (three million copies sold), a cookbook with a message: eat foods low on the food chain. Since it came out in 1971 she has also worked unstintingly for that cause, insisting that hunger is brought about by the way elite groups control and distribute food. Her other books include *Food First: Beyond the Myth of Scarcity*, *World Hunger: Twelve Myths*, and *What to Do After You Turn Off the T.V.*

Timothy Leary *1920-*

As the "prophet of LSD," Timothy Leary turned on the 60s generation to the world of psychedelic drugs. Educated at UC Berkeley (Ph.D. in Psychology), Leary was an assistant professor there from 1950-55, later directing psychiatric research at the Kaiser Foundation in Oakland before leaving to teach at Harvard. There, Leary discovered psychedelics, and quickly became one of America's most controversial figures with his calls to "turn on, tune in, and drop out." After being fired by Harvard and converting to Hinduism, he founded the League for Spiritual Discovery (abbre-

Frances Moore Lappé. Photo by Bob Hsiang.

viated LSD) to legally protect the taking of acid as a "sacrament." In 1968, Leary was sentenced to twenty years in prison after police found two marijuana roaches in his car, but within six months the radical Weather Underground had helped him escape and flee to Algeria. Eventually he was kidnapped by American agents and returned to prison, from which he was finally released in 1976. In 1982 Leary returned to Berkeley for a bizarre debate with Watergate conspirator G. Gordon Liddy. He now lives in Los Angeles and markets computer software.

William Mandel *1917-*
William Marx Mandel is best known today for his long-running and controversial "Soviet Affairs" show on radio station KPFA. When Mandel's family moved to the Soviet Union in 1931, he had just finished high school, and while there he learned Russian and studied biochemistry at Moscow University. Returning to the U.S., he was kicked out of college in New York for participating in political

William Mandel at KPFA. Photo by Don Pitcher.

demonstrations. He went on to work at Stanford's Hoover Institution in 1947 as a Soviet specialist before being called to testify at Joseph McCarthy's 1953 witch-hunt of communists and their sympathizers. As the cameras rolled, he told McCarthy, "This is a book-burning. You need only the tinder to set fire to the books as Hitler did twenty years ago." The next day Mandel was fired from his job and for many years was only able to find work as a translator of Russian scholarly journals. About 1960, he began broadcasting the nation's first radio talk show on KPFA. As the only radio program on the Soviet Union anywhere in the U.S., the broadcasts roused the ire of conservatives, and Mandel was subpoenaed to testify before the House Un-American Activities Committee. Mandel later lectured at the University for a brief period, and he was active in the Free Speech Movement.

Billy Martin *1928-*
Berkeley's favorite bad boy, Billy Martin (born Alfred Manuel Pesano), grew up in West Berkeley, playing baseball in James Kenney Park. Martin became a stellar basketball and baseball player at Berkeley High School, and only a few years after graduating he played in the 1950 World Series. He went on to manage the New York Yankees in the World Series in 1976, 1977, and 1978, and the Oakland A's in 1981. In recent years he has had a rocky career as a revolving-door manager of several other well-known baseball teams. In an amusing 1982 confrontation, Martin's inflated ego collided head-on with Berkeley politics. The city planned to

rename James Kenney Park after him, but when he arrived for the honor, Martin was told that the city council had changed its mind and only the baseball diamond would be named for him. Furious, Martin told Berkeley not to bother him anymore with its political games.

Country Joe McDonald *1942-*
Folk/rock musician Country Joe McDonald was born into a political family—his mother, Florence, was a Berkeley councilmember, city auditor, and rent board commissioner. McDonald, a Vietnam veteran, soon found himself deeply involved in the anti-war movement. His group Country Joe and the Fish was one of the top acts in the 60s, starring at Woodstock and providing the sound track for numerous demonstrations. Their best known anti-war song, *I Feel Like I'm Fixin to Die Rag*, asks the audience to get into the act by singing along with "Gimme an F, gimme a U,..." Today Country Joe remains active in veterans' issues, and runs Rag Baby Records out of the Fantasy Records building. He still puts out an occasional album and tours smaller venues.

Helen Wills Moody *1905-*
Born in Berkeley and a long-time member of the Berkeley Tennis Club, Helen Wills Moody grew up to be one of history's finest women tennis players. She won a record eight singles championships at Wimbledon between 1923 and 1938, and her domination of the sport was so complete that for five years she did not lose a single set to any opponent. A beautiful and aristocratic woman, Moody was best known for her stony silence and complete lack of visible emotion,

even when she won. The press labeled her "Queen Helen," and "Miss Poker Face," and her cold, merciless manner while playing inevitably led the crowd to cheer for her opponent. Ironically, her most intense rival was another Berkeleyan and fellow Cal graduate, Helen Jacobs, winner of the 1936 Wimbledon. Helen Moody later achieved a reputation for her water-color work and now lives in Carmel.

Julia Morgan *1872-1957*
America's most successful woman architect, Morgan designed more than 800 buildings in her half-century career. The first woman to study engineering at Cal and later the first woman to graduate from the elite Ecole des Beaux-Arts in Paris, she earned an early reputation as a hard worker. Architect Bernard Maybeck acted as her mentor, and her first job was designing the Hearst Greek Theatre for UC's Supervising Architect John Galen Howard.

Morgan designed many other structures in Berkeley, including the Berkeley City Club (her favorite), Hearst Women's Gym at UC Berkeley, the Julia Morgan Center (originally St. John's Presbyterian Church), and dozens of brown shingle homes. Her most famous effort is the rambling 144-room Hearst San Simeon Castle, complete with Hearst's own private zoo. Originally William Randolph Hearst had directed her to create a simple group of buildings, but his ideas became more and more pretentious and eccentric, driving Morgan and the carpenters to the edge of sanity. Working fourteen-hour days, she oversaw every detail of the twenty-year-long construction process. (In recent years, visitors to

San Simeon have been brought to see cuts from old movie footage about Hearst in which Morgan, standing beside him and carrying paper and pencil, is described by a canned voice as Hearst's secretary.) When she retired in the 1940s, she left behind an incredible variety of structures. Morgan never married, and despite being a successful businesswoman, died penniless.

J. Robert Oppenheimer *1902-1967*
A professor of physics at UC Berkeley from 1929-1947, Oppenheimer is often referred to as "the father of the atomic bomb." Oppenheimer wrote his first professional paper at age twelve, and after graduating summa cum laude from Harvard headed for Germany where he received a Ph.D. from the University of Goettingen in 1927. At Berkeley, Oppenheimer established the nation's first school of theoretical physics, but his rapid teaching pace

Malvina Reynolds. Photo by Eleanor M. Lawrence.

frequently overwhelmed even his most advanced students. In 1943, he joined the secret team that developed the first atomic bomb in Los Alamos, New Mexico, although he was a vocal opponent of its use against Japan. He later helped develop the far more powerful H-bomb, but again argued against its use. Oppenheimer proposed that the United Nations control all atomic power, and headed the UN Atomic Energy Commission from 1946-1952, but the cold war hysteria of the 1950s soon led to doubts about his allegiances. He was eventually falsely accused of being a Soviet spy and his security clearances were stripped. Despite this, in 1963 Oppenheimer was awarded the Enrico Fermi Award for his work in atomic energy. In the last years of his life, he directed the Institute for Advanced Study at Princeton University.

Malvina Reynolds *1900-1978*
Born into an immigrant socialist family—her father was a charter member of the American Communist Party—Malvina Reynolds combined a love for music with a desire to transform society. After receiving three English degrees from Cal—B.A. (1925), M.A. (1927), and Ph.D. (1939)—Reynolds became a professor, but she was repeatedly fired for her leftist beliefs. By 1946 she had found a new calling—writing and performing folksongs, based on her activism in environmental, socialist, and feminist causes. Her music was later recorded by Pete Seeger, Judy Collins, Joan Baez, and Diana Ross. Reynolds spent the last 40 years of her life at 2027 Parker St. in Berkeley. Her best known song, "Little Boxes," was inspired by the rows of Daly City houses.

Ed Roberts and Joan Leon at the World Institute on Disability. Photo by Don Pitcher.

Edward Roberts *1939-*

When Ed Roberts came down with polio in 1953, doctors told his mother her son would be a vegetable for life. She didn't buy the prognosis and neither did he. He graduated from Burlingame High School in 1959, where he was a much loved figure. When he entered UC Berkeley, he was the first quadriplegic to attend. Not knowing where to put someone who spent most of his time in an iron lung, the University housed him in Cowell Hospital. While there, he and another disabled student, Phil Draper, founded the Berkeley Center for Independent Living. Their success helped open the doors for other wheelchair-bound students. After Roberts received his M.A. in political science in 1966, he began teaching, using his spare time to help organize and train others with disabilities. When Governor Jerry Brown appointed him head of the State Department of Rehabilitation in 1975, Roberts used the post to greatly broaden the department's role in helping those with severe disabilities become employable. In 1984 Roberts was awarded the prestigious $250,000 MacArthur Foundation "genius" grant to fund his interest in helping others. With it, he founded the World Institute on Disability, a Berkeley-based public policy and advocacy group. The father of a young son, Roberts has appeared on *60 Minutes* and has become the most famous advocate for the disabled in America.

Galen Rowell *1940-*

One of America's best known landscape photographers, Galen Rowell is also a mountaineer who has made more than a hundred first ascents in the Sierra Nevada and numerous expeditions to the Himalayas. Born in Berkeley and a graduate of Berkeley High, Rowell spent a decade working as a mechanic before quitting to work full-time as a photographer and writer. His books include *In the Throne Room of the Mountain Gods, Mountains of the Middle Kingdom,* and his book on photography, *Mountain Light.*

Jerry Rubin *1938-*
One of the most colorful characters from the 1960s, Jerry Rubin arrived in Berkeley to attend graduate school in sociology. Within six weeks he had dropped out, joining Free Speech demonstrations and then working to organize the 1965 Vietnam Day teach-in that attracted 12,000 protestors. In 1967, he decided to run for mayor on

Jerry Rubin. Photo by Harold Adler.

a pro-marijuana and anti-war platform and won a surprising 22% of the vote. Eventually Rubin linked up with fellow radical Abbie Hoffman to form the tongue-in-cheek Youth International Party—the Yippies. They and five others were charged with inciting riots in Chicago during the 1968 Democratic convention, and their trial and conviction brought added fame to the "Chicago Seven." In the 1980s, Rubin—who had once created pandemonium on the floor of the New York Stock Exchange by throwing dollar bills from the balcony—emerged in an ironic new role, as a "networking facilitator" for fellow Wall Street yuppies.

Leigh Steinberg *1949-*
One of the most notable sports agents in the business, Steinberg has represented great gladiators of sport, including Steve Bartkowski, Bill Ring, Will Clark, and Warren Moon. He also has something almost unheard of among agents, a reputation for fairness, honesty, and moral commitment. A darling of the media, Steinberg was once voted by *Cosmopolitan* one of the nation's most eligible bachelors. Perhaps the wealthiest sports agent in the business, he is a major contributor to liberal causes. Steinberg holds a J.D. from Boalt Hall.

Douglas Tilden *1860-1935*
Hailed as the "Michelangelo of the West," sculptor Douglas Tilden left such works as the *Baseball Player* and *Mechanics Monument* in San Francisco, and the *Football Players* on the UC campus. At age five, Tilden lost his hearing from scarlet fever. He became the first student at the Berkeley School for the Deaf in 1866, and spent a lifetime trying to correct people's dis-

torted views of his disability. Although he was the first professor of sculpture at what is now San Francisco Art Institute, his romanticized pieces have fallen out of vogue. His best known piece, the *Bear Hunt*, is now at the School for the Deaf and Blind in Fremont.

Jay T. Ward *1922-1989*
People in the market for a home probably scratch their heads when they drive by J. T. Ward Realtors—the name seems vaguely familiar. A graduate of both UC Berkeley and Harvard Business School, J. T. Ward opened a real estate business in a converted garage near the Claremont Hotel in 1947. Shortly afterwards, his life was suddenly changed when a cement truck smashed into the office, injuring him so severely that doctors feared he would be blinded and crippled for life. He escaped both fates, but during a six-month convalescence Ward tried his hand at cartooning, working with an artist friend from Terrytoons. The characters that resulted—Crusader Rabbit, Bullwinkle the Moose, and Rocky the Flying Squirrel—became television classics. Ward continued to sell real estate until 1959, when the *Bullwinkle Show* appeared. It ran for five years, and reruns still delight children and adults. To be closer to his new business, Ward moved to Los Angeles, but kept ownership of his real estate operation until 1986.

Saul Zaentz *1921-*
President and owner of the Berkeley-based Fantasy Corporation, Saul Zaentz administers an empire based upon records and films. Zaentz started out as a Fantasy employee in 1955 and eventually bought the company. He was responsible for turning the company into the world's largest jazz producer, and also produced many films, including the Academy Award winners *One Flew Over the Cuckoo's Nest* and *Amadeus*.

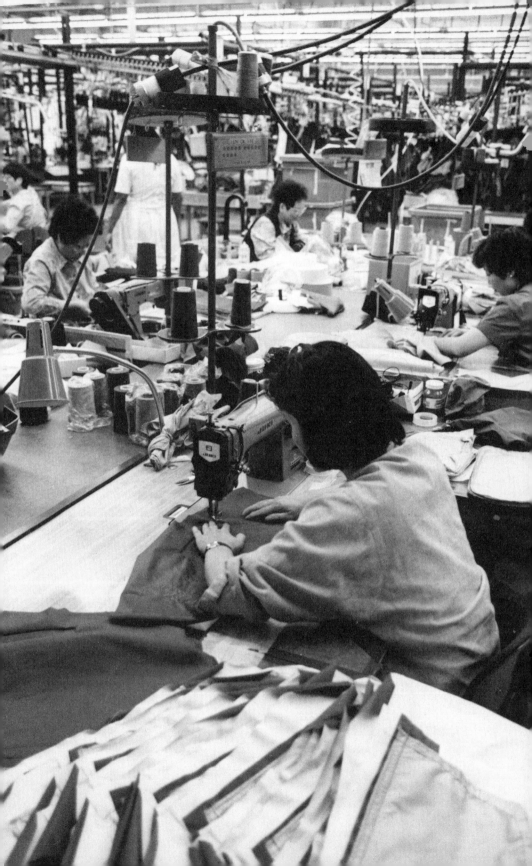

Economy and Business

Since Berkeley's inception, the University has dominated the city, setting the tone for its social, cultural, and economic life. With more than 9000 employees, the University system is by far the largest employer, creating "ripple effects" (more like tsunamis) throughout the local economy. Research programs at Cal have been instrumental in drawing biotechnology, computer software, and other technology-based businesses to the city. Many stores also depend on students, both as customers and as a source of cheap labor. The University's stable job base helps protect Berkeley from the boom and bust cycles of other cities.

Another characteristic of Berkeley is its abundance of government workers. Berkeley's five largest employers are publicly funded. Berkeley's robust private sector is based in service as well as high technology industries. Nearly all the city's manufacturing plants are located in West Berkeley, the oldest part of Berkeley (see "A Tour of Victorian Ocean View" in *The Buildings of Berkeley*). In 1855 workers logged redwood from the Oakland hills to construct Berkeley's first plant, the Pioneer Starch and Grist Mill. Other businesses soon flocked to the area—Cornell Watch Company, Standard Soap, Heywood Lumber, Raspiller Brewing Co., and the giant

An early photo of the Berkeley Daily Gazette. Courtesy of the Berkeley Historical Society.

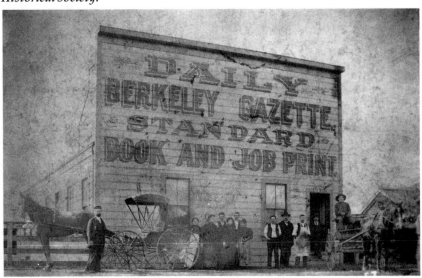

Opposite: Manufacturing outdoor gear at The North Face. Photo by Don Pitcher.

Berkeley's Largest Employers

Business	Employees
UC Berkeley Campus (full and part-time)	9500
Lawrence Berkeley Lab (University research center)	3000
Berkeley Unified School District (full and part-time)	2000
City of Berkeley (full and part-time)	1350
State of California, Health Department	900
Alta Bates Hospital	820
Teknekron Financial Systems (research and development)	800
Herrick Hospital	670
Cutter Labs (blood plasma products, intravenous solutions)	530
ASUC (Associated Students of UC—mostly part-time)	500
The North Face (backpacking equipment and apparel)	480
U.S. Postal Service	400
Pacific Bell	330
Pacific Steel Casting	300
Airco Temescal (high vacuum equipment)	260
Spenger's Fish Grotto	200

Primary source: City of Berkeley Office of Economic Development, 1988

Niehaus Brothers Planing Mill. By the late 1920s, West Berkeley had nearly 200 manufacturing plants, producing everything from egg cleaning machines to railroad cars. The city was home to the largest processor of coconut oil in the world and reputedly the finest machine shop on the West Coast. During World War II, these factories were turned full tilt to the war effort, as steel mills and foundries supplied material for the Richmond shipyards.

After the war, however, West Berkeley's industrial base began a long decline; today there are approximately 150 plants left in the city. The plants that once manufactured boats and planes, well drilling equipment and furnaces are now gone. The biggest loss came in 1982 when Colgate-Palmolive closed its plant, throwing 400 people out of work.

Despite the slow decline of traditional heavy industry in West Berkeley, the city's manufacturing sector remains strong as companies from such high-tech fields as biotechnology, computers, and medical products move in. In general, the city of Berkeley has been better able to control industrial development than its neighbors, and the resulting blend of traditional, high-tech, and service-oriented establishments create a prosperous economic environment. Today, the largest manufacturing firm is Cutter Labs, a manufacturer of medical products since 1903, best known for its insect repellent.

The Backpacking Industry

Technology and ideology both made wilderness camping the recreation of the late 60s. Since Berkeley was a few hours' drive from the Sierra Nevada and had a history of environmental activism as well as a large and adventurous student population, it was the logical place for the new backpacking industry to develop.

Berkeley's camping industry began with the Ski Hut, established in 1935. The owners, both avid skiers, gambled that even during the Depression people would be willing to spend $2.75 a day to rent ski gear. With the 1937 opening of Sugar Bowl, California's first major ski resort, the ski industry took off, and Southern Pacific Railroad added a baggage car on their weekend runs to Donner Summit. The trains were soon filled with University students off for fun in the snow. After World War II, Ski Hut began to develop its own versions of the Army's camping equipment—nylon tents and sleeping bags, dehydrated foods and backpacks—and Trailwise became Berkeley's first mountaineering manufacturer.

In 1968, three years after its founding, The North Face, a small backpacking retail store in San Francisco, moved its base to Berkeley, opening a 10,000-square-foot factory to manufacture backpacks, tents, and other gear. The North Face soon developed a reputation for its high quality equipment and for its revolutionary geodesic tent designs, which were inspired by the work of Buckminster Fuller. By the 1970s it had become the largest manufacturer of quality outdoor gear in the United States, and its products were sold throughout the world. Then, following a now-familiar story, California innovation sold out to foreign financial interests. The company was bought by a Hong Kong firm in 1987 and now manufactures many of its products in Asia (although the Berkeley factory still employs 500 workers). The North Face Factory Outlet at 1238 5th Street is worth a visit for some of the best bargains on camping gear and clothes in the Bay Area.

In spite of a shake-out in the backpacking trade over the past decade as several companies succumbed to competition and a changing market, several other backpacking companies remain healthy: The North Face, Copeland's (at the former Ski Hut location), Marmot Mountain Works, and Sierra Designs (now owned by North Face) all maintain successful stores. The largest retailer is the Seattle-based cooperative giant, Recreational Equipment Inc. (REI). Opened in 1975, the store carries the latest in clothes, canoes, daypacks, tents, bikes, and almost anything else for outdoor enthusiasts. The annual spring and fall sales at REI draw crowds of hundreds.

The Book Trade

By any standards, Berkeley is a giant on the American literary scene. Not only does a selective list of authors who have lived in Berkeley run like a page out of the literary *Who's Who* — Joan Didion, C.S. Forester, Allen Ginsberg, Pauline Kael, Frank Norris, Jack Kerouac, Carolyn Kizer, Ursula Le Guin, Czeslaw Milosz, Jessica Mitford, Ishmael Reed, Ann Rice, Gary Snyder, George Stewart, Alice Walker, Thornton Wilder—but the people of the city support and relish

Berkeley's Oldest Businesses

Listed chronologically below are some of the city's oldest commercial operations—places established before 1920, or that have at least kept the same name over the years. The oldest local store still operating in Berkeley is Gorman & Son Furniture store, opened in 1880. It is still operated by members of the Gorman family.

- Wells Fargo Bank, 2144 Shattuck Ave. (1879 for Express Office)
- Gorman & Son Furniture, 2599 Telegraph Ave. (1880)
- ASUC Store, UC Campus (1887)
- Mason-McDuffie Co., 2860 Telegraph Ave. (1887)
- Spenger's Fish Grotto, 1919 4th St. (1890 for grocery store)
- Cal Ink, 711 Camelia St. (1891)
- W. J. Mortimer & Co., 2101 Milvia St. (1892)
- Berkeley Hardware, 2145 University Ave. (1894)
- Bekins Moving and Storage, Ward and Shattuck Ave. (1895)
- East Bay Municipal Utility District, 2130 Adeline St. (1900)

Gary Gorman of Gorman & Son. Photo by Don Pitcher.

- Cutter Labs, 4th and Parker Sts. (1903)
- Alta Bates Hospital, 3001 Colby St. (1904)
- Herrick Hospital, 2001 Dwight Way (1904)
- Berkeley Sewing Machine Company, 2030 University Ave. (1905) (America's oldest independent sewing machine dealer)
- Campanile Hotel, 2070 University Ave. (1905)
- Pacific Gas & Electric, 2111 M.L. King Way (1905)
- Macaulay Foundry Inc., 811 Carlton St. (1906)
- Tupper & Reed Music, 2277 Shattuck Ave. (1906)
- Berkeley Dog and Cat Hospital, 2126 Haste St. (1907)
- Berkeley Market, 2369

Telegraph Ave. (1907)
- Carlton Hotel, 2338 Telegraph Ave. (1907)
- Huston's Shoes, 2216 Shattuck Ave. (1907)
- Virginia Cleaners, 1650 Shattuck Ave. (1907)
- Lee Frank Jewelers, 2200 Shattuck Ave. (1908)
- Radston's Office Supply Co., 1950 Shattuck Ave. (1908)
- Morrison's Mfg. Retail Jewelers, 2108 Allston Way (1909)
- College Cleaners, 2942 College Ave. (1910)
- Rochester Electric Co., 2524 Shattuck Ave. (1910)
- Shattuck Hotel, Shattuck Ave. and Allston Way (1910)
- Berkeley Theatre, 2425 Shattuck Ave. (1911)

- White Electric Co, 1511 San Pablo Ave. (1912)
- California Cinema, 2115 Kittredge St. (1914)
- Claremont Resort Hotel, 41 Tunnel Rd. (1914)
- Elmwood Theater (originally The Strand), College and Ashby Ave. (1914)
- Ehret Co. Plumbing and Heating Inc. 1936 Shattuck Ave. (c. 1915)
- Berkeley Florist, 1688 Shattuck Ave. (1916)
- Magnani's Poultry, 1586 Hopkins St. (1917)
- U. C. Theater, 2036 University Ave. (1917)
- E. H. Morrill Co., 999 Anthony (contractors) (1918)
- Blue & Gold Market, 2257 Shattuck Ave. (1919)

A Berkeley grocery on Telegraph, 1910. Photo by Louis Stein. Courtesy of the Berkeley Historical Society.

Moe Moskowitz at Moe's Books on Telegraph Avenue. Photo by Robert Eliason.

their literary advantages. Twice yearly the local paper, the *Express*, devotes a dense issue to newly published local books; and it is not uncommon to see people lining up outside a bookstore, as they might at a movie theater, waiting to hear an author read. Nor is the community confined to writers and readers: Berkeley is rich with typesetters, calligraphers, graphic artists, editors, printers, reviewers, publishers, distributors, and, of course, booksellers.

Many factors led to Berkeley becoming the publishing center it is today. The Free Speech and the anti-Vietnam War movements attracted thousands of activists and intellectuals to the city. In the bustle of movement politics, folks were forced to get their hands dirty in the printing process. From back room presses rolled political diatribes, marijuana grow-it-yourself books, psychedelic posters, magazines about communal living, and sex guides—subjects more traditional publishers avoided. As the counterculture grew, companies such as And-Or Press, Nolo Press, and Ten Speed Press grew up to fill a demand for out-of-the-mainstream books.

Changes in the national publishing industry helped Berkeley publishers to develop. Technological advances in typesetting and offset printing made it easier to produce books and posters on a small scale and local level. West Coast Print Center, established by poet Don Cushman, printed many beautiful volumes for small presses publishing new fiction and poetry. Funding from the National Endowment for the Arts, generous in the 1970s, helped many publishers make it through the lean years. In addition, the strong Bay Area book market afforded local publishers an audience, without their having to undertake expensive national advertising campaigns.

Another positive influence has been the wholesale distributor **Bookpeople**, established in 1968 as a cooperative to serve the counterculture. Bookpeople's support of small presses and off-beat titles helped get books to the public that would not otherwise have been distributed. It has prospered, and now distributes books from over 900 publishers. **Small Press Distribution** is another unusual book distributor based in Berkeley. This non-profit corporation distributes books for more than 300 independent presses, predominantly fiction, essays, and poetry that other distributors find "non-commercial."

As a result of all this, today there are nearly 50 different small publishers in Berkeley, as many as are in the entire state of Texas. Most of these are small outfits that produce fewer than a half-dozen titles a year. A few Berkeley publishers have managed to break into the mass market—**Ten Speed Press** with *What Color is Your Parachute*, and the *Moosewood Cookbook*, and **North Point Press** with *Son of the Morning Star* and *West with the Night* —while others such as **Creative Arts Book Co.**, **Heyday Books**, and **Nolo Press** have successfully created their own niches. Berkeley's largest publisher, **UC Press**, produces over 150 new titles a year, primarily for the academic market.

Berkeley's most obvious connection to the book trade is at the retail end. There are at least 65 booksellers and rare book dealers in Berkeley, not including the dozens of retailers, such as bike shops, backpack stores, and health food stores which stock specialized books. Some bookstores focus on relatively narrow fields like science fiction, architecture, or Marxism, while the largest stores cut a much broader swath. Telegraph Ave. is Berkeley's book mecca, with the giant **Moe's** and **Cody's** stores, plus *fifteen* nearby booksellers. Locals and not-so-locals stop by for an evening-long browse. The highly popular readings at **Black Oak Books** and Cody's have helped these bookstores become centers for social life. And, for the devoted bibliophile, there are at least seventeen rare book dealers in Berkeley.

Berkeley Bookstores

ASUC Store Book Department
UC Campus, 642-7294
General and scientific

Avenue Books
2904 College Ave., 549-3532
General, family, and children

Berkeley Book Consortium
1700 Shattuck Ave., 486-0166
Used books

Berkeley Book Store-Ed Hunolt
2476 Bancroft Way, 848-7906
New and used textbooks

Black Oak Books
1491 Shattuck Ave., 486-0698
Excellent choice of new and used books

Book Stop
1816 Euclid Ave., 843-1816
General books and magazines

Builder's Booksource
1801 4th St., 845-6874
Architecture, design, and landscaping

Campus Textbook Exchange
2470 Bancroft Way, 848-7700
New and used textbooks

Cartesian Bookstore
2445 Dwight Way, 549-3973
Used general scholarly

Castalia Books
1554 Solano Ave., Albany, 526-0375
Children's and teacher's books

Cody's Books
2460 Telegraph Ave., 845-7852
A Berkeley institution—50,000
new books

Comic Relief
2138 University Ave., 845-4091
New and used comics

Comics & Comix
2461 Telegraph Ave., 843-5405
New and used comics

Crown Books
2504 Telegraph Ave., 548-8247
Chain store—general

Dark Carnival
2978 Adeline, 845-7757
Fantasy, science fiction, and horror

Deja Vu Metaphysical Book Store
1706 University Ave., 524-0436
Metaphysical books

Dharma Publishing Bookstore
1815 Highland Place, 843-6812
Tibetan Buddhist works

Eastwind Books & Arts
1986 Shattuck Ave., 548-2350
Asian studies and travel books

Easy Going
1400 Shattuck Ave., 843-3533
Large selection of travel guides and
maps

Elmwood Bookshop
2924 College Ave., 848-4582
General books

Gaia Bookstore & Catalog Co.
1400 Shattuck Ave., 548-4172
Recovery, eco-feminism, shamanism
and more

**Graduate Theological Union
Bookstore**
2465 LeConte Ave., 649-2470
Religion and ethics

Gray's Book Company
1821 Solano Ave., 527-9677
General books

Half/Price Books
2525 Telegraph Ave., 843-6412
General used books

Heartsong Bookstore
1412 Solano Ave., Albany, 527-1245
Metaphysical

Ironhorse Comic and Toy Co.
1705 Solano Ave., 528-3302
Comics

Logos Bookstore
2398 Telegraph Ave., 548-2626
Christian and other

Mama Bears
6536 Telegraph Ave., Oakland, 428-9684
Women's books, coffeehouse

Moe's Books
2476 Telegraph Ave., 849-2087
Giant choice—used, new, and
antiquarian

Mr. Mopps' Children's Bookshop
1405 M.L. King Way, 525-9633
Children's books

Nature Company
1999 El Dorado Ave., 524-6336
Nature books

Nature Company
4th St. and Hearst Ave., 524-9052
Nature books

New Medicine Tapes and Books
1308 Gilman St., 527-3643
Recovery, self-help, and psychology

Other Change of Hobbit
2433 Channing Way, 848-0413
Science fiction and fantasy

Pegasus Fine Book
1855 Solano Ave., 525-6888
General new and used, magazines

Pendragon Fine Used Books
5560 College Ave., Oakland, 652-6259
General new and used

Revolution Books
2425 Channing Way, 848-1196
Progressive and revolutionary books
and periodicals

Ross Valley Book Co.
1407 Solano Ave., 526-6400
Western Americana, new and used

Serendipity Books
1201 University Ave., 841-7455
Used books, scholarly, and general

Shakespeare & Co. Books
2499 Telegraph Ave., 841-8916
Large choice of used books

Shambhala Booksellers
2482 Telegraph Ave., 848-8443
Metaphysical

Sierra Club Bookstore
6014 College Ave., Oakland, 658-7470
Outdoor guides and nature

Small Press Distribution
1814 San Pablo Ave. 549-3336
Small press fiction and poetry

Sound Choices
2510 San Pablo Ave., 845-2219
Eastern religion and New Age books

Sunrise Book Shop
3054 Telegraph Ave., 841-6372
Eastern and Western mysticism,
new and used

T'Olodumare Bookstore
2440 Durant Ave., 843-3088
African books and resources

University Art Museum Bookstore
2625 Durant Ave., 642-1475
Art, photography, film

University Press Books
2430 Bancroft Way, 548-0585
University press publications

Waldenbooks
2150 Shattuck Ave., 644-1360
Chainstore—general

Waldenbooks
2391 Telegraph Ave., 548-2159
Chainstore—general

The Map Center/Wilderness Press
2440 Bancroft Way, 843-8080
Hiking books, outdoor guides, and
topographical maps

Fantasy Records

Fantasy, the largest producer of jazz
records in the nation, is housed in a
concrete tower at 10th and Parker
Streets. The company has provided
editing facilities for many acclaimed
films, among them *One Flew Over the
Cuckoo's Nest, Amadeus, The Right
Stuff,* and *The Unbearable Lightness of
Being.*

Saul Zaentz, the owner of Fantasy,
produced both *Cuckoo's Nest* and
Amadeus. Fantasy, which has one of
the finest motion picture production
facilities in Northern California, has
sheltered and incubated a variety of
independent filmmakers and recording artists. It also has one of the largest recording studios on the West
Coast and is perhaps best known for
bringing Credence Clearwater Revival
to the top of the pop charts.

Collectives and Cooperatives

More than 50 collectives and cooperatives exist in Berkeley today. These range from worker-owned collectives in which new employees receive the same wages as ten-year veterans and decisions are made only by unanimous vote, to consumer-owned cooperatives such as REI, which returns profits to members in a yearly dividend.

The importance of cooperative organizations has waxed and waned over the years. During the 30s and the revolutionary early 70s, dozens of worker-run organizations appeared in Berkeley, while more complacent times such as the 50s and 80s resulted in a winnowing out process. John Curl of Berkeley's Heartwood Collective offers an excellent historical overview in *History of Collectivity in the San Francisco Bay Area* (Homewood Press, 1982).

A Brief History

The earliest local cooperatives had their roots in the Grange Movement, established in the 1870s to provide a cooperative marketing and banking system for farmers and unions. The Bay Area became a national center for the cooperative movement, and at its peak in 1902, the Pacific Coast Cooperative Union had more than 100 grocery stores. Most of these gradually failed due to conflicts with other groups and national economic upheavals, leaving only a few cooperatives by the 1920s.

The Crash of 1929 forced people to find their own solutions to unemployment and poverty. One of the most effective of these was the Self-Help cooperative movement, which emphasized barter and labor exchanges. By 1933 there were 21 Self-Help units in Alameda County alone. One of the largest was the Berkeley Unemployed Association, which maintained a machine shop, a rug-weaving operation, a shoe repair shop, a mattress factory, and several other operations. The Self-Help movement and Upton Sinclair's influential EPIC program (End Poverty in California) laid the groundwork for two of Berkeley's largest and most influential cooperatives, Barrington Hall and Consumer's Cooperative of Berkeley (the Co-op). University

students established Barrington Hall in 1938 to house and feed students. It was one of the only places (other than International House) to provide housing for minority students in the 30s. Barrington became the model for other student coops on the West Coast, and today the student cooperative in Berkeley operates seventeen houses. Finnish immigrants and other locals followed Barrington's lead by forming the Consumers' Cooperative of Berkeley in 1938. At its peak in the early 1970s, the Co-op, as it was called, operated nearly a dozen stores. It was a major social and economic institution in Berkeley until poor investments, inept management, and a lack of capital forced it into bankruptcy in 1988.

After World War II, America slipped into a conservative spirit that left little room for such socialist ideas as the cooperative. The 60s and 70s brought a shift in attitude, however, and with it a renewed enthusiasm for communal arrangements, both in work and in life. Communal houses opened "food conspiracies" to purchase food; farmers' markets supplied organic produce; the Free Clinic offered low cost medical care; and people pooled money and skills to form small collectives where decision-making was by consensus. Soon collectively run shops like Missing Link Bicycle Shop, Leopold's Records, and Cleo's Copying appeared on the streets of Berkeley. (Cleo's was established in the late 60s after the University banned student protesters from using its duplication facilities.)

Most of the several hundred collective ventures lasted but a few months before the members burned themselves out on hard work, low pay, and internal dissension. Others, such as Whole Earth Access, Leopold's, and Cleo's abandoned their collective structure and evolved into successful commercial operations. One of the longest lasting cooperatives, Taxi Unlimited, was established in 1961. Its crudely painted multi-color fleet became a symbol of the counterculture in the 60s, but an anachronism by the 80s. Taxi Unlimited went under in 1985 (see *Touring Revolutionary Berkeley*).

Two collectives have been instrumental in sustaining cooperative life in Berkeley: the Bay Warehouse and the Cheese Board. In 1970 the Bay Warehouse was established as an alternative high school, offering training in trades such as auto repair, woodworking, and printing. When conflicts between teachers and administrators arose, the shop teachers kicked out their administrators and broke away to form the Bay Warehouse Collective. The collective lasted for less than two years, but its pieces became three of the East Bay's most successful collectives: Heartwood woodworking collective, Inkworks print shop in Berkeley, and Carworld auto repair in Oakland.

Originally created as a for-profit business, the Cheese Board became a collective in 1972. It proved an immense success and an influential local shop—Alice Waters (founder of Chez Panisse) cites it as a primary factor in North Berkeley's evolution into a gourmet center. The Cheese Board provided financial and practical support to a number of other collective enterprises, such as the Juice Bar Collective, Swallow Restaurant, and Uprisings Bakery. Member support for political organizations such as the Livermore Action Group has also been substantial.

The 1985 *Directory of Collectives* (available in local libraries), provides a complete listing of collectives on the West Coast, including more than 200 in the Bay Area. Listed below are some of the best known in Berkeley. Many of these are described in greater detail elsewhere in this book.

Berkeley Collectives

Alternatives Center
2375 Shattuck Ave., 644-8336
Cooperative development

Bananas*
6501 Telegraph Ave., Oakland, 658-7101
Parental and child care services

Berkeley Free Clinic*
2339 Durant Ave., 548-2570
Free or low cost health services

Berkeley Tenants Union*
2022 Blake St., 843-6601
Tenants' rights and direct action

Berkwood-Hedge School
1809 Bancroft Way, 843-5724
Non-profit private grade school

Blake Street Hawkeyes*
2019 Blake St., 849-3013
Non-profit theatre company

Cheese Board*
1504 Shattuck Ave., 549-3183
Cheeses and breads

Community Memory Project*
2617 San Pablo Ave., 841-1114
Computerized community bulletin board

Earthworks*
2547 8th St., No. P, 540-9267
Pottery and ceramics

Ecology Center*
1403 Addison St., 548-2220
Ecology information and bookstore

Heartwood
2547 8th St., No. K, 845-4887
Woodworking and cabinetwork

Inkworks Printshop
2827 7th St., 845-7111
Printing

Juice Bar Collective*
2114 Vine St., 548-8473
Lunches and snacks

KPFA*
2207 Shattuck Ave., 848-6767
Listener-sponsored FM radio station

La Peña Cultural Center*
3105 Shattuck Ave., 849-2568
Cultural center and cafe

Livermore Action Group
3126 Shattuck Ave., 644-2028

Anti-nuclear direct-action group

Missing Link Bicycle Shop
1988 Shattuck Ave., 843-7471
Bicycles and bike repair

Nabalom Bakery*
2708 Russell St., 548-7800
Whole grain bakery

Nexus Institute
2707 8th St., 549-0703
Woodworking, construction, and arts

Northern Calif. Land Trust
3120 Shattuck Ave., 548-7878
Community land ownership

Pro Per Legal Education Project
2100 MLK Way, 845-0699
Legal help

Swallow Restaurant*
Art Museum, 2625 Durant St.,
841-2409

Uprisings Bakery*
2424 Ridge Road, 644-1165
Wholesale, whole grain bakery

University Students Co-operative Association
2424 Ridge Road, 848-1936
Housing for students

*Described in greater detail elsewhere in this book

Unusual Shops

A few shops in Berkeley are worth a special trip for their idiosyncratic offerings. The **Laotian Handicraft Center** (1579 Solano Ave.) is a tiny shop that sells embroidered clothing, pillows, quilts, and other items made by refugees from the Hmong and Mien tribes. It was founded in 1982 as a non-profit outlet to provide these

Muey Sio Saefong, assistant manager at the Laotian Handicraft Center. Photo by Don Pitcher.

women valuable training in English language skills, employment, and business management.

A good place to explore is the unusual **Tail of the Yak Trading Co.** (2632 Ashby Avenue). Its brilliant religious icons and trinkets from Asia and the Americas make the store wildly fun.

For handmade ceramic pieces, Berkeley has many choices, the largest being **Berkeley Potters Guild** (731 Jones St.), **Earthworks** (2547 8th St.), **The Potters' Studio** (2397 San Pablo Ave.), and **The Mug Shop** (1659 San Pablo Ave.) The Mug Shop and Potters Guild also offer classes.

Berkeley also has a remarkable collection of **antique shops**. Near the intersection of Ashby Ave. and Adeline St., thirteen such shops crowd together. My favorite is the sprawling **Thomas Livingston Antiques** (2994 Adeline St.), but it's impossible to visit only one store once you're in the area. On weekends the nearby Ashby BART Station parking lot turns into one of the Bay Area's best **flea mar-**

kets. Two-hundred and fifty vendors offer used clothing, old furniture, 60s era records, and all the other possessions that travel along with us through life. The market began in 1976 to raise funds for local community groups after Proposition 13 slashed funding, and now it helps support a coalition of groups that includes the Free Clinic, the Gray Panthers, and KPFA.

Dave's Smoke Shop (2444 Durant Ave.) specializes in international magazines and newspapers, but also sells hundreds of different American magazines. It's a great place to skim articles in an atmosphere thick with the scent of imported tobacco.

Games of Berkeley (2010 Shattuck Ave.) is one of the largest games stores in California. There are role-playing favorites such as Dungeons and Dragons, toy soldiers, boomerangs, dart boards, strategy games, and even a 12,000 piece jigsaw puzzle for folks with plenty of free time.

The walls of the **Tattoo Archive** (2804 San Pablo Ave.) are covered with books, posters, and magazines on tattooing: it's a clean, educational place. The owner will also gladly leave you with a permanent souvenir of your visit.

Weavers, knitters, and spinners will find everything they need in the huge **Straw into Gold** store (3006 San Pablo Avenue). Although primarily a wholesale distributor, the retail shop here sells many kinds of yarns, dyes, spinning wheels, and fibers. Straw into Gold also stocks books and magazines on the textile arts and offers classes in knitting, crocheting, and spinning.

As the ultimate hippie-turned-establishment store, **Whole Earth Access** (Ashby and 7th Ave.) epitomizes

C.W. Eldridge at the Tattoo Archive.
Photo by Don Pitcher.

the last fifteen years of Berkeley history. Established in 1978 as an outlet for counterculture products—simple tools for living off the land—it has evolved into one of the Bay Area's most successful discount chains. Wood stoves, axes, and flannel shirts can still be found among the microwave ovens and dinnerware sets.

The **Body Shop**, established in 1970, sells hundreds of lotions, oils and creams, and you can choose from a wide variety of unique scents. The stores emphasize recycling by refilling your bottles and using simple packaging. In addition, the knowledgeable staff will fill you in on the uses of the various products. There are three local Body Shop outlets: 2911 College Ave., 1942 Shattuck Ave., and the original shop at 2509 Telegraph Avenue. A mail order business serves folks farther afield.

Street Vendors

Berkeley's most intrepid business people are the dozens of street vendors who hawk their wares along Telegraph Avenue. The tradition began in 1967 when Fred and Pat Cody let several craft sellers set up in front of their bookstore. Soon hawkers were offering belts, marijuana pipes, tie-dyed clothing, and other handmade work all down the Avenue. As the vendors spread out along Telegraph, competition over space became severe, and some vendors hired guards to protect their strip of sidewalk or chained their tables to signposts.

The chaos and occasional violence led the city council to divide the sidewalks into 156 spaces in 1973. Today the city sells 500 street vending licenses; nonetheless, turnover is low and competition for newly available spaces is keen. The waiting list for a license is two years, and even then a vendor is not guaranteed a place during the Christmas season, when lots are drawn! The big seller on the Avenue is always jewelry; but woodwork, plants, photos and T-shirts are also popular items. While everything sold is supposed to be made by hand, a few vendors stretch the definition, stringing factory-produced pieces together and calling the result "handmade." Most pieces are of high quality, however, and often cost much less than similar items would cost at a crafts fair.

Politics

Perhaps more than any other American city, Berkeley is known for its political activism. Critics label it "the only city with its own foreign policy," or "The People's Republic of Berkeley"—stereotypes with more than a grain of truth. The people of Berkeley care deeply about their government and about the injustices in the world around them. Many of them were first attracted to the city by its reputation as a haven for those with liberal values and as a place where people act upon their beliefs.

The University Loyalty Oath controversy of the early 1950s and attacks against radio station KPFA during the anti-communist hysteria of that era first called attention to Berkeley as a liberal enclave, but it was not until the 1960s that Berkeley leapt into the national political consciousness. The images are still vivid in many people's minds—Mario Savio on the roof of a police car, the city council chambers dense with marijuana smoke during a debate over its decriminalization, and the pitched street battles over the Vietnam War and People's Park. More recent issues such as rent control, divestment from South Africa, and sister-city relationships have continued to attract national and even international media coverage.

Politics seeps into everything in Berkeley, even such seemingly mundane issues as garbage disposal, waterfront development, the naming of streets, the beer you drink, or the tearing down of an old smokestack. Former resident John Kenneth Galbraith once called Berkeley voters "the most intelligent constituency in the nation," and citizens pride themselves on staying at the forefront of important national and international issues. Activists canvass the neighborhoods with petitions, they join protests against apartheid and nuclear weapons, and they argue vehemently at city council meetings. Residents participate in elections at an exceptional rate. Registration approaches 90% of those old enough to vote, and turnout during presidential election years exceeds 70% (the statewide average is 40%).

Berkeley is a city that flouts the national trend towards conservatism, making Republicans—only 12% of the voters—something of an endangered species. In 1988, when George Bush carried California by four percentage points, he lost in Berkeley by a greater than 6-1 margin. No Republican has even bothered to run for the city council since 1973.

Sit in on a city council meeting and you're likely to hear an unusually informed and highly vocal gathering of people. This is not the staid gathering of business leaders so dominant in most cities, but is instead something closer to a sporting event, with the more divisive issues bringing out posters and chants, and angry voices screaming into the microphone as allotted time runs out.

In reality, however, Berkeley city government is something of a dichotomy. Underneath the political theater lies another side virtually ignored by

the news media. The nuts and bolts of city government—repairing potholes, paying employees, arresting criminals, managing the parks, developing a planning document—these functions are not conducted all that differently than in other American cities. What does distinguish Berkeley is that the entire political playing field has been shifted to the left, and that the players represent a public with a strong desire to change the world around them.

The dominant feature of Berkeley politics over the past several decades has been a confusing number of groups representing a constantly changing field of candidates and issues. Due to the weakness of Berkeley's Republican Party in recent decades, the political slates now represent only factions within the Democratic Party. Most elected officials, even those from moderate slates, would be considered liberals in other American cities. (Leo Bach, a member of the city council from the conservative end of the spectrum during the 1970s, called himself "an old communist"—the kind of statement that would be political suicide most places.)

The two primary camps in recent Berkeley politics have been the moderates ("conservatives" to their opponents) and the progressives ("radicals" to their opponents). Today most moderates in the city are affiliated with the Berkeley Democratic Club (BDC), while progressives are represented by Berkeley Citizens' Action (BCA).

A Brief History of Berkeley Politics

For much of its history, Berkeley has marched to its own political rhythm. The first municipal election following incorporation in 1878 was won by the West Berkeley-based Workingman's Party, elected on a then radical platform aimed at kicking the capitalists out of office and sending the Chinese laborers packing for China. The Workingman's Party proved a transitory, albeit important populist organization. Although it helped push through a new state constitution, it was labeled communistic and anarchistic by the powerful businessmen of that day, and its tax-the-rich provisions were gutted by a timid legislature.

By 1911, Berkeley had become the first American city to elect an avowed socialist mayor, J. Stitt Wilson. For many years thereafter, Berkeley served as a model of progressive government, becoming in 1923 one of the first cities in the nation to adopt the council/manager form of government, then considered the most effective way to reduce the power of machine politics. The city of Berkeley established a nationally recognized police force, developed a master plan for growth, opened the first accredited high school in California, and even created a Civic Arts Commission. Berkeley became a model for other cities and was chosen in 1934 as one of five American cities where people could best achieve the "goodness of living."

Opposite: Berkeley stop signs. Photos by Don Pitcher.

A Republican Era

Berkeley's city government failed to keep pace with the sudden changes brought on by the influx of minorities during World War II and the rapid growth of the University after the war. Just as its population was moving in the opposite direction, Berkeley came to be dominated by conservative Republican businessmen. Election races in the complacent Eisenhower Era of the early 1950s barely made a ripple in the press, as the headlines noted that the incumbents had again been re-elected. They were supported by the *Berkeley Daily Gazette* which remained a bastion of conservatism until its demise in the early 80s.

The mid-1950s was a period of gradual Democratic ascendancy in Berkeley, as the strong grassroots presidential campaign of Adlai Stevenson brought new life to the local Democratic Party. In 1955 the Democratic Caucus crossed the color barrier, for the first time endorsing a black man, Lionel Wilson, for city council. Wilson lost, but went on to become a judge, and, in 1977, the first black mayor of Oakland.

The Democratic 60s

The year 1961 proved a turning point for liberal Democrats as they gained control of the city council and began a slow process of change. Commercial development in West Berkeley was slowed, affirmative action programs were applied to city departments, and a Fair Housing Ordinance was enacted (though it was later narrowly repealed by the voters). In 1968, Berkeley became the first city of its size to use voluntary school busing for integration, an act that attracted national attention.

While the council was moving slowly, other events in Berkeley were altering the political map much more rapidly. Rallies against the 1960 San Francisco hearings of the House Committee on Un-American Activities, and the 1964 Free Speech Movement quickly turned Berkeley into a center for student protest. This new generation looked upon traditional liberal members of the city council as a polite face on the same old policies of the military-industrial complex. The tumultuous anti-war protests during the Vietnam War, the People's Park riots, and the sense of rebellion that filled the air soon began to upset the traditional moderation of Berkeley city government, proving a strong challenge to the bewildered Democrats.

The schism between members of the New Left who opposed the Vietnam war and liberals who supported it broke into the open in 1966 when radical Robert Scheer, a member of the Red Family commune and editor of *Ramparts Magazine,* challenged the incumbent liberal Congressman Jeffrey Cohelan in the Democratic primary. The pivotal issue was Vietnam, with Scheer demanding an immediate U.S. pullout from the war, while Cohelan favored a slower approach. The race attracted national media attention, being viewed as something of a referendum on President Johnson's war policies. (Johnson was apparently so concerned that his press secretary called Alameda County election headquarters three times on election night to check up on the race.) Scheer lost, but the relative closeness of the election galvanized the coalition of anti-establishment radicals and anti-war liberals. The next year they helped elect the first radical to the city council, an articulate black social worker named Ron Dellums.

A Radical Agenda

By 1970 even greater changes were afoot. Dellums ran for Congress, narrowly defeating the incumbent, Jeffrey Cohelan. Berkeley's longtime conservative Republican State Assemblyman was defeated by Democrat Ken Meade, who soon made a name for himself by the then-radical action of refusing to wear a tie during legislative sessions. The 1971 elections were a watershed for change in Berkeley. Controversy raged over a Black Panther-sponsored measure to carve up the Berkeley police department into three "neighborhood divisions." The measure lost by a 2-1 margin, but not before the *National Review* warned of "an honest-to-God New Left Democratic People's Republic on the Continental United States."

Although 42 different candidates ran for city council in 1971, radicals united under the umbrella of the April Coalition slate with the strong support of Congressman Dellums and hundreds of volunteers working to get out the student vote. Their opponents, led by the city's Republican mayor, were terrified over the prospect of a radical government in Berkeley. Governor Reagan warned of "an impending radical takeover," and the national media descended upon the city en masse.

The election resulted in a split city council, and conflicts between radicals and moderates surfaced almost immediately. Unlike traditional Democrats who emphasized local problem-solving, the radicals focused upon the idealistic goals of changing American society and stopping the war. When the radicals refused to stand for the Pledge of Allegiance (on the theory that U.S. actions in Vietnam were so heinous that they could no longer support their country), it made front-page news across the nation. The photo of the three seated radicals and the six standing moderates seemed to epitomize the split within Berkeley. (Albany's more conservative city council did penance for

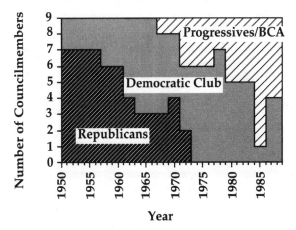

BERKELEY'S CHANGING CITY COUNCIL

Number of Councilmembers vs *Year*

Progressives/BCA

Democratic Club

Republicans

Berkeley by saying the pledge twice at its meetings. The Albany Soroptimists club also did their part by purchasing a giant American flag to fly over the Buchanan overpass of Highway 80, and it continues to wave there.)

The least radical of the April Coalition's candidates was Ilona (Loni) Hancock, a young activist and organizer of the Mother's March for Peace, who was later to be elected mayor. Much more controversial was D'Army Bailey, a fiery black man known for his flashy clothes, Jaguar automobile, and $25,000 campaign war chest. Bailey turned city council sessions into a three-ring circus of accusations and racial provocations. In his eyes, moderate black council member Wilmont Sweeney became "Uncle Willie," and liberal black Mayor Warren Widener, "the Chief Pig." Even fellow radical Loni Hancock was labeled "a white bitch" for

fighting to include white women in Affirmative Action programs. The constant badgering by Bailey caused both the city manager and city attorney to resign. Eventually Bailey's abusiveness led voters to recall him from office (in a special election conveniently timed to ensure that the students were out of town for the vote). He was replaced by a more conservative black leader, William Rumford, Jr.

The open split between the city council factions created chaos in Berkeley during the early 70s. Appointments to the city's many boards and commissions broke down; as a result, many were left without a quorum, and decision-making ground to a halt. City council meetings reflected the wild mood that reigned in Berkeley, some continuing through the night as arguments were thrown back and forth and every means pos-

Mayor Loni Hancock in her office, 1989. Photo by Don Pitcher.

sible was used to question city actions. The debates turned violent in May 1972. Following a council vote to refuse a $1000 appropriation of city funds for rebuilding a North Vietnamese hospital destroyed by U.S. bombers (one council member called it "treason"), a crowd of 3500 anti-war activists vented their anger by trashing the city.

A Divided Left

The 1973 election found those on the left deeply divided between "ideologues" and "pragmatists," while the well-funded mainstream Democrats ran as a unified group and won three of the four open seats. Initiatives from the left fared much better, resulting in a Police Review Commission (the first in the nation), a Neighborhood Preservation Ordinance, and an act to limit enforcement of marijuana laws. To raise funds, a "win a kilo or bust" marijuana raffle offered as first prize "a kilo of what people think it is." The measure was quickly invalidated in the courts by Judge Lionel Wilson.

Stung by their inability to wrest control of the city council, the April Coalition disbanded, with the less radical members regrouping into Berkeley Citizens' Action (BCA) in 1974. BCA proved to be a more pragmatic coalition than its predecessor, quickly developing into a grassroots organization with dozens of volunteers, tons of leaflets, and the support of Congressman Dellums. Despite the more conservative Berkeley Democratic Club's haphazard organization, backroom politics, and few campaign workers (but lots of money), BDC won three of the five open seats on the city council in 1975 as well as the mayor's race. The city council that resulted included, in addition to a

black mayor, two black men, three white women, an Asian woman, and one white male.

BCA Takes Over

In 1979 a political unknown, BCA's Gus Newport, became one of only three openly socialist mayors elected in the U.S. in recent years (the others were elected in Burlington, Vermont and Santa Cruz, California). "Galloping Gus" Newport soon attracted the media's spotlight. He traveled to Cuba, Mexico City, and Helsinki to hobnob with others on the left, met with officials from the People's Revolutionary Government of Grenada, and attempted to visit Berkeley's sister city in El Salvador while it was under fire from government troops. Republicans in the State Assembly took to calling him "Comrade Newport." Forming an alliance with an independent on the council, BCA put together a working majority that lasted for two years and that brought the "radicals" to power. In 1981, moderate Democrats struck back, claiming all four of the open seats and regaining their council majority.

BCA was slowly gaining ground despite these setbacks, not simply because of its members' more moderate positions (exemplified by calling themselves "progressives" instead of "radicals"), but also by their identification with the issue of rent control in a city of renters. Another factor was moving municipal elections to the fall to coincide with national elections, a change that dramatically increased voter turnout in BCA student strongholds.

In 1984, a year when President Reagan was racking up huge victory margins across the country, Berkeley was electing what the news media

Berkeley City Council meeting, 1988. Photo by Don Pitcher.

called "the most radical city council in the nation." BCA's Newport was re-elected mayor, and progressives won all four open council seats, giving them an 8-1 majority. In 1986, mainstream Democrats struck back with an initiative to change from city-wide elections to district voting. The measure passed easily, immediately forcing new elections for everyone on the city council. Loni Hancock, one-time radical from the BCA with a strong Quaker background, was elected mayor along with a bare majority of BCA stalwarts on the council.

The next two years were remarkably docile by Berkeley standards. Although Mayor Hancock found herself faced with homeless rights activists who established a protest camp behind City Hall ("Loniville"), most city council meetings began to revolve around such issues as permit parking zones, crime, street maintenance, and

the University's growth.

The city council election of 1988 proved a rerun as all incumbents were re-elected, maintaining the narrow BCA majority. The most divisive issue of the election was a proposal to establish a sister-city relationship with the Palestinian refugee camp of Jabaliya. The measure was defeated by a wide margin on the November ballot, but not before the issue severely split both BCA and the Jewish community. Although the Jabaliya issue dominated pre-election hype, perhaps the pivotal issue of the election was an old one, rent control. In the closest election in memory, tenant activists maintained a bare majority on the Rent Board by a single vote out of the 40,000 votes cast.

In some respects, the last 30 years have seen Berkeley come full circle in its politics. Although council meetings still sometimes have an air of political theater, the sense of constant up-heaval and confrontation has dissipated. The good-old-boy network of city government in the 1950s has been replaced by a liberal-dominated network. District elections have forced council members to acquaint themselves with a smaller group of people and to focus more on problems within their own neighborhoods. If the city council has become less partisan, offering a welcome respite from decades of political bloodletting, the positive legacies of earlier years remain in terms of neighborhood preservation, accessibility for the handicapped, and greater than usual racial tolerance.

City Government

Although Berkeley was incorporated in 1878, its present council/manager form of government did not emerge until 1923. Prior to that, elected city commissioners acted as both legislators and administrators, creating a conflict of interest when budget time rolled around each year. The new government of 1923 included a policy-making city council, auditor, and mayor elected by the voters, and a professional city manager appointed by the city council.

Berkeley is run by a mayor and by eight council members who are elected for two-year terms to represent a particular district. The mayor is elected every four years and presides over the city council as a voting member, but without veto or executive power. His or her responsibilities are actually more pomp than substance—meeting with other governmental leaders, representing Berkeley before federal agencies, and setting the tone for the city government.

The city council meets the first four Tuesdays of each month at 2134 M. L. King Way (the old City Hall), with sessions starting at 7:30 pm. The meetings are all broadcast over KPFB (FM 89.3). Berkeley is a city of politically-active citizens, and city council meetings have a reputation for rancorous debate. Anyone can address the city council on any subject by filling out a speaker's card at the city clerk's desk. Thirty minutes are reserved at the start of the first and third meeting each month for public comments (limited to three minutes each).

Council members enact ordinances, approve an annual budget, and levy taxes and fees. They also appoint members to 44 different boards, commissions, task forces, committees, and subcommittees (such as the Landmark Preservation Commission, Mental Health Advisory Board, City Humane Commission, Youth Commission, and Cable TV Task Force). Most of these groups are simply advisory in nature, but some, such as the Board of Adjustments, the Board of Library Trustees, and the Police Review Commission, have considerable clout. The citizen-elected Rent Stabilization Board is independent of the city council and oversees implementation of the Rent Control and Stabilization Ordinance .

The city manager wields the real power in Berkeley. The manager administers the five city departments: Management Services Agency, Health and Human Services, Planning and Community Development, Public Safety, and Public Works. He or she also appoints department heads (they must be also approved by the council), develops a budget for the city, and presents departmental recommendations to the city council. Although councilmembers and the mayor get most of the limelight, the city manager gets most of the respon-

Opposite: Old Berkeley City Hall, now offices of Board of Education. Photo by Mark Sarfati.

What's in a Name?

Martin Luther King, Jr.'s visits to Berkeley in the early 60s attracted thousands of students to Sproul Plaza, many of whom were also involved in the Civil Rights and anti-war movements. Because of his leadership in the push for peaceful change, his murder in 1968 shocked society and forced a re-evaluation of the way in which American society works. In recent years, the admiration of Berkeley's leaders for Martin Luther King, Jr. has led to a renaming of streets, squares, and buildings reminiscent of what happened after the equally sudden and tragic death of President John F. Kennedy. In Berkeley, the Martin Luther King, Jr. Civic Center Building looks over Martin Luther King, Jr. Park, which contains the Martin Luther King, Jr. Memorial Peace Wall, and faces onto Martin Luther King Jr. Way (formerly Grove St., but also jokingly called MiLKy Way). The entire Civic Center complex is officially known as Martin Luther King, Jr. Square. Berkeley also operates the Martin Luther King, Jr. Swim Center and the Martin Luther King, Jr. Youth Services Center, while the University recently renamed the Student Union Building the Martin Luther King, Jr. Student Union. There is even a Martin Luther King, Jr. Junior High.

sibility. This is reflected by the tremendous salary discrepancy between them—the mayor receives $21,100 per year, the city manager $88,200, and this is after a 300% pay raise for the mayor in 1988. The elected mayor and city council have the last laugh, however, since they can both hire and fire the city manager with a simple majority vote.

Berkeley citizens have not been content to let elected representatives establish all city policies. Through a referendum process, voters can overrule a city council action (as they did in overturning an anti-discrimination housing law in 1963), and through an initiative process they can bring an issue directly to the voters. Initiatives require signatures from at least 5% of the total number of votes cast in the last mayoral race (generally around 2300 signatures). In recent years citi-

zen initiatives have established the Police Review Commission, a city-wide Fair Campaign Practices Ordinance, the Rent Control and Stabilization Ordinance, a nuclear-free zone, district elections, and recycling programs, to name just a few. Voters can also recall elected officials, as they did in the 1973 recall of councilmember D'Army Bailey.

To vote in Berkeley, you must be over eighteen, have been a resident of the city for at least 29 days, and have registered at least 29 days in advance of the election. Registration cards are available at public libraries, fire stations, the League of Women Voters office, and from the city clerk's office. For more information on city government structure, including names and phone numbers of council members, contact the city clerk's office in City Hall (2180 Milvia St., 644-6480), or see

CITY REVENUE SOURCES 1987

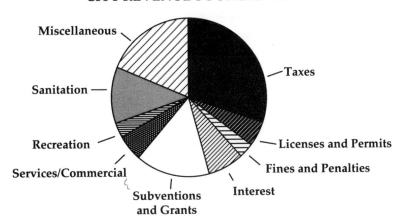

CITY EXPENDITURES 1987

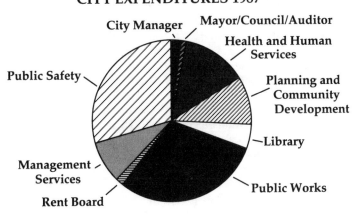

the extensive collection of city government documents in the public library. The League of Women Voters (1836 University Ave., 843-8824) publishes several excellent political publications including *A Guide to Berkeley City Government* and *Who Represents Berkeley?* The annual report by the city auditor details all the financial aspects of Berkeley city government.

Berkeley's Sister Cities

One of the unique features of local politics is its frequent focus on events outside the tiny eighteen square miles of earth that bear the name Berkeley. Many residents have long considered it Berkeley's duty to speak out on national and international issues, sometimes to the exclusion of more pressing problems on the home front. During the Vietnam War, the city became a hotbed of anti-war protests, demonstrations, teach-ins, city council condemnations of the war, draft-card burnings, and other actions. In more recent years, sister-city relationships have been used both as gestures of opposition to U.S. government policies and as support for liberation struggles.

Traditional sister-city relationships involve exchange programs and other brotherhood-of-all efforts. Berkeley has one such relationship (with Sakai, Japan), but its politically motivated sister-city ties capture far more media attention and bring out the boxing gloves. Conservatives charge that devoting energy to such issues squanders time better spent on local matters, while others retort that you can't put your head in the sand and ignore the world outside. The most controversial proposed relationship was that between Berkeley and the Palestinian refugee camp of Jabaliya. The proposal's 1988 defeat by Berkeley voters seemed to reflect a continued move away from controversial international issues.

Berkeley's oldest sister-city contact was established with **Sakai, Japan**, in 1967. Sakai is a large industrial port city that was home to Yosano Akiko, famed in Japan for her anti-war poetry and her emphasis on social activism, sexuality, and women's issues. The most visible reminder of Berkeley's sister-city relationship is the giant sundial at the foot of the Berkeley Pier, donated by Sakai in 1974. The two cities have an active student exchange program in which high school and college students spend a month visiting families in the sister city. Students from the Jefferson School exchange letters with Sakai students.

Berkeley has pseudo-sister-city relations with two Chinese cities. These include a "Friendship Relationship" with **Haidian**, a suburb of Beijing that contains the University of Beijing, and an education and cultural exchange program with **Changsha**.

More controversial is Berkeley's sister-city relationship with **San Antonio Los Ranchos**, **El Salvador**, a town of several thousand and the home of two U.S. nuns killed by Salvadoran death squads in 1980. Located in the rebel-held Chalatenango Province, Berkeley's sister-city relationship was meant both to help the people there, and as a political statement in opposition to U.S. support for the Salvadoran government. Shortly after the relationship was established (1983) word leaked out that Berkeley's relationship was with a former village—San Antonio had been abandoned after being bombed into rubble. The villagers fled to Honduran refugee

Berkeley City Council being sworn in in the fall of 1988. Left to right: Don Jelinek, Maudelle Shirek, Ann Chandler, Fred Weekes, Auditor Anna Rabkin, Mayor Loni Hancock, Shirley Dean, Alan Goldfarb, Nancy Skinner, and Mary Wainwright. Photo by Mark Sarfati.

camps, but government-placed mines prevented its reoccupation until 1988. For more information on how to help the people of San Antonio Los Ranchos, contact New El Salvador Today (864-7755). They provide medical, educational, and housing supplies for the refugees.

Another of Berkeley's controversial Central American ties is with **León, Nicaragua**, the second largest city in Nicaragua and home to the country's main university. Like Berkeley, it has a reputation for rebelliousness, political activity, academic excellence, and fine food. The FSLN was born here, and it was the first city to fall to the Sandinistas. It has also been the target of U.S.-funded Contra attacks. The 1986 establishment of this sister-city relationship was viewed as an open challenge to the Reagan Administra-tion. It included an effort to help the people by privately raising money for health, literacy, and educational assistance. Berkeley citizens sent ten tons of school supplies and bikes in a 1987 shipment—supplies otherwise unavailable due to a U.S. economic boycott.

In 1979 Berkeley was the first American city to stop doing business with companies involved with South Africa. Nine years later the city council took a further step by declaring the embattled settlement of **Oukasie, South Africa** a sister-city. Oukasie is a 10,000-person black slum bordering on the white town of Brits. The South African government, claiming that the schools were overcrowded and that the town lacked water or sewers, has tried to relocate the villagers fifteen miles north to an area bordering one of the "tribal homelands." The real intentions were obvious—to get blacks away from Brits and then force them into the "homeland" where they would have no control over their own lives. Berkeley's sister-city relationship was an attempt to prevent such forced relocations by focusing attention on the South African government's actions.

Law and Disorder

In some parts of Berkeley, particularly the southern and western edges, crime is a constant companion. The windows of houses are covered with grates, and if you look closely you may see pockmarks from the stray bullets of a drug turf battle. Workers in corner markets face holdups, and residents return to parked cars to find smashed windows and a tangle of wires where the stereo once was. Yet in other parts of the city, the news reports of drive-by shootings and families ruined by crack might as well be stories of civil war in Lebanon. Here the residents are reminded of crime only sporadically, when they return home to find an apartment that has been ransacked, or that their neighbor's bicycle has been stolen in broad daylight. Berkeley, like most large American cities, has its share of rapes, muggings, and lesser problems—noisy neighbors and slashed tires. When all these offenses are totaled, a crime is committed an average of once every six or seven minutes in the city.

The Berkeley Police Department seems to get mixed reviews. A lasting legacy of the 1960s is an undercurrent of anti-police feeling from a time when a cop seemed to represent not

Bay Area Crime Rates in 1987

City	Population	Crime Rate per 1000 people
Alameda	74,466	43
Albany	15,728	8
Berkeley	106,742	126
El Cerrito	23,520	16
Fremont	157,462	68
Hayward	104,086	74
Lafayette	23,089	7
Moraga	15,512	3
Oakland	365,983	450
Orinda	17,707	4
Palo Alto	57,364	35
Piedmont	10,683	3
Pinole	15,287	9
Richmond	79,828	103
San Francisco	767,933	584
San Jose	730,079	369
San Leandro	67,463	51
San Pablo	22,105	33
Union City	52,012	27
Walnut Creek	60,132	28
California	27,663,000	65
U.S. total	243,400,000	55

Source: *Crime in the United States,* 1988, U.S. Department of Justice.

someone who risked his life to save yours, but someone who busted your friends for a joint. Today, this perception is misplaced, since most Berkeley cops tend towards the live-and-let-live end of the spectrum. In police circles, the city of Berkeley has a reputation as a place that promotes educated and ethical cops. Part of this reputation comes from a tradition of hiring top applicants and of adequately funding the department. Other positive aspects include a citizen-run Police Review Commission that watches over those who enforce the laws, and a Police Reserve program that puts more than 50 community volunteers on the streets each month.

Despite efforts to control crime, Berkeley is still plagued with one of the highest crime rates in the Bay Area—126 crimes per 1000 people in 1987. The reasons for this are varied—a tolerant social climate that attracts ex-cons, easy pickings around the UC campus, and a willingness by residents to report all crimes, no matter how petty. In contrast to some other Bay Area cities, Berkeley officials encourage such reporting, as they are aware that a higher crime rate encourages federal and state financial assistance.

Berkeley's crime rate varies greatly around the city. By far the worst places are West and South Berkeley where robberies, burglaries, aggravated assaults, rapes, and even homicides are disturbingly common. The areas bordering on the south and west sides of campus (downtown and Telegraph Ave.) also have a high crime rate, though the problems tend to be theft-related. In recent years the crack epidemic has taken a startling toll in the poorer parts of town, leading to thefts, harassment of residents, and drug-related murders. A special drug strike force, and even a mobile station house, have been brought in to attempt to control the South Berkeley crack dealers.

History

Berkeley's police department has a long history of innovation and professionalism that has made it a national model for at least 27 other departments. This reputation stems from one man, August Vollmer. In 1905 this 29-year-old letter-carrier and ex-Marine was elected Town Marshall. He inherited a department that was in

Berkeley Crime Rate

	1979	1980	1981	1982	1983	1984	1985	1986	1987
Homicide/ Manslaughter	6	11	20	20	15	9	15	14	12
Rape	90	69	72	70	40	50	43	57	45
Robbery	601	607	598	497	603	549	660	695	580
Agg. Assault	405	342	381	340	464	454	450	467	538
Burglary	3126	3186	3518	2661	2899	2892	2930	2951	2442
Theft	7581	7866	9147	8718	8251	8846	8236	8111	7823
Auto Theft	1016	958	872	657	639	782	869	826	1045
Arson	-	-	-	64	90	75	89	72	80
Totals	12825	13039	14608	13027	13001	13657	13292	13193	12565

shambles. Violence by hoodlums in West Berkeley was so bad that Southern Pacific transcontinental trains refused to stop there. As an opponent of capital punishment and brutality against criminals, Vollmer believed in attacking the social roots of the problems. Although he had only six years of schooling, he made education a top priority among his recruits. Vollmer had clear ideas of what he was looking for: "The policeman's job is the highest calling in the world. The men who do that job should be the finest men. They should be the best educated. They should be college graduates. That's what policemen should be. And what are they? Dumbbells." He spent his life trying to change that.

Vollmer tried other innovations, making Berkeley the first American city to put all its officers on bicycles and later in automobiles. The department was also the first to test radio communications, to develop a fingerprinting program, and to stress crime prevention. Vollmer established the nation's first scientific crime lab in 1916, encouraged development of the polygraph machine (lie detector) by Leonard Keeler (son of noted Berkeley poet, Charles Keeler), and was among the first to use women as police officers. Vollmer's innovative work did not go unnoticed. He was called on to develop major police reforms for such cities as Los Angeles, Chicago, Dallas, and Havana (Cuba), and to head the national Commission on Law Enforcement under President Hoover. Vollmer retired in 1932, but continued to teach and write for many years. Vollmer Peak in the Berkeley hills is named in his memory.

The Berkeley police department's vaunted reputation came crashing down during the tumultuous 60s, as anti-war protests, People's Park confrontations, and riots turned the city upside down. The basically conservative department proved unable to handle the abrupt changes in Berkeley society. The city council responded to the unrest with an increase in Berkeley's police force, but the new officers' lack of experience led to an escalation of the conflicts between young people and the "pigs." Berkeley's police responded to the confrontations with much force and verbal abuse, particularly against blacks and anyone with long hair and jeans. To counteract this, the Black Panthers produced a "Community Control of Police" initiative that would have divided the police department into three neighborhood sections run by elected local boards. The measure proved too radical for the electorate in 1971, but two years later they did pass an initiative to create the first civilian Police Review Commission (PRC) in the country. The new law was immediately attacked by officers who claimed it was biased against them and by city council "moderates" who refused to appoint members in an attempt to kill the commission. Portions of the law were struck down by the courts, but the PRC eventually became an accepted part of Berkeley city government.

Today, Berkeley's Police Department consists of nearly 250 employees, approximately half of whom patrol the streets. A variety of other law enforcement agencies can also be found in their respective roles—BART police, Highway Patrol, East Bay Regional Park officers, University police, and federal officers are all entitled to make arrests in Berkeley. The 50-year-old city jail was remodelled in 1988 to accommodate up to 80 people. Usually there are only twenty inmates on weekdays; on weekends there are sometimes 40. Most prisoners are held overnight and then transferred to the county jail in Santa Rita.

City Crime Prevention

The Berkeley police department's crime prevention bureau (2171 McKinley Ave., 644-6696) has a number of publications suggesting methods to control crime. They help organize neighborhood watch programs, conduct free home security surveys, fingerprint children, and etch identification numbers onto valuables on request. They also offer special group programs in rape prevention and safety education for children. The Police Department has an excellent ride-along program where you can go on patrol with one of the officers to get a firsthand picture of crime in Berkeley.

Police Review Commission

This organization consists of nine members appointed to two-year terms by the city council. It hears complaints against officers, investigates the incidents, and makes recommendations to the public, the city council, or the city manager; but it does not have any actual enforcement power. For information on filing a complaint with the PRC, call 644-6716.

Crime Prevention on Campus

In 1987, California's Little Hoover Commission named UC Berkeley the "Number one campus for crime in America." USA Today labeled it the third worst campus in the nation in terms of violent crime, with a rate twice the national average. After both reports, University officials quickly leapt to Cal's defense—UC claims the numbers were inflated by inclusion of such areas as People's Park and Telegraph Ave.; that many major universities do not publicly reveal crime figures and so are not listed; and that the campus itself is actually much safer than surrounding neighborhoods. Despite these disclaimers, UC has its share of criminal activity, and visitors are often stunned at the sight of open drug dealing on Telegraph Avenue. There have been a number of rapes reported on campus. Students make easy targets for theft or robbery of car stereos, wallets, and daypacks. Bikes are a particularly popular target, with more than 240 stolen each year. The U-shaped bicycle locks are the best defense.

The most dangerous areas on campus, particularly at night and for women alone, are the eucalyptus grove on the west side and the fire trail in Strawberry Canyon. The University Police Department (basement of Sproul Hall, 642-6760) has a number of free pamphlets that cover theft and burglary prevention, rape, domestic violence, and night safety on campus. The Housing Office (642-3642) also has flyers listing housing safety tips for students.

One of the most practical crime prevention services is the nightly escort service, offered 6:30 pm-2:30 am. (As schedules change, it is important to check all services listed here at the phone number below.) Escort aides are student employees of the University Police Department who walk students between the campus and nearby parking or living areas. Call 642-9255 (642-6763 on Fri or Sat) to arrange an escort. The University also has free nighttime bus service to BART and residences around campus. The service is offered Sun-Fri 7 pm-2:20 am, and becomes door-to-door after 10 pm. For a complete schedule of shuttle services call 642-5149.

Touring Revolutionary Berkeley

More than 25 years have passed, but for many people the images of Berkeley during the tumultuous 1960s and 70s—protests, acid trips, free love, sit-ins, and draft card burnings—have permanently established the city in their minds as a center of free thinking and radical action. Berkeley, along with San Francisco's Haight-Ashbury district, was once an epicenter of change in American society. An entire network of communal living arrangements and collective businesses sprang up, causing an almost palpable fear in the establishment. Daily headlines bemoaned new threats emerging from Berkeley; the city had become a "liberated zone" for the youth culture. There were alternative schools and anarchist communes; there were rock masses in the Free Church, and windows bloomed with pot plants. People bought groceries from food conspiracies and headed to the Free Clinic for medical help. They set up alternative newspapers, an Ecology Center, and dozens of collectives.

Apart from a few "psychedelic relics," most people in Berkeley have long since moved beyond the 60s; yet there remains a certain sense of nostalgia for this exciting period. The "flower children" are long gone, and Berkeley's street scene looks more like skid row than a vibrant setting for social change. Today's UC students have only vague notions of the 60s, since most were barely out of the womb at the time and grew up under vastly different social conditions.

The tour that follows is intended to awaken a desire to learn about this period and understand how it has affected Berkeley (and even the rest of the country) by taking you through some landmarks from the 1960s and 70s. Locations are arranged in roughly chronological sequence. Boxed numbers refer to this chapter's map.

Before 1960

Despite the obvious differences between Berkeley in the 60s and the city that existed only a decade earlier, the roots of social activism go deep. In addition to electing radicals in the city's first election in 1878 and a socialist mayor in 1911, the people of the city had a long heritage of cooperatives (see *Economy and Business*), and of co-existing (albeit uneasily) with leftists such as the Red Finns of West Berkeley (see "A Tour of Victorian Ocean View" in *The Buildings of Berkeley*).

Although Sproul Plaza on the University campus was the focus for much of the student activism in the 60s and 70s, prior to 1960 the Plaza did not exist and Telegraph Ave. extended all the way to Sather Gate. For many years the University would not allow any political activities on campus, and during the 1930s flatbed trucks would pull up to Sather Gate to serve as rallying platforms. In 1933, the Social Problems Club (accused by

Opposite: Summer of Love. Photo by Michael Rossman.

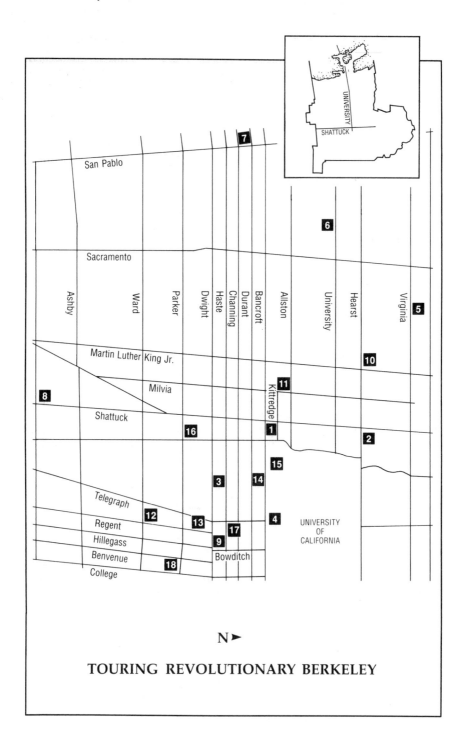

N►

TOURING REVOLUTIONARY BERKELEY

some of being a communist front) held rallies in front of the gate, protesting Japan's invasion of Manchuria. They were dispersed by the police, but similar protests against war and fascism continued throughout the 30s. Even as late as 1941, a rally against U.S. involvement in the war in Europe attracted 2000 students. Eventually, students were allowed to speak out from the Wheeler Oak in front of Wheeler Hall, and after it was cut down in 1934 they moved to the steps of Wheeler. With the completion of Dwinelle Hall in 1954, the center of campus political activities moved west a few feet to Dwinelle Plaza. Within a decade, the relative quiescence of the Berkeley campus would be replaced by a level of activism previously unseen anywhere in the nation.

TOURING THE REVOLUTION

One of Berkeley's oldest institutions on the left is **1 radio station KPFA** at 2207 Shattuck Ave., founded in 1949. While the station has won nearly every major radio award, its out-of-the-mainstream broadcasts have frequently provoked the wrath of conservatives. When Soviet Affairs commentator William Mandel was called to testify before the House Un-American Activities Committee (HUAC) in 1960, he galvanized the youth with his response—"If you think, for one minute, I am going to cooperate with this collection of Judases, of men who sit here in violation of the United States Constitution, if you think I will cooperate with you in any way, you are insane." Both HUAC and the Senate Internal Security Subcommittee continued to investigate KPFA for subversion and communist infiltration until 1963. The station reported extensively on People's Park and other pro-

Night rioting on Telegraph Avenue, 1968. Photo by Alan Copeland.

tests during the 60s and 70s, offering an alternative to the corporate media version of events.

During the mid-50s, poets **Allen Ginsberg** and **Gary Snyder**, influential members of the Beat Generation, lived at 1624 Milvia St., while author **Jack Kerouac** lived in a "little rose-covered cottage in the backyard of a bigger house" at 1943 Berkeley Way. Poet **2** **Robert Duncan** lived nearby at 2029 Hearst Street. Apartment complexes have replaced all but Duncan's house. The writing of the Beats helped propel Berkeley out of the complacent 50s.

Berkeley Heats Up

Student activism in Berkeley built slowly during the early 60s. Large rallies were held on Dwinelle Plaza against the 1961 Bay of Pigs invasion and the 1962 American naval blockade of Cuba. When President Kennedy—a hero to most students—spoke to 88,000 people at the 1962 Charter Day ceremony in Memorial Stadium, 500 students picketed the event, in protest of his sending military advisors to South Vietnam.

One of the other centers for early activism was the cooperatively-run student house, **3** **Barrington Hall,** at 2315 Dwight Way. During the infamous HUAC hearings in San Francisco, 700 students gathered here on May 14, 1960 to plan massive demonstrations. More than 5000 people converged on San Francisco the next day to protest the hearings; San Francisco police responded by hosing the students down the steps of City Hall and hauling dozens off to jail. Members of the John Birch Society made copies of news footage from the protests and distributed 9,000 films around the

country to show how the "communists" were trying to halt HUAC. (Jerry Rubin, then working as a Cincinnati newspaper reporter, heard radio accounts of these protests and decided that Berkeley was the place for him. It took him another five years, but when he did arrive, he became one of the New Left's most flamboyant leaders. See *The People of Berkeley* for more.) Barrington Hall has always attracted students on the fringe of academic culture—many became involved in the Free Speech Movement, while others were arrested for drug use, and still others turned the building into a crash pad for anyone needing a spot for the night. (Similar problems almost led to Barrington's closure in 1987.)

During this period, civil rights had also become a hot issue across the country, and many students spent their summers registering black voters in the South. Back in Berkeley, racial problems weren't much better; in 1956 the only black employee in downtown Berkeley was a maid at Hink's department store. In 1963, hundreds of protesters from the Congress on Racial Equality (CORE) picketed these downtown stores, trying to force them to hire blacks, but without success. A year later CORE focused its attention on the Lucky Supermarket at 2455 Telegraph Ave., a store that had long refused to hire blacks. In addition to pickets (numbering as many as 100 students), protestors used a new tactic—the "shop-in." CORE members filled shopping carts with groceries, unloaded them at the checkout stands, and then walked out, creating chaos in the store. After ten days of this, Lucky knuckled under, agreeing to hire minorities at all of its Bay Area stores.

Free Speech demonstrators at Sather Gate, 1964. Courtesy of the University of California. Photo by Don Kechely.

The Free Speech Movement

Although earlier protests had drawn some attention to discontent on campus, it was the Free Speech Movement (FSM) that catapulted Berkeley into national headlines. With the completion of **4 Sproul Plaza,** the area in front of Sather Gate was now on campus. The University attempted to restrict political speakers and tables to the corner of Bancroft and Telegraph, where students had to talk over the din of traffic. Activists decided to confront the new restrictions directly. On September 30, 1964, a group of 50 students staged the first sit-in at Sproul Hall, protesting the school's restrictions on political activity, recruitment

of volunteers for civil rights actions, and collection of political contributions. When activist Jack Weinberg set up two card tables and pulled out his political leaflets the next morning, campus police immediately arrested him. Before he could be hauled away, however, hundreds of students surrounded the police car, demanding his release. The Free Speech Movement was born.

By evening, 3000 students crowded Sproul Plaza in protest, with speakers using the police car roof as a platform to address the crowd. After 32 hours, a compromise was finally reached and Weinberg and the car were released, but two months later the University pressed charges against student leaders Mario Savio and several others. The campus again erupted into action. The charismatic Savio roused the crowd of 2000 with his now famous speech: "There is a time when the operation of the machine becomes so odious, makes you so sick at heart, that you can't take part; you can't tacitly take part, and you've got to put your bodies upon the gears and upon the wheels, upon the levers, upon all the apparatus and you've got to make it stop. And you've got to indicate to the people who run it, to the people who own it, that unless you're free, the machines will be prevented from working at all." Led by Joan Baez singing *We Shall Overcome*, they moved into Sproul Hall for a sit-in. That night 773 students were arrested, and the long battle between the students and the University began in earnest.

Many people in California found this new spirit of confrontation a threat, and those who opposed the FSM called it the "Filthy Speech Movement." Whatever it was, it proved a windfall to a political neophyte named Ronald Reagan. He made the student protests a symbol of the sort of action he would not tolerate as governor. Shortly after his election two years later, Governor Reagan forced the resignation of UC President Clark Kerr.

Acid Comes to Berkeley

The 60s saw an explosion of drug use in Berkeley. Marijuana, mushrooms, LSD, uppers, and downers were sold openly on the streets and a new culture grew up around the mind-expanding experiences they seemed to offer. According to Tom Wolfe in *The*

Electric Kool-Aid Acid Test, the "world's greatest acid manufacturer, bar none," was Augustus Owsley Stanley III, a student at Cal in the early 60s, and the grandson of a wealthy U.S. Senator from Kentucky. After learning a few tricks from a girlfriend majoring in chemistry, Owsley dropped out of Cal to set up his **5** **first LSD factory** at 1647 Virginia Street. He did a booming business here—once ordering raw materials for 1-1/2 million doses—until the police busted him in 1965. Acid was legal in California until October 1966, however, and Owsley walked free. Owsley's LSD, always labeled with some whimsical emblem, eventually gained an international reputation among acid-heads. He joined up with writer Ken Kesey's Merry Pranksters in La Honda and later bankrolled the newly-formed Grateful Dead, the originators of acid rock. (The Jefferson Airplane song "White Rabbit" is taken from Owsley's nickname.)

Protesting the Vietnam War

Although the Free Speech Movement had attracted activists to Berkeley, it was opposition to the war in Vietnam that united the New Left. In 1965 the rapidly escalating conflict led activists Jerry Rubin, Robert Scheer, mathematics Professor Stephen Smale, and others to form the Vietnam Day Committee (VDC). Based in an office at 2407 Fulton St. (now gone), the group organized marches and protests several times a week during 1965 and 1966, while VDC mimeograph machines spewed out hundreds of anti-war leaflets. The office elicited strong reactions in people, and in April of 1966 someone set off a bomb in front

of the office, injuring five VDC workers and severely damaging the building. The bomber was never found, but
some in Berkeley still consider the FBI
a prime suspect.

As a major transfer point for troops
en route to Vietnam, Oakland Army
Terminal became an all-too-real symbol of the Vietnam War. On August
10, 1965, Berkeley's city council chambers were invaded by 200 protestors
from the VDC intent on having the
council deny the Santa Fe Railroad's
permit to carry soldiers through
Berkeley to the army base. Right-wing
city council member John DeBonis
called the students "cowards, slack-
ers, bums, and idiots," and the city
council voted unanimously against
the proposal. Two days later 500 anti-
war protestors, led by Jerry Rubin,
marched to the **6** **Santa Fe Station,**
now a restaurant, at 1310 University
Ave., where they sat on the tracks.
When the train slowed, protestors
jumped on board, pulling the emergency brake and climbing on the roof.
One protestor was hauled into court
and charged with "littering" for
throwing anti-war leaflets into a window of the troop train.

VDC's most successful events were
two gigantic teach-ins held in May
and October of 1965. The first attracted 30,000 students and anti-war
activists to Union Field (now occupied by Zellerbach Hall), where they
listened to 36 hours of speeches by
Irving F. Stone, Dr. Benjamin Spock,
Paul Krassner, Norman Mailer, Senator Ernest Gruening, and Dick Gregory, among others. That fall, a
smaller crowd of 12,000 came for
more music and speeches against the
escalating carnage in Vietnam. After
speakers, comedians, and singers had
fired up the crowd, Ken Kesey and his

*Mario Savio speaking at an anti-war
rally, 1966. Photo by Michael Rossman.*

Merry Pranksters ambled onto the
stage, all high as kites and dressed in
Day-Glo military garb. Kesey called
the rally a waste—"You know, you're
not gonna stop this war with this
rally... Just look at it and turn away
and say Fuck It...." He then played
through a ragged harmonica rendi-
tion of "Home on the Range." The
energy level that had been building
all day plummeted, and the final
speaker tried unsuccessfully to rally
the crowd. The concluding march to
the Oakland Army Terminal met an
army of 400 Oakland police who di-
verted the crowd into Provo Park for
the night.

The next day, a second group of
several thousand marchers again
headed towards Oakland, but at Adeline and Ashby Aves. they were met
by a phalanx of police and National

Guardsmen, along with a dozen or so Hell's Angels, chanting "America first! America for Americans!" and "Go back to Russia, you fucking communists!" The Hell's Angels rushed the protestors, seizing the banner of the leaders and pummeling members of the crowd before the Berkeley police intervened to end the melee. Many marchers fled, and the rest sat down for an hour-long teach-in on the spot before finally giving up and heading home.

On October 4, 1967, an anti-war radical named Lenny Heller sent shock waves across the country when he declared in front of 750 students on Sproul Plaza, "Remember, you're a human being first and a super-patriot and an animal second." Then, risking a $10,000 fine, he soaked his Selective Service card in nail-polish remover and lit it on fire. Two weeks later Heller led more than a thousand others in San Francisco as they turned in their draft cards, yelling "Hell no, we won't go!"

A *Barb* in Society's Side

In 1965, Max Scherr, owner of the **7 Steppenwolf Bar** at 2136 San Pablo Ave. (a radical hangout that now sells used bathroom fixtures), decided the time had come to offer an alternative source of news. Scherr was soon hawking copies of his new weekly tabloid, the *Berkeley Barb*, on Telegraph Avenue. Published at 2886 Telegraph Ave., the underground *Barb* served both as a mouthpiece for leftists and as a chronicle of the counterculture. It shocked America.

The marriage of anti-war protestor General Waste-More-Land (Tom Dumphy) to Elizabeth Schwartz with General Hershey Bar in the background. Photo by Harold Adler.

Governor Reagan attacked it, libraries banned it, and critics blamed it for inciting the People's Park riots. By 1969 the *Barb's* weekly circulation had soared to 90,000, far more than that of the conservative *Berkeley Daily Gazette*. The *Barb* was an odd amalgamation—Black Panther and anti-war statements appeared next to photos of nude revelers and ads for rock concerts and avant-garde films.

The paper became a must-read for the Berkeley counterculture, and attracted a national following with its libertarian ideas and chaotic, wild layout. Scherr's interest turned increasingly to groups such as the Sexual Freedom League and others promoting free sex and nudity. The personal ads in the back of the *Barb* began to distract attention from the other features—"Chick alone or with one or two children to live with commune on Macrobiotic Retreat in New Mexico...." As they became more outrageous and explicitly sexual, the ads were not only a major source of controversy but also the paper's primary source of income. In 1978, the *Barb* tried to make it on more respectable terms by spinning the ads off into a new publication, *The Spectator*. Although *The Spectator* has survived, the *Barb's* circulation dropped below 3000, and the last issue was published on July 3, 1980.

Into the Community

By 1967—the "Summer of Love"—much of the anti-war activism had spilled over from campus into a new cultural center, Telegraph Avenue. A number of shops opened to serve the burgeoning hippie crowd: headshops, ethnic clothing stores, health-food stores, and vegetarian restaurants.

Street vendors began selling bongs, tie-dyed shirts, and other wares from blankets on the sidewalk (see *Economy and Business*), while activists organized street closures, partly as protest actions, and partly as a way of creating an alternative culture on the streets.

One of the most influential radical organizations in Berkeley during the late 60s and early 70s was the Berkeley Free Church. In 1967 the Episcopal hierarchy assigned Dick York, fresh out of Berkeley's Episcopal Church Divinity School of the Pacific, to be a "street priest" to the hundreds of young people flooding into Berkeley. York's Free Church startled the religious hierarchy with its rock masses, draft card burnings, Christian be-ins, and guerilla liturgy—"Oh God, who is hung on the cross of this terrible Vietnam War, help us to love peace... Oh God, who is a civilian blown to bits by bombs 'dropped exclusively on military targets,' help us to stop this war...." The Free Church services turned into major media events, making Reverend York something of a hippie Billy Graham. Occasionally, however, he was reprimanded for his radicalism. In 1973, York flew to L.A. to perform a free-form wedding ceremony for former Berkeley radical Tom Hayden and an obviously pregnant Jane Fonda. Under pressure from conservatives, the Episcopal Bishop of California issued York a "Letter of Godly Admonition" for performing the marriage ceremony of a divorced woman.

Before the demise of the counterculture led to its closure in 1972, the Free Church succeeded in helping thousands of transients by directing them to "crash pads" and offering medical help, drug and legal counseling, hous-

Reverend Dick York (center) with friends at the Berkeley Free Church. Courtesy of the Berkeley Free Church.

ing referrals, and free meals. (York's house frequently had as many as 90 hippies sleeping inside.) Many of these services evolved into present-day assistance programs: the Free Clinic, the Emergency Food Project, and Berkeley Support Services (see *On the Street*). Interestingly, in 1988, Reverend Alexia Bowley was appointed to serve a similar "street priest" role for the hundreds of homeless people who have flooded Berkeley in recent years.

The First Riots

On June 28, 1968, the "good vibrations" of the counterculture grew to seismic rumblings as Berkeley got its first taste of rioting. Three days earlier Peter Camejo of the Young Socialist Alliance had announced to the city council that, whether they liked it or not, a rally would close Telegraph Ave. in solidarity with student uprisings in France. The council denied the alliance a permit, but by the time organizers began setting up in front of Cody's bookstore, a crowd of 4000

had gathered. When a phalanx of 276 police moved against demonstrators blocking the street, they faced a barrage of rocks, and responded with all the tear gas they could throw. A full-scale riot ensued between the crowd and the police. Protestors said the "pigs" provoked the violence; officers said the demonstrators came armed to fight. By the time the aftershocks began to die down five days later, 58 people had been injured, 218 had been arrested, the windows of shops all along the street had been shattered, and the city's reputation as a center for revolutionary action had been firmly established in the American mind.

Black Power Emerges

When Martin Luther King, Jr. spoke to 6000 students gathered on Sproul Plaza on May 17, 1967, he called Berkeley "the conscience of the academic community in the nation"; less than a year later another crowd packed the plaza to mourn his assassination, sitting in silence for 50 minutes. But after the silent memorial the singing of *We Shall Overcome* deteriorated into a shouting match between those calling for violence and others pleading for calm. The tide had already begun turning away from King's non-violence and towards the Black Power promoted by activist Stokely Carmichael, and in the wake of King's murder, black high-school students rioted, breaking windows in downtown Berkeley.

The Black Panther party, the best known of all the militant organizations promoting black self-determination, originated in North Oakland in 1966. Its leaders—Bobby Seale, Huey Newton, and Eldridge Cleaver—had all lived in Berkeley at one time or another, and much of the party's support came from Berkeley radicals, both black and white. Dressed entirely in black, the Panthers openly carried firearms while preaching that blacks should be exempt from the draft. To fund their gun purchases, they sold copies of Mao's *Little Red Book* on the Berkeley campus.

By 1968 the Panthers had a national membership of more than 2000, and *The Black Panther*, their weekly newspaper, had a circulation of 100,000. Over the course of the Panthers' fifteen-year history, 27 members died in the violent confrontations with police that characterized the struggles of the Party. Many on the left charged that police openly provoked the Panthers to set up these confrontations. Outside the **8** **Black Panthers' National Headquarters** at 3106 Shattuck Ave., students and others frequently protested arrests, tailings, and gunbattles between the police and the Panthers. Bobby Seale was co-founder of the party and one of the Chicago Seven (a group of seven radicals, later eight,

accused of provoking riots during the 1968 Democratic National Convention). After Seale was arrested in his apartment at 1927 Stuart St. in 1968, protestors organized a disruption in the city council chambers to call for an investigation of the police department. An intimidated city council finally agreed to let Seale speak, and the protestors left quietly. The charges were eventually dropped.

In 1971, the Black Panthers sponsored a "Citizens' Control of Police Initiative" that would slice the city into three sections, each with its own neighborhood police department. The measure failed by a wide margin, but not before terrifying the establishment that the freaks and black radicals were about to set up their own police departments within the city.

Demonstrators supporting Huey Newton and the Black Panthers, 1969. Photo by Alan Copeland.

Not far from the old Panther office is the home of Black Panther-turned-conservative-Christian, Eldridge Cleaver. Cleaver had come from a very rough background—by age 31 he had already spent fifteen years in prison on charges ranging from selling marijuana to rape. But this internal rage also led him to write the powerful autobiography *Soul on Ice*, a national bestseller. In 1966, Cleaver joined the Panther party as "Minister of Information," writing for *Ramparts* magazine, one of the New Left's primary outlets. On April 6, 1968, just two days after Martin Luther King, Jr.'s murder, Cleaver and another Black Panther, Bobby Hutton, became involved in a gunbattle with Oakland police. Hutton was shot dead, and his Berkeley funeral attracted over 2000 mourners. Charged with parole violations, Cleaver became an even more vocal spokesman for black power.

When UC students requested that Cleaver teach a special class on racism, the Regents turned thumbs down, leading to large student protests. During one protest radicals barricaded themselves inside Moses Hall, renaming it Cleaver Hall. The police who rushed the building were under the direction of Edwin Meese III, then a deputy district attorney for Alameda County, and later the Attorney General under President Reagan.

In 1968, Eldridge Cleaver ran for president on the newly-created Peace and Freedom Party ticket; his campaign director was Bob Avakian, now Chairman of the Revolutionary Communist Party. Too young to be president, Cleaver received only a minimal percentage of write-in votes. Shortly after the election, Cleaver's parole was revoked, and he fled to Algeria. He later voluntarily returned to the U.S., brandishing a new set of beliefs. He now pops up in nearly every election as a Republican candidate for a local office.

Third World Strike

By 1969 black militants were intent on forcing major changes in the University as well as in American society. Cal's College of Letters and Science approved the development of a black studies program, but members of a student group called Third World Liberation Front (TWLF) demanded creation of a Third World College at the University to be entirely controlled and staffed by blacks, Asians, and Chicanos. To force the issue, on January 22, 1969, they began a student strike, blocking entrances to the campus and physically accosting those who continued to attend classes. Fist fights broke out between strikers and non-strikers, causing dozens of people to be arrested and others to be injured, both by strikers and by police. Each day hundreds of students formed serpentine chains, marching around campus and through buildings to call other students out to join the strike.

The protests turned increasingly violent as windows were smashed, non-strikers attacked, and tear gas bombs set off in classrooms, forcing their evacuation. A fire gutted Wheeler Auditorium, causing $300,000 in damage; several weeks later police found a timing device connected to two quarts of gasoline in Dwinelle Hall. The TWLF denied responsibility for both actions.

After a particularly disruptive day in February when a plainclothes policeman was beaten by strikers and a strike leader was beaten by police, Governor Reagan declared a "State of Extreme Emergency" and ordered the California Highway Patrol onto campus. The University administration then suspended all protest rallies. Students responded angrily to the "pigs," and when baton-swinging police charged rock-throwing picketers, the walls of Sproul Plaza rang to the voices of a thousand students chanting "Sieg Hiel! Sieg Hiel!" When Reagan met with the Regents at University Hall that February, 3000 students massed on the lawn across the street to yell "Fuck Reagan!"

Most students, however, continued to attend classes, and by the time finals rolled around in mid-March, the strike was called off. The TWLF failed to shut down the campus or create an autonomous Third World College, and it alienated many by its violence. Yet that fall the University created the first Ethnic Studies department in the nation.

People's Park

During the 50s and 60s the University destroyed dozens of homes and apartments on Southside to make room for new parking garages, dorms, and other structures. Although residents had often complained, it was not until the late 60s that things really came to a head in what turned out to be the biggest confrontation of Berkeley's "revolutionary war." In 1968, the University bulldozed several aging houses near the intersection of Telegraph Ave. and Haste St., leaving behind a trash-covered, muddy plot of land that became a de facto parking lot. Radicals believed the University had wanted to remove supposed agi-

tators living in the old houses. When the University delayed establishing the planned parking garage/soccer field on the plot, Michael Delacour, owner of a Dwight Way dress shop called Red Flag, came up with a different idea—turning the lot into a center for hippie culture. Originally christened "Power to the People Park," it became simply ▉ People's Park. An announcement in the April 18, 1969 *Berkeley Barb* proclaimed, "On Sunday we will stop this shit. Bring shovels, hoses, chains, grass, paints, flowers, trees, bull dozers, top soil, colorful smiles, laughter, and lots of sweat.... We want the park to be a cultural, political, freak out, and rap center for the Western world.... This summer we will not be fucked over by the pigs 'move-on' fascism, we will police our own park and not allow its occupation by imperial power." That weekend, several hundred people showed up for a combination construction project and festival of independence.

People's Park quickly became a focal point for student protest—a protest that evolved into open resistance. The Vietnam War was heating up, Richard Nixon had just been elected president, both Martin Luther King, Jr. and Robert Kennedy had been gunned down, the Chicago Seven were standing trial, and the Black Panthers were calling for an armed struggle against those in control. Frustrated by their inability to change national policy, protestors turned to a local issue where they had some control, the new People's Park.

On May 11, People's Park was consecrated by Reverend Richard York of the Free Church in a ceremony that mixed religion and people-power. Two days later, Chancellor Roger Heyns announced that the area would

Above: People's Park before the fence. Photo by Alan Copeland.

Left: Police and protestors at People's Park fence. Photo by Harold Adler.

Above: Police, tear gas, outside Sather Gate. Photo by Alan Copeland.

Right: Running from tear gas on Telegraph Avenue. Photo by Harold Adler.

be fenced off "to re-establish the conveniently forgotten fact that the field is indeed the University's, and to exclude unauthorized persons from the site." Finally, on May 15, the drama began. At 4:45 am Berkeley police ejected 50 people who had crashed out in the park and the University brought in workers to construct an eight-foot-high, chain-link fence around the lot. Before 3000 protestors on Sproul Plaza, ASUC president-elect Dan Siegel (now a San Francisco lawyer) declared, "Let's go down and take over the park!" The crowd headed down Telegraph and ran head-on into an army of police under the direction of Edwin Meese III. In the battle that erupted, the police ran out of tear gas and began throwing stones back at the demonstrators. Eventually they resorted to birdshot and buckshot. By the end of "Bloody Thursday," 128 people had been injured and a rooftop bystander, James Rector, had been mortally wounded by a deputy sheriff's shotgun blast. He died four days later. Claiming that "what is going on in Berkeley is not only a threat to our youth, but a menace to our whole land," Governor Reagan imposed a curfew and called in 2000 National Guardsmen. For the next seventeen days Berkeley looked like a military camp.

Five days after the riot, the death of James Rector led to more rallies in support of People's Park. In response, a National Guard helicopter dropped tear gas bombs on a crowd of 800 protestors in Sproul Plaza. Wind spread the gas for more than a mile around the campus, angering even those who supported a heavy military presence in Berkeley. (Fred Cody described an incident on the Plaza in which two well-dressed women were caught up in one of the protests. "Noting that the two women were lagging behind in an attempt to preserve their dignity, a young black paused in his flight to shout, 'Better run like hell—we're all niggers now!'")

These events, especially the helicopter gassing, galvanized student support across the nation, and virtually every other major campus in California—from UC San Diego to Chico State—joined in sympathy strikes to protest the heavy-handed use of police force in Berkeley. In an ASUC referendum on removing the People's Park fence, the vote was 12,719 in favor and 2175 against. Even the University faculty sided with the protestors, voting 642 to 95 that the fence around People's Park should come down. That June, University Regents ignored such sentiments and voted to proceed with building plans for the site. On Bastille Day (July 14), an angry crowd of 1000 stormed the fence, cutting holes in it before being repelled by police tear gas.

The fence stood for another three years, but on May 8, 1972, a violent demonstration against President Nixon's mining of Haiphong Harbor in North Vietnam turned into a storming of the park. Protestors tore the fence down and pried up the asphalt courts built by the University, throwing the pieces into the street. The fence was never replaced, but the western third of the lot remained a free parking lot for several years. In 1979, after the University proposed turning it into a student fee lot (a move suspected to be the first step in its development), protestors reacted by attacking the remaining asphalt with picks. Since then there has been an uneasy truce, and for several years it seemed that the land would become a permanent city park. In 1988, however, the University again proposed that student housing be built on what had deteriorated into a sleazy hangout for drug dealers and the homeless. A surprise riot by 2000 people on the night of May 19, 1989 left two destroyed fire trucks and 28 looted shops along Telegraph Avenue. Some blamed the organizers of a People's Park Twentieth Anniversary rally, but the trouble-makers appeared to be mainly a few anarchists, some drunk college students, and some Oakland gang members. The final chapter in the People's Park saga has obviously not yet been written.

Immediately after the creation of People's Park, other parks sprang up on lots throughout Berkeley. Most were simply a few plants (often pot plants) in a vacant lot, but on BART property at Grant and Hearst Sts. something more lasting emerged. Now known as Ohlone Park (the name "Ohlone" being that of the Indian tribe which once lived in the area), the narrow strip of land still contains the odd playground structures built during the time when it was **10 People's Park Annex**. In downtown Berkeley, Civic Center Park (now Martin Luther King, Jr. Park) was taken over by hippies and unofficially re-named **11 Provo Park**, after the anarchist Dutch activists. This and **12 Ho Chi Minh Park** (Willard Park) became playgrounds for the children of the counterculture; places for Sunday "happenings" where blissfully stoned hippies danced and sunned. The more political history of People's Park is captured in a mural at Haste and Telegraph painted in 1976.

Telegraph Comes Alive

During the summer of 1969, the city council created the Telegraph Avenue Concerns Committee to serve the particular needs of people on the Avenue. With help from the school district and local churches, they established an ambitious Summer Program in the decrepit McKinley School on Haste between Telegraph and Dana (a site now occupied by the Rochdale Village student apartments). The program offered classes in dance, music, theater, puppetry, crafts, and art, along with limited counselling services and housing, health, and employment referrals. The school also became the home of the Free Clinic and a free food program, along with a free day care center. Pat and Fred Cody called the Summer Program a "counterculture Chautauqua." Moe Moskowitz (of Moe's Books) donated hundreds of paperbacks for a Free Library, while the basement of the school housed a popular Free Store where second-hand clothes and shoes went out the door on happy new owners. One story from this era tells of a kleptomaniac who frequented the Free Store, always carefully concealing the free clothing he'd chosen.

One of the most influential of the many collective stores founded during this era was **13 Ma Revolution** located at 2575 Telegraph Avenue. Established in 1970, the grocery store was a founding member of the People's Food System, a loose network of counterculture stores and organic farmers. As one of the only natural food stores around, it soon became the hip place to shop. Unfortunately, in a 1977 shootout at the group's San Francisco Cooperating Warehouse, one person was killed and a Ma Revolution employee was seriously injured. Within a year the store had declared bankruptcy.

The Free Clinic

After the "Summer of Love," it became obvious that traditional health services could not handle the influx of hippies and drug-users, whose unfamiliar problems and lack of medical insurance made them a liability. A temporary **14** **Free Clinic** opened upstairs from Moe's Books and later moved to the McKinley school, before finding its home at 2339 Durant Avenue. The Free Clinic was a genuine community effort led by Southside churches and businesses and staffed by doctors, nurses, and medics who volunteered their time and expertise. Funds came partly from donations collected on the street. The Free Clinic really got rolling during the People's Park riots when the trained cadre of twenty medics treated those injured by rocks or tear gas and picked the buckshot out of people caught in the crossfire. After one riot, injured protestors inside the clinic began yelling "Pig! Pig!" at several officers making an arrest outside. In response, three tear gas canisters flew in the clinic door, injuring many medics and patients who had to be carried outside.

Taxi Unlimited

During the worst riots, the hippie drivers of Taxi Unlimited painted white crosses on the sides of their multi-colored jalopies and used them as ambulances to transport injured protestors out of the battle zones to the Free Clinic. Established in 1961,

the collective's funky fleet of psychedelically painted cabs offered free rides to hitchhikers, low-cost service to the elderly, and free transport for people on their way to a protest. Anyone could add their own paint to the cars, which gradually became a patchwork of colors and patterns. Based at 3058 Shattuck Ave., the taxis were an integral part of street life for many years, until business slumped in the late 70s. The company finally folded in 1985.

Peace Returns to Telegraph

During the times of violence, Cody's Books at 2460 Telegraph Ave. remained a neutral zone. Fred and Pat Cody's generous treatment of street people, along with their support for the Free Clinic, the Emergency Food Project, and other causes may have helped make Cody's one of the only places on Telegraph that never had its windows smashed by rioters.

One incident threatened the store's financial survival more than any other. During a demonstration, a police tear gas container bounced across the sidewalk and crashed through the front window before going off. The overwhelming stench forced the store's temporary closure, and it was many weeks before the smell finally dissipated. Fred Cody noted that the gas became a symbol of the protests to many people: "Indeed, visitors to the area seemed almost regretful that only a few 'pockets' of tear gas were still to be sniffed at in odd parts of the store space and they seemed pleased that the books still retained a tearful aura as a souvenir...."

The Codys expressed their sympathies in both words and deeds. Just two weeks after the People's Park riots tore Berkeley apart, they joined other pacifists to form the Berkeley Peace Brigade, helping keep a gigantic Memorial Day March a peaceful event. With the help of 30,000 daisies supplied by the Quakers, more than 700 Peace Brigade members stood between the police and 50,000 protestors. There was widespread fear of rioting and violence. Reagan declared himself ready to use "what force is necessary," and the sheriff threatened to "use shotguns to stop the riot." However, there were only three arrests.

This was not, of course, the last of the protest rallies. In the fall of 1969, as U.S. casualties in Vietnam topped 40,000 men, Berkeley students joined students from 400 other colleges and universities in a "Vietnam Moratorium." Despite a heavy downpour, 3000 students packed Sproul Plaza on October 15 to demand an immediate withdrawal of all troops from Vietnam. An attempt to take over the campus ROTC center in **15** **Callaghan Hall** was foiled by campus police. As the war finally began to wind down in the early 70s, student protests gradually lost their fever pitch as activists turned their attention to local issues.

Housing Wars

As far back as the 1940s, rent control and tenant activism were central to Berkeley's political culture, so it is not surprising that housing issues became major points of contention during the 60s and 70s. Radical tenants formed the Berkeley Tenants' Union (BTU). The group responded to overcrowding, poor maintenance, and rapidly

escalating prices and challenged the property rights of landlords and their control over housing for the two-thirds of Berkeley residents who rented apartments and houses. By 1970, some 500 renters were withholding their rent in an effort to force landlords to sign favorable rental agreements and recognize the BTU as the tenants' sole bargaining agent. Most of their efforts failed and many tenants were evicted, but in a few cases the tenants actually gained ownership of the property after forcing the landlords into foreclosure.

The most controversial local property owner was Richard Bachenheimer. Radicals plastered "Wanted" posters of him around town, claiming he was "known for his psychotic fits of temper at the sight of organized tenants." His houses were the sites of frequent clashes with the BTU.

Although many believe that rent control has been an unqualified success, the University claims there has been a 40% drop in rental housing in the city since 1980, which has severely exacerbated the housing crisis experienced by students. Two things are probably true. Those who have rent-controlled apartments are loathe to leave them, and few self-respecting Berkeley citizens want to become "fascist landlords."

Communal Living

Starting in 1968, the **16** **Red Mountain Tribe** occupied Bachenheimer's houses at 2233 and 2235 Parker Sts. A radical collective that eventually gained ownership of one of the buildings, members of the tribe treated incoming Cal freshmen to "Red Tours" of the campus, showing off the sites of

Hippies at a commune. Photo by Alan Copeland.

earlier protests, marches, and sit-ins. Directly in front of the Parker St. houses, you can still see the traces of a giant Vietcong flag, its red and blue stripes and yellow star just visible in the street's asphalt. A similar giant Vietcong flag adorned Telegraph Ave. for many years.

One way people countered the rise in rents was by establishing communal houses in which the rent would be divided among the members. The time was ripe for bold experiments with new ways of living, and by the early 1970s, over 500 communes and collective group houses were scattered throughout Berkeley. Some

were organized around political or religious principles, while others were based on vegetarianism, drugs, lesbianism, utopianism, feminism, common work, or group sex. All of them tried to create a social structure different from the establishment dream of a house in the suburbs with 2.3 children. While some communes were relatively stable, others changed members constantly, becoming crash pads for anyone who needed a place off the street. To the University's chagrin, many of its newly constructed high-rise dorms emptied as students chose the cheaper communes where they could hang out, have a try at restructuring society, smoke dope, enjoy free love, or otherwise thumb their noses at society's norms.

In 1969, Robert Scheer, Anne Weills, and Tom Hayden established what became Berkeley's best known radical commune, the Red Family, with a dozen or so members living in four houses on quiet Bateman Street (alias Batman Street) and Hillegass Avenue. Robert Scheer had helped found the Peace and Freedom Party; his wife Anne Weills (later married to Dan Siegel, the ASUC President-elect charged with inciting the People's Park riots) had travelled to Hanoi in 1968 as part of a three-person group of anti-war activists; and Tom Hayden had helped create the Students for a Democratic Society (SDS) and been one of the Chicago Seven. Neighbors believed the commune to be heavily armed, and rumor had it that the FBI was concerned enough to stake out Tom Hayden's house (3073 Bateman St.) by renting an apartment directly across the street.

The Red Family was involved in a range of radical activities, including the Blue Fairyland Nursery School at 3031 Bateman Street. While not overtly political, the school was known as an open and integrated school where one was likely to hear a folksinger crooning political folk songs while the kids "did their own thing." The nursery school moved to its present location at 1645 Milvia St. in the mid-1980s. Members of the Red Family also sponsored a "Peace Initiative" in 1971 that gave the people of Berkeley a chance to vote on a separate peace treaty with North Vietnam; a Superior Court ruled the ballot measure ineligible.

In 1971, while filming Steelyard Blues, Jane Fonda stayed at 3016 Bateman St. and enrolled her daughter Vanessa in Blue Fairyland. Hayden had just been kicked out of the commune, but he and Fonda became close friends and eventually headed together to North Vietnam, where Fonda made the notorious anti-U.S. comments for which conservative critics have reviled her ever since. As described above, the Free Church minister Dick York married the couple in Los Angeles in 1973.

One Berkeley commune, the **17 One World Family**, stands out from the rest. In 1970 they moved into the old Lucky Supermarket at 2455 Telegraph Ave., turning it into the One World Family Natural Foods Restaurant, offering macrobiotic vegetarian meals and music by the One World Family Band and Chorus. The building's walls (both inside and out) were covered with paintings of spaceships and scenes of Aquarian bliss. Initiates to the commune (at nearby 2405 and 2415 Prospect St.) donated all their belongings to the group and contributed seven hours of work each day, either at the restaurant or in the commune. The One World Family's beliefs mixed yoga, birth control, "nature's botanicals" (drugs), and communal child rearing with a blend of Christian, Utopian, and "Aquarian" ideas.

One World Family's spiritual leader, Allen Noonan, claimed to have been struck by a bolt of light which sent his astral self to the Galactic Command Space Complex. While there, the extra-terrestrials asked him to serve as Earth's Messiah, and told him that his head would serve as a transceiver for their messages. After an arrest for marijuana possession, Noonan spent two months at the California State Correctional Institute at

Vacaville, where he tried to convince the psychiatrists that his communion with space beings was genuine. At the height of its popularity the commune had a core of 60 or so members, but the group eventually faded away.

The SLA and Patty Hearst

By the early 70s, many Berkeley revolutionaries had begun the long trek back to more traditional lives. Then, just as things were quieting down, the Symbionese Liberation Army (SLA) emerged, making national headlines in 1974 by kidnapping newspaper heiress **18** **Patty Hearst.** After commandeering an old Chevrolet from a Shattuck Ave. Supermarket, they headed to her apartment at **2603 Benvenue St.** and threw her into the car, bound and gagged. Her kidnappers delivered messages to the outside world through taped communiques dropped off for broadcast over KPFA. In the massive manhunt that followed, more than 75% of the nation's 8500 FBI agents were involved in checking leads to the case, and Patty Hearst's picture made the cover of *Newsweek* seven times. Hearst (who later claimed to have been brainwashed) eventually joined forces with the SLA and assisted in a bank robbery and other shootouts. (Warren Zevon's song "Roland the Headless Thompson Gunner" glorifies this action in the line "Patty Hearst heard the burst of Roland's Thompson gun and bought it.")

Although most people on the left viewed the SLA as a bunch of frightening loonies, a few radicals leapt to support them, plastering Berkeley with posters of "Tania" (Patty's new revolutionary name), and SLA slogans such as "DEATH TO THE FASCIST INSECT THAT PREYS UPON THE LIFE OF THE PEOPLE!" (At the northeast corner of San Pablo Ave. and Channing Way, the faint letters 'SLA' are still visible on a concrete block.) Most of the SLA members were killed in a gunbattle and subsequent fire in Los Angeles later in 1974. Among those killed were Camilla Hall (a former employee of the East Bay Regional Park District) and Patricia "Mizmoon" Soltysik (a former employee of the Berkeley Public Library), who lived for a time as lovers at 2021 Channing Way. Others with connections to the SLA, Steven Soliah and Jack Scott, still live in Berkeley. Wendy Yoshimura, who served time in prison for her role in a Sacramento bank robbery by the SLA and for a cache of guns in a garage she had rented at 2575 LeConte St., later came back and worked at North Berkeley's Juice Bar Collective. Patty Hearst was arrested in 1975. Convicted of bankrobbery in 1976, she served three years in prison before being pardoned by President Carter. She now lives in Connecticut with her former police guard husband and two children.

The Revolution Postponed

At one time the hippie counterculture seemed poised to take over American society, but the revolution was indefinitely postponed by a variety of events—the end of the Vietnam War, a disillusionment over failed hopes and unrealistic dreams, and the evident mess drugs were making of people's lives. As this generation matured they began raising families and looking for more stable lives. As time passes, many vestiges from the 1960s and 70s disappear—spray-painted slogans fade, buildings are torn down, and rebels join the system they once fought. Many institutions that began or had their heyday during this time—Taxi Unlimited, the Berkeley Co-op supermarkets, the Free Church, and most of the communal houses—are gone. But the impact of Berkeley's progressive heritage is still felt. Today's rent control program grew out of the communal and tenants' rights efforts, and such institutions as the Free Clinic, Berkeley Support Services, Berkeley Food Project, the Cheese Board, Bookpeople, and the Ecology Center survive and continue to contribute to and influence the community. Take a walk along Shattuck Ave. near the old Black Panther Party headquarters and you'll find La Peña, Berkeley Citizens Action, Berkeley Community Law Center, and Long Haul Community Center,

all progressive organizations with strong community ties.

The citizens of Berkeley remain on the liberal end of an increasingly conservative national spectrum; for many locals, the "L" word is a badge of honor, not a pejorative label of disrepute. The ideas continue to influence the way the people of Berkeley respond to the world around them, though the intensity and full-on energy of the 1960s may have been redirected. It is no coincidence that the city has become a national center for creative people—artists, writers, dancers, poets, chefs, computer programmers, scientists, potters, and others. This creativity does not emerge from a vacuum; it requires a society that supports it, a place where creators do not face rejection simply for violating the norm. Perhaps this continuing desire to stay on the cutting edge is the ultimate legacy of the 60s.

Religion

The words "religion" and "Berkeley" seem at first to be antonyms. Street preachers on Sproul Plaza are routinely jeered, and the city's moral center is steeped in secular humanism and activist liberalism. Despite this reputation, however, Berkeley is an important religious center. There are more than 200 churches, temples, and ashrams, serving a diverse spectrum of beliefs from Southern Baptist to Druidic. The Berkeley Area Interfaith Council (2340 Durant Ave., 841-0881) coordinates twice-yearly interfaith services and publishes a comprehensive directory of all these religious groups.

Religion in Berkeley has deep historic roots. Archaelogists have unearthed religious and ritual objects from the West Berkeley Indian shellmound that date back for centuries. The first Spanish explorers of the area were led by a Catholic priest, Juan Crespi, and the prime mover in the University's establishment was a Congregationalist minister, Henry Durant. Even the city's name comes from a Bishop of the Church of England!

Berkeley's first Christian religious services were held in Ocean View in 1856 by Reverend Cox, a circuit-riding preacher. The earliest chartered church, the First Congregational, grew out of services held in 1874 at the Berkeley Hotel that once stood at Telegraph and Bancroft. In 1878, parishioners constructed Berkeley's first church building, the Episcopal **Church of the Good Shepherd** (1823 9th St., 549-1433), requiring just one month to complete the task.

Tradition and Diversity

Although unusual faiths and splinter groups have been welcomed in Berkeley, if you look at the congregations in many local churches on a Sunday morning, you might think yourself in middle America. Places such as **St. Mary Magdalen Church** (2005 Berryman St., 526-4811), **Northbrae Community Church** (941 The Alameda, 526-3805), **Chinese for Christ Berkeley Church** (2715 Prince St., Berkeley, 654-8137), **Congregation Beth El** (Arch and Vine Sts., 848-3988), and **St. John's Presbyterian Church** (2727 College Ave., 845-6830) maintain an informal family-oriented openness that unites neighbors. There are all the usual events—potluck dinners, holiday crafts fairs, and summer car washes—that are such an important part of America's social fabric. Visit St. Mary Magdalen for a Christmas or Easter Mass and you'll discover that some families fill entire pews, or head to **Congregation Beth Israel** (1630 Bancroft Way, 843-5246) on a Saturday morning to join Berkeley's Jewish community.

Several local churches focus on the

Opposite: Reverend James Stewart at the McGee Avenue Baptist Church. Photo by Don Pitcher.

University campus, providing a welcome respite from the hectic, secular world surrounding them. Some of the best known campus ministries are **Newman Hall** (2700 Dwight Way, 848-7812), **St. Mark's Episcopal Church** (2300 Bancroft Way, 848-5107), **B'nai B'rith Hillel Foundation** (2736 Bancroft Way, 845-7793), **University Lutheran Chapel** (2425 College Ave., 843-6230), and the **First Congregational Church** (2345 Channing Way, 848-3696).

Black churches are also an integral part of Berkeley community life. Their long history of social activism makes them not just places to worship, but places to rally, to strategize, and to socialize. Many black churches are also strengthened by a tradition of lifetime pastorship, providing a sense of continuity that is rarely seen in white congregations. As a result,

St. Mary Magdalen Church on Sunday morning. Photo by Don Pitcher.

black political leaders have frequently come not from the ranks of law school graduates, but from the ministry— Martin Luther King, Jr., Marcus Garvey, Malcolm X, and Jessie Jackson all began as preachers.

The dozen or so black churches in Berkeley, whether tiny storefront operations or large community centers, continue this activist heritage. The largest and most influential of these is the **McGee Avenue Baptist Church** (1640 Stuart St., 843-1774), founded in 1918 to serve a post-World War I influx of blacks to the Bay Area. Every Sunday nearly 500 people attend services by Reverend James Stewart, who, since his arrival in 1970, has made the church a social and political center for South Berkeley. The church sponsors a Head Start program, marshalls support behind efforts to fight crime and drug dealing in South Berkeley, and feeds up to 200 hungry people three times a week.

Founded by the South Korean Reverend Sun Myung Moon, the **Moon Unification Church** has a notorious reputation as a cult. It is one of the few openly right-wing groups in Berkeley. On campus its front organization is the "Collegiate Association for the Research of Principles" (CARP, 644-0789). The church owns a large mansion on upper Hearst St. and the church's national director, Mose Durst, is from Berkeley.

Asian Religions

Eastern Religions have long held a particular attraction to Berkeley residents. The **Nyingma Institute** (1815 Highland Place, 843-6812) was founded by a Tibetan Buddhist Lama, Tarthang Tulku Rinpoche, who fled Tibet in 1959 ahead of the invading Chinese, carrying 30 rare texts with

Hare Krishnas at the UC campus, 1970. Photo by Jerald Morse.

him. The first Tibetan meditation center, it also publishes many Tibetan books and manuscripts. Public lectures and meditations are given on Sundays at 5 pm. The Institute of Buddhist Studies (2727 Haste St., 486-9083), founded in 1966, was the first school outside Japan to be accredited by the world's largest Buddhist denomination. It is now linked to the Graduate Theological Union. The **Berkeley Zen Center** (1929 Russell St., 845-2403), established in 1967, is an excellent place to learn about meditation without becoming a monk. Members come from a variety of religious backgrounds (especially Jewish and Catholic) and from all walks of life. Saturday services are open to the general public and there is free zazen meditation instruction beginning at 9 am. A free meal follows the meditation.

Berkeley Higashi Honganji (1524 Oregon St., 843-6933) is a religious center for Japanese Americans. The **Thai Buddhist Temple Mongkolratanaram** (1911 Russell St., 540-9734), has a primarily Thai congregation, and the **Buddhist Temple of Berkeley** (2121 Channing Way, 841-1356) serves the Chinese community in Berkeley.

A center for the Sikh religion in the East Bay is the **Sikh Dharma Brotherhood** (2669 Le Conte Ave., 548-5688). The irisdescent dome on its building strikes quite a contrast to the subdued Northside neighborhood.

In a city where almost anything is tolerated, controversial religious groups naturally find a home. Well known are the **Hare Krishnas**, with their saffron-colored robes, shaved heads, finger cymbals, and constant chanting, "Hare Krishna, Hare Krishna, Krishna Krishna, Hare Hare...." Despite a checkered history in Berkeley, the Krishna Temple (2334 Stuart St., 540-9215) is an interesting place to visit, especially to partake in the Sunday feast of vegetarian fare after a first course of Krishna doctrine.

Religious Activism

Despite the outwardly traditional appearances of local churches, many of them are involved in causes beyond the standard religious sphere. As Berkeley's political allegiance shifted over the years from gray-tweed Republican to blue-jeans leftist, its religions also moved toward the liberal end of the spectrum. Today, Moral Majority types would feel ill at ease in many Berkeley churches where the religious message is linked to social activism. The Free Church, established in the 60s, was a leader of such activism—a poster from that time pleads that the Free Church "desperately needs crash pads for the large number of sisters and brothers arriving daily in Berkeley," and concludes, "Revolution begins with solidarity in survival." Although the Free Church folded in 1972, it left a legacy of social services in its wake (see *Revolutionary Berkeley*). Other local churches, particularly the **University Lutheran Chapel** (2425 College, 843-6230) and **St. Joseph the Worker's Catholic Church** (1640 Addison, 843-2244), have continued this support of those in need. Reverend Gus Schultz of University Lutheran has a history of political activism dating back to 1971, when he made national headlines by offering sanctuary to any sailor who would desert the Oakland-based *U.S.S. Coral Sea*, then en route to Vietnam. (None took him up on the offer.) The church also houses the Berkeley Emergency Food Project. In recent years more than 25 of Berkeley's churches have joined the East Bay Sanctuary Covenant, offering board and shelter to Salvadoran and Guatemalan political refugees. The program is based at Trinity Methodist Church (2320 Dana St., 540-5296).

Graduate Theological Union

Most people in Berkeley have only a vague notion about the quiet area just north of campus called "Holy Hill." Scattered through this neighborhood are buildings housing the Graduate Theological Union (GTU), a non-sectarian school that has become an internationally renowned center of religious cooperation in education. The GTU includes nine schools representing a range of Protestant denominations and Roman Catholic orders, as well as a dozen research

centers for special areas such as Ethics and Social Policy Studies and Urban Black Studies. The staff of 135 professors works with approximately 1500 graduate students. In the late 1950s, several religions established graduate schools in Berkeley, and the idea for cooperation seemed a logical next step. A prime mover was the Pacific School of Religion, the oldest seminary in the western U.S. Founded in 1866 as a Congregational school, it is now interdenominational. Two years after the formal creation in 1962 of the GTU, the first of several Roman Catholic schools joined it, and a few years later the first research center, the Center for Judaic Studies, opened. While most of the schools now cluster around Holy Hill, the GTU includes two schools on southside and the San Francisco Theological Seminary in San Anselmo.

The most significant unifying step in the development of the GTU occurred in 1981 when all the schools' libraries were combined into a central library. The 350,000 volume library on Ridge Road (open to the public) contains one of the largest theological collections in the nation. UC students have special borrowing privileges (before 5 pm) as part of a cooperative association established between the schools that also allows for cross-registration for students of both institutions. In addition to the library, the GTU bookstore (2465 Le Conte Ave., 649-2470), the most comprehensive theological bookstore in the western U.S., contains a gold mine of books on everything from ancient Biblical languages to liberation theology. The **Pacific School of Religion Museum** (see *Arts and Entertainment*) is also well worth a visit.

The Buildings of Berkeley

One of Berkeley's outstanding characteristics is its heritage of beautiful and creative homes—buildings by unknown skilled carpenters working from standard plans and by nationally acclaimed architects such as John Galen Howard, Bernard Maybeck, and Julia Morgan. This heritage stretches from simple Pioneer homes to playful Hansel and Gretel apartments, from carefully crafted brown-shingles to monumental Beaux Arts buildings. To some extent this diversity stems from the University's dynamic Department of Environmental Design (architecture) and the artisans it attracted. Also important were stringent zoning ordinances (the first passed in 1916) that led boosters to proclaim Berkeley a "City of Homes."

In recent years the people of Berkeley have had the foresight to preserve the city's architectural wealth. The 1973 Neighborhood Preservation Ordinance limited demolition of single-family homes and forced a quarter of any replacement construction to be for low-income tenants. The result was an increased emphasis upon saving the city's older homes. In 1974, the city council enacted a Landmark Preservation Ordinance to identify and preserve historic buildings; over 100 such landmarks now exist.

The influential **Berkeley Architectural Heritage Association (BAHA),** established in 1974, publishes books on local architects and their buildings, leads neighborhood architectural tours, and initiates a variety of educational and preservation-oriented efforts. The BAHA office (P.O. Box 1137, Berkeley, 94701; 841-2242) offers an outstanding collection of publications including dozens of self-guided walking tours and detailed information about practically every old building in the city. Membership is $15/yr.

Berkeley Architectural Styles

The information below about architectural styles and architects in Berkeley is based upon BAHA research work. For a more complete description of local architectural styles and homes see Mark A. Wilson's *A Living Legacy* (Lexikos Press, San Francisco 1987) or BAHA's *41 Walking Tours of Berkeley,* which briefly covers buildings in most of Berkeley's neighborhoods.

Pioneer *1850-1885*
These simple wood-frame buildings were built to resemble the homes that the pioneers had left behind in New England. Many have raised base-

Pioneer style. Photo by Don Pitcher.

ments as protection against the once-frequent flooding of the creeks or unusually high tides of the Bay. Windows and doorways are often topped by decorative trim. Some pioneer houses also have false fronts with additional molding along the cornice. The homes were built quickly from locally milled wood and were called "balloon frames" because they looked as if the first wind might carry them away. Commercial buildings of this style often used false fronts to suggest the establishment's importance. Good examples are the Continental Garden Restaurant at 2377 Shattuck Ave. and several Ocean View houses (see "A Tour of Victorian Ocean View," following).

Italianate *1860-1885*
The designs for these Victorian homes were influenced by romantic 19th-century paintings showing the villas of northern Italy. Italianate homes have a strong vertical orientation accentuated by tall, narrow windows with rounded arches and bracket-supported eaves. Many also have angled bay windows and porches supported by columns. The nicely restored raised-basement Italianate cottage at 2601 Dana St., built about 1860, may be the oldest building in the Southside area. Berkeley recently lost one of its most majestic homes, the Italianate villa of Napoleon Bonaparte Byrne at 1301 Oxford St., built in 1868 near Codornices Park, to arson.

Stick-Eastlake *1870-1895*
Stick houses are the simplest and most box-like of the Victorian styles, with wooden strips along corners, doors, and windows (stickwork), and square rather than angled bay windows. The intricate decorative motifs

and stained glass windows were named for George Eastlake, an English author and designer of simple, angular furniture. Eastlake's simplicity was lost in the translation of his designs into the mass-production of American furniture, which turned out pieces with elaborate decorative motifs. Eventually the decorative pieces began to show up on the exterior of Victorian houses as the floral, sunflower, and other ornamented patterns now associated with the Victorian Era. Not surprisingly, Eastlake was appalled to hear that his name was being used to describe an ornamental style that expressed the opposite of his philosophy!

The largest Stick-Eastlake houses commonly have square corner towers and are known as villas. The best local examples are the Niehaus Villa at 839 Channing Way (described in "A Tour of Victorian Ocean View"), and the Flagg-Wright House (1880) on Milvia and Francisco Streets. Built by a ship carpenter, John Paul Moran, the latter house bears his trademark of carved anchors along the rear gables.

Queen Anne *1880-1900*
Queen Anne homes best display the Victorian Era's obsession with decoration. Ornaments include stickwork, stained glass, sunburst panels, gabled roofs with scrolled wood at the peaks, spindlework along the porch, and fish-scale patterned walls. The largest frequently boast a curved corner tower topped by a witch's hat. Berkeley also has dozens of Queen Anne cottages, some of which incorporate Stick-Eastlake styles. The Captain Boudrow House at 1536 Oxford St. (1889) is an elegant example of the Queen Anne style with a stained glass window depicting Captain Boudrow's

flagship. Another interesting Queen Anne house is the Gough House (1886), 1431 Arch St., built by Ira Boynton, which has an hexagonal tower.

Berkeley Victorian. Photo by Don Pitcher.

Beaux Arts *1895-1925*
The Beaux Arts style originated in Paris at the École des Beaux Arts and became popular in America after its use in the 1893 Columbian Exposition in Chicago. Beaux Arts was used primarily in large public buildings such as those on the University campus (see *The University*). Its advocates supported the idea of a "palatial urbanism" with broad boulevards, elaborate buildings, and grandiose landscaping; the buildings combined classical columns, heavy window casements and high ceilings. The Main Post Office (1914) at 2000 Allston Way and the old City Hall (1908), now the School Board offices, at 2134 M. L. King Way, are other examples of Beaux Arts buildings.

Craftsman/Brown-Shingle
1900-1920
Although Berkeley had dozens of lovely Victorian homes, its architecture was rather ordinary until the 1890s, when a back-to-nature movement emphasizing natural materials and rustic designs began to take root. Craftsman homes came out of this early environmental movement and became dominant in the early years of this century. The buildings generally had overhanging eaves and exposed wood beams, brown-shingled exterior walls, and large pillared porches. Craftsman homes had a hand-crafted design, while the more common brown-shingles were rather plain two-story rectangular houses. There are hundreds of examples of brown shingles throughout Berkeley, particularly in the Elmwood area. The rambling Anna Head School built in 1892 (now University offices) at Haste and Bowditch Sts. is one of the oldest and finest examples.

Berkeley brown-shingle. Photo by Don Pitcher.

First Bay Tradition *1890-1935*
The First Bay Tradition grew out of the Craftsman movement, and employed a similar emphasis on hand-crafted construction and natural materials such as unpainted redwood. First Bay Tradition architects took the concept a step further by incorporating such diverse styles as Swiss Chalet, English Tudor, and Gothic. The

Bay Area's most influential architects—among them Ernest Coxhead, John Galen Howard, Julia Morgan, Willis Polk, John Hudson Thomas, and A. C. Schweinfurth—designed First Bay Tradition homes throughout Berkeley. The best known architect was Bernard Maybeck.

In some ways the First Bay Tradition was more a philosophy than an architectural style. Its primary exponent was Charles Keeler, a Berkeley poet and ornithologist and friend of Bernard Maybeck. In his influential book, *The Simple Home,* he railed against the machine-produced architectural excesses of the Victorian period and suggested simpler designs that could provide a "shelter for daydreams." (His broad horizons also led to the establishment of the "First Berkeley Cosmic Society," a venture that was 50 years ahead of its time.) Maybeck crafted one of the earliest of these "simple homes" for Keeler. His house at 1770 Highland Place (built in 1895) caused a sensation in local architectural circles with its steep Japanese-style roofs, exposed redwood timbers, double band of windows wrapping around the exterior, and unpainted redwood shingles (now replaced by stucco). After its construction Keeler became an advocate for Maybeck's vision, and within a few years his neighbors began to commission similar homes. The Berkeley Hillside Club was particularly influential in these commissions. Limited to women until 1902, the club was dedicated to making homes an integral part of the natural environment. A club statement proclaimed: "The California hills are brown, therefore, the house should be brown. Redwood is the natural wood of the country, therefore, it is natural to use it. A house should not stand out in a landscape, but should fit in with it. This is the first principle that should govern the design of every house." (In an ironic twist, many people who were once proponents of redwood construction later joined The Save the Redwoods League to prevent destruction of the remaining redwood groves.) A magnificent example of a First Bay Tradition structure is the Julia Morgan Performing Arts Center (1908) at 2640 College Ave., originally St. John's Presbyterian Church. Designed by Morgan, the brown-shingled structure has an interior of large redwood rafters and a rustic, comfortable feeling.

Period Revivals *1900-1940*
During the late 19th and early 20th centuries, revivals of historic styles became popular in California. **Colonial Revival** houses are found throughout Berkeley. The large, boxy houses have a distinctive hip-roof (like a pyramid with the top knocked off) and often have column-like building corners (pilasters), columned porches, and leaded-glass dormer windows. The McCreary House (2318 Durant Ave.), built in 1902, has been home to the Berkeley Architectural Heritage Association, and is a fine example of this style, with its stained-glass windows and elaborate curved porch. Around the Ashby BART station every second house seems to be of this style: there are six nearly identical Colonial Revival houses in a row between 1621 and 1631 Parker Street.

Opposite: Berkeley Hansel and Gretel apartments. Photo by Don Pitcher.

The **High-Peaked Gable Cottages** common around Berkeley may derive their Scandanavian flavor from the designs of a local Finnish contractor. The steep roof is the most obvious characteristic, but other features include a porch with columns, dormers on the roof, and a mixture of pieces from other turn of the century styles. Good examples are the three colorful cottages at 3020-28 M.L. King Way.

Inspired by early California Spanish missions, the **Mission Revival** style —favored for public or commercial use—features exposed rafter beams, arched window openings, stucco walls, balconies, towers, and the distinctive red-tile roofs. The former Santa Fe Depot (1904) at 1310 University Ave. and the old Southern Pacific Railway Depot (1913) at 700 University Ave. are good examples. Both are now used as restaurants. St. Mark's Episcopal Church (1901), 2300 Bancroft Way, has copies of the bell towers present on the original Spanish mission structures. Inside the nave you'll find Tiffany stained-glass windows. One of Berkeley's strangest homes is the Marquis House (1910) at 2827 Russell St., built as a parody of the Mission Revival style.

John Hudson Thomas's design for the École Bilingue at 1001 Heinz Ave. (1915) is a lovely example of a **Dutch Colonial** style building with a gambrel roof, heavy support posts, and half-timbering.

The wonderfully playful Normandy Village apartments at 1781-83 and 1817-39 Spruce St. (1928) in the **Hansel and Gretel** style were originally built to be a complete village with stores as well as apartments. Once there, you'll feel you have stepped back into childhood: carved gargoyles sneer at you from beam ends; dropping rooflines are reminiscent of the Black Forest. William R. Yelland designed these and the equally whimsical Tupper & Reed building at 2777 Shattuck Ave. (1926), the chimney of which is topped by a weather vane in the shape of a figure blowing a horn.

English Tudor-style houses are common in wealthier parts of Berkeley, particularly near the Claremont Hotel. (The Claremont Hotel was completed in 1915 and incorporates its own English half-timbering along with other styles.) English Tudor homes are distinguished by steep rooflines, half-timbers, exposed gable ends, stone-accented doorways, and decorative chimneys. Good examples include the Douglas House (1910), 35 Parkside Ave., built by Albert Farr, and the Graduate School of Public Policy (1893) at Hearst at Le Roy Aves., designed by Ernest Coxhead, with the front added later by Bakewell and Brown.

California Bungalow *1900-1930*

Certainly the most common house on the Berkeley flatlands is the lowly California bungalow, a one-story stucco building with a porch or veranda. Originally an English adaptation of the *bangalas* found in India, the idea really took off in California, where the mild climate and availability of cheap land made them a sensible housing solution. The structures were inexpensive (under $1000), and prefabricated units required few carpentry skills. Although such famous architects as Greene & Greene designed magnificent Southern Cali-

A California bungalow. Photo by Don Pitcher.

fornian versions of the bungalow, with sleeping porches and Japanese-inspired woodwork, most are more prosaic boxes with low roofs, stucco walls, and gracious porches. West Berkeley has hundreds of examples of the latter.

Prairie Style *1905-1930*
Frank Lloyd Wright's creations reflected the midwestern prairies in their broadly horizontal structures with overhanging eaves and low-pitched roofs. The angular appearance and geometric decorative pieces of his work revolutionized American architecture. A good example of Wright's influence is the Loring House, 1730 Spruce St. (1914), designed by John Hudson Thomas. Another of Thomas's creations is the Sellander House, 35 Oakvale Ave. (1914), which provides the unusual combination of Tudor Revival and Prairie styles.

Art Deco and Moderne *1925-1950*
Art Deco originated in the 1925 Paris Exposition Internationale des Arts Decoratifs et Industriels Modernes, in which historical styles were rejected in favor of clean, futuristic shapes. Art Deco buildings are adorned with chevrons, zigzags, and stylized floral motifs etched into their streamlined concrete exteriors. The Main Public Library (1930) at Shattuck Ave. and Kittredge St. is a good example of the style: there are playful zigzag patterns above the windows and Egyptian decorations on the panels, while small iron cobra heads crown each window. Moderne-styled buildings are simpler and incorporate plain industrial materials. Moderne was used in many government buildings built in the 1930s, such as Berkeley City Hall at 2180 Milvia Street. Berkeley High School, also built during the New Deal, reflects the sentiments of that era with its stylized WPA relief sculpture on the exterior.

Brutalism *1960-*
Modern day parking garages are examples of a common theme in recent architecture—form follows function. Structures that frequently dominate city skylines use heavy walls of exposed concrete with cavernous openings for windows and balconies. The name Brutalism comes from the French words for exposed rough concrete (*breton brut*), but could just as well apply to the style's lack of style. Particularly egregious local examples are Wurster Hall (1964) and Evans Hall (1971) on the UC campus. An attractive version is the University Art Museum (1972).

A TOUR OF VICTORIAN OCEAN VIEW

Berkeley's origins lie not in the University, but in the gradual development of its shoreline into the settlement of Ocean View, the area now known as West Berkeley. Before the establishment of the University in 1873, this was a small, thriving community of farmers, innkeepers, saloon owners, and dockworkers. Between 1873 and 1900 the local population nearly tripled. Students were attracted to the numerous saloons that grew up beyond the one-mile limit from the University, and a number of major factories moved in. In the last decades of the 19th century a number of Victorian-style homes—Pioneer, Italianate, Stick-Eastlake, and Queen Anne—were built for local workers and for others who commuted to San Francisco by ferry.

Throughout much of the present century Ocean View was left as somewhat of a backwater, as more vigorous developments centered around the University and throughout the Berkeley hills. Many of the older homes were lost to industry, community redevelopment projects, or simply to age and neglect. Since the 1970s, however, Berkeley residents have come to appreciate the area for its architectural and historic values. Several of the finest old homes have been saved from the bulldozer, restored, and moved to the Delaware Street Historic District at 5th and Delaware Streets. Others—some renovated, many not—remain among the factories, warehouses, and more recently built eyesores. An excursion through Ocean View will never rank as a major architectural Grand Tour; the homes of this area nevertheless offer a charming and, especially for long-time residents, a surprising vision of what small-town Berkeley was like in its infancy.

Start at the magnificent (though poorly-maintained) **1** **Niehaus Villa** (1889) at 839 Channing Way. Built by Edward F. Niehaus, a carpenter who ran the West Berkeley Planing Mill, this Stick-Eastlake house was a show-

Niehaus Villa in the Stick-Eastlake style. Photo by Don Pitcher.

piece for the sash, moldings, scroll-sawed and turned wood produced by his mill. (At one time the largest mill on the West Coast, the planing mill burned down in 1901 and was never rebuilt.) Inside the Niehaus Villa each room has panels of a different type of Central American hardwood. Note the ornate three-story corner tower that dominates the neighborhood; the intricate sunflower scrollwork beside the second-story windows; the lattice-arched porch; and the wrought-iron fence along 7th Street.

At 2320 7th St. (1892) is a Queen Anne built by Niehaus. Note the fish-scale shingles and the wrought-iron fence.

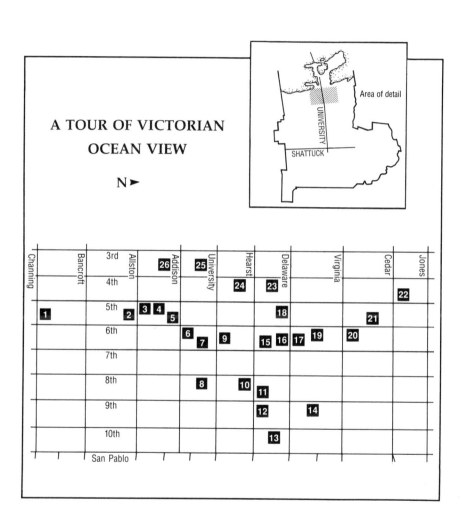

A TOUR OF VICTORIAN
OCEAN VIEW

N►

The **2 Schuster House** (812 Allston Way) and **Frey House** (808 Addison Way) (1893) are twin Queen Anne houses built by the Niehaus brothers. Gustavus Adolphus Schuster was a partner with Niehaus in the planing mill. Both houses have an abundance of the ornamental bric-a-brac produced by the Niehaus mill.

The **3 Valasca House** (1878) at 2109 5th St. is an early Italianate built by Juan Valasca, a tanner and hides dealer. This part of Ocean View was once known as "Nob Hill" since it stood 25 feet higher than surrounding land.

Ocean View has quite a few twin Victorian houses. The twin raised-basement Italianate houses at **4 2105 and 2107 5th St.** (1886) were built by Peter Haller, an Ocean View blacksmith. Note the bay windows, fancy bracketwork, and finials on the gable peaks. Number 2107 was home to the "West Berkeley News" for several years.

One of the oldest buildings in the area is the Charles Geirrine House (1877) at 2127 6th Street. The simple raised-basement house is now covered with asbestos tiles, but its Victorian features still show through.

The beautifully-restored **5 Joseph B. McVey House** (1888) at 814 Addison St. is a Queen Anne cottage built by McVey, a carpenter. His brother, the teamster Edward McVey, lived at 816 Addison in a slightly older two-story Victorian house. Both of them bought their property from Rosario Sisterna, a Chilean rancher who owned much of this land.

The **6 Berkeley Day Nursery** (now West Berkeley Health Center) at 2031 6th St. was designed by Walter Ratcliff in 1927, with help from Julia Morgan. While it is not a building in the Victorian style, it is important as one of the first childcare centers in the nation and was a valued institution in working-class Ocean View. The building combines Tudor half-timbering with touches of English Cottage-style architecture.

7 Library Hall (1879) at 2016 7th St. was built by volunteers from the Workingman's Club, a radical political party formed in part to fight the arrival of Chinese laborers. The hall was used as a reading room for club members. The building was moved from 6th and Delaware to its present location, where it presently serves as Christ Church Chapel. Library Hall is a plain white box in the New England meeting-house style.

Across the street at 2027 8th St. is the Black Pine Circle School (1912). Designed by Ernest Coxhead, one of California's most respected architects of the First Bay Tradition era, its original brown-shingle exterior has now been stuccoed over.

The Queen Anne house at **8 2017 8th St.** (1895) was built by carpenter John G. Rose, as was the now stuccoed-over 2015. The houses have an interesting history. Concerned for children in rough-and-tumble West Berkeley, Pheobe Apperson Hearst created the West Berkeley College Settlement at 2015 8th Street. For several years she paid all expenses for a program that provided children with student teachers from the University, use of a gymnasium and tennis courts, and training in such trades as shoe repair and net making. Unfortunately, when she withdrew her financial support in 1904 the ambitious program was unable to survive.

At 844 University Ave. is the Dansco Indoor Garden Center, originally the **9 Walter Mork Metal Works Co.**

(1890). This false-front building has interesting lattice windows and is in excellent condition. It was one of many commercial establishments that appeared along University Ave. after completion of the horsecar line between the University and Ocean View.

10 St. Procopius Latin Rite Church (1879) at 926 Hearst Ave. was built in the prevailing Gothic Revival style, and has 200-year-old stained glass windows taken from a bombed church in Belgium after World War II. Originally established as the First Presbyterian Church of West Berkeley, its members were mostly working-class folks, predominantly seafarers. In 1906 its pastor, George Wilkins, preached prohibition, so riling up the hard-drinking town of Ocean View that he was hung in effigy. Over the years the flock dwindled, and in 1972 the church was sold to a Latin-language Old Catholic Church, whose founder was later jailed for child molesting. The congregation now has only a couple of members and a stand-in priest, so the lovely old church is in a sad state of disrepair.

11 At **931-935 Hearst Ave.** you'll find a row of three nicely-restored Queen Anne cottages with raised basements. They were built in the 1880s. Hearst Ave., originally known as Bristol Ave., was renamed in honor of Phoebe Apperson Hearst, the University's fairy godmother.

The **12 Church of the Good Shepherd** (1878) at 1001 Hearst Ave. is the oldest church in Berkeley. Built in the Greek Revival style on land donated by the influential Bowen family, the church was completed in a month. The 75-foot louvered spire has a thousand-pound bell donated in 1882

Church of the Good Shepherd. Photo by Don Pitcher.

by the Volunteer Fire Department. It is no longer rung for fear of damaging the church.

The large and barn-like **13 Finnish Hall** at 1819 10th St. is a treasure trove of early West Berkeley culture. The three-story hall was built in 1908-09 by refugees from Finnish famines and drought. Unable to find carpentry work in Berkeley, the Finns decided to apply their skills to their own construction project, while their wives raised the money by working as domestics and through fundraising. The completed hall was used for theater events, dances, sewing circles, concerts, dinners, and reading clubs for the large and vibrant Finnish community of West Berkeley. (The hardwood maple floor was unusually springy, and the Finns claimed this allowed dancers to carry on late into the night without tiring their legs.) The Finns had a strong history of socialism—the building was also known as Comrade's Hall—and were a primary force behind the founding of Berkeley's Co-op in 1938. In 1934 their ties to the labor movement brought trouble when organizers used the hall as a base during the violent San Francisco general strike. Local vigilantes

Finnish Hall. Photo by Don Pitcher.

attacked the Finnish supporters here, smashing all the windows, destroying the front door, and chopping three pianos into pieces. Berkeley police claimed they were unable to respond due to a "paralysis" of their switchboard; the Finns sued the city over selective law enforcement and won. Eventually, political differences led to a splintering of the community, as moderate "White" Finns formed an alternative Finnish Brotherhood Hall and the "Red" Finns remained in Finnish Hall. Berkeley's Finnish population gradually became assimilated or moved away, and the hall was sold in 1972. It is still occasionally used by local Finnish groups, but is primarily a meeting hall for classes and activist groups. The hall's exterior has been painted a garish blue on white, but the building remains in good condition.

The lovely **14 Bluett House** (1893) at 1729 9th St. is the only West Berkeley Victorian that has a witch's hat tower. John J. Bluett, a carpenter, built the house with sawtooth shingles, a double-gabled roof, and a corbelled chimney.

The old **15 Seventh Street School** (1887) at 1814 7th St., a large and attractive structure with a distinctive pent eave, was built to house the overflow from the original Ocean View School during the population surge in the 1880s. The building was designed by A. H. Broad, also a respected painter. It is now used as an artist's studio.

The recently restored Neoclassical building at 834 Delaware St. is believed to be **16 Bowen's Inn** (1853), built by Captain William Bowen, one of the first settlers of Ocean View. One of the oldest buildings in Berkeley, it has served at various times as a hotel, grocery store, post office, and Baptist church. A dirt path (the future Delaware St.) ran from Bowen's Inn to Jacob's Landing, a short pier from which Captain James Jacobs ran his freight business on the San Francisco Bay.

At 831 and 835 Delaware St. are the **17 Wilkes Houses** (1891), built for the English families of Frederick and George Wilkes. One is a restored Queen Anne cottage with a raised basement, enclosed porch, and arched entryway, while the other has an Italianate bay window and an elaborate gable.

In 1971, the Berkeley Redevelopment Agency proposed removing many of West Berkeley's aging, dilapidated homes to establish an industrial park, but when the bulldozers arrived, angry neighbors sat in front of the houses, halting their destruction. After years of political wrangling, the newly elected "radical" city council of 1979 revised the plan and created the **18 Delaware Street Historic District**. Relocation of many of the doomed homes was completed in the mid-80s, and today you will find thirteen lovingly-restored Victorian buildings here. Restoration on nearby houses continues.

The old **19** **O'Keefe Saloon** (1877) at 1723 6th St. was one of more than twenty liquor establishments and four breweries that appeared in West Berkeley shortly after the new University opened. (Ocean View was just outside the one-mile, booze-free circle around the campus.) John O'Keefe, an Irish immigrant, ran the saloon, which also served as a boarding house and kindergarten. The commercial use of the structure is apparent in the raised porch and its proximity to the street.

When the **20** **Paschold House** (1886) at 1647 6th St. was built, the surrounding land was still relatively open. The old willow in front of this Italianate house is a reminder of a time when willows crowded the banks of nearby Schoolhouse Creek. The house's barns are gone; its windmill is now part of the Delaware Street Historic District. The homestead was built by Carl Paschold, a German tailor who bought the half-block site for $750 in 1883. He was later convicted of attacking his stepdaughter, and after his death the family was forced to sell the property to pay off his debts.

The **21** **Brown House** at 1614 6th St. is a lovely, raised-basement Queen Anne cottage built along Schoolhouse Creek. The house has a large angled bay window, fish-scale shingles, and an elaborate bargeboard along the eaves. Charles R. Brown bought this and two adjacent lots in 1889 for $10 in gold coin.

Two remaining signs of Ocean View's agricultural past are the old John Brown Barn (1880s) in the alleyway between 5th and 6th Sts. near Cedar St. and Arcieri's Dairy (1908) at 1201 6th Street. The latter two-story building, with bay windows and a corner entry, still has an operating windmill and water tower. Cows continued to graze on open ranch lands in this area until industrial development pushed them out.

The **22** **Ehret House** (1886) at 1516 5th St. was restored in the 1970s as the "Integral Urban House" with solar heating, organic gardens, and complete recycling. The institution is no more, but the building remains one of the finest examples of Italianate Victorian homes in West Berkeley. Note the hipped roof supported by elaborate brackets and large arched windows. Its first owner was Anatole Ehret, founder of Ehret Plumbing Co., one of Berkeley's oldest businesses.

Berkeley Windmills

Before the era of EBMUD and water shipments from the Sierra Nevada, many residents of Berkeley depended on backyard windmills and storage tanks for their water supply. Just five of these structures remain standing, only one of which still provides water (the old Arcieri Dairy described above). Two remain intact, one at the Delaware Street Historic District, the other near the intersection of Francisco St. and San Pablo Ave.; the others have lost their blades and storage tanks, though the support towers still remain: 3342 California St. and 1930 Delaware Street.

On 4th St. next to Caldwell Roland Roofing Co. (1635 4th St.) is an elm tree that has grown up through four old Conestoga wagon wheels left in drayman Dick Moore's storage lot. They have apparently been here since the 1880s. Dating from the 1850s are two old Monterey cypresses—one in the yard behind and another at the corner of 4th and Cedar St. (the latter the source for the mistakenly-named Cedar Street.). These trees are believed to have been planted by Mrs. Bowen (of Bowen's Inn).

The Heywood House (1878) at 1808 5th St. was built by Charles W. Heywood, a future mayor of Berkeley. The Heywoods were an important family in early Berkeley, serving the city as mayors, legislators, and city councilmembers. Zimri B. Heywood settled in Ocean View in 1856, after establishing a ferry wharf and lumber business with Captain James Jacobs. The Heywood House was later home to another well-known businessman, Frank Spenger. It is a raised-basement Pioneer cottage with three corbelled chimneys, a bay window, and a hipped roof supported by decorative brackets.Surrounded by new upscale shops, the **23 Heywood/Ghego House** (late 1870s) at 1809 4th St. seems out of place. The rather plain structure is a raised-basement Italianate cottage built by Walter Heywood, one of Zimri Heywood's thirteen children. The house originally had a fine view of San Francisco Bay, then only two-and-a-half blocks away. **24 Spenger's Fish Grotto** (1895) at 1921 4th St. is a remnant of Berkeley's checkered history. The parking lot facing it was once an Indian shell mound, the ancient site of shellfish harvesting by the Ohlone Indians. In the late 19th century the shell mound was turned into Willow Grove Park, though its actual purpose was as a beer-garden. Throngs arrived by train at the nearby Southern Pacific station. Johann Spenger, a German fisherman, first used the building opposite as a grocery store and later converted it to a bar that gave free fish to patrons. Eventually the fish business became a bigger draw than the bar. If you look closely at Spenger's today (see *Restaurants and Cafes*) you'll see that at the center of the newer additions is a wood-frame raised-basement cottage. (It's still used by members of the Spenger family.) Out front are two Swiss Guard iron statues that came from San Francisco's old Sutro Baths.

25 China Station Restaurant (1913) at 700 University Ave., once Berkeley's Southern Pacific depot, is one of dozens of Mission Revival stations that were built during the railroad's heyday. Amtrak closed the train station in 1971, and after careful remodelling in 1976 it opened as a Chinese restaurant. It's a fitting change: Chinese laborers were not only an important part of early Ocean View, they were also essential in the completion of the railroad, Berkeley's first link with the East Coast. Inside China Station are a number of interesting photos of Chinese workers and old railway construction. The interior paneling comes from the now-demolished Alaska Commercial Building (1906-08) in San Francisco.

The tour ends at two interesting Berkeley wineries. The **26 Takara Sake Plant** (1947) at 708 Addison St. was built as the Challenge Cream and Butter plant. After it closed, the building became the largest sake factory in America. Just down the street at 2nd and Addison is a small tasting room for **Audubon Cellars**. The metal warehouse doesn't compare with the historic structures of old Ocean View, but the wines are excellent. Both places have tasting rooms. On sunny days you may also enjoy walking along the neighboring shore of Aquatic Park.

Architect Bernard Maybeck

"You cannot produce a living architecture as a system of applied logic. Architecture is life-poetry; the logic is not something to be taught by intellectual machinery, however clever its cogs and shifts. Architecture is the imprint of a greater logic of Man and Nature which no smart brain can take apart and make simpler." —*Bernard Maybeck*

Bernard Maybeck was one of America's most loved architects, both because of his delightful and mystical personality and, more importantly, because his unusually creative buildings seemed so appropriate to their sites. His ability to incorporate both old and new construction materials in whimsical ways and his skill in combining elements of Craftsman, Japanese, Classical, and Gothic design set Maybeck apart from other Bay Area Craftsman architects.

Born in New York in 1862, Maybeck was the son of a German woodcarver. Intending to follow his father's lead, he left for Paris to study furniture design, but became fascinated instead by its magnificent buildings. While there, he attended the leading architectural school of the day, École des Beaux Arts, before returning to New York in 1888. After a short stint in Florida where he co-designed the famous Ponce de Leon Hotel in St. Augustine, Maybeck headed to Missouri (where he met his wife) and then to California. In San Francisco he found work as a draftsman and taught classes both at the University and from his home.

Bernard Maybeck was highly influential in developing Pheobe Apperson Hearst's master plan for the campus

Architect Bernard Maybeck. Photo courtesy of Jacomena Maybeck.

(see *The University*), but once it was underway, he quit his teaching posts and began designing buildings in earnest. His structures ranged from the Roman-inspired Palace of Fine Arts in San Francisco to at least 45 Berkeley homes in a variety of architectural styles.

Maybeck's first local architectural commission (1895) came from Charles Keeler, who recognized that the earthy character of Maybeck's work, along with his attention to detail, were appropriate for the tranquil but culturally stimulating town of Berkeley. To some of Keeler's neighbors the new style was simply strange. Maybeck enjoyed telling the story of two elderly ladies he heard commenting on one of his First Bay Tradition houses: "Who lives in that funny house?" asked one. "Oh," the other replied, "That's the house of Mr. Maybeck. He's the architect that plans all those freak houses, you know."

Maybeck's personal life and behavior were also unusual. He was a balding, bearded vegetarian who lived modestly and often wore work smocks, sandals, and a red beret. This was not the aura one expected of a famous architect. Though he was well known, Maybeck was not wealthy because he was frequently paid in land instead of cash for his work. He was forced periodically to sell these lots to remain solvent.

Maybeck's best known building is the First Church of Christ Scientist at 2619 Dwight Way. In this 1910 masterpiece Maybeck combined six architectural styles—Gothic, Renaissance, neoclassic-Classic, Japanese, Mediterranean, and Industrial. The church was built from a variety of materials, including asbestos tiles, cheap leaded factory windows, and corrugated tin on the roof (later replaced by tiles). Although stained glass was used

First Church of Christ Scientist; Bernard Maybeck. Photo by Don Pitcher.

sparingly, the courtyard garden was planned so that the bright colors could be seen through the opaque windows. Tours of the church are given on Sundays at 12:15 pm. Have the guide point out the initials of Maybeck's wife in the ceiling beams. An even better time to view the church's interior is at sunset when the western windows glow with light.

Maybeck continued to design homes up to his death in 1957 at the age of 95. Two good books on Maybeck are *Bernard Maybeck, Artisan, Architect, Artist* by Kenneth Cardwell (Peregrine Smith, Salt Lake City, 1977) and *Maybeck, the Family View* by Jacomena Maybeck (Berkeley Architectural Heritage Association, 1980).

A TOUR OF MAYBECK COUNTRY

Many of the beautiful First Bay Tradition homes are in the hills just north of the University campus. The following walk should help acquaint you with the various architects' styles. Before beginning the walk it may be helpful to see where it all began. The **Keeler House** (1770 Highland Place) angles back from the street, with a crazy pattern of steeply curving rooflines over stuccoed walls. At one time the area had many similarly graceful homes, but the fire in 1923 destroyed nearly 600 of the area's structures. Many were replaced by less attractive buildings. To see what the Hillside Club was trying to prevent, walk half a block down Highland to the massive apartment boxes crowded along the straight streets. This should put you in the mood to appreciate the beauty that remains in the North Berkeley hills.

Attractive ◼ **Codornices Park** is a good place to begin this walk. The park is accessible by AC Transit (line No. 7) and has free parking.

Bayview Place has two homes by First Bay Tradition architects. Bernard Maybeck's ◼ **Senger House** (1907) at No. 1321, faces away from the street onto a back garden. Across the street at No. 1322 is a Swiss chalet-style house designed by Henry Gutterson. Notice the stenciled patterns on the stucco surface of the Senger house.

In the ◼ **Schneider-Kroeber House** (1907) at 1325 Arch St., Maybeck's European interests are evident. This impressive Swiss chalet, for many years the home of Alfred Kroeber, has a deep roof overhang with exposed beams, large gables,

Schneider-Kroeber House; Bernard Maybeck. Photo by Don Pitcher.

and a Dutch front door. The garden was originally landscaped by John McLaren, the landscape architect of Golden Gate Park. Professor Kroeber is popularly known for befriending Ishi, one of California's last Indians to live the old way of life. Theodora Kroeber's book, *Ishi in Two Worlds,* is a classic, and their daughter, Ursula LeGuin, is one of America's best-known fantasy writers.

Take a look at the old hitching post (1890) on your left just before you turn from Arch St. onto Glen Avenue. The ◼ **Dempster House** (1908) at 2204 Glen Ave., a large brown-shingle home, has a turret tower with a witch's hat. The porch is supported by massive wooden beams to bolster its earthquake resistance.

The ◼ **Fred Wallace House** (1905), 1340 Arch St., is another Swiss chalet-style house, with balconies supported by massive brackets with scrolled ends. The house was designed by Maybeck's brother-in-law John White, another well-known Bay Area architect.

Julia Morgan designed the ◼ **Paul**

Schindff House (1910) at 1425 Arch St., one of many brown-shingle homes built in Berkeley's boom years after the 1906 San Francisco earthquake. Note the curved bay window.

G **Vine Lane** is one of dozens of walkways in the North Berkeley hills created by the Hillside Club. Notice the ironwork gate over the Euclid St. entrance. John White designed the **McFarlan House** (1924), No. 3 Vine Lane, to replace a Maybeck home destroyed by the 1923 fire. Maybeck's original chimney was incorporated into the new Tudor style house.

The **H** **Schmidt-Kennedy House** at 1537 Euclid Ave. consists of two stucco buildings connected by a bridge. Both were rebuilt in 1923 after the Berkeley fire. The house has a mixture of Tudor half-timbering and Mediterranean-style red and green eaves. One part, the Maybeck Recital Hall, is used for intimate jazz and classical concerts and has featured such performers as Dizzy Gillespie, Charlie "Bird" Parker, Toshiko Akiyoshi, and Bobby Hutchenson. Call 848-3228 for upcoming concerts.

The **I** **Estelle Clark House** (1921) at 1408 Hawthorne Terrace is Maybeck's version of an Italian Renaissance house. Its twin chimneys, stucco walls, arched windows, and tile roof are visible from the street.

Bernard Maybeck designed **J** **Rose Walk** (1913) as part of a planned hillside community. After the devastating 1923 fire, Henry Gutterson designed the homes along the pathway with Maybeck's assistance. The flower-lined walk curves gracefully up pink concrete steps from Euclid Avenue.

The **K** **John Galen Howard House** (1912) at 1401 LeRoy Ave. was for many years the home of the re-nowned Beaux Arts architect John Galen Howard (see *The University*). Julia Morgan designed an addition to the house in 1927.

The house at **L** **1500 LeRoy** (1928) was designed by architect Carr Jones. Its fanciful exterior has sloping redwood-shingled roofs and old brick walls. **M** **La Loma Steps** climb to Buena Vista Way on a flower-lined path with a sharp jog in the middle.

One of the more hidden Maybeck houses is at 2683 Buena Vista Way (1915). Built for **N** **Charles Seeger**, a music professor at Cal and father of folksinger Pete Seeger, the house was one of the few in the area to survive the 1923 fire. The house is a simple stucco structure with a European provincial exterior.

The **O** **Mathewson House** (1915) at 2704 Buena Vista Way is a graceful example of Maybeck's versatility: it combines a low, Prairie-style roofline with overhanging eaves in the First Bay Tradition. The stucco and redwood composition and large windows give this home a pleasant, open feeling.

A few houses down at 1515 La Loma Ave., the **P** **Lawson House** (1908) suggests a Roman villa. Arches set off the upstairs porches, bright tiles make a colorful pattern inset in tinted stucco walls, and a pergola encloses part of the rear yard. The intricate floral designs on the rear wall were carved by Italian artisans. Professor Andrew Lawson, who discovered the San Andreas fault and was an advocate of strong building standards, had this fire-proof and earthquake-proof home built with reinforced concrete two years after San Francisco's devastating earthquake.

The 1923 fire destroyed many of

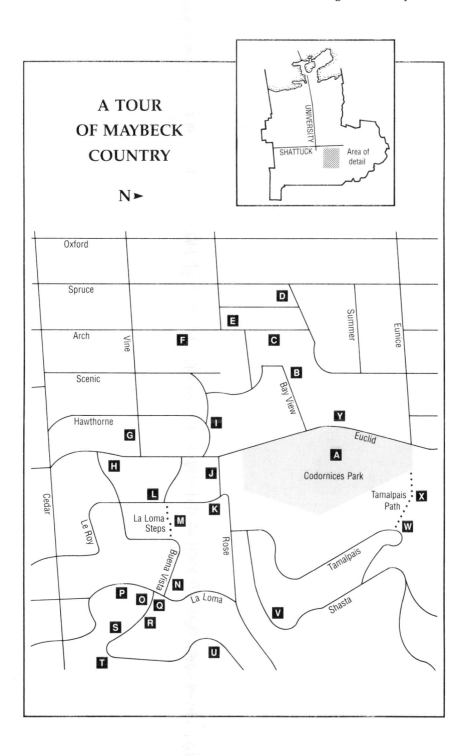

Bernard Maybeck (foreground) and neighbors building the Codornices Park clubhouse in 1916. Courtesy of the Berkeley Architectural Heritage Association.

Maybeck's architectural works, including his own home. On the old foundation at 2711 Buena Vista Way, he rebuilt using materials salvaged from destroyed buildings and junkyards. The sliding glass door at the entrance is believed to be the first such door used in a residence. Maybeck framed the walls in the traditional way, but decided to experiment with construction materials less flammable than redwood shingles. He invented a frothy concrete (reputedly light enough to float on water) that he named "bubblecrete." The resulting **Q** **"Sack" House** was built the year after the fire by dipping gunny sacks in the airy concrete and hanging them like shingles over thin wires. It has now been expanded in several directions using the "bubblecrete" shingles for walls. This simple, fanciful home was Maybeck's studio for many years. He built homes for his grown children just up the hill on Maybeck Twin Dr.

and Buena Vista Way.

Maybeck Twin Drive shows the Hillside Club's influence again with a road that splits for uphill and downhill traffic as it contours along the slope. Its name comes not from the split road, but from Maybeck's twin grandchildren. Near the intersection with Buena Vista Way are four Maybeck houses. The **R** **Tufts House** (1931), 2733 Buena Vista Way, has concrete walls and a steep roofline with tall front windows that suggest a Bavarian cottage. Maybeck painted playful designs on the garage. Directly opposite at 2751 Buena Vista Way is the **Wallen Maybeck House** (1932), built for the architect's son and daughter-in-law. Note the large picture windows, the whimsical balcony, and the steep roofline that mimics the adjacent hillside. Maybeck designed the balcony so the parents could check on the twins in the downstairs nursery through an arched window.

Next door is **Arillaga** (1950), one of the last houses Maybeck designed (he was 88). Built by his son, this plain split-level structure has concrete block walls and a floor created from Navy hatch covers. **No. 1 Maybeck Twin Dr.** was Maybeck's home for the last 25 years of his life. He moved an abandoned real estate office to the site in 1924, expanded it, and covered the building with "bubblecrete." Be sure to walk to the top of Maybeck Twin Dr. for a panoramic view of North Berkeley. The Japanese-influenced **Johnson House** (1959) at 14 Maybeck Twin Dr. crowns the hill. Nearby is a Monterey cypress tree planted in 1850 by José Domingo Peralta, Berkeley's first European-heritage settler. The tree marked one boundary of the Peralta property.

Back on Buena Vista Way at 2780 is the **S** **Gannon House** (1924), built for Maybeck's daughter and her husband. Maybeck used a distinctive bell-bottomed chimney, and the wood-shingled roof gives this First Bay Tradition home a rustic log-cabin appearance.

Berkeley's oddest home is the **T** **Temple of the Wings** (1914) at 2800 Buena Vista Way. Maybeck was involved in the initial plan, but quit the project after disagreements with the headstrong owners, Ira and Florence Boynton. (Later the Maybecks and Boyntons became involved in a fourteen-year boundary dispute that culminated in Mr. Boynton's threats to have the Maybecks, then in their 70s, arrested.) The Boyntons found a more amenable architect in A. Randolf Monro, who designed the finished structure. Thirty-four large Corinthian columns of concrete supported the roof, but the sides were open to the air, except during storms when sailcloth was unfurled to protect the inhabitants. An open central portion was designed to be used for

"Fort Soap"

Captain Richard Parks Thomas owned the highly successful Standard Soap Company in West Berkeley, which at one time produced 300,000 lbs of laundry soap every week. A former ship captain and cavalry lieutenant in the Civil War, Thomas also headed California National Bank of San Francisco and owned the Berkeley Ferryboat Line. He was one of the Bay Area's leading business figures. Thomas called his 32 acres of hillside land in North Berkeley, La Loma Park and built there a residence, log house, barn, and a fort-like building complete with howitzers and a Civil War cannon. Every Fourth of July the patriotic Captain Thomas invited hundreds of people for catered festivities that concluded with the booming of his cannon. In 1887 a mother abandoned her baby at the party. Unable to locate the woman, the Thomas' (who were childless) adopted the baby. The fort-like building (on the site of the present Hume Cloister) was jokingly known as "Fort Soap." The Standard Soap Company closed shortly after Thomas' death in 1898 and the building burned in 1925.

dance instruction; living quarters were in the side wings. The Boynton family's style of living probably inspired the area's nickname "Nut Hill"—they subsisted for a time on peanuts and dried fruit, and were exponents of the naturalistic dance of their friend Isadora Duncan. The 1923 fire destroyed the house but left behind the 34 columns. Architects Edna Deakin and Clarence Casebolt rebuilt the house with a more traditional stucco enclosure.

The unusual **U** **Hume Cloister** (1927), 2900 Buena Vista Way, was built for Samuel and Portia Hume by John Hudson Thomas, an architect best known for his Prairie-style homes. The design replicates the 13th-century Augustinian monastery in Toulouse, France. The view across San Francisco Bay from the castle is worth the steep climb up from Temple of the Wings. After retracing your path down Buena Vista Way, turn right onto Greenwood Terrace and step

Hume Cloister; John Hudson Thomas. Photo by Don Pitcher.

back into the 20th century. John Galen Howard designed the house at **1488 Greenwood Terrace** (1912). It's a beautiful craftsman-influenced, Swiss chalet-style home graced by majestic Monterey pines planted in the 1870s.

The impressive three-story house at **V** **2645 Shasta Rd.** (1911, rebuilt in 1926) was designed by architects Williamson and Winterburn. Chalet-like porches overlook the creek below, and an unusual red-tile roof completes the house.

Rowell House; John Hudson Thomas. Photo by Don Pitcher.

The **W** **Rowell House** (1914), 149 Tamalpais Rd., is one of my favorite First Bay Tradition designs. It is best viewed from Tamalpais Path. Surrounding redwoods and Douglas firs complement the beauty of John Hudson Thomas' elegant combination of half-timbering and masonry.

Follow **X** **Tamalpais Path** back to Codornices Park through a forest of redwoods, live oak, and ivy. Off to the right in the canyon, Codornices Creek drops over a series of small waterfalls. Get to the creek by a dirt path that takes off halfway down the trail.

End your walking tour in the **Y** **Berkeley Rose Garden** (1937), 1300 Euclid St., built by the WPA. Maybeck designed the curved redwood pergola. The garden offers a panoramic view of the Bay, and when the roses are in bloom the place is spectacular. You can return to Codornices Park through a pedestrian tunnel near the tennis courts.

Arts and Entertainment

Art is a big part of Berkeley life. Open the *Express* for any given week and you'll find a dozen different plays, fifteen or so gallery exhibitions, concerts of all types, movies from A to Z, and a wide range of readings, dance performances, and special events. It seems that everyone in Berkeley is an artist or performer of some kind, lives with an artist or performer—or at the very least lives next to one. Berkeley has always attracted artists of all kinds, from photographer Dorothea Lange to poster artist David Lance Goines, and from composer Ernest Bloch to painter William Keith.

Although the University remains a powerful force in local arts, a new center for the art scene is emerging in West Berkeley, an area previously known for its industrial architecture, pot-holed streets, and working-class neighborhoods. As the city's industrial base has changed, many of the established manufacturers in West Berkeley have moved away or gone out of business, leaving spacious warehouses and factories that make ideal live/work spaces for artists, artisans, and small businesses. One of the most successful of such remodelling efforts is the Kawneer Building (2547 8th St.), now the site of more than 40 different operations—dance studios, woodworking shops, a theater, a potters' studio, and a variety of other small enter-

prises. Nearby, you'll find Nexus, Kala Institute, Artworks Foundry, and a number of other art studios and exhibition spaces.

Despite Berkeley's heritage in the arts, local artists complain that they get almost no support from either the city or the University. Escalating commercial rents have forced the closure of two acclaimed textile arts schools, Fiberworks and Pacific Basin School of Textile Arts, while inadequate facilities and complaints from neighbors led to the Berkeley Shakespeare Festival's move to Orinda. The **Berkeley Civic Arts Commission** (644-6084), an advisory board that promotes the arts in Berkeley, is hampered by a small budget and a volunteer staff, but it is finally starting to take a more active role in supporting local artists.

Conga drummers at the UC campus. Photo by Don Pitcher.

Whale sculpture outside the Lawrence Hall of Science. Photo by Don Pitcher.

The most complete source of information on upcoming events, performances, readings, exhibitions, and concerts is the weekly *Express.* The *Daily Californian* is an excellent source of listings of events on and around campus, and both KALX and KPFA broadcast extensive arts programming. The bulletin boards in the hallway outside the art and music room in the main public library are plastered with announcements of all types, from folk art sales and conga drum workshops, to upcoming Gregorian chant performances and recorder society meetings.

Museums

Lawrence Hall of Science
Centennial Drive, 642-5132, open daily, adults—$3.50, UC students —$2.50, *children—free.* High atop the Berkeley hills squats an octagonal concrete structure that would seem at home in a low-budget sci-fi film. The Lawrence Hall of Science (LHS), completed in 1968 and named after the Nobel Prize-winning scientist Ernest O. Lawrence, offers exhibits that include everything from earthquake simulations to moving life-size dinosaur models, plus a planetarium, computer terminals, science film programs, and many hands-on experiments in its innovative Wizard's Lab. Popular with kids, LHS is always a delight. On weekdays take advantage of the free shuttle bus from the Hearst Mining Circle on campus (call 642-5149 for the schedule).

A number of interesting sculptures surround LHS. A giant fiberglass whale on the plaza serves as a play structure for children, and behind the building a life-size model of the space shuttle Challenger's cabin memorializes those killed in America's worst space disaster. The stunningly realistic Challenger interior is open Saturdays from noon to 1 pm. An unusual piece nearby combines astronomy and art. Richard O'Hanlon carved three granite stones to create an orientation device that aligns with the equinox, the North Star, noon, and other celestial phenomena.

Just down the hill is a wind organ consisting of 36 aluminum poles, slotted to produce sounds that are simultaneously eerie and soothing. The sounds change constantly depending on the wind speed and direction, and can be altered by turning the pipes or covering the stop holes. Nearby benches make this a popular place to enjoy the sunset.

Every Saturday night when the sky is clear you can view the stars from the LHS plaza with the **Sidewalk Astronomers, Inc.** (527-4026). The volunteer group's telescopes, including one with a 24-inch mirror, offer the chance to see planets, galaxies, and other heavenly objects.

Lowie Museum of Anthropology

Kroeber Hall, 642-3681, closed Wed, adults-$1.50, children-$.25, UC students free. Although the Lowie has the largest anthropological collection west of the Mississippi, its modest display space only hints at the more than half-a-million specimens stored here, including archaeological material from Egypt, Peru, the Mediterranean, and North America. Contemporary ethnographic material here comes from California, Africa, the Pacific Islands, and Asia. The museum gift shop has unusual books and attractive, often inexpensive folk art.

Judah L. Magnes Museum

2911 Russell St., 849-2710, closed Fri, Sat, and Jewish holidays, free. Hidden away on a quiet street near the Claremont Hotel is the Magnes Museum, a major center for Jewish art and artifacts from around the world. The third largest such collection in America, it occupies a landmark mansion built in 1908. Inside are several galleries exhibiting work by well-known contemporary artists, special collections from vanishing Jewish cultures, and a room commemorating the Holocaust. The Blumenthal Library has over 10,000 rare books and manuscripts from around the world, and the Western Jewish History Center houses photographs, oral histories, newspapers, and other archives from the western U.S. The museum's gardens were designed by John McLaren, the landscape architect for Golden Gate Park. Docent tours are available.

University Art Museum

Bancroft Way below College Ave., 642-0808, closed Mon and Tues, adults-$3, UC students and children free . This spacious concrete structure is one of the largest university art museums in the world. In addition to a permanent collection that includes works by Cezanne, Miro, Magritte, Picasso, Renoir, Rubens, and many 20th-century American painters, the museum houses the world's largest collection of paintings by abstract expressionist Hans Hoffman (1880-1966). Hoffman escaped pre-war Nazi Germany with the help of two Berkeley professors and later donated to the University 45 of his paintings and a $250,000 bequest to house them—a gift that helped create the new museum.

Designed by Mario J. Campi and completed in 1970, the museum is an

enjoyable, airy place, built in a series of rising terraces. Student pieces are shown on the ground level, while the other galleries show changing exhibitions. Out front is a giant plow-like metal sculpture, one of the "stabiles" created by Alexander Calder, inventor of the mobile. The University Art Museum also has a fine bookstore and the cooperatively run Swallow Restaurant, a good place for light meals. Pacific Film Archives, in the basement, has more than 6000 films, making it an important center for cinema studies (see "Movie Theaters" below).

Museum of Paleontology

Earth Sciences Building, 642-1821, open daily, free . This is one of the nation's richest and most diverse paleontological collections. In its small display space you'll find dinosaur fossils, Irish elk antlers, collections of rocks and minerals, and a range of other paleontology exhibits. In the basement are two seismographs. (Several tons of dinosaur bones are also stored out of sight in the Campanile.)

Pacific School of Religion Museum

1798 Scenic Avenue, 848-0528, open Mon-Fri. Berkeley's least-known museum is housed in the lovely old library reading room at Pacific School of Religion. The museum includes both the Bade Institute of Biblical Archeology and the Howell Bible Collection, with nearly 300 rare Bibles and other books, several printed soon after the invention of the moveable type press in 1455. Dr. William Bade (1871-1936), a professor at Pacific

School of Religion and onetime Sierra Club president, directed five excavations at Mizpah of Benjamin, an ancient Israelite city, that yielded the bowls, jars, cuneiform tablets, jewelry, lamps, and other items now housed in the Bade Institute's collection. The round mahogany table in one corner, originally a gift to John Muir by the Philippine government, was donated to the museum by Muir's grandchildren. (Dr. Bade was John Muir's biographer.)

Art Galleries

Artwork is all over Berkeley. In addition to the University Art Museum and Magnes Museum (described above), the walls of local coffeehouses and restaurants are often lined with artwork, and numerous shops sell a range of pieces. You'll even find periodic exhibitions in the **Municipal Parking Garage** (2020 Addison Street). Of note is the **A.C.C.I.** (Arts and Crafts Cooperative, Inc.) at 1652 Shattuck Ave. (843-2527), run cooperatively by artists and craftsworkers who since 1963 have offered ceramics, jewelry, paintings, and photographs.

On campus, visit the **Worth Ryder Art Gallery** in Kroeber Hall (642-2582, open Mon-Thurs) for exhibits of new works by Cal students and faculty members. The **Heller Gallery** (642-4636) in the Student Union Building (closed Sun) exhibits both student and non-student works on walls surrounding the first floor lounge. Hidden in the recesses of Lower Sproul Plaza, the **ASUC Art Studio** (call

Opposite: Inside the University Art Museum. Photo by Don Pitcher.

Plop Art

Perhaps the most controversial art work in Berkeley is the fourteen-foot monster at the Berkeley Marina. Fred Fierstein, a Berkeley electrician, copied the sculpture from a 7th-century Chinese piece, calling it "The Guardian." He offered it to the Berkeley Civic Arts Commission, but their delays frustrated him. Instead of waiting for a final yea or nay, he hired a crane and early one morning plopped it down on a median strip facing the Berkeley pier. Fierstein and his friends claimed the piece was there to protect the waterfront from greedy developers. The city bureaucracy was shocked but afraid to take any action lest they be viewed as despoilers of art work. Art experts were appalled at the tasteless and banal sculpture, and the fact that water drains off the piece through its penis seemed to annoy others, but the do-it-if-you-can-get-away-with-it crowd in Berkeley was thrilled. To keep the city from removing it, supporters of "The Guardian" managed to get a non-binding resolution on the 1986 ballot. Local voters passed the initiative by a narrow margin, and since then city bureaucrats have been nervously waiting for more "plop art" to show up in Berkeley parks.

642-3065) has a gallery exhibiting photographs, paintings, ceramics, and sculpture by local artists. It also offers excellent arts classes. Students and non-students can use the darkroom, ceramics workshop, and printmaking equipment and facilities on an hourly basis for a reasonable fee.

In bucolic Live Oak Park the **Berkeley Art Center** (1275 Walnut St., 644-6893, open Thurs-Sun) sits along tree-lined Codornices Creek. The center exhibits paintings, sculpture, and other works of art, and each spring offers a series of classical concerts.

You'll discover a number of un-usual exhibition and performance spaces in West Berkeley, where many artists have moved to escape the high commercial rents of other Berkeley neighborhoods. In a Heinz ketchup factory from the 20s, the non-profit **Kala Institute** (1060 Heinz Ave., 549-2977) provides space for teaching, creating, and exhibiting prints by some of the best known printmakers. Kala also has an acclaimed performance art series. The **Artworks Foundry and Gallery** (729 Heinz Ave., 644-2735), run by Italian immigrant Piero Muso, is one of the few places in America where you can watch bronze sculptures being produced using what is termed the "lost wax process." Sculptors from throughout the U.S. use the foundry. Another unusual place to see artwork is the **Urban Sculpture Garden** at 5th and Harrison Streets. Here, in a large weed-filled lot surrounded by industrial buildings, truck parts, and garbage dumpsters, several giant steel sculptures are slowly rusting away. Reach the site through a gate at the adjacent trucking company.

Other Berkeley galleries worth a visit are **New Pieces** (1587 Solano Ave., 527-6779) for fabric sculptures, and two West Berkeley exhibition spaces: **Nexus Institute** (2701 8th St., 549-0703), and the Nature Company's **Wrubel Gallery** (740 Hearst Ave., 524-9052).

Theater

Berkeley Repertory Theatre

2025 Addison St., 845-4700. Originally known simply as "The Theatre," the Berkeley Rep began in 1968 with performances at International House on campus. When director Michael Liebert first moved his troupe of actors to a new theater in the Elmwood district, the company barely kept its head above water. Gradually they gained a reputation for imaginative performances, and their popularity outstripped the building's 85-seat capacity. The present 400-seat theater, completed in 1980, has both state-of-the-art equipment and a well-paid, professional troupe of actors; it is one of the most respected theaters in

The stage at the Berkeley Repertory Theater. Photo by Kevin Gilson.

The Black Repertory Group performing **The Green Pastures.** *Photo by Jacob Blanchette.*

California. Because most plays sell out, the troupe performs a simultaneous "parallel season" in other local theater houses. Still, the demand for tickets is so great that rumors circulate about the Rep's leaving Berkeley to find adequate performance facilities. The Rep is now directed by Sharon Ott, who took over after Michael Liebert died in 1984.

Tickets aren't cheap, but half-price tickets are sold after noon on weekdays for performances that evening. (The queue often forms before noon, so get there early.) Seniors and students can also purchase half-price tickets half an hour before the performance, if any are left unsold. For information on volunteer ushering at the Rep call 841-6108.

Berkeley Shakespeare Festival/ California Shakespeare Festival

John Hinkle Park through 1989, Siesta Valley in Orinda thereafter, 548-3422. One of Berkeley's best known theatrical institutions, the Berkeley Shakespeare Festival, brought Elizabethan pageantry to John Hinkle Park from 1973-1989. Like many other Berkeley successes, however, the festival became too popular and outgrew its city park facilities. Its new home is a new 600-seat amphitheater in Orinda. The festival generally produces four plays in a season that stretches from July to mid-October. It also conducts a popular summer apprentice program for teens, and offers a special winter conservatory to the general public. Ticket discounts are available for students and seniors.

Black Repertory Group

3201 Adeline St., 652-2120. From its origins in the Downs Memorial Methodist Church, the Black Rep moved to a tiny southwest Berkeley storefront location in 1973; after four ground-breaking ceremonies, donated city land, and a $300,000 city grant, they finally settled into a 250-seat theater in 1987. Under the direction of Nora Vaughn, the group produces plays by, for, and about black Americans, and encourages new playwrights in its "New Arts Experience Program." The Rep produces five plays in a season that runs from November to June. Special senior discounts are available for Saturday matinee performances.

Blake Street Hawkeyes

2019 Blake St., 849-3013. One of Berkeley's most unusual troupes, the Blake Street Hawkeyes was the home base for both George Coates and Whoopi Goldberg, and continues to produce avant-garde and often absurdly funny shows. The Hawkeyes were originally three transplanted Iowans (hence the name "Hawkeyes") who opened a theater in 1975. It's nothing fancy (we're talking folding chairs in a converted garage), but the shows are sometimes memorable.

Julia Morgan Center for the Arts

2640 College Ave., 548-7234 . In 1908, work began on St. John's Presbyterian Church, a beautiful redwood structure designed by famed architect Julia Morgan. When St. John's moved to new quarters in 1973, the old church was transformed into a performance space, the Julia Morgan Center for the Arts. The center is now used for everything from ballet classes to a Chinese-American preschool.

Pacific Jewish Theater

820 Heinz St., 849-0498. The Berkeley Jewish Theater started in 1981 with a series of Yiddish poetry readings at a North Berkeley deli; in 1989 it moved into its new West Berkeley location. The group stages works by Jewish playwrights that deal primarily with Jewish religious and cultural issues, as well as broader social issues. Four plays are produced each season from September to June.

Theater of the Blue Rose

2525 8th St., 540-5037. The Theater of the Blue Rose is a small repertory ensemble that puts on nine plays a year on weekend nights. These are classic works rather than the modern or experimental performances you'll find elsewhere. At only $3, this has to be the best theater bargain in the Bay Area.

Zellerbach Playhouse

UC campus, 642-1677. The Playhouse stages University faculty and graduate student productions as well as occasional performances by other groups such as the Berkeley Opera. The 500-seat playhouse has a flexible design which allows for an unusual variety of seating and production arrangements. Get program listings from the Cal Performances office in Zellerbach Hall.

Dance

Many people are not aware of Berkeley's long heritage as a center for experimental dance. The Temple of the Wings in North Berkeley served for many years as a teaching space for lyrical free-form dance classes in the style of Isadora Duncan. There, Sülgwynn Quitzlow taught hundreds of schoolgirls dressed in flowing robes right up to her death in 1983.

As a result of the University's support of modern dance and the enthusiasm of the people of Berkeley for these productions, top New York dance troupes such as the Martha Graham Dance Company or Twyla Tharp Dance frequently prefer to perform in Berkeley's Zellerbach Hall rather than in a San Francisco venue. For details of events pick up the Cal Performances schedule from Zellerbach ticket office (642-9988).

Those interested in dance instruction soon discover the outstanding **Shawl-Anderson Dance Center** (2704 Alcatraz Ave., 654-5921). Established in 1958 and still directed by founders Frank Shawl and Victor Anderson, the non-profit center has grown into a major institution for modern, jazz, and ballet dance. Instructors are among the finest in Northern California.

Two excellent local schools also provide instruction in ballet only, the **Berkeley Ballet Theater School** (2640 College Ave., 843-4687), based in the Julia Morgan Center, and the **Berkeley Conservatory Ballet** (1800 Dwight Way, 841-8913). Students from the Conservatory Ballet stage a production of the Nutcracker at Zellerbach Hall every December.

The spacious **Ashkenaz** (1317 San Pablo Ave., 525-5054) offers classes in Greek and Jewish folk dancing, belly dancing, ballet, ballroom dancing, and other forms of dance. Pick up a schedule for a complete list of current offerings. The **Starry Plough** (3101 Shattuck Ave., 841-2082) has free Irish dance lessons and music every Monday night. Check with the University's **International House** (2299 Piedmont Ave., 642-9460) for other ethnic dancing classes. There are four differ-

Dancers at the Temple of the Wings. Courtesy of San Francisco Bay Area Dance Coalition. Photo by Margaretta Mitchell.

ent dance studios within the Kawneer Building (2525 8th St.), the most unusual being the **Motivity Center** (482-4729) where students combine ballet, modern dance, and gymnastics on flying trapezes.

The San Francisco Bay Area Dance Coalition (255-2794) is a non-profit organization that promotes, represents, and supports the local dance community, offering everything from telephone referrals to liability insurance. Their book, *Dance Around the Bay,* lists more than 650 Bay Area dance companies, teachers, performance facilities, festivals, and other dance resources, while their free paper, *In Dance*, lists dance events.

Shawl-Anderson Dance Studio. Photo by Maggie Miller.

Music

University Department of Music
Hertz Hall, UC campus, free. Concerts feature Cal students, staff, and alumni performing a variety of classical music. A schedule is available from the Music Department in Morrison Hall (642-4864), or check the *Daily Californian*. Tickets are available from the ASUC Box Office in the Student Union Building or at the door. Each spring the Music Department hosts a free exhibit of historical musical instruments, offering a good chance to see and hear such oddities as the ophicleide, the sackbut, and the er-hu.

The ASUC sponsors rock and jazz performances on lower Sproul Plaza several times a week during the school year, and on weekends you'll find conga drummers setting up infectious rhythms there.

Cal Performances
Zellerbach Hall, 642-9988. A wide range of music and dance productions appear each year. Most are held in the 2100-seat Zellerbach Hall, considered one of the finest performance facilities anywhere. Pick up a program listing in Zellerbach Hall. Students and faculty of the University receive discounts on tickets, or you can get in free if you're willing to usher. For details call 642-0212.

Berkeley Symphony
Usually at the First Congregational Church, Dana St. and Durant Ave., Five programs per year between September and March, 841-2800 for tickets and information. The year was 1969 and Berkeley's mood was defiantly counterculture. Enter the "Berkeley Promenade," an alternative arts group that presented classical music in street clothes (tuxedos were passé), and held performances in churches, the Art Museum, and other "community spaces." Under the directorship of Thomas Rarick, the Promenade's Boston Pops-like sound quickly attracted

Inside Zellerbach Hall. Courtesy of Cal Performances. Photo by Vernon DeMars.

enthusiastic crowds. As the euphoria of the era faded, however, the group began to founder economically and its director resigned. In 1977 the Promenade started its transformation from a groovy little orchestra into a nationally known symphony. The force behind this transformation was Kent Nagano, a California native who had been conducting for Sarah Caldwell's Opera Company in Boston. The general prescription for an orchestra in financial trouble is to stick to basics and play the safe, popular tunes. Under Nagano, the Promenade did the opposite, tackling complex, innovative new compositions and performing well-known classical works less frequently. The move toward experimentation was paralleled by a return to formal concert attire and a new name, the Berkeley Symphony. A turning point was the performance of a 1984 Frank Zappa composition complete with life-sized puppets, moving stage sets, and dancers. Zappa's expensive production nearly drove the Berkeley Symphony into bankruptcy, but it drew national publicity.

Nagano himself also once attracted attention by stepping in at the last minute to direct the Boston Symphony without even a rehearsal. The performance was a triumph, earning him a standing ovation and invitations to direct the Boston Pops, the New Japan Philharmonic, and the London Symphony. Nagano became director of the Opera de Lyon in 1989, but continues to direct most of the Berkeley Symphony's productions. His dedication and the excellence of the musicians have turned the symphony into one of the most highly acclaimed young orchestras in the country. Unlike many other symphony audiences who seem more interested in being among the elite than listening to the music itself, Berkeley Symphony audiences tend to be musically educated, but unpretentious.

Berkeley Opera

715 Arlington, 524-5256. Operating on a small budget, the non-profit Berkeley Opera produces a number of excellent English-language operas each year, many of them pieces seldom heard elsewhere. Richard Goodman, a professor of engineering at the University, established the company in 1979, and although the performers work more for love than money, the productions are first-rate. (Many of the singers also work with the San Francisco Opera.) The Berkeley Opera puts on three operas a year, two at the Julia Morgan Center and one popular summer opera at the Hillside Club (2286 Cedar Street). Tickets are inexpensive by opera standards.

Kent Nagano, conductor of the Berkeley Symphony Orchestra. Courtesy of the Berkeley Symphony Orchestra. Photo by Christian Steiner.

Other Musical Opportunities

The city-run **Berkeley Art Center** in Live Oak Park (1275 Walnut St., 644-6893) produces a Spring Performance Series each May featuring a wide range of music. There are also twice-monthly classical and jazz concerts in the small but acoustically-perfect **Maybeck Recital Hall** (1537 Euclid Ave., 848-3228), usually on Sunday afternoons. Reservations are recommended. Folk, classical, and jazz concerts are held in a tiny room at the **New Pieces** fabric shop (1597 Solano Ave., 527-6779). Another place for Classical, Renaissance and Baroque concerts is **MusicSource** (1000 The Alameda, 528-1685). On Tuesday evenings you can enjoy hearing live opera while dining in **Ristorante Venezia** (1902 University Ave., 644-3093). See the *Express* for additional musical listings.

Movie Theaters

Berkeley is home to a dozen different movie theaters, mostly of the squeeze-screen, multiplex variety. Two out-of-the-ordinary Berkeley theaters are very special places and recommended for film fanatics.

UC Theater

2036 University Ave., 843-6267. No Berkeley apartment is complete without a UC Theater schedule stuck to the refrigerator door. The UC has been around since 1917, and its cavernous 1400-seat interior still packs them in. In 1976 the theater was purchased by three partners intent on offering a changing repertoire each night. Today the partnership has grown to become one of the nation's largest independent chains, owning more than 30 other theaters across the country under the heading of Landmark Theaters Corp. The UC doesn't simply show golden oldies; the films are often connected by a theme such as a Humphrey Bogart festival, or Japanese Samurai films, or films about apartheid. (Many people consider this the finest repertory film theater in the nation.) The cult classic *The Rocky Horror Picture Show* is shown each Saturday at midnight to a crowd almost as weird as the movie itself. There are discount cards for theater regulars.

Pacific Film Archives (PFA)

2625 Durant Ave., 642-1124. Berkeley's other claim to cinematic fame is housed downstairs in the University Art Museum (see above). The theater has 200 of the hardest seats in town, and you won't find anyone munching popcorn here, but the movies are sometimes unforgettable. With over 6000 titles in its archive, PFA is regarded as one of the three finest film collections in the world, sharing the stage with New York's Museum of Modern Art and the Cinematheque Française in Paris. Almost every day of the year PFA shows two different films that may be obscure pieces by obscure directors from obscure countries, or well-known but rarely seen classics. PFA also attracts directors and guest lecturers who talk with the audience about their work and about cinema in general. If you're a serious film student, PFA has viewing rooms, an exhaustive Archive Library, and a clipping file with reviews covering more than 15,000 films. The Art Museum publishes a free monthly calendar with a detailed schedule of the films shown—pick up a copy at local bookstores and coffeehouses.

Readings

Berkeley's literary passion is revealed not only by its numerous bookstores and libraries, but also by its devotion to authors. In recent years there has been a proliferation of open readings, discussions, and book-signings by internationally known authors. The best source of information on these readings is *Poetry Flash* (548-6871), a free monthly paper that covers literary events. It is available in local libraries and bookstores. The most popular places for readings and book-signings are **Black Oak Books** (1491 Shattuck Ave., 486-0698) and **Cody's** (2454 Telegraph Ave., 845-7852). Sci-fi enthusiasts will enjoy readings at **Dark Carnival Bookstore** (2978 Adeline St., 845-7757).

There are poetry readings on Sunday nights upstairs at **Cafe Milano** (2522 Bancroft Way, 644-3100), and Saturday evenings at **Cafe Sierra** (2512 Bancroft Way, 849-3979). The **Bay Area Poets Coalition** (845-8409), **Mature Poets** (644-6107), and the **Berkeley Poets Cooperative** (843-8793) all offer monthly readings with open mikes.

Berkeley is also home to what may be the oldest poetry contest in the nation, the Annual Poets Dinner, held every March since 1926. Check *Poetry Flash* for information. Radio station KPFA has daily readings of poetry and prose, while KALX has a Saturday morning show featuring interviews with authors.

Painting the Town

Wall painting is at least as old as Neanderthal cave art. An important part of many cultures, it did not really

Architect-author Wytold Rybcznyski reading at Black Oak Books. Photo by Rosina Fleming.

flower in this country until the New Deal when Diego Rivera and other Mexican artists achieved fame for their proletarian scenes. The 1960s and 70s were another heyday for mural painting, and most of Berkeley's murals date from that time.

The first Berkeley murals of the counterculture generation evolved from graffiti art on a wall near what later became People's Park. The mural was named *People's Wall* and contained calls for revolution; images of Che Guevara, Huey Newton, Bobby Seale; and slogans such as "Serve the People, Stop the Pigs." The *People's Wall* was later painted over by a local communal group (see *Touring Revolutionary Berkeley*), and replaced with a sun and flying saucer calling for "The People's Spiritual Revolution." In 1976 the wall was again painted over, becoming *A People's History of Tele-*

graph Avenue, the city's best-known mural. It was painted by Osha Neumann, Daniel Galvez, Janet Krenzberg, O'Brian Thiele, and others who volunteered their labor. The mural reads from left to right starting with Mario Savio addressing a Free Speech Movement rally from the roof of a police car, and ending with a panhandler along the Avenue. In between are details that include part of Savio's speech, Julia Vinograd (the Bubble Lady), Sproul Hall's columns dropping bombs, the creation of People's Park, and television images of Ronald Reagan, Lyndon Johnson, and a Vietcong soldier. The dominant scene depicts "Bloody Thursday," May 15, 1969, when a street battle erupted over People's Park. A Vietcong flag is painted on the closed street and National Guardsmen aim weapons as friends lean over James

Rector, killed by the shot from an Alameda County deputy sheriff's gun. When the building's new owner decided to open a cafe here in 1988, he obliterated part of the famed mural with white paint, claiming the whitewashing was a simple mistake by the painters. To celebrate the twentieth anniversary of People's Park in 1989, volunteers repainted fading sections and restored the whitewashed portion .

The city of Berkeley is now replete with murals, some sponsored by the building's owners and others funded by the government. Many are heavy on politics, with allusions to the struggles of oppressed peoples. Covering the entrance to La Peña (3105 Shattuck Ave.), is perhaps the most ambitious mural in Berkeley, *Song of Unity*. The mural was created by Osha Neumann, O'Brian Thiele, Ray Patlán, and Anna de Leon in 1978 and updated in 1988 to include new scenes. *Song of Unity* combines Latin and other ethnic music themes into a dynamic piece that mirrors La Peña's vibrancy. The mural centers around Chilean protest singer and human-rights activist, Victor Jara. After the overthrow of Salvador Allende in 1973, thousands of people were herded into a Santiago stadium. When the soldiers found Jara playing his guitar and singing, they smashed his guitar. After he refused to stop singing and the crowd began to sing along, they cut off his hands saying, "Now sing, you bastard!" When he still continued, he was shot to death. In this sculptured mural Jara's three-dimensional hands can be seen play-

ing the guitar while his disembodied head sings from below. On the right side are North American musicians including Malvina Reynolds (from Berkeley) and Satchmo. At the top, the eagle of North America and the vulture of South America rise above a brilliant green quetzal, all in bas relief. The quetzal's tail flows out onto the sidewalk.

In addition to these two famous murals, Berkeley has at least two dozen other wall paintings. Some of the best (or hardest to ignore) are:

- *Ancisco* (1277 Gilman Street). San Francisco Bay fantasy scene painted in 1979 by John Wehrle. Once extraordinary, but now in need of restoration.
- *Berkeley High School* (Milvia St. and Allston Way). Student-painted pieces from 1976 of school scenes and animals.
- *California Wildlife* (2430 Bancroft Way). Nature scenes filled with leaping whales and circling eagles; painted in 1979 by Lou Silva.
- *Cocaine Slavery* (3198 Adeline Street). Painted by "guerilla artists" in 1989, this mural depicts cocaine as a new form of slavery.
- *Intersections* (Willard Jr. High, Telegraph Ave. and Prince Street). Disconcerting giant mural with a collage of images painted by Osha Neumann and Daniel Galvez in 1982.
- *Recycling Center* (Dwight Way at M.L. King Way). Earth-devouring metal monster being pulled apart and recycled. Painted by Osha Neumann and Peralta College students in 1978.

Opposite: Osha Neumann restoring People's History of Telegraph *mural. Photo by Don Pitcher.*

- *Still Life and Blossoming Almond Trees* (inside Stern Hall at Hearst Ave. and Highland Place). Completed in 1931 by famed muralist Diego Rivera, this bucolic scene shows farm workers and flowering trees as seen through an open window.
- *Viva La Raza* (3217 Adeline Street). Semi-trailer rig with Chicano themes; painted by Daniel Galvez, Osha Neumann, O'Brien Thiele, and Stephanie Barrett in 1977.

City Parks

Berkeley has always been a city for those who appreciate the environment. Tree-lined Strawberry Creek and the rolling hills to the east were chosen deliberately as the bucolic setting for the new University when it was established in 1868. In the early years this utopian landscape led some to flights of poetic fancy:

The sun lies warm on Berkeley hills:
The long, fair slopes bend softly down
To fold in loving arms the town;
The sun-kissed uplands rise and
    swell,
And blue-eyed grass and pimpernel
Dot the young meadow's velvet
    sheen.
The air with spring-time music thrills,
Sweet songs of birds in halls of green
On Berkeley hills…

—*Adeline Knapp (1909)*

This quiet landscape was soon lost in a blitzkrieg of growth and development that followed the San Francisco Earthquake of 1906. By 1915, when community interest in open space finally began to rise, virtually all land within the city had already been developed. In 1974 voters took concrete steps to regain some open space by passing a temporary property tax override to purchase and develop city park land. Although the city has since created a dozen new parks, the acreage of parkland in Berkeley remains small—less than 3% of the land area.

Still, there are more than 40 city parks scattered throughout Berkeley, providing a wide range of recreation possibilities. You can visit recreation centers, sports facilities, playgrounds, a pier, wooded creeks, lawn bowling greens, and even rock-climbing areas. Local children also enjoy a number of

Berkeley Rose Garden. Photo by Don Pitcher.

mini-parks—tiny playground areas sandwiched between houses on residential streets.

The park and recreation programs reflect the chaotic nature of city government, with separate offices that seem to work against each other. Berkeley's parks are managed from the small Parks/Marina office at the Marina (644-6371), while recreation facilities are directed from the Recreation Office in City Hall (644-8515), except for certain recreation programs directed by the Health and Human Services Department. (For further information about recreation facilities, see *Recreation*.) If you're interested in influencing local policy and management, attend one of the Park and Recreation Commission's meetings held the fourth Monday of each month. Call 644-6530 for meeting location and times. The city has an Adopt-A-Park program (644-6371) that provides community volunteers to help with specific landscaping or maintenance projects; they can be as small as the adoption of a planter.

Several of the city's more notable parks are discussed below.

Aquatic Park

Heinz and 7th Sts. Berkeley's largest recreation area, Aquatic Park occupies 100 acres in West Berkeley and includes a mile-long saltwater lake connected to the bay by tidewater gates. At one time the area encompassed an ecologically rich marsh bordered by a sandy beach, but during the Depression Era the Works Progress Administration (WPA) constructed a road (later to become the Eastshore Freeway) on bay-fill a thousand feet from the old shoreline. The road cut off the shallow, muddy lake that became Aquatic Park. Today, the constant roar of traffic is the backdrop to the park—but if you're looking for an escape from civilization, you can paddle a kayak around a protected stretch of water, or bicycle down an exercise course/bike path. There's a frisbee "golf course," boat ramps and docks, a popular water ski jump, and a long, narrow lawn with picnic areas and a playground. On the northeast shore you'll find Seabird Sailing Center and Golden Gate Brewery Cafe, while the Berkeley Rowing Club maintains a boathouse along the southwest shore. Aquatic Park is also a good place to view the many species of ducks and shorebirds that stop here during their migration. At the south end of the park is the International Bird Research Center which works to save injured marine birds, particularly those coated by oil spills.

Berkeley Rose Garden

Euclid Ave. and Eunice St. The sweet scent of roses permeates the air in one of the city's best loved parks, the Berkeley Rose Garden. Many consider this the finest rose garden in Northern California; more than 250 different varieties of roses of varying colors cascade down a series of semi-circular terraces. Completed in 1937 by the WPA, the garden features a central terrace ringed by a Bernard Maybeck-inspired redwood pergola draped with climbing roses. A small pool at the base of the garden is fed by the culverted Codornices Creek. There is also an official testing and display site for the "All-American Rose Selections" at the base of the garden. The rose bushes are pruned in early January in preparation for Mother's Day, but some roses are always blooming. The Rose Garden offers a lovely setting for outdoor weddings. The city charges $100 for four hours use of the garden, and reservations may be made up to a year in advance by calling 644-6530. As many Berkeley residents have discovered, the benches atop the Rose Garden also provide spectacular sunset views out through the Golden Gate.

Cedar-Rose Park

Cedar and Chestnut Sts. One of Berkeley's nicest parks, Cedar-Rose has tennis, basketball, and volleyball courts, playgrounds, and picnic areas. The large grassy field is a good place for soccer games and provides tent-space for the very popular Pickle Family Circus each May.

Codornices Park

Euclid Ave. and Eunice St.—across the street from the Rose Garden. Kids love the long concrete slide and other playground equipment here, while the large lawn is perfect for frisbees, picnics, or simply lying in the sun. There is also a softball diamond and basketball court for those with more ambition. At the north edge of the park, Tamalpais Path climbs through the woods along Codornices Creek.

Martin Luther King, Jr. Memorial Park

M. L. King Way and Allston Way. Until recently the big lawn next to Berkeley High School was called Civic Center Park. Then the city council decided to rename the lawn, the city hall building, and adjacent Grove St. after the slain civil-rights leader. To many folks, however, the park will always be known by a third name, Provo Park. Following massive Vietnam War demonstrations in 1966, a local group launched the "Free" movement, styled after Amsterdam's anarchist Provos (the word originated

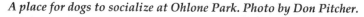

A place for dogs to socialize at Ohlone Park. Photo by Don Pitcher.

from the French "provocateur"). Provos distributed food and organized free rock concerts at the park for the hundreds of hippies who had converged on Berkeley, and over time the name Provo became attached to the park. It has a children's playground on one end, and provides a hangout for high school students. In 1988 a Peace Wall, consisting of over 1000 hand-painted tiles, was added to the fountain area. People of all ages and groups painted the tiles, including Nobel Laureate Bishop Desmond Tutu and a group of Russian students.

Ohlone Park

Hearst Ave. near M. L. King Way. The city developed this narrow strip in place of the buildings that were destroyed in the 1960s when BART was being constructed underground. The park resulted in part from a "People's

Basketball players at Ohlone Park. Photo by Don Pitcher.

Park Annex" planting project in 1969. A remaining climbing structure from a children's playground built from junkyard material is evidence of this community effort. Originally named Hearst Strip Park, it was renamed in 1981 for the area's first inhabitants, the Ohlone Indians. Today the park has an exercise course (with signs unreadable under the graffiti), a baseball field, basketball and volleyball courts, playground areas, and three community gardens (644-6371). The most uncommon feature is the fenced-in Dog Park, where dogs and their owners socialize—it's the only place in the city where dogs can run without a leash.

Rock Climbing Areas

The hills of North Berkeley are dotted with volcanic rock outcroppings, seven of which are managed as city parks. The best known is **Indian Rock Park** (Indian Rock and Shattuck Aves.). It takes its name from the profile of an Indian chief, which supposedly can be seen from Indian Rock Avenue. Surrounded by hillside homes, the park is a large mass of basalt with steps carved to the top. The view spans the western horizon from the towers of downtown Oakland and the smog blankets of San Jose to the gentle summit of Mt. Tamalpais and the tree-topped knoll of Albany Hill. The rock (along with others in the area) provides not only a spectacular vista, but also an opportunity to practice the art of bouldering—attempting short but difficult climbs without a rope. Modern U.S. rock climbing originated on Indian Rock as local Sierra Club members learned techniques here that they later used in their assaults on Yosemite's larger precipices. You will still see climbers practicing difficult moves, as bags of chalk dangle from their belts. Nearby telephone poles are plastered with notices about climbing films and equipment for sale, along with ads for prospective climbing partners.

A few hundred feet up the hill is **Mortar Rock Park,** where you'll find old mortar holes once used by the Ohlone Indians to grind acorn meal, as well as buckeye trees that they may have planted. The lesser-known **Grotto Rock Park** (Santa Barbara Rd. and Indian Rock Ave.) and **Contra Costa Rock Park** (Contra Costa and Los Angeles Aves.) provide unobstructed views of the Bay Area. The tiny **Great Stoneface Park** (San Fernando Ave. and Thousand Oaks Blvd.) is pleasant, but does not offer the same vistas, and the rocks cannot be climbed easily. My favorites are Berkeley's two highest parks, **Cragmont Rock Park** (Easter and Regal Rds.), where picnic tables seem perched on the edge of the world, and **Remillard Park** (Keeler Ave. and Poppy Lane). The climb in Remillard is more difficult (for the non-climber), but the view is well worth the scramble.

Strawberry Creek Park

Allston Way and West St. The city created this park in the 1980s along the abandoned Santa Fe railroad tracks in West Berkeley. Strawberry Creek, once home to salmon and steelhead, is little more than a culvert for much of its length today, but this park brings the creek briefly to the surface again. The park has lighted basketball, tennis, and volleyball courts as well as a nice playground and open lawn area. The Berkeley

Boys on the slide at the park by Martin Luther King, Jr. Junior High. Photo by Don Pitcher.

Youth Alternatives (BYA) center is in a brick building adjoining the park.

Totland

Virginia St. and McGee Ave. Notice those two young "rock jocks" heading up the street toward Indian Rock, talking as if they've known each other all their lives? They have. They learned to parallel play at Totland Park. And those two couples laughing at a table at Chez Panisse—how long have they known each other? Since they took their babies to Totland the same afternoon. Sequestered in a quiet corner of the Berkeley Flatlands, and secured by a chain-link fence, Totland is the best spot in Berkeley for friendly toddlers, mothers looking for companions, and parents trying to dream up the perfect spot for their three-year-old's birthday party.

BERKELEY CITY PARKS

Park	Location	Picnic tables	BBQ	Softball
Aquatic Park	Bancroft and Bolivar	X	X	
Bateman Park	Colby and Prince	X		
Berkeley Rose Garden	Euclid and Bay View			
Berkeley Way Mini-Park	Berkeley Way and West	X		
Dorothy M. Bolte Park	Spruce and Michigan			
Cedar-Rose Park	Cedar and Chestnut	X	X	
Charlie Dorr Mini-Park	2200 Acton	X	X	
Codornices Park	Euclid and Eunice	X	X	X
Columbus School Park	9th and Allston	X	X	X
Contra Costa Rock Park	Contra Costa and L.A.			
Cragmont Rock Park	Regal Road	X		
George Florence Park	Addison and 10th	X	X	
Frederick Mini-Park	Arlington and Yosemite			
Glendale La Loma Park	La Loma and Glendale		X	X
Greg Brown Mini-Park	1907 Harmon	X		
Grotto Rock Park	Santa Barbara			
Grove Park	M.L. King and Oregon	X	X	L
Haskell-Mabel Mini-Park	Haskell and Mabel			
John Hinkel Park	Southhampton and San Diego	X	X	
Horseshoe Park	Seawall			
Indian Rock Park	Indian Rock at Shattuck	X		
James Kenney Park	8th and Delaware	X	X	L
King School Park	Hopkins and Colusa	X		
Lawn Bowling Green	2270 Acton			
Le Conte School Park	Russell and Fulton	X		
Live Oak Park	Shattuck and Berryman	X	X	
Malcolm X School Park	Ashby and King			
M.L. King, Jr. Park	M.L. King and Allston			
Mortar Rock Park	Indian Rock and San Diego			
Monkey Island Park	Garber and Oak Knoll			
John Muir School Park	Claremont and Ashby			
North Waterfront Park	Spinnaker			

Basket-ball	Tennis	Volley-ball	Jogging	Play-ground	Lawn	Size (Acres)	Special Features
			X		Large	100.0	Boating, frisbee golf
			X	F		0.4	
	5					3.6	Roses galore
				X	Small	0.4	
			X	X	Small	1.2	Concrete slide
X	3	X		F	Large	4.9	
				F		0.2	
X				F	Large	10.6	Concrete slide
L				F	Large	0.5	
					Small	0.2	Rock climbing
X					Medium	3.0	Rock climbing
				F	Small	0.5	
					Small	0.2	
				F	Small	5.6	Clubhouse
X				X	Small	0.6	Clubhouse
						0.3	Rock climbing
2L	3L			F	Small	3.1	Recreation center
				X		0.1	
					Small	3.4	
			X			1.2	Rock climbing
				F	Small	4.2	Ampitheater, clubhouse
2L	2L			X	Medium	4.2	Recreation center
8	5			F	Medium	1.7	Concrete slide, pool
						1.8	2 lawn bowling greens
X				X	Small	1.3	
2L	2L	L		F	Medium	5.5	Theater, art & rec center
3			X	X		0.2	
				F	Large	2.8	
						0.4	Rock climbing
					Small	0.3	
2				X	Medium	1.0	
					Large	90.0	Trails, bayviews

L=Lighted F=Fenced

BERKELEY CITY PARKS (cont.)

Park	Location	Picnic tables	BBQ	Softball
Ohlone Park	Hearst and M.L. King	X	X	L
Oak Park	Domingo and El Camino Real			
Prince Street Totlot	Prince and California	X		
Remillard Park	Keeler and Poppy			
Roosevelt Totlot	2424 Roosevelt			
San Pablo Park	Park and Oregon	X	X	2L
Shorebird Park	Seawall Drive	X	X	
63rd Street Mini-Park	63rd and California			
Solano-Peralta Park	Solano and Peralta	X		
Stoneface Park	San Fernando and Thousand Oaks	X		
Strawberry Creek Park	Allston and West	X	X	
Terrace View	Fairlawn and Queens			
Thousand Oaks Sch. Park	Colusa and Tacoma	X		
Totland Park	Virginia and McGee	X	X	
Walker Park	Walker and Derby			
Washington School Park	McKinley and Bancroft			
Willard Park	Hillegass and Derby	X		X

Basket-ball	Tennis	Volley-ball	Jogging	Play-ground	Lawn	Size (Acres)	Special Features
L		L		F	Large	9.8	Dog park, par course
					Small	0.3	
				X		0.2	
			X	X	Small	5.9	Rock climbing, woods
				F		0.2	
3L	6L			X	Large	13.0	Rec center, soccer
		X	X		Medium	6.2	Par course, beach
				X		0.2	
				F		0.1	
						0.7	Rock climbing
2L	2L	L		X	Medium	3.7	Cable ride
2				X		0.7	Rec bldg, concrete slide
3				X	Large	2.6	
				F	Small	0.4	
						0.2	
X				X		1.5	"Environmental yard"
3	2L			X	Large	2.7	Rec area

L= Lighted F= Fenced

Totland Park. Photo by Kit Duane.

The Marina

Unbeknownst to many Berkeley residents, the city's shoreline offers a variety of activities. You can sail small boats, fly a kite, fish for striped bass, watch birds, hike over grassy rolling hills, or look across to San Francisco and the Golden Gate Bridge from a waterfront restaurant. Within the Berkeley Marina there coexist a variety of environments that change with the time of the day, tides, and seasons. In the winter, the sky is often filled with migrating birds on the Pacific Flyway. During winter storms, snowy egrets arrive from the ocean beaches and walk among the rocks spearing crabs. In the summer, cool ocean air, sucked toward the hot inland valleys, whips wildly across the water, making this an ideal time for boat races.

For a fine view on a summer evening there is no nicer walk than that on the Berkeley pier. After the sun sets on the Pacific behind Mt. Tamalpais, the lights go on in San Francisco and in the Berkeley hills. Seagulls come in to rest on the pier and cormorants sit drying their wings on the breakwaters. You also may catch sight of San Francisco's familiar summer fog, which, when it comes billowing through the towers of the Golden Gate, heads straight for Berkeley.

The marina is easily accessible by car (take University Ave. west across the freeway) or AC Transit bus 51M. The bike route passes under the freeway, up a flight of stairs, and then across a busy off-ramp intersection.

Marina Facilities

The Berkeley Marina includes a boat harbor and several parks, as well as its pier. The Parks/Marina office (644-6371) is along the marina's south shore. Berkeley also operates a Marina Environmental Education Program (644-8623) with public tours each Saturday from the new nature center. Programs center around the marine environment, dock life, fishing, and other topics.

Construction of the yacht harbor along Berkeley's shore began in 1936. Landfill gradually created open space around the harbor, and by 1960 the general outline of the shoreline was complete. Between 1966 and 1975 Berkeley developed the new marina with berths, walkways, and buildings, producing one of the largest and finest marinas on San Francisco Bay. The marina now has 52 acres of water surface. The 975 berths, protected from surge and rough water by an entrance breakwater, have storage lockers, fresh water, electrical outlets, night lighting, 24-hour security, parking, restrooms and showers, and locked gates. The marina can accommodate boats as large as 110 feet, and facilities include a fuel dock, launching ramps, repair facilities, a two-ton boat hoist, spaces for 38 visiting boats, and 90 storage spaces.

The many other parts of the marina area, and activities related to them, are described below.

Opposite: Windsurfing at the Berkeley Marina. Photo by Don Pitcher.

Adventure Playground. Photo by Don Pitcher.

Adventure Playground

644-6530. After World War II, children in Europe grew up in a bleak environment, but its abundance of war debris proved a treasure trove for creative minds. European playground designers, noting how children played with seemingly useless material, began to create playgrounds that allowed children to build and paint things for themselves. Berkeley's wonderfully funky Adventure Playground follows the same tack. The playground provides hammers, nails, paint, and wood for children to build forts, clubhouses, toys, and anything else. Adventure Playground also has a net kids love to climb, an old rowboat with hundreds of layers of bright paint, and a cable slide for the truly adventurous. During winter months it is open only on weekends and holidays 11 am-5 pm; during the summer every day 9 am-5 pm. The playground accepts donations of wood, tools, rugs, or other things for creative play.

Berkeley Yacht Club

540-9167. Located on the south edge of the marina's entrance, the Berkeley Yacht Club's lounge commands a spectacular bay view. The club is primarily for boat owners, though others can join. Members pay a $500 initiation fee, plus $80 each quarter. Facilities include a full bar, lounge, and dining area, while activities include cruises, dinners, races, and a variety of parties.

Cal Sailing Club

527-7245. If you've always wanted to learn to sail but have been put off by the cost, the Cal Sailing Club is a good place to start. The non-profit club costs $40 for a three-month membership ($35 for UC students), less than what some sailing schools charge for a single day. Members must spend at least two hours every three months helping to maintain the equipment (some of which is a bit beat up), but there are no additional charges. The club's fleet includes 30 small sailboats (13-foot Lidos), two larger boats (22- and 26-foot), and a dozen windsurfers. You can use them Mon-Fri, noon-sunset and Sat-Sun 9 am-sunset. Sailing and windsurfing lessons are offered on Mon and Thurs afternoons and Sat mornings. Club members also head out for longer weekend cruises to Angel Island or San Francisco in the larger boats. Twice a month the club throws its doors open, offering free sailing lessons to the public.

Design Associates Working with Nature (DAWN)

644-1315. This non-profit group specializes in restoring and managing California's native ecosystems. Employees collect seeds from around the state and grow more than 150 plant species at their nursery, many un-

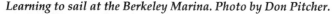

Learning to sail at the Berkeley Marina. Photo by Don Pitcher.

The Berkeley pier. Photo by Don Pitcher.

available elsewhere. DAWN is open Mon, Thurs, and Sat 9 am-noon, but sells only to members ($12/year) and public agencies. Their annual plant sale, however, is open to the public.

Marina Sports Center
849-2727. Want to try your hand at deep-sea fishing? The Bait and Tackle Shop at the marina coordinates fishing expeditions for a number of independent charter boats. Trips outside the Golden Gate cost $40/day (plus $8.50 extra for bait and tackle; $6 for rod and reel; $4.50 for a fishing license). During the busy king salmon season (mid-February through November), it's a good idea to make reservations two weeks in advance for weekend trips.

North Waterfront Park
Berkeley's newest and least developed city park came into existence in the mid-80s as the old garbage dump was covered with fill, graded into hills, and planted to grass. Paved trails cover the 90-acre site, whose grassy hills have become popular kite-flying, frisbee-throwing, and bay-watching spots. There is a nice grouping of native plants (courtesy of DAWN) on the hill next to the traffic circle. Half of the park is still a muddy, weed-covered field, but the city hopes to (someday) develop ponds, cycling and running paths, and playgrounds on the northern edge.

Olympic Circle Sailing Club
843-4200. Unlike most yacht clubs, Olympic Circle is for people who don't own a boat, but want to learn how to sail. Its 40 yachts (24-40 feet long) make it the largest training center on the West Coast. Beginners can rent yachts after they have been through 60-80 hours of instruction. Annual fees are not for those with small bank accounts (close to $2000/year), but the training and boats are top-notch. Olympic Circle also has instruction for non-members ranging

from introductory classes to advanced celestial navigation, and it offers flotilla-style charters to such places as Tahiti and the Caribbean.

The Pier

Berkeley's long pier now has only recreational use—it draws people who enjoy fishing, watching windsurfers, or sauntering along the Bay as the dusk deepens and the city lights up. The first of Berkeley's piers, Jacob's Landing, was constructed in 1853 to facilitate transport of supplies to the new community of Ocean View. Twenty-two years later a small municipal pier was built to provide direct ferry access to San Francisco. Landfill has since covered these first piers, but the old pilings are still present under University Ave. west of the freeway. Uneven settling has turned a drive along the road into a washboard ride.

In 1926 the Golden Gate Ferry Company built a wooden automobile pier from the base of University Ave. three miles into the Bay, extending to water deep enough to dock the large electric-diesel ferries. These car ferries proved so popular that ferry police urged Berkeley motorists to drive at least 60 miles per hour on the pier to keep them filled! With completion of the Bay Bridge in 1936, however, ferry service proved unprofitable, and within two years the last Berkeley ferry was retired. The pier gradually deteriorated until a barge collision severed the last two-thirds of it and forced its closure. Between 1958 and 1961, however, the city rebuilt 3000 feet of the pier, adding new rails, benches, lighting, and an observation platform in 1972. The remaining pilings from the old pier still extend far into the Bay, serving as perch sites for pelicans, gulls, and cormorants, and presenting a navigational hazard for boats.

Today the Berkeley pier is open day and night and is one of the premier fishing areas in the San Francisco Bay. No fishing license is required to catch the smelt, striped bass, perch, sharks, skates, and rays that inhabit the water.

Shorebird Park

Built in the late 1960s, Shorebird Park sets picnic tables in a wooded area facing the south basin. Nearby is the Adventure Playground and the Cal Sailing Club. A few brave the cold waters to swim here.

Protecting the Bay

Sediment and Landfill

An incredible 40% of California's land area is drained by the Sacramento and San Joaquin rivers. As they enter San Francisco Bay on their way to the sea, they deposit sediment from decades of environmental abuse. Between 1850 and 1954 the Sacramento brought 2.4-trillion cubic yards of sediment into the Bay, enough to cover the city of Berkeley with nearly four miles of muck. Much of this material was flushed out to sea, and dredging continues to remove more, but sedimentation nevertheless chokes many parts of the Bay. At its most extreme, sedimentation has advanced the shoreline by a half mile along the north shore of Carquinez Straits, where the water was once 90 feet deep!

Sedimentation is not, however, the biggest problem in San Francisco Bay. Two-thirds of the Bay is less than eighteen feet deep, which makes it easily polluted and easily filled by developers. First in San Francisco and later throughout the Bay Area, filling and subsequent development reduced the water surface and destroyed ecologically important marshlands. In 1960 a report from an Army Corps of Engineers found that the Bay's surface area had already been reduced by 30% to 540 square miles, and that over two square miles were being lost each year. At that rate the Bay would be little more than a river by the year 2020.

Despite these warnings, in 1961 the Santa Fe Corporation proposed a 2000-acre fill along Berkeley's shoreline to establish a new "city" of islands stretching thousands of feet into the Bay. In the 1920s Berkeley citizens were the first to push for protection of the East Bay hills, and in the 1960s they were the first to support protection of their other boundary, the Bay. Catherine Kerr, Esther Gulick, and Sylvia McLaughlin formed the Save San Francisco Bay Association and convinced the city to turn the proposal down. By 1965 the Association had 10,000 members and had succeeded in persuading the state legislature to create the San Francisco Bay Conservation and Development Commission (BCDC). Since its creation there have been no major fills—only smaller ones, such as Berkeley's now-closed dump.

The Shoreline
Berkeley's oddly shaped shoreline was improvised by garbage collectors, highway engineers, and city bureaucrats. In 1923, after garbage burning had been banned in Berkeley, the city council opened a new dump along the shoreline, first along the highway, and after 1960 in the area north of the marina. The final site was completely filled by 1981 and non-recyclable garbage is now hauled 45 miles to a Livermore landfill.

While the marina area belongs to the city, Santa Fe Corporation owns 174 acres of landfill adjacent to the Eastshore Freeway. Santa Fe and other developers have for many years attempted to develop this land. Causeway-linked islands, an airport, a convention center, a junior college, and a large shopping center have all been proposed at one time or another in the last 25 years, but each time the citizens of Berkeley have blocked development. In 1965 the city council labeled the land "U" (unclassified), which means that city approval is required for any development. Frustrated by its inability to profit from the land, Santa Fe sued the city, but the lawsuit was eventually dismissed in Berkeley's favor. In 1983 Santa Fe submitted a new proposal for a massive development (four-million square feet) that would include shops, hotels, office buildings, and parking garages. Citizen response was negative, and in a 1986 election an alternative low-scale development plan put forth by the Sierra Club was approved by city voters. That plan stands in limbo as Santa Fe has again filed suit. Meanwhile, citizen pressure calls for another option, an Eastshore State Park that would reach from Albany to the Bay Bridge. Measure AA, passed by Alameda and Contra Costa County voters in 1988, supplies $15 million to help establish this park between Oakland and Richmond, but whether Berkeley's Santa Fe-owned land will be included remains to be seen.

The Berkeley Beach
Until the late 19th century the Berkeley shoreline had both an extensive marsh and a sandy beach that stretched south from Strawberry Creek. The beach became a popular place for summer outings from the growing settlement of Ocean View. (Sand was so plentiful that the landowner, Samuel Heywood, sold it for 50¢ a wagonload.) Berkeley's shoreline did not change appreciably until the 1930s, when the WPA used this sand as fill material for a new road that paralleled the shoreline a thousand feet out, leaving a shallow mudflat along the bayshore. Additional fill was placed here in the early 1950s with the creation of the Eastshore Freeway and Frontage Road.

Pollution Control
Over the years San Francisco Bay has served as a dumping site for waste materials of all types, from garbage to petrochemicals. Until recently, the major focus of Bay cleanup has been better sewage treatment, with the result that the Bay is much cleaner today than it was twenty years ago. Major problems remain, however. One is caused by the fact that much of San Francisco Bay's natural water inflow is now rechanneled at the Bay delta toward Southern California, depriving the Bay of its natural pumping system. Another problem is Berkeley's aging and cracked sewer system, which leaks into the storm drains, into the water table, and, during storms, onto the streets. Although repairs are underway, completion is a long way off and will cost more than $40 million. The result is a badly contaminated shoreline. Recent studies have found high levels of coliform bacteria, the standard measure of sewage pollution, at the mouth of Strawberry Creek. Clams and mussels found on the Berkeley shoreline should not be eaten. Recently, new concerns have surfaced in the form of toxic chemicals that are affecting marine life in the Bay. Striped bass populations have plummeted 80% in the last two decades, and there are periodic warnings against eating Bay-caught fish due to chemical contamination—so beware!

Regional Parks/Wildlands

More than 100 years ago, architect Frederick Law Olmsted knew that his vision of a rustic campus in Berkeley would require parks. Many years later his "scenic lanes" came into being through the efforts of several far-sighted individuals, as described below. Today they include 46 regional parks, over 1000 miles of trails, and 63,000 acres of land in Alameda and Contra Costa counties. Three of these parks are in the hills adjacent to Berkeley: Tilden Regional Park, which is considered the cornerstone of the East Bay Regional Park District, plus the less developed Wildcat Canyon Regional Park, and Claremont Canyon Regional Preserve.

History

In the early years of this century, a number of companies (which later merged to become the East Bay Water Company) purchased watershed land in the Berkeley hills and built dams on the creeks in order to compensate for the lack of fresh water available west of the hills. Lake Temescal, Upper San Leandro Reservoir, Lake Chabot (built in 1875), San Pablo Reservoir, and Jewel Lake are some of the resulting reservoirs. A drought and the devastating 1923 Berkeley fire demonstrated that even with these reservoirs, the water supply was inadequate, and as a result, the East Bay Municipal Utilities District (EBMUD) was created to build aqueducts that would bring water from the Sierra Nevada.

In 1928 EBMUD acquired the East Bay Water Company's land and reservoirs. The reservoirs were kept for water storage, but EBMUD attempted to sell the other 15,000 acres of watershed land, claiming they were surplus property. Developers leapt at the opportunity of filling the East Bay hills with roads and homes, but those concerned with protecting the open space had other dreams.

Robert Sibley and Hollis Thompson organized the East Bay Metropolitan Park Association in 1928 with the goal of creating a chain of parks along the hills. They commissioned the son and stepson of Frederick Law Olmsted, as well as Ansel F. Hall of the National Park Service, to study the recreational needs of the East Bay. The final report recommended public acquisition of upper Wildcat Canyon and establishment of a regional park system. Although EBMUD remained opposed to the park concept, the Park Association received state legislative support for a new regional agency, the East Bay Regional Park District (EBRPD), that would acquire and manage the land.

The legislature developed an ingenious shell game to finance the new Park District. Property owners were to be assessed 5¢ per $100 valuation, but as the money was paid to EBMUD for the land, the Utility District would have to lower its rates equivalently.

Opposite: Nature walk at Jewel Lake in Tilden Park. Courtesy of East Bay Regional Park District.

Tilden Park hills. Photo by Don Pitcher.

Although it was in the midst of the Depression, there was strong public support for the new parks, and in 1934, voters passed the Regional Park proposal by a 3-1 margin.

History has touched the Park District in different ways. The Depression Era brought federal labor and financial support for the new parks through the Works Project Administration and the Civilian Conservation Corps. Crews constructed roads, trails, fire breaks, camps, and even a golf course, while also planting thousands of Monterey pines to reduce erosion problems. World War II then turned the East Bay parks into military training grounds—if you look closely you'll discover old foxholes in the eucalyptus forests of Tilden. After the war the Army established a Nike missile base along San Pablo Ridge to defend against Soviet bombers; the site was abandoned a decade later after the missiles became obsolete. (Today the narrow paved entrance

road to the barracks, Nimitz Way, has become one of the most popular running, dog walking, and cycling paths in the Berkeley hills.)

Since 1964, when the people of Contra Costa County voted to join the EBRPD, the system has grown dramatically, but population growth has simultaneously increased pressure on the remaining open space and led to crowding of the existing parks. In 1988 voters passed a $225 million bond measure to fund additional land acquisitions and development, and by the year 2005 the park system is expected to cover more than 100,000 acres in the East Bay.

The Parks Today

Although the three nearest regional parks are described below in more detail, a few general points apply to all. None of the Berkeley area parks allow camping, except for groups such as the Boy Scouts. Illegal campers risk citations. The only regional parks that do allow public camping are Anthony Chabot, east of San Leandro, and three parks south of Livermore—Del Valle, Ohlone (backpack sites only), and Sunol. Public pressure may eventually force the Park District to provide additional camping facilities, but don't count on it.

Dogs are allowed in the Regional Parks but must be kept on a leash in developed areas. They are allowed off-leash in open space or undeveloped areas as long as they are under control. Horses may be ridden only on certain paths, generally the larger fire roads. Both dogs and horses are prohibited from the land around the Environmental Education Center in Tilden and the Lake Anza beach. See the Tilden and Wildcat Canyon maps (available at the Environmental Education Center) for specific trail restrictions.

To stay up-to-date on East Bay Park events, join the Parks Foundation (531-9300). Membership costs $35/year ($17 for students, the disabled, and seniors) and includes a subscription to the monthly *Regional Parks Log*. The *Log* covers local environmental trips, describes various park planning issues and events affecting the parks, and has educational games for kids.

Charles Lee Tilden Park

The 2065-acre Tilden Park, largely open meadows and forests, also contains the most developed land in the Regional Park system, with attractions to suit nearly everyone. You can cycle along a spectacular ridgeline; hike on miles of trails; swim in Lake Anza; ride ponies, a carousel, or a miniature railroad. You can learn about Califor-

nia's plant life in a botanical garden, about the natural world in an environmental center, or about barnyard animals at a Little Farm. You can even play eighteen holes of golf. Tilden is easily accessible and is large enough to allow you to "get away from it all" without having to travel far away.

The oldest of the East Bay Regional Parks, Tilden Park opened in 1937. The Park District's first president, Major Charles Lee Tilden, offered his home for board meetings and even lent his own money to purchase the first 60 acres of park land. A bust of Tilden sits in front of the Park's Brazilian Room.

To get there by car or bike, follow Spruce St. to Grizzly Peak Blvd. and enter the park from several intersecting roads. AC Transit bus routes No. 7 and No. 8 take you from the Berkeley BART station to the park entrance at the intersection of Golf Course Drive and Grizzly Peak Boulevard. Bus No. 67 will take you from downtown Berkeley to the upper end of the Canyon Dr. entrance. From there it's two-thirds of a mile downhill to the Environmental Education Center and the start of several trails. During the summer, special buses equipped to carry bicycles leave downtown Berkeley for Tilden every hour, 11 am-6 pm daily. Budget cuts may alter this service, so call AC Transit (839-2882) for an update.

Botanic Garden
In 1940 the U.S. Forest Service donated 2000 potted plants to help start a botanic garden on six-and-a-half acres in Tilden Park. Today it is the largest native plant garden in Northern California, with over 1500 different species, including the largest collection of manzanita anywhere (over

100 different species) and more than 200 rare or endangered plants. Wildcat Creek flows through the garden, whose ten sections each represent a different part of California—sea bluff, Pacific rainforest, Sierran, etc. Slide shows are shown in the small visitors' center on Saturday mornings at 10:30 during the winter months. The center has native plant seeds for sale, and each April holds a special sale of native plants from the garden. Free group tours (841-8732) are available all year.

Brazilian Room

One of the Bay Area's most popular wedding halls is the Brazilian Room, located just north of the Botanic Garden. Outside the lovely stone structure, a pleasant garden offers views into the rolling hills, while inside are panels of tropical hardwoods originally used in the Brazil Building of the 1939 World's Fair on Treasure Island. The 30 x 54-foot hall is generally booked up for a year in advance with five weddings, anniversaries, and bar mitzvahs each weekend! On weekdays when the building is used for business meetings or training seminars the schedule is lighter. Acoustics are not the best here, however. Rates are $500 for five hours on weekends or $200 on weekdays with extra charges for non-locals and for use of such "amenities" as the fireplace, patio tables, etc. Call 540-0220 for details, or visit the room on Tuesdays 1-8 pm to make reservations.

Environmental Education Center

On the northern edge of Tilden is the Environmental Education Center, built in 1974 to orient park-goers to the natural world. Inside you'll find an active beehive, an exhibit on noc-

turnal animals (including a "scratch 'n sniff" skunk display), and a variety of other imaginative exhibits about the natural world of the East Bay hills. Staff members lead nature walks every Thurs, Sat, and Sun. Call 525-2233 for a schedule of events. The Center is open Tues-Sun, 10 am-5 pm.

Hiking and Trails

Approximately half of Tilden's 40 miles of trails, dirt fire roads, and paved service roads are open to bikes and horses. The **Skyline National Recreation Trail,** created in 1970, was the first in the National Trails System. It stretches 31 miles from the northern end of Wildcat Canyon Regional Park to Chabot Regional Park in Castro Valley. It is open to hikers and horseback riders for its entire length, and to cyclists along extensive portions. The Skyline Trail covers five miles in Tilden, including the Seaview and Nimitz Way Trails.

Seaview Trail, a three-mile dirt road, follows the crest of San Pablo ridge from Inspiration Point to the miniature steam trains. From Vollmer Peak (1913 feet), just off the Seaview Trail, you get a 360-degree panorama of the entire East Bay. (The peak was named after August Vollmer, a famous Berkeley police chief.)

Nimitz Way, a nearly level paved path, follows San Pablo Ridge northwest from Inspiration Point. Runners, families, cyclists, horse riders, and dog walkers all crowd this gentle, scenic trail. Along the way you'll see the remains of three Nike missile pads from the former Army base.

Surrounding the Environmental Education Center near the north end of Tilden Park is a maze of trails and fire roads that take you through a variety of vegetation. There are trails for

The Little Train. Photo by Don Pitcher.

every fitness level. You can take a short loop hike to Jewel Lake or follow longer and steeper paths up the grassy slopes of Wildcat Peak. One of the most interesting paths is the **Wildcat Gorge Trail** that follows Wildcat Creek from the playfield just south of the pony rides on Central Park Dr., goes past a 100-foot-high cliff needled with caves, and then winds around Lake Anza to the Regional Park Botanic Gardens, gaining 400 feet in elevation along one-and-a-half miles.

Lake Anza

Lake Anza was built in 1938 to provide irrigation water for the nearby golf course. Today, the sandy beach and wooden float at this nine-acre lake provide an enjoyable place for sunbathing and swimming during the summer months. Boats aren't allowed, but with a state fishing license you can try for bass, catfish, or perch (although you shouldn't expect to catch anything). On warm weekends the Park District sometimes turns

away people for a lack of space, so get there early. Lake Anza is open daily between May and October with lifeguards on duty 11 am-6 pm. Admission is $2 for adults; $1 for seniors, the disabled, and those under eighteen; 50¢ for children ages two to five; and free for tots. There's a snack bar and changing facility at the beach.

Little Farm

Adjacent to the Environmental Education Center is the Little Farm, with a half-scale barn built in 1955 by a Berkeley High School carpentry class. The farm houses a family of friendly sheep, chickens, goats, donkeys, pigs, and cows, all accustomed to humans. For many city children this is their first chance to see farm animals up close.

Little Trains

Built in 1952, the Redwood Railway provides a delightful diversion. For $1 (or $4 for five rides) the miniature engines haul gondola cars filled with

Tilden Carousel

Near the center of Tilden a beautiful antique merry-go-round thrills children and parents alike. Built in 1911 by the Herschell-Spillman Co., it was operated in Southern California until 1948, when it was sold to a Tilden Park concessionaire. The merry-go-round was put up for sale in the 1970s, and Berkeley residents launched a campaign to buy it. With $8000 in donations as seed money and a commitment from the Park District to put up the remaining $77,000, the merry-go-round was purchased and com-

Tilden carousel. Courtesy of East Bay Regional Park District.

pletely restored in 1978. The carousel is one of only 200 hand-carved wooden carousels remaining in the nation and is listed in the National Register of Historic Places. Riders choose from a zoo-full of 59 animals—zebras, camels, reindeer, frogs, giraffes, roosters, dogs, cats, pigs, storks, goats, dragons, tigers, lions, and a herd of horses. The carousel is open daily (10 am-5 pm) through the summer and on weekends and school holidays during the rest of the year. Rides are 50¢ or twelve rides for $5. A small snack bar is next door.

people one-and-a-half miles through the southern end of Tilden Park, offering views of San Pablo Bay and Wildcat Canyon. Trains run on weekends and school holidays all year and daily during the summer months from 1-6 pm. Nearby, the Golden Gate Live Steamers Club (established in 1936) has a wonderful collection of scaled replicas of the steam trains that once hauled freight and passengers throughout the nation. You can ride these models for free on Sundays (weather permitting) between 10 am and 3 pm. Call 548-6100 for details on both trains.

Pony Rides

Near the northern edge of the park you'll also find the pony rides ($1), a children's favorite since 1959. The rides are open daily (for children aged two and up) through the summer, over spring break, and on weekends during the school year. Hours are 11 am-5 pm.

Tilden Golf Course

One of Northern California's finest golf courses lies within Tilden Park. Built by the CCC in 1937, this popular eighteen-hole course charges $11 on weekends and $9 on weekdays, with discounts for late afternoon games. The clubhouse includes a snack bar and pro-shop.

Claremont Canyon Regional Preserve

A recent addition to the Regional Park system, the 200-acre Claremont Canyon Regional Preserve has no facilities, although Claremont Canyon Rd. passes through it and trails extend from the ends of Stonewall Rd. and Dwight Way. Claremont Canyon has its own historical footnote: it served as the location for the first transcontinental telegraph line. The cable was strung along a route that became known as Telegraph Rd., splitting off to head up Claremont Canyon and over the hills to the east. The routing led not only to the creation of Telegraph Ave., but also to the odd way Claremont Ave. angles away from it in Oakland. Claremont Canyon Regional Preserve is bordered by the University's Strawberry Canyon Ecological Preserve to the north; together, the two provide an extensive area of open space adjoining Berkeley. One of the most interesting and scenic trails in this magnificent preserve follows the ridge between Claremont and Strawberry canyons from the end of Panoramic Way to Grizzly Peak Blvd. in Tilden Park.

Wildcat Canyon Regional Park

Shortly after Tilden Park was established, EBMUD offered additional property to the Park District in lower Wildcat Canyon. Lacking sufficient funds, the district declined the offer, and EBMUD eventually turned to private interests in 1952. The new owners only completed an entrance road (Wildcat Canyon Parkway) and a sewer line for a massive residential development before the bucks ran out. Finally, in 1965, the Regional Park District began to purchase the 2378 acres of land that became Wildcat Canyon Regional Park in 1973. Although most of the present park has been used for ranching since the mid-19th century and cattle grazing is still allowed, Wildcat Canyon is essentially undeveloped.

Getting There
Although there is no road through Wildcat Canyon, you can drive near it by ascending Spruce St., and turning down Canon Dr. at the "Y" in the road. Bear left and park near the Environmental Education Center. (There is no direct bus service to Wildcat Canyon. From Berkeley, bus route 67 will take you to the upper end of Canon Drive. From there you can walk two-thirds of a mile to the Environmental Education Center.) The Center has park maps and information on both Tilden and Wildcat Canyon Regional parks. Follow the Jewel Lake Trail (marked with blue duck signs) a mile past the lake to the Wildcat Canyon Park entrance. The main entrance to the park can be reached by following Arlington Blvd. until it dead ends and then turning right onto Wildcat Canyon Parkway. The Parkway ends at a 50-car parking lot within the park.

Hiking and Trails
Compared to Tilden, Wildcat Canyon has fewer eucalyptus and Monterey pines and has been kept more open by cattle grazing. There are nearly a

dozen different hiking trails through the beautiful grassy knolls and densely wooded canyons. Bikes are allowed only on the paved Nimitz Way Trail, but horses may be ridden on all Wildcat trails. The Skyline National Trail covers six miles within the park, beginning at the Wildcat Canyon Parkway entrance and following the creek (via Wildcat Canyon Trail) for a mile before branching off to the Havey Canyon Trail. The Havey Canyon Trail rises through a wooded canyon to San Pablo Ridge, where it joins Nimitz Way and continues south through Tilden Park. A return loop via the Mezue Trail provides panoramic vistas of the Bay Area and pleasant grassland country.

EBMUD Watershed Lands

The East Bay Municipal Utility District owns 27,000 acres of land in the East Bay hills, including extensive watershed land around San Pablo and Briones Reservoirs bordering on Wildcat Canyon and Tilden Parks, plus smaller areas between Tilden and Sibley Regional Parks. In 1973 EBMUD opened its lands to the public with a system that now includes 55 miles of trails. Those around San Pablo Reservoir, Lake Chabot, and Lafayette Reservoir are open to the public, but in other areas you will need to purchase a permit ($5/year) from EBMUD. (Call 835-3000, ext. 237 for a list of the several locations where permits can be purchased). No dogs are allowed on any of the trails and there is no swimming in these water supply reservoirs, but horseback rid-

ing is allowed. You can fish at Lafayette Reservoir, San Pablo Reservoir, and Lake Chabot. Camping is not allowed on EBMUD land.

From Inspiration Point in Tilden Park, the two-mile Inspiration Trail drops downhill to San Pablo Reservoir, where it crosses under San Pablo Dam Road. The frontage road along the lake shoreline suffers from the noisy traffic on the nearby San Pablo Dam Road. For a more enjoyable hike turn right (south) onto the old road and follow it to the upper end of San Pablo Reservoir, where you can walk the trails around Briones Reservoir (permit required). The Skyline Trail that goes through Wildcat Canyon and Tilden Park also passes through a short section of EBMUD land just south of Tilden Park. No permit is needed to use this trail.

University Wildlands

The University owns hundreds of acres of undeveloped land in both Claremont and Strawberry canyons. Driving, bicycling, and camping are prohibited, but the many fire roads and trails offer hikers and runners excellent views of the Bay Area. One of the more interesting is the trail to the 50-foot tall concrete letter "C" (as in Cal) that faces campus (see *The University* for its origins). Access is via a dirt fire-road directly behind Stern Hall. Follow the road up the steep hill, bearing left (uphill) each time the road splits until you reach the "C."

The most popular of Berkeley's running or walking paths is in Strawberry Canyon, a quarter mile up from

Opposite: UC Botanical Garden. Photo by Don Pitcher.

the swimming pools. Follow the fire road uphill to Panoramic Way, or continue on to the Space Sciences Lab. Those with less energy can take the free shuttle bus (Mon-Fri only) from the University to Lawrence Hall of Science and walk up to the Space Sciences Lab, where the trail heads down through Strawberry Canyon.

University Botanical Garden

Established on campus in 1891, the University Botanical Garden is the oldest campus botanical garden in America. During the early years it included a magnificent glass conservatory (like the one in Golden Gate Park), but in 1924 the garden moved to the 30-acre site of the old Stutt Dairy Ranch in Strawberry Canyon and the conservatory was torn down. Today the University Botanical Garden is home to more than 8500 different species from around the world. It is divided into more than a dozen geographic regions (Australian or Mexican-Central American, for example) plus a palm garden, an herb garden, several greenhouses, and a "garden of plants for mankind." The latter section has an exhibit of dye plants, fiber plants, and the ancestors of modern vegetables such as corn. The California section (covering nearly fifteen acres) is devoted to endemics—native plants found only in a limited region. One of the most unusual is the Pygmy Forest of coastal Mendocino County, where a dense hardpan of soil slows tree growth and blocks root penetration, producing stunted trees. This garden reproduces the situation with a layer of concrete beneath imported Mendocino soil.

On the west side of Centennial Drive, a redwood grove planted in the 1930s offers a contrast between plants typical of a present-day redwood forest and, above them, shrubs and trees typical of a redwood forest in the Miocene Era.

The three public greenhouses contain plants that could not survive the Bay Area's climate. The Tropical House has banana trees, Arabian coffee bushes, taro plants, and a 95% relative humidity that is guaranteed to fog your glasses. The Fern House contains a fascinating collection of insectivorous plants as well as ferns so thick you can barely walk down the aisles. The Desert and Rainforest House has cacti and succulents at one end, and tropical plants such as flowering orchids at the other.

Strawberry Creek flows through the center of the Botanical Garden, past flowering rhododendrons (some over 50 years old), cacti from the southwest, tropical palms, and many California plants. There are a few picnic tables and an open lawn with benches facing the Golden Gate, making this a wonderful place to spend a sunny afternoon. The Botanical Garden is open daily 9 am-4:45 pm, with free docent-led tours at 1:30 on Sat and Sun afternoons (except during football home games). Group tours ($1/person) are possible Mon-Sat by advance reservation (call 642-3343). The group, **Friends of the Botanical Garden** (Centennial Drive, University of California, Berkeley, CA 94720), helps support maintenance, tours, and development of the garden. Membership costs $20/year or $7.50 for students. Every year on Mother's Day they hold a sale of plants, many that you won't find anywhere else. The University's free bus stops at the Botanical Garden on weekdays, and there is a parking lot for bikes and cars inside the gate.

Saving the Great Outdoors

Berkeley's environmental awareness stretches back into the previous century. Bernard Maybeck and other local architects began to emphasize the relationship between buildings and their surroundings in the late 1800s. Local citizens, among the most active anywhere on environmental issues, have founded many influential organizations—among them the Save the Redwoods League, East Bay Regional Parks District, Save San Francisco Bay Association, Friends of the Earth, and Earth Island Institute.

The best local source of information about the environment is the **Ecology Center** (1403 Addison St., 548-2220). Established in 1969, a year before the first Earth Day, this is the oldest ecology center in the nation, and still one of California's most effective local environmental organizations. It coordinates the city's curbside recycling program, sponsors the Berkeley Farmers Market, holds classes and meetings, and organizes petition drives on a variety of environmental matters. The free monthly newsletter (available in many local shops) includes a comprehensive calendar of upcoming meetings, walks, talks, trips, and other events. The center sells books about ecology as well as organic gardening supplies, and has nearly two dozen file drawers filled with clippings on environmental issues. Its knowledgeable staff can answer your questions, or at least steer you in the right direction for more information. Listed below are a number of other influential local environmental organizations:

- **Audubon Society**, Golden Gate Chapter, 1250 Addison St., No. 107B, 843-2222.
- **California Native Plant Society**, 2380 Ellsworth St., Suite D, 841-5575.
- **California Natural Resources Federation**, 2830 10th St., 848-2211.
- **Citizens for a Better Environment**, 2131 University Ave., 841-6163.
- **Environmental Defense Fund**, 2606 Dwight Way, 548-8906.
- **International Bird Rescue Research Center**, Aquatic Park, 841-9086 (coordinates bird rescues, especially for oil-soaked seabirds).
- **Northern California Land Trust**, 3120 Shattuck Ave., 548-7878.
- **Save San Francisco Bay Association**, 2140 Shattuck Ave., 849-3053.
- **Sierra Club**, San Francisco Bay Chapter, 6014 College Ave., Oakland, 658-7470.
- **Urban Ecology**, 1939 Cedar St., 548-7801 (involved in creek restoration and other local urban issues).

Recreation

In addition to the spate of private health clubs offering Jazzercise, Nautilus weights, big mirrors, and hard bodies, Berkeley residents can choose from activities ranging from skating on one of the largest ice rinks in the West to signing up for a research expedition in Kenya. The list below emphasizes inexpensive activities that are available to the general public.

Bicycling

In many ways, bicycles offer the best transportation in Berkeley: they provide exercise, are easier to park and often faster than cars, and don't cause pollution. Although the city produces a map listing local bike routes, many people ignore them and simply ride on streets blocked to through traffic by diverters. AC Transit does not carry bikes, except for its summertime Tilden Park routes, but BART does allow bikes during non-commute hours. Bike lockers are available at both the Ashby and North Berkeley BART stations for $30/yr. For details call 464-7133. You can also park inside the city's Center Street Garage (2075 Center Street, 644-6383) for only $1/day. CalTrans (923-4444) operates a special **Bay Bridge Commuter Bicycle Shuttle** (50¢ each way) on weekdays between the MacArthur BART Station in Oakland and the Transbay Terminal in San Francisco. CalTrans also publishes several excellent free cycling maps, including a Berkeley-to-Lake Tahoe route map, a bicycle commute map of the East Bay, and a Bay Area bike map. Cal Adventures (642-4000) rents bikes for $15/day.

A widely ignored law in California, intended to make it easier to trace stolen bicycles, requires registration of all bikes. The Berkeley Licenses Department (2171 McKinley Ave., 644-6547) and the UC Police Department (Sproul Hall, 642-6760) provide three-year licenses for $6.

Cycling Advocacy Groups

A number of organizations work to improve access for bicyclists. The **East Bay Bicycle Coalition** (P.O. Box 1736, Oakland, 94604, 452-1221) focuses on Alameda and Contra Costa counties, while the **Regional Bicycle Advisory Committee** (3313 Grand Ave., Oakland 94610, 452-1221) includes the entire Bay Area. The **Bicycle Trails Council of the East Bay** (P.O. Box 9583, Berkeley, 94709) promotes mountain biking and tries to minimize conflicts with other trail users on public lands.

Group Rides

Two excellent local clubs give you a chance to ride with other cyclists, including some of national caliber. Rides are posted at the **Missing Link** (1988 Shattuck Ave., 843-7471) and **Velosport** (1650 M.L. King Way, 849-0437), and they are listed in the free *California Bicyclist* publication available in most local bike shops. The **Berkeley Bicycle Club** (531-1400) is for the more dedicated cyclist. Almost every day of the year racers from the club take off for a 25-70 mile jaunt over the Berkeley hills, and on good

Cycling on Nimitz Way in Tilden Park. Photo by Don Pitcher.

weekends as many as 50 riders show up. Rides start from Sproul Plaza (weekends), or Velosport(weekdays). Club members take part in regional races several times a year and have weekly events during the summer. The **Grizzly Peak Cyclists** (P.O. Box 9308, Berkeley, 94709) emphasize touring rather than racing. Every weekend, the club sponsors rides which vary in length and destination and offer a more relaxed pace than the rides taken by the Berkeley Bicycle Club. The Grizzly Peak Cyclists also sponsors the popular Century ride (100 miles) in Tilden Park each summer. For the Ironman crowd, the club puts on a Triple Century ride (300 miles) where cyclists circle the Bay in 24 hours.

Local Rides

The East Bay hills offer excellent cycling for those with plenty of energy. A very popular loop is up Spruce St. to Grizzly Peak Blvd., and then back down to Berkeley via Claremont Avenue. I prefer the steeper climb up Centennial Dr. through Strawberry Canyon, with a stop at Lawrence Hall of Science for the view. For a longer ride, follow Grizzly Peak Blvd. south to Skyline Blvd. in the Oakland hills. You will eventually intersect Joaquin Miller Rd. near the East Bay Regional Parks District headquarters. From there you can either retrace your path or follow roads paralleling Highway 13 (Monterey Blvd., Moraga Ave., and Broadway Terrace). Automobile traffic can be heavy on all these roads, particularly on a sunny weekend.

You can avoid all traffic by using Nimitz Way in Tilden Park, a paved trail that provides an easy and scenic ridgeline ride. Many people drive to Inspiration Point and then cycle along the path, but purists prefer to cycle over the hill to Inspiration Point first. Grant Petersen's *Roads to Ride* (Heyday Books) is an excellent guide to local cycling routes. For information on riding trails within Tilden and other East Bay Regional Parks, call the Park District office at 531-9300.

City Recreation Centers

The City of Berkeley offers dozens of free or inexpensive recreation classes for all ages. Get a complete listing from the **Berkeley Recreation Office** in City Hall (644-8515). Berkeley also has four city recreation centers, all of which have lighted tennis courts, basketball courts, playgrounds, and spacious lawns. **Live Oak Recreation Center** (Berryman St. and Shattuck Ave., 644-8513), along Codornices Creek, includes several rooms for social meetings or arts classes. The Live Oak Theater performs plays here, and across the street you'll find art work on exhibit at the Berkeley Art Center.

In **Willard Park** (Hillegass Ave. and Derby St., 644-8517), the city maintains a small clubhouse for after-school recreation and classes.

The city's most complete recreation areas are the **James Kenney Recreation Center** (8th and Virginia Sts., 644-8511), and the **Frances Albrier Community Center** (Ward and Mabel Sts., 644-8515). The James Kenney Center has an indoor gym with an exercise and weight room. Children enjoy the whimsical frog statue in the playground. Both parks also have volleyball courts and lighted softball diamonds.

The **Martin Luther King Youth Services Center** (1730 Oregon St.,

Playing the Numbers

A surprise hot spot in Berkeley is the bingo hall at 1294 San Pablo Ave. (524-9302). Opened in 1987, the room fills up every night of the week with chain-smoking, Cheetos-munching bingo players, ready to dab away at a maze of eighteen different versions of bingo ($15). The top prize is $250. For something less brain-taxing there are pull tabs at 50¢ each. Proceeds go to local non-profit groups (which is why the place is officially called the Berkeley Community Service Center) whose volunteers staff the games, looking a bit lost in the crowd.

Bingo players at Berkeley Community Service Center. Photo by Don Pitcher.

644-6031) has a separate program of classes for kids run by the city's Young Adult Project. These include karate, basketball, sewing, and homework assistance, along with a Girl's Club and a Teen Club.

The city rents all its recreation facilities and senior centers for meetings, parties, and other events. Call 644-6530 for details.

Games

If you're interested in games of any type, a good place to start is **Games of Berkeley** (2010 Shattuck Ave., 540-7822), the largest game store in California. In addition to hundreds of different games and puzzles for sale, the store has useful bulletin boards and staff who can help you find other players.

Billiards
Billiard players will find tables in many Berkeley bars and the **ASUC Recreation Center**, but the best place to see pool sharks in action is **Town and Country Billiard Parlor** (1551 University Avenue).

Bowling
Many longtime Berkeley residents have probably never heard of the city's only bowling alley. Hidden away in the basement of the ASUC Building, the **ASUC Recreation Center** (642-3825) includes an inexpensive bowling alley, pool tables, and video games, and is open to the public. Reservations are recommended for weekend nights.

Chess
Berkeley has long been a mecca for

Victor Perez and Morton Levine playing chess outside the French Hotel Cafe. Photo by Don Pitcher.

avid chess fans, and Cal teams consistently rank among the nation's best. Chess players will often find fellow enthusiasts at **Cafe Strada** (2300 College Ave.) and the **French Hotel Cafe** (1540 Shattuck Ave.) for afternoon games. The **Berkeley Chess Club** (652-5324) holds matches every Friday at 7:30 pm in the Berkeley YMCA. Although members play USCF-rated games all the way up to the master level, they welcome drop-ins and beginners. The **Cal Berkeley Chess Club** (642-7477) has weekly tournament games at 7 pm Wednesday nights during the school year in the

Tan Oak Room (Student Union, 4th floor). They also put on chess exhibitions, tournaments, and speed chess matches.

Darts

Three Berkeley pubs have dart boards, **Pappy's** (UC campus), **Starry Plough** (3101 Shattuck Ave.), and **Albatross Pub** (1822 San Pablo Avenue). Both the Starry Plough and Albatross hold weekly competitions between players at various levels. The Albatross offers the most complete setup (six lanes) and the best atmosphere. **Loft Dart Shop** (1543 Hopkins St.) has supplies and information on other dart competitions.

Go/Dominoes

The **Berkeley Go Club** meets Thursdays at 7:30 pm in the Men's Faculty Club on campus (642-4536). The **Berkeley Lawn Bowling Club** (2270 Acton Way, 841-2174) sponsors dominoes tournaments and is a good place to challenge the best local players.

Hackey Sack

Fans will find some of America's best players in Berkeley. The **Berkeley Footbag Club** (643-8024) is an ASUC-sponsored group with participants at all levels. Drop by Lower Sproul Plaza almost any noon hour if you're interested in playing.

Lawn Bowling

Berkeley's **lawn bowling greens** (2270 Acton Way, 841-2174) are very popular with senior citizens. A city-owned facility since 1928, this is a great place to learn the old genteel sport of "bowls." Membership fees are $68-$73, but visitors are welcome any time. To protect the fragile turf, newcomers must take free etiquette lessons and wear flat-soled shoes.

Role-Playing Games

Enthusiasts will find a directory of players, club listings, and other announcements on a bulletin board at Games of Berkeley. **Gamers of Berkeley** (848-6396) is a club for

Lawn bowling. Photo by Don Pitcher.

Dungeons and Dragons and other role-playing games that meets Sundays, noon-6 pm in 85 Evans Hall on campus. Non-students are welcome. While the University is in session, the

Berkeley Campus Adventurers' Club (643-4536) has role-playing and space games for students, faculty, and staff each Saturday, noon-6 pm at 123 Dwinelle Hall on campus.

Ice-skating

Many people are surprised to find that Berkeley not only has an ice rink, but one of the largest in the western states. When it first opened in 1939, Iceland (2727 Milvia St., 843-8800) attracted crowds from all over the Bay Area. The rink has been home to some of the most famous American skating champions—Peggy Flemming, Gene Turner, and Charlie Tickner— and its St. Moritz Figure Skating Club is still considered one of the finest in the nation. Today, the aging, cavernous structure of Iceland encloses a 100 x 200-foot ice arena surrounded by benches capable of seating 3,700 spectators. They are generally empty except for a few tired skaters and daydreaming parents. On the far wall a kitschy "winter wonderland" mural looks out on skaters of all levels as they circle the ice to piped-in muzak. The rink is open daily at a cost of $4.50 for adults or $3.50 for children. Skate rental is $1. 25. Iceland also offers lessons.

Skating at Iceland. Photo by Don Pitcher.

Shuffleboard

Both **Triple Rock Brewery** (1920 Shattuck Ave.) and **Raleigh's** (2438 Telegraph Ave.) have popular table shuffleboard games.

Video Games

The best places for video games are the **Silver Ball Arcade** (2518A Durant Ave.), the **ASUC Recreation Center** (on campus), and **Town and Country Billiard Parlor** (1551 University Avenue).

Gardening

Two of Berkeley's city parks contain garden plots available to the public for private cultivation. These public gardens are complete with water systems, fences, wood chips, mulch, and sometimes tools. No pesticides or herbicides are allowed in these organic gardens. **Ohlone Park** (Hearst Ave. and M.L. King Way) has 20-30 plots available in three areas. Call the site coordinator at 841-3453 for more information. The **Peralta-Hopkins Garden**, on a small plot at this intersection, is usually full, but you can get on the waiting list by calling 525-0865. The non-profit group **Common Arts** (658-5660) maintains a community garden next to the South Berkeley Public Library (1901 Russell Street). If you are interested in the People's Park "garden," show up most any Saturday afternoon to lend a hand.

Running Trails

The most scenic of Berkeley's running paths is the **Strawberry Canyon Fire Trail**, which starts next to a small parking lot a quarter mile up from the Strawberry Canyon pools. Although many folks drive up, you can also hop on the free bus that leaves the campus from Hearst Mining Circle. The tree-draped dirt fire road climbs 685 feet in elevation over a distance of 3.75 miles. After the relatively gentle first mile, the path climbs steeply to an upper fire trail then flattens out for 1.7 miles. The upper trail offers excellent panoramic vistas and ends at the Space Sciences Lab off Grizzly Peak Boulevard. For information on other running trials in Berkeley and the Bay Area see *55 1/2 Running Trails of the San Francisco Bay Area,* by Tony Burke (Heyday Books). Races are listed in *Citysports* magazine, distributed free throughout Berkeley.

Summer Camps

Operated by the city of Berkeley since 1921, **Tuolumne Family Camp** is located in Stanislaus National Forest along the Tuolumne River, a few miles from Yosemite National Park. Campers live in tent cabins furnished with cots, mattresses, and cabinets. The staff of 30 provides family-style meals and recreational activities of all types, including fishing, hiking, swimming, and folk dancing. It's a good idea to apply early (before April) to guarantee a space in this popular camp program. The camp runs for nine weeks each summer, starting at the end of June, and is a three-generation tradition in many Berkeley families, who periodically join forces to prevent the area of the camp from being dammed as a reservoir for the City of San Francisco. **Camps, Inc.** (549-2396) operates

Cazadero Camp, located in a redwood grove along the Russian River in Sonoma County, and Echo Lake Camp in the high Sierra, just south of Lake Tahoe. "Caz" provides lively youth and family music camps; Echo Lake Camp, environmental programs. Lair of the Golden Bear (642-0221) is for those affiliated with the University or for Alumni Association members; and there are a variety of Science Camps run by Lawrence Hall of Science (642-5133). Bananas (658-0381) has a complete listing of summer camps, and *Parents Press* also runs ads for summer camps.

Summer Day Camps

In the summer, the city runs various day camps for kids from six to sixteen, as well as organized play or other activities at the city recreation centers and schools. Contact the Recreation Office (644-6530) for details on these programs.

Each summer the University offers a number of recreation camps, sports camps (intensive training in volleyball, swimming, tennis, and gymnastics), and other classes open to all kids aged six to fifteen. Call the Strawberry Canyon Recreation Area at 643-6720 for details. During the school year the YMCA runs a Kid's Club, with pre- and post-school activities and daycare at various Berkeley schools. The Y also has a Summer Kid's Club at several locations, along with other daytime and residence camp programs. For details, call the central Y at 848-6800 or the South Berkeley Y at 843-4280.

Swimming

In addition to the ever-popular Lake Anza in nearby Tilden Park, you can swim at a dozen different Berkeley pools. If you're only interested in swimming, the Y's two indoor pools are less economical than other local pools.

City Pools

Berkeley High School (Milvia St. at Durant Ave., 644-6843) has two indoor pools that are open all year to the public, though the warm (88-92°F) south pool is open only for the disabled, seniors, and Berkeley Adult School classes. The other pools in Berkeley are outdoors. The finest, King Swim Center (Hopkins St. at Colusa Ave., 644-8518) is open all year, and has an adjacent track and children's playground. Willard Swim Center (Telegraph Ave. and Derby St., 644-8519) is open from April through November, while the West Campus Swim Center (Browning and Addison Sts., 644-8520) opens only for the summer.

Berkeley's public pools cost $2/swim, $30/mo, or $25 for fifteen swims. Youth rates are 75¢ during family swim hours. There are also special rates for seniors and the disabled at Berkeley High School's south swim center. Swimming classes (also offered to disabled swimmers) and a Masters Swim Team are available. Call 644-6530 for times and other pool information. All city pools can be rented for lessons and parties.

UC Pools

On the UC campus, members of the public pay $6 for a day's access to the sumptuous black-tiled Hearst Pool in

Swimming pool at the Golden Bear Recreation Center. Photo by Don Pitcher.

the Women's Gym or to the huge 50 x 25-yd **Spieker Aquatics Complex** in the Recreational Sports Facility (2301 Bancroft Way, 642-8342). Better rates are available if you join the Cal Rec Club or take a swimming class through the Adult Sports Program (see below). Cal students can use any campus pool without charge. The University also operates two popular outdoor pools in **Strawberry Canyon** (643-6720) above campus, both of which have grassy areas for sunbathing. For the general public, access costs $3/day, or fifteen visits for $38. Alumni, faculty and staff have lower rates and can purchase special swim passes. For hardcore swimmers, the Strawberry Canyon Aquatic Masters (SCAM) program offers coached workouts, videotape training, and stroke analysis six days a week for $30/month. Swimming lessons are also available.

My favorite Berkeley pool is in the **Golden Bear Recreational Center** (642-9821) on the Clark Kerr Campus (Sports Lane, UC Berkeley). From its redwood benches or small grassy lawn you can look out over much of the Bay Area. Rates for the general public are $2.25/swim or $30 for fifteen swims.

University Sports and Recreation

Cal Sports Clubs
These clubs had their origins in 1889 when a group of students formed a Handball Club. Today the clubs offer students, faculty, and staff an alternative to intramural sports or PE classes. Most of the clubs are closed to the

Cal Adventures

If you enjoy the outdoors and want to learn new skills, check out Cal Adventures, the University's outdoor recreation program. To students and the general public it offers travel seminars and special evening slide programs, as well as dozens of classes in sailing, windsurfing, kayaking, backpacking, skiing, rock-climbing and other outdoor activities. Cal Adventures also offers longer trips, such as rafting in Peru, sea kayaking in Baha, rock climbing in Joshua Tree National Monument, Trans-Sierra ski tours, and photo workshops in Yosemite. Cal Adventures also rents skiing, camping and climbing gear at reasonable rates, and has a small bike repair shop. The notice boards here are a good place to find used gear, or to hook up with fellow climbers, kayakers, and other outdoor enthusiasts. Pick up a catalog of current classes from their office at 2301 Bancroft Way (642-4000) in the Recreational Sports Facility building. Sign up early, since the classes often fill quickly.

Cal Adventures class at the Berkeley Marina. Photo by Don Pitcher.

general public. They are supported primarily by private donations, and include more than 30 competitive sports, including badminton, boxing, cycling, fencing, frisbee, skiing, synchronized swimming, and wrestling. The level of competition varies greatly; some of the Sports Clubs have achieved national rankings, such as the men's volleyball team which won the national title in 1989. For more information call the Recreational Sports Facility (RSF) at 642-8342.

The University has a special recrea-

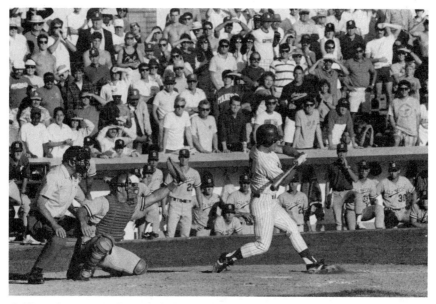

Cal/Stanford baseball game, 1988. Photo by Don Pitcher.

tion program (Cal Special Training and Recreation, or **CalSTAR**) for people with physical disabilities. RSF administers it both for UC students (free) and disabled members of the community (nominal fee). Training is specifically tailored to individual needs and includes access to hundreds of classes or activities. Call the RSF for details.

Golden Bear Clubs

The University operates a series of outstanding training programs for budding athletes in gymnastics, swimming, and volleyball. The **Golden Bear Gymnastics Club** provides a full range of gymnastics instruction and competition for boys and girls up to eighteen at the **Golden Bear Recreation Center's gymnasium** (642-9821). All classes have limited enrollment and many have long waiting lists. The **Golden Bear Swim**

Club (642-9821) uses coaches from UC Berkeley's strong aquatics staff to train young swimmers (ages 5-25) in competitive techniques. The club trains at the Golden Bear Rec Center. The **Golden Bear Volleyball Club** (643-7122) provides competition and expert coaching for young volleyball players aged eleven to eighteen at the RSF. Prices for all of these programs vary according to age and level.

Men's Intercollegiate Athletics

Although the University isn't known as a major intercollegiate sports center, Cal teams have won numerous national championships within the past decade, and over the years Cal has produced more than 100 Olympians. The strongest programs—swimming, water polo, and rugby—have collected sixteen national and NCAA titles in recent years and produced Olympic gold medal winners Matt

Biondi (1984 and 1988), Par Arvidsson (1980), and Bengt Baron (1980).

In the sport that garners most of the news media's spotlight—football—Cal doesn't have such a stellar record. While in the 1920s Cal enjoyed five years as an unbeaten "Wonder Team"—just in time for completion of the new 80,000-seat stadium in 1923—the team has not won a division championship bid to the Rose Bowl since 1959 (Cal lost to Iowa 38-12). Nevertheless, a number of well-known NFL players have attended Berkeley, including Joe Kapp, Craig Morton, Chuck Muncie, Steve Bartkowski, Vince Ferragamo, and Ray Wersching. The team's history includes a 1929 Rose Bowl loss to Georgia Tech complete with a football that collapsed when the Cal punter tried to kick it, and a 66-yard wrong-way run by a Cal player. (His teammate tackled him on the one yard line, but Georgia managed a two point safety on a subsequent blocked punt.)

Tickets for men's sporting events may be purchased at the Harmon Gym ticket office (642-5150) or at the gate, if the event is not sold out. For information on all upcoming sporting events, phone 642-5363.

The Big Game

The Big Game against arch rival Stanford has been played every year since 1892, and though both teams are frequently struggling near the bottom of the division, loyal fans turn out to fill the stadium. Like the traditional Harvard-Yale encounter, the Big Game reduces intellectual and economic rivalries between the two schools to a meaningful level—a mock war fought by helmeted soldiers on a 100-yard-long battlefield.

The symbol of this rivalry is the Stanford Axe, a red ten-pound logger's axe with an eighteen-inch blade that first appeared in the late 1890s. Stanford fans used to flourish the Axe in front of Cal, yelling, "Give 'em the Axe!" In 1899, the taunts became too much to take. Cal fans ambushed the Stanford Axe guardians in San Francisco and stole it, creating near riot as they fled back to Berkeley with the booty. For many years the Axe remained there, locked in a safe deposit box and brought out only for Big Game rallies. In 1930 Stanford fans posing as reporters recaptured the Axe: one Stanford student ignited flash powder and another threw a tear-gas bomb, while others grabbed the Axe and fled. The Cal guardians took off in hot pursuit, but the Stanford crowd escaped when a Stanford alumnus bridge operator raised the San Mateo drawbridge on pursuing Cal fans. Three years later tensions between the schools decreased (they buried the hatchet?), and it was agreed that the Axe should be awarded to the winner of each year's Big Game. Ironically, similar thefts of school mascots in the 1980s led to a repeat of the earlier events. Rivalry with Stanford remains Berkeley's longest and fiercest competition.

The best known of the Big Games was played in 1982. Both Cal and

Stanford entered the match with 6-4 records. Stanford was expecting a bid for a bowl game if it won, and this was Stanford quarterback John Elway's last college game. As the clock wound down in the fourth quarter, Stanford kicked a field goal and took the lead 20-18, and with only four seconds remaining they kicked off to Cal. The resulting Cal runback became known as "The Play," and is the stuff of legends.

Cal's Kevin Moen caught the kickoff on his 43 yard line and crossed midfield before lateralling to teammate Richard Rogers. Rogers stumbled a few more yards before handing off to Dwight Garner. It looked as though the play was over as the Stanford defense stopped Garner on the 44, but just as he was being tackled, he lateralled it back to Richard Rogers. Rogers in turn lateralled to Mariot Ford, who carried the ball to Stanford's twenty-yard line. There, things really got interesting. As Ford was being tackled, he threw the ball backwards over his shoulder without looking. The ball went straight into the arms of Kevin Moen, who was now running at full speed. The Stanford band, thinking the game was already over, had marched onto the field and were suddenly shocked to see a Cal player weaving his way through them. As Moen scored, he flattened the tuba player. The cannon on Tightwad Hill sounded, signaling a Golden Bear score. Cal had won 25-20. Complete pandemonium broke out as 75,000 fans ran onto the field in glee. The game remains perhaps the strangest finish ever to a college football game. One commentator noted that this "was the first time I ever saw a tuba player leading the interference on a touchdown—or on any other play. It appeared to me that the weakest part of Stanford's defense was the woodwinds."

Big Game, 1988. Photo by Don Pitcher.

Cal's nationally ranked women's volleyball team, 1988. Courtesy University of California, Berkeley. Photo by Rob Delaney.

Recreational Sports Facility

Campus recreation centers around the spacious Recreational Sports Facility (RSF) located at 2301 Bancroft Way (642-8342). Inside are seventeen handball and racquetball courts, five squash courts, a weight room, a 53-meter x 25-yard pool, three gymnasiums, a Jacuzzi spa, a martial arts room, a dance studio, and a pro-shop. Funded by a self-imposed student fee, RSF was completed in 1984 and became an immediate hit, making the commercial "fitness centers" look paltry by comparison. RSF charges students only a small equipment fee, but other users must pay $6/day unless they are members of the Cal Rec Club or taking a class through the Adult Sports Program. The building is usually open daily, but hours vary depending upon the academic calendar.

UC students can choose from dozens of physical education classes of all types. The University also provides sports facilities and training to the general public through its **Adult Sports Program**; costs average $50 for a six-week class (free to students). Pick up a schedule of adult classes from the RSF.

Membership in the **Cal Rec Club**

(642-8342) gives you access to all the RSF facilities plus discounts on various sports and recreation programs. Dues for community members will set you back a stiff $420/yr plus a $125 initiation fee. Alumni, faculty, and staff pay less.

University Research Expeditions Program

642-6586. This program matches folks from all walks of life with UC scholars in need of assistance on research expeditions. No special academic or field experience is necessary, but you pay for transportation and other costs (tax deductible) to help subsidize the research. UREP has projects all over the world, from excavations of Indian shell middens in California to studies of Brazilian sharecroppers. Expect to pay at least $1000 plus airfare. Meals,

Men's Spectator Sports

Sport	Season	Meet Location
Baseball	January-May	Evans Diamond
Basketball	November-February	Harmon Gym
Crew	April-June	Oakland Estuary
Football	September-November	Memorial Stadium
Golf	September-May	Orinda Country Club
Gymnastics	November-April	Harmon Gym
Rugby	January-April	Haas Field
Soccer	September-November	Memorial Stadium
Tennis	October-May	Hellman Courts
Track and Field	March-June	Edwards Stadium
Swimming and Diving	October-March	Spieker Aquatic Complex
Water Polo	September-November	Spieker Aquatic Complex

Women's Spectator Sports

Sport	Season	Meet Location
Basketball	November-March	Harmon Gym
Crew	April-May	Oakland Estuary
Cross-Country	September-November	Various locations
Field Hockey	September-November	Kleeberger Field
Gymnastics	January-April	Harmon Gym
Soccer	September-November	Kleeberger Field
Softball	February-May	Strawberry Field
Tennis	November-May	Hellman Courts
Track and Field	February-June	Edwards Stadium
Swimming and Diving	October-March	Spieker Aquatic Complex
Volleyball	September-December	Harmon Gym

lodging, research equipment, ground transportation, and camping gear are included in the costs. Most trips last approximately two weeks and require that you be in good physical condition. Call for a catalogue of current projects.

Women's Intercollegiate Athletics

The origins of Berkeley's women's sports can be traced to a basketball game with Stanford in 1896 (Stanford won 2-0). Although the programs have yielded several Olympic champions—most recently Mary T. Meagher, a triple gold-medal winner in swimming at the 1984 Olympics—women's sports have long held a back seat to men's events. Intercollegiate competition did not begin in earnest until the late 1960s, and the program was underfunded until 1976, when the Department of Women's Intercollegiate Athletics was established. It became one of the best in the nation: every Cal team has since been in national championship competition, and field hockey, soccer, swimming, and tennis teams have finished seasons in the nation's top five, although in recent seasons the field hockey team has slipped to a lower ranking.

Purchase tickets from the Women's Athletics Office in Hearst Gym (642-2098) or at the gate.

The Y's

Central YMCA

2001 Allston Way, 848-6800. Berkeley's central Y has a full complement of exercise equipment and classes available to men and women. There are swimming pools, weight-lifting facilities, a sauna and steam room, racquetball courts, and a gymnasium and dance studio. Half-price discounts on memberships are available in mid-summer and December. Individual visits are $6-8/day, depending upon facilities used. Special programs are available for children. The YMCA also has inexpensive temporary lodging for men (see *Hotels and Motels*).

South Berkeley YMCA

2901 California St., 843-4280. This Y has a games room, a meeting/exercise room, and a weight-lifting center. Classes and memberships are cheaper here than at the Central YMCA, and there are even monthly children's slumber parties to give parents a break from their kids.

University YWCA

2600 Bancroft Way, 848-6370. In contrast to the YMCA, this center emphasizes student career counseling, less strenuous exercises, health seminars, and volunteer programs. Open to both women and men, this is the place to come for aerobics, yoga, ballet, or bellydancing classes. The Career Center has job listings and research material plus a series of career and employer information programs. Membership in the YWCA is inexpensive, but there are additional charges for most programs and classes. You'll find unusual bargains here at the sale of used clothing and other items on the first Thursday of each month.

Youth Activities

In addition to the parks, centers, and camps already mentioned, there are many activities in Berkeley designed just for kids. The **Alameda/Contra**

Costa Youth Soccer League (528-1146) organizes local soccer games for all skill levels and all ages from eight to nineteen. **North Oakland Little League** (428-9844) continues this American tradition in the Berkeley area. For more listings of private organizations, contact the **Berkeley Recreation Department** (644-6530). It also sponsors youth baseball, basketball, football, and tennis programs at all of the city recreation centers.

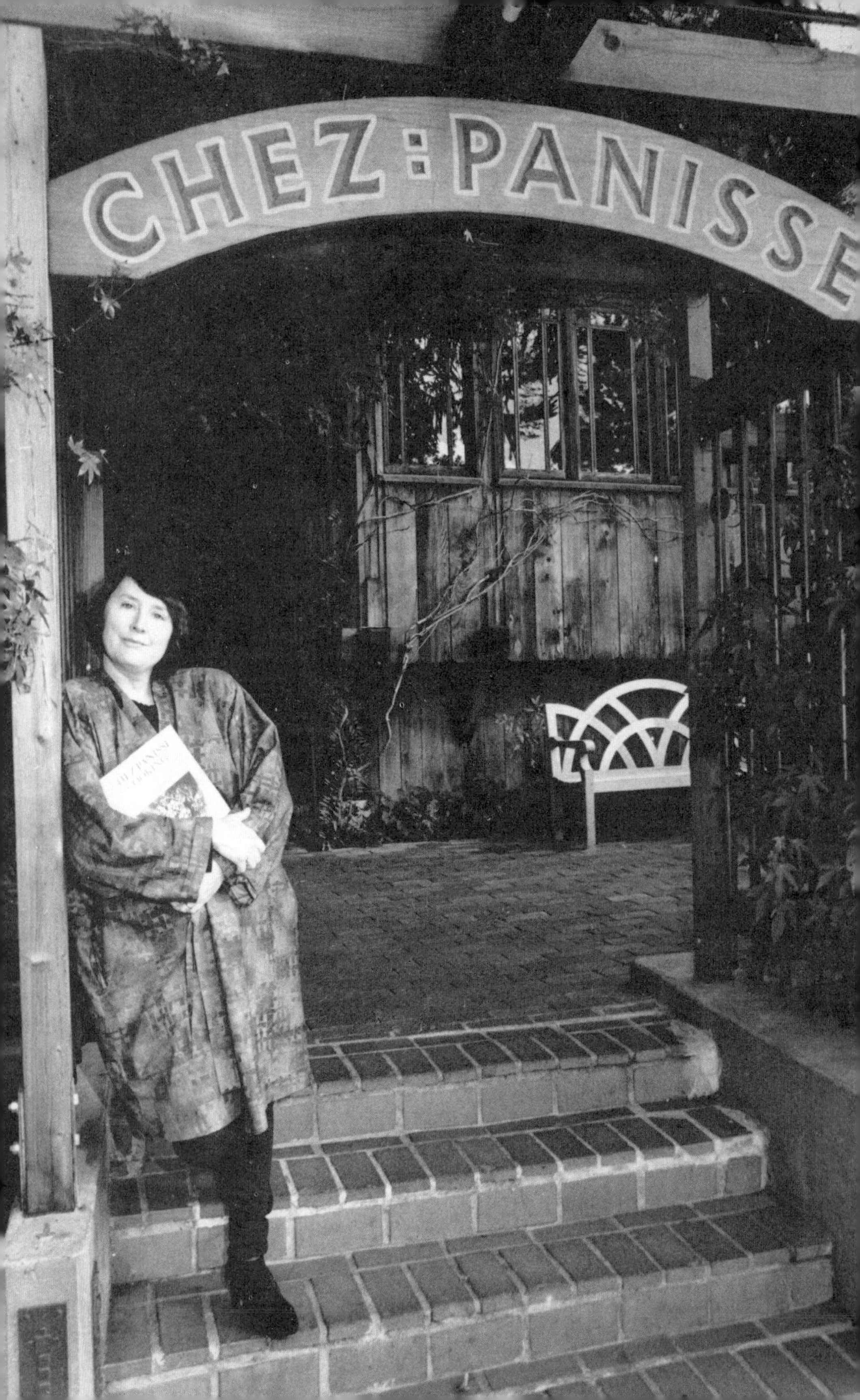
CHEZ : PANISSE

Restaurants and Cafes

On a per capita basis, the Bay Area is America's top restaurant market. Berkeley's 300 restaurants and cafes took in $118 million in 1987, an average of $1094 for each Berkeley resident. While San Francisco's comparable figure is $1910 (a number partly inflated by the higher cost of meals there and the greater number of tourists), both cities are far above the national average of just $281 per person.

Good restaurants and cafes abound in Berkeley, covering the spectrum from slap-it-on-the-counter fast food outlets to outstanding ethnic restaurants and internationally known gourmet establishments. Many of the hundred or so places described briefly below are in the less expensive price ranges, reflecting the author's personal bias (of necessity) towards affordable meals. For more detailed descriptions of Berkeley area restaurants (particularly the pricier ones), see restaurant guides such as *Restaurants of San Francisco* by Patricia Unterman and Stan Sesser, or *200 Good Restaurants* by Russ Riera.

Prices at Berkeley restaurants tend to be lower than those for equivalent meals almost anywhere else in the Bay Area. This is due to both the stiff competition among restaurants and the low income levels of students. If you're interested in saving more money, watch for discount coupons in local free papers, particularly *The Monthly* or *Bay Food*.

Because everyone's definition of "expensive" is different, I have used dollar signs to symbolize the approximate dinner costs at the restaurants listed below: $ = under $6/person; $$ = $6-$12/person; $$$ = $12-$18/person; and $$$$ = over $18/person. In general, these per-person prices assume a dinner with house wine, tip, and tax. Most places charge approximately 25% less for equivalent lunchtime meals and 35% less for breakfasts. Weekend brunches are closer to dinner prices.

Eating establishments in Berkeley tend to change frequently, particularly in Southside and North Berkeley, where expensive leases force out places that don't rake in the cash. Some corners seem to be cursed—each new place opens with great fanfare, only to be gone by year's end. In addition to the inevitable failure of some of the places listed below and the arrival of new ones, restaurants often change their chefs, ownership, or staff, transforming great places into mundane ones or bland hash houses into centers of gastronomic delight. In other words, don't take this information as the final word, but as a starting point in your exploration of Berkeley's restaurants and cafes.

Twenty years ago it would have been easy to categorize local restaurants, since they stuck to more or less traditional styles. Today, however, the borders are less definitive, particularly in places generally labeled "Cali-

Opposite: Alice Waters at Chez Panisse. Photo by Don Pitcher.

fornia Cuisine." Many of these take their inspiration from French and Mediterranean staples, but they are as likely to draw on the incendiary spices of the American Southwest or the intricate flavors of Asia, and to exploit the availability of fresh California produce. I have somewhat arbitrarily divided the restaurants into fifteen categories:

- African
- American
- Breakfast Places
- California Cuisine
- Cambodian, Korean, and Vietnamese
- Chinese
- European and Mediterranean
- Indian
- Japanese
- Mexican and South American
- Middle Eastern
- Pizzerias
- Seafood
- Thai
- Vegetarian and Natural Foods

Nearly all of the places listed below offer outstanding meals; any exceptions are noted.

AFRICAN

Blue Nile

2525 Telegraph Ave., 540-6777. Open Sun 5-10 pm; Mon-Sat 11:30 am-10 pm. $ to $$. Ethiopian food is unlike any other. The delicious and spicy stews (wat) are served on a spongy, tasty pancake (injera), and are eaten with your fingers. Sweet honey wine is a specialty. The Blue Nile has a friendly staff and a comfortable, rustic two-

Diners at the Blue Nile Restaurant. Courtesy of the Blue Nile Restaurant.

level interior. The lunch specials are a bargain.

Other Ethiopian Restaurants

The East Bay is blessed with four other Ethiopian restaurants, all fiery palate burners and well worth a visit: **Asmara**, *5022 Telegraph Ave., 547-5100,* **Cafe Eritrea d'Afrique**, *4069 Telegraph Ave., 547-4520,* **Sheba**, *3109 Telegraph Ave., 654-3741,* and **Zula**, *4909 Shattuck Ave., 654-2830.*

Casbah

1920 San Pablo Ave., 540-0784. Open Sun, Tues-Thurs 5:30-10:30 pm, Fri-Sat 5:30-11 pm. $$. No credit cards. A spacious West Berkeley restaurant with palm trees, the Casbah has the atmosphere of a Marrakesh cafe. There is live music or belly dancing on weekend evenings. Here you'll find authentic Algerian couscous and a variety of lamb dishes, plus delicious round loaves of bread, shish kebabs, and other North African specialties.

AMERICAN

Note: see also the sections on Breakfast Places, California Cuisine, Seafood, Vegetarian/Health Food for other American restaurants.

Addison Annex

2107 Addison St., 841-2156. Open Mon-Fri 7:30 am-5:30 pm; Sat 9 am-5 pm. $. Addison Annex is one of the best downtown places for a light breakfast or quick lunch of soup, sandwich, or salad. The friendly staff and reasonable prices keep the tiny cafe crowded at lunchtime with office workers and students.

Brennan's

720 University Ave., 841-0960. Cafeteria open daily 11 am-9 pm; bar open 11 am-2 am. $. The Brennan name is an old one in the Ocean View area of Berkeley: three Brennan brothers set up a livery stable and saloon here in 1878. It wasn't until 1959, however, that a grandson of one of the stable founders, retired contractor John Brennan, opened this popular barn-like cafeteria and pub. With its Irish heritage, Chinese cooks, and all-American chow, Brennan's has to be the oddest conglomeration in town, and its diverse clientele make it a fun place to meet a cross-section of Bay Area society. Along with Spenger's down the street, this is one of the few local restaurants with a union shop. If you're a fan of meat and potatoes, white bread and jello, this is the only place in Berkeley. Prices are low (especially for lunch) and portions are substantial— both the turkey and roast beef sandwiches are excellent. Brennan's is noisy, tacky, and old-fashioned, and bartenders at the huge central bar pour reasonably priced Irish coffees.

Coffee Renaissance

2512 Durant Ave., 548-6997. Open Sun-Thurs 8 am-10 pm; Fri-Sat 8 am-8 pm. $. One of the few 60s-style survivors, Coffee Renaissance still has inexpensive espresso coffees and unusual square crepes. These filled crepes make a real bargain for lunch or dinner. Get them à la carte. From the front tables you can watch the weirdness always happening on Durant Avenue.

Everett & Jones Barbeque

1955 San Pablo Ave., 548-8261. Open Sun-Thurs 11 am-2 am; Fri-Sat 11 am-3 am. $ to $$. Everett & Jones has been searing lips with its excellent hot-sauce-drenched ribs since 1973. There is now a small chain of shops, each run by one of the nine Everett daughters. The setting on San Pablo Ave. is an old drive-in with a couple of picnic tables plunked down out front and a back wall papered with corny signs. It's one of the few local restaurants open after midnight.

Fatapple's

1346 M.L. King Way, 526-2260. Open Mon-Fri 6 am-11 pm; Sat-Sun 7 am-11 pm. $ to $$. Fatapple's offers fries, desserts, and juicy hamburgers cooked over a charcoal grill and served with a choice of freshly-grated cheeses. For dessert, have a slice of Fatapple's justly famous apple pie made from tart green apples. Breakfasts include crisp buttermilk waffles, pastries, and hot Peet's coffee. There's a long wait most evenings or anytime on a weekend, but you can pick up freshly baked goods and coffee from the adjacent bakery to stave off the hunger pangs while in line.

Flint's Bar-B-Q

6609 Shattuck Ave., Oakland, 653-0593. Open Sun-Thurs 11 am-2 am; Fri-Sat 11 am-4 am. $ to $$. Just across the Berkeley line is one of the Bay Area's best barbecue restaurants. You'll find freshly-cooked ribs or hot links smothered in a sizzling sauce. The ribs come with a side of potato salad and a slice of white bread. All food is served to go.

Elmwood Pharmacy

2900 College Ave., 843-1300. Open Mon-Fri 9 am-6 pm; Sat 9 am-5 pm. $. For a taste of traditional Americana spiced up with Berkeley politics, drop by the Elmwood Pharmacy's old-fashioned soda fountain. For years one of Berkeley's favorite citizens, Ozzie Osborne , (a fighter pilot in World War II) could be found behind the counter, cutting slices of pie, mixing malts, or putting together a double-decker sandwich. When new landlords tried to force the pharmacy—a 30-year-old neighborhood fixture—out in 1981, so that they could build a shopping mall, Ozzie and his many neighborhood friends fought back. They circulated a petition for an ordinance to control rents in Elmwood, and as a result, voters passed the nation's first commercial rent control measure. Eventually, the California state legislature made all such laws illegal.

Although Ozzie retired in 1989, the pharmacy is now run by two friends, Robin Richardson and Norm Shea, who can still be found behind the counter, keeping alive American's soda fountain tradition in a city famous for its culinary revolutions.

Ozzie Ozborne's old-fashioned soda fountain at the Elmwood Pharmacy. Photo by Don Pitcher.

International House Cafe

2299 Piedmont Ave., 642-9458. Open Sun, Tues-Thurs 3 pm-12:30 am, Fri-Sat 3 pm-1 am. $. The "I House" has cheap lunches and a varied menu. In the evening, the cafe turns into a popular student pub (no meals, but great nachos), with outstanding sunset views of San Francisco Bay. While you're in the I House itself, wander around to see the Persian rugs, huge fireplace, chandeliers, and comfortable furniture ("students and their guests only"). For language tutors check the I House bulletin boards.

Sandwiches A-Go-Go

2456 Bancroft Way, 848-8271. Open Mon-Fri 7 am-5 pm; Sat 10 am-3 pm. $. When I first arrived in Berkeley more than ten years ago, Sandwiches A-Go-Go was already a source of amusement. The dated name, cheap pre-wrapped sandwiches, and aging blue exterior mark this as a survivor from an earlier time. Fortunately, the prices are also dated, making this Berkeley's cheapest sandwich shop.

Saul's Deli

1475 Shattuck Ave., 848-3354. Open Mon-Fri 10:30 am-9 pm; Sat-Sun 9:30 am-9 pm. $ to $$. Billing itself as an authentic Jewish deli, Saul's offers many favorites usually found only in New York or Chicago—lox, potato knish, beet borscht, pickled tomatoes, kishka, matzo ball soup, and blintzes. In addition to the standard restaurant items, the deli also prepares combination sandwiches to go. Try the delicious rice pudding for dessert.

Soup Kitchen Heike

2498 Telegraph Ave. Open daily 8:30 am-10 pm. $. One of the few hippie-era holdouts left on Telegraph, the Soup Kitchen serves cheap, earthy meals in a bus-your-own setting. Don't expect California Cuisine here, just sandwiches on dense homemade bread, hearty soups, and fresh salads. If you like to people-watch, find yourself a place by the large corner windows.

Stuffed Inn

1829 Euclid Ave., 849-0378. Open Mon-Fri 10:30 am-8 pm; Sat-Sun 12:30-5 pm. $. This Northside shop is one of the most popular sandwich places in town. Dish up your own soup or order one of the nourishing sandwiches. Lunch here will fill you up without thinning your wallet. The restaurant's wooden walls and tables impart a 60s-era feeling.

The Swallow

2625 Durant Ave., 841-2409. Open Sun 11 am-5 pm; Mon-Sat 11 am-8 pm. $ to $$. One of several local cooperatives that originated as an offshoot of the Cheese Board, The Swallow is a bright cafe that faces onto the sculpture garden of the University Art Museum. Get fresh quiches, pâtés, soups, salads, and a variety of sandwiches from a cafeteria-type setting. Prices are higher than other Southside eateries, but where else can you enjoy a meal while surrounded by fine sculptures and an open expanse of green grass?

Top Dog

2503 Hearst St., open roughly Mon-Fri 10 am-midnight; Sat-Sun 11 am-midnight; 2534 Durant Ave., open Sun 11 am-2 am; Mon-Thurs 10 am-2 am, Fri 10 am-3 am; Sat 11 am-3 am. $. No pretense here, just fast, cheap, and delicious hot dogs. Since 1966 the shoebox-sized Top Dog outlets have been selling several kinds of links, including German bockwurst and

Louisiana hot sausage, as well as the lowly all-beef frankfurter. The black-and-white TV is always on. Check out the various cartoons and anti-government diatribes on the wall.

Cart and Campus Food

The University campus itself has much to offer hungry students and visitors. Along Bancroft Way several carts sell burritos, Chinese dishes, falafels, pastries, coffee, and other take-away food. As the lines attest, the food is tasty and cheap. Several eating places along lower Sproul and in the Dining Commons just across the plaza offer additional choices. Wurster Hall and the Bechtel Engineering Building also have small cafes.

BREAKFAST PLACES

For many Berkeleyans, a leisurely breakfast that includes freshly baked goods and is served in a fine cafe is the only civilized way to begin the morning. Head to the Homemade Cafe, Fatapple's, or Westside Bakery and Cafe on a Saturday or Sunday morning, and you'll discover patient *Chronicle*-reading crowds waiting to enjoy a proper breakfast. Listed below are some of the best places for a breakfast out, though some also serve lunches and dinners. See "American Restaurants" and "California Cuisine" in this chapter for other places offering breakfasts and brunches. Of particular note are Augusta's, Fatapple's, Saul's Deli, and Sedona Bar and Grill. For something different, try the Chinese Sunday dim sum brunches at Long Life Vegi House and Taiwan Restaurant.

Bette's Oceanview Diner

1807 4th St., 644-3230. Open Mon 6:30 am-2:30 pm; Tues-Sun 6:30 am-4 pm. $ to $$. An extremely popular morning spot, Bette's has *chic* written all over it, from the red vinyl booths and checked floor to the shiny jukebox with 10¢ oldies. The place is a takeoff on the diners that dot America's East Coast towns. As with many renovated diners, the food at Bette's isn't especially cheap, but it is good. For breakfast, in addition to standard fare there are some real treats, such as homemade scones, banana-rum pancakes, and tasty huevos rancheros.

Brick Hut Cafe

3222 Adeline St., 658-5555. Open Mon-Fri 7:30 am-2 pm; Sat-Sun 8:30 am-3 pm. $. Originally a collectively run cafe, the Brick Hut was established by seven lesbian women and one man in the early 70s. He left in 1975 (after refusing to join an orange juice boycott in response to Anita Bryant's anti-gay statements), and the Brick Hut has been an all-female enterprise ever since. In 1982, the Brick Hut ceased to be a collective, but you'll still find substantial breakfasts served in a pleasant cafe that has exhibits of artwork on the brick walls. The omelettes and blueberry waffles are especially tempting. As with the other popular Berkeley breakfast spots, weekends mean long waits unless you arrive early.

Continental Garden Restaurant

2377 Shattuck Ave., (843-4857). Open Tues-Fri 9:30 am-2:30 pm; Sat-Sun 8:30 am-3 pm. $ to $$. This brilliant yellow false-front Victorian building built in 1886 is one of the few survivors from downtown's early days. Most breakfasts (including the house specialty, "Blue Max") arrive with Swiss-style rösti potatoes. Out back is a charming courtyard garden for weekend brunches and lazy, romantic lunches.

Gramma's Inn

2740 Telegraph Ave., 549-2145. Open Sun 10 am-2 pm. $$$$. Reservations required. Gramma's serves a terrific Sunday champagne brunch for a fixed price of $19. The quiet setting is perfect for a romantic breakfast getaway without leaving town.

Homemade Cafe

2554 Sacramento St., 845-1940. Open Mon-Fri 7 am-2 pm; Sat-Sun 8 am-3 pm. $. A simple, unpretentious place, the Homemade has the reputation as Berkeley's best breakfast spot, as the weekend crowds testify—don't get there after 8:30 on a Saturday or Sunday morning unless you're ready for a long wait. You can't go wrong ordering "the basic" with homefries and a dollop of sour cream. The coffee cakes are also outstanding. Homemade Cafe serves lunch after 11 am, though breakfasts are available anytime.

Lois the Pie Queen

851 60th St., Oakland, 658-5616. Open Wed-Fri 8 am-7 pm; Sat 8 am-3 pm; Sun 9 am-6 pm. $. Lois has a fine selection of pies (including sweet potato pie), but is perhaps better known for the heavy-on-the-fat breakfasts. For those from the South, this is one of the few places around that serves grits and homemade biscuits. Lois' place is just across the Berkeley border off Adeline Street. Check out the photos of a long-time regular, Reggie Jackson.

Mama's Royal Cafe

4012 Broadway, Oakland, 547-7600. Also at 811 San Pablo Ave., Albany, 526-6066. Both are open Mon-Fri 7 am-3 pm; Sat-Sun 8 am-3 pm. $ to $$. Neither is in Berkeley, but both Mama's are extremely popular breakfast spots for locals. The Oakland cafe has a longer heritage, a more laid-back atmosphere, and a more devoted following. Omelettes are the specialty here—there are more than 30 kinds. Watch for the annual napkin art contest that attracts an amusing array of talent.

Meal Ticket

2025 Blake St., 848-6325. Open Mon-Fri 7 am-4 pm. $. One of the lesser-known breakfast hangouts, this friendly neighborhood cafe has a diner-inspired decor of polished furnishings and a checkered floor. Try the homemade granola or tasty egg frittata, or for lunch the Texas-style chili. Because Meal Ticket lacks a stove, everything is cooked in the convection oven.

Westside Bakery and Cafe

2570 9th St., 845-4852. Mon-Fri 7 am-3 pm; Sat-Sun 8 am-2 pm. $ to $$. Surrounded by the West Berkeley blend of new and old industries, this bright, modern cafe is very popular with local workers and the weekend breakfast crowd. Westside offers freshly baked breads and pastries, thirteen different kinds of omelettes, and light lunches.

CALIFORNIA CUISINE

Note: see also restaurants listed under "European and Mediterranean."

Augusta's
2955 Telegraph Ave., 548-3140. Open Tues-Thurs 11:30 am-2:30 pm, 5:30-9:30 pm; Fri 11:30 am-2:30 pm, 5:30-10:30 pm; Sun 11:30 am-8 pm. $$$. Augusta's specializes in fresh-grilled fish and meats, but also serves delectable vegetable dishes and pastas. The atmosphere is homey and friendly, yet at the same time elegant, and the spacious back terrace is wonderful for

lazy, alfresco lunches. For something completely different, ask about the annual "unmentionable cuisine dinner" that includes turkey testicles, crickets, starlings, and duck tongues.

Cafe Fanny
1603 San Pablo Ave., 524-5447. Open Sun 8 am-3 pm; Mon-Fri 7 am-3 pm; Sat 8 am-4 pm. $$. Alice Waters (of Chez Panisse fame) named her latest culinary hit for her daughter Fanny. With Acme Bread next door on one side and Kermit Lynch Wines on the other, the parking lot fills early. Fanny offers open-faced sandwiches, tasty small

Thoughts on Running a Restaurant

When I was young I dreamed of being the chatelaine of a great, slightly shabby estate with a life of soirees and charming weekends, conversation, music and games. It just may be that having a restaurant is a socially responsible expression of that dream.

A restaurant offers a very sociable setting, a way to support many causes and pursue many interests, express your own style and feed people at the same time. That's not half bad for a way to earn a living if you don't mind working eighteen hours a day seven days a week.

But perhaps I am simply continuing a family tradition in the food industry. My great grandfather came to California in 1848 to farm in the Santa Clara Valley and my father was a sheep rancher who also grew rice, tomatoes and asparagus...and they worked long hours too.

Bonnie Hughes, owner of Augusta's restaurant. Photo by Don Pitcher.

—*Bonnie Hughes, Augusta's*

pizzas, cafe au laits served in giant bowls, and a variety of other light meals to be eaten standing at the counter or sitting on the benches. The tiny cafe fills quickly at lunchtime.

Cafe Pastoral

2160 University Ave., 540-7514. Open Sun 5-9:30 pm; Tues-Thurs 11:30 am-2:30 pm, 5:30-10 pm; Fri 11:30 am-2:30 pm, 5:30-10:30 pm; Sat 5:30-10:30 pm. $$$. Many pricey Berkeley restaurants offer California Cuisine, but few with as much class as Cafe Pastoral. Its co-owner and chef San-Ju Dong, a painter, emphasizes the value of food as a work of art (portions tend to the small side, however). Bright paintings and a floor splashed with colors give the airy restaurant a gallery-like feeling. Try the Korean chicken salad for lunch. This is a nice cafe for lunches or special evening meals.

Chez Panisse

1517 Shattuck Ave., 548-5525. Open Tues-Sat with 6, 6:30, 8:30, and 9:15 pm seatings. $$$$: Fixed price of $55 (plus wine, tax, and tip). Everyone who has spent time in Berkeley knows of Chez Panisse, the city's claim to gastronomic fame; fewer have been able to afford to try it. Chez Panisse's menu changes daily, forcing the chef to come up with new and unusual combinations. In spite of its high prices, the restaurant is so popular that weekend reservations should be made up to three months in advance. Located in a lovely old home in North Berkeley, Chez Panisse is one of the few dress-up places in town.

Chez Panisse Cafe

1517 Shattuck Ave., 548-5049. Open Mon-Fri 11:30 am-3:30 pm, 5-11:30 pm; Sat 11:30 am-4:30 pm, 5-11:30 pm. $$$

to $$$$. For those who cannot afford the acclaimed Chez Panisse restaurant, an upstairs cafe serves similarly grand meals at more accessible prices ($15-$20 per person). The cafe's menu changes daily, but it always includes calzones and pizzas (baked in a wood-fired oven), fresh pastas, and salads. This is California Cuisine at its best. Reservations for the cafe (highly recommended) can only be made for lunch, so expect a long wait during peak hours.

Christopher's Cafe

1843 Solano Ave., 526-9444. Open Sun 5:45-9:15 pm; Mon-Thurs 11:30 am-2:15 pm, 5:45-9:15 pm; Fri 11:30 am-2:15 pm, 5:30-10 pm; Sat 5:30-10 pm. $$$ to $$$$. I must confess an aversion to the starkly-modern design that permeates Christopher's and many other local California Cuisine restaurants. Here it is expressed in the splashy neon sign out front, the bright art on white walls, and chefs in an open kitchen preparing mesquite-grilled foods. But even fellow cynics will find the food here of exceptional quality and variety. The menu changes daily and covers an eclectic choice of appetizers and entrees that blend Far Eastern and Southwest American styles. The house specialty, sauteed marinated Chinese lamb, and the exceptional fish dishes are worth trying. For quality fare at lower prices (everything under $5), try **Christopher's Nothing Fancy Cafe** at 1019 San Pablo Ave., Albany, 526-1185.

Fourth Street Grill

1820 4th St., 849-0526. Open Sun 5-9:30 pm; Mon-Thurs 11:30 am-2:30 pm, 5:30-9:30 pm; Fri 11:30 am-2:30 pm, 5:30-10:30 pm; Sat 5-10:30 pm. $$$ to $$$$. One of the Bay Area's best known purveyors of mesquite-grilled meats and other California Cuisine, Fourth Street Grill dishes up consistently high quality meals. Choose from a wide variety of daily specials. Portions tend to be small. Fourth Street Grill is often crowded, so reservations are highly recommended. Its appealing interior includes fine artwork, and a bright enclosed patio. Owner Susie Nelson (like Alice Waters at Chez Panisse) once taught at Berkeley Montessori School.

Lalime's

1329 Gilman St., 527-9838. Open Mon-Thurs 5:30-9:30 pm; Fri-Sat 5:30-10:30 pm. $$$$. Fixed price Fri-Sat ($30), or Mon ($18); standard menu on other days. One of the newest of Berkeley's many California Cuisine restaurants, Lalime's gets raves from both critics and patrons. The constantly changing menu blends Mediterranean and Far Eastern flavors, and the wine list is unusually varied. Monday night regional dinners are a real bargain.

Omnivore

3015 Shattuck Ave., 848-4346. Open Sun 5-9 pm; Mon 5:30-10 pm; Wed-Sat 5:30-9:30 pm. $$$. The food at this neighborhood restaurant is just what the name implies—a selection of the best in California Cuisine, including both vegetarian and non-vegetarian meals. Omnivore's specialty is mesquite-grilled fish cooked in a central open kitchen and served in a rustic (but noisy) exposed-wood dining room.

Panini

2115 Allston Way, 849-0405. Open Mon-Fri 7:30 am-5 pm; Sat 9 am-4 pm. $ to $$. No smoking. Located in Trumpetvine Court, Panini offers creative gourmet sandwiches at surprisingly affordable prices. Fresh Semifreddi sourdough baguettes are sliced and topped with sun-dried tomatoes, roast beef, artichoke hearts, fresh spinach, home-cooked chicken, or various cheeses. The restaurant also serves soups, salads, and desserts. Eat at tables inside the airy cafe or outside in the vine-bedecked courtyard.

Sedona Grill and Bar

2086 Allston Way, 841-3848. Open Mon 11:30 am-2:30 pm; Tues-Fri 11:30 am-2:30 pm, 5:30-9:30 pm; Sat 5:30-9:30 pm; Sun 10 am-2 pm, 5:30-9:30 pm. $$$$. When the Shattuck Hotel was remodelled in 1986, the restaurant was turned into an elegant space with food to match its revitalized decor. Everything is fresh and innovative, and the menu includes an ever-changing variety of meals with a Southwest flavor. Desserts are also a strong point. For a special Sunday brunch, order the huevos rancheros. (The restaurant was originally known as Dakota Grill and Bar; litigation from a Dallas chain restaurant, Dakota Club, forced adoption of the new name Sedona in 1988.)

Skates

100 Seawall Dr. (at the Marina), 549-1900. Open Sun 10:15 am-3 pm, 4-10 pm; Mon-Sat 10:15 am-3 pm, 5-10 pm. $$$ to $$$$. Trendy—that's the only way to describe Skates. House specialties are fresh fish and pasta, but the menu offers everything from sushi to mesquite-grilled ribs. The food is well-cooked, however, and window seats provide panoramic views of San Francisco Bay from both the restaurant and the rather noisy cocktail lounge. Expect a high-spirited, chic crowd. Reservations are recommended.

A Revolution in Cooking

Until the late 1970s Berkeley was something of a culinary backwater, the food indistinguishable from that of dozens of other college towns. Today, the city offers a remarkable range of creative restaurants, some considered among the finest of their kind. Central to this transformation are Alice Waters and the restaurant she founded, Chez Panisse.

After graduating from UC Berkeley in 1967, Alice Waters worked as a teacher in Missouri and spent a year in France. Her formal training in food preparation consisted of waitressing and a few odd jobs at fast food places, so when she and two partners approached local banks to request a start-up loan for a new Berkeley restaurant, they were practically laughed out the door. Turning instead to friends and relatives for money, they opened Chez Panisse in 1971.

During her travels, Alice Waters had been impressed by a meal at a small French inn that served truly local food—fresh trout caught in a backyard creek and wild strawberries from the creek bank. She tried to repeat that experience at Chez Panisse with a limited menu that changed daily and offered only what was fresh that day. It was the sumptuousness of French cooking with a fresh California twist. Seeking a handle, people began calling it "California Cuisine," or "Nouvelle California Cuisine," or "New American Cuisine."

It didn't take long for people to discover Chez Panisse (especially with dinners in the early days for only $8.50), and when enthusiastic restaurant critics also wandered in, its popularity sky-rocketed. Chez Panisse soon spawned a legion of imitators around the country, as the idea of using the freshest ingredients caught the fancy of those whose taste buds had been dulled by traditional fare.

Chez Panisse has since become somewhat of a launching pad for chefs, producing Jeremiah Tower (Star's in San Francisco), Judy Rodgers (Zuni Cafe in San Francisco), Anne Isaak (New York's Petaluma), Lilly Lecocq (La Farine Bakery), Charlene Rollins (formerly of Boonville Hotel), Mark Miller (Coyote Cafe in Santa Fe), and Steve Sullivan (Acme Bread). Paul Bertolli, the chef at Chez Panisse since 1982, has added a Mediterranean emphasis. The restaurant's success has conferred celebrity status on Alice Waters and has led to three cookbooks. Coinciding with (and in part owing to) Chez Panisse's rousing success, gourmet foodshops proliferated in North Berkeley, leading to the area's nickname "Gourmet Ghetto."

CAMBODIAN, KOREAN, VIETNAMESE

The Cambodiana's
2156 University Ave., 843-4630. Open Mon-Thurs 11:30-9:30 pm; Fri 11:30-10 pm; Sat noon-10 pm. $$. Head to Cambodiana's for authentic, spicy Cambodian dishes. The delicious beef brochettes are a house specialty. Lunches are an excellent bargain.

The Milvia
2237 Milvia St., 644-1343. Open daily 11:30 am-2:30 pm, 5-10 pm. $$. This tiny restaurant just across from Berkeley High offers a varied selection of Korean, European, and American dishes in a pleasant semi-formal setting. Try the huge mushroom burger or the tasty Korean ribs served with rice and kimchee. A lovely courtyard patio in the back is perfect for sunny days.

Viet Nam Village
2521 Durant Ave., 845-1626. Open Sun 11 am- 9:30 pm; Mon-Fri 11 am-11 pm (closed Saturday). $. For authentic, cheap Vietnamese cooking with no MSG, head to this hole-in-the-wall restaurant in Southside's grimy Durant Center. Service is quick and the friendly staff pile your plastic plate high. Each table is topped by a veritable village of spicy sauces.

CHINESE

Note: see "Vegetarian/Health Food" for two other Chinese restaurants—Long Life Vegi Food and Vegi Food.

Hong Fu
2126 Center St., 845-4020. Open Mon-Thurs 11 am-9:30 pm; Fri-Sat 11 am-10 pm. $ to $$. Hong Fu is relatively unknown in spite of its low prices, tasty Chinese dishes (try the spicy eggplant), and unusually friendly service. The lunch specials make this an excellent place to stuff yourself for almost nothing, and almost everyone takes a doggie bag home after the huge dinner portions.

Hong Kong Villa
2042 University Ave., 486-8328. Open daily 11 am-10 pm. $$. Most folks know Hong Kong Villa for its distinctive front windows filled by hanging roast ducks with their heads flopped over their shoulders. Food here is not as spicy as other local Chinese restaurants and is served with lighter sauces. House specialties include BBQ pork, Hong Kong-style roast duck, and unique won ton noodles. Check the blackboard for daily specials.

Lilly's
1580 Hopkins St., 526-3127. Open Tues-Sat 11:45 am-2:30 pm, 5-9:30 pm; Sun 5-9:30 pm. $$. Tucked away near Monterey Market, this small restaurant has wonderfully spicy Hunan Chinese cooking. The pork dishes, onion pancakes, and hot and sour chicken are all outstanding. Try the popular take-out lunch counter.

Oriental Food-to-Go
1782 Shattuck Ave., 644-1005. Open M-Sat 10:30 am-10 pm. $. Oriental Food-to-Go has Berkeley's cheapest Chinese lunches and dinners. Everything is under $3, and the food is surprisingly good and filling. There are several tables inside for those who want to eat there instead of taking the food home.

Rich Potsticker House

1428 San Pablo Ave., 528-2013. Open Mon-Sat 11 am-9 pm. $. It's hard to miss this fluorescent pink West Berkeley restaurant. Popular with locals for lunch, it's a friendly, inexpensive place where you can get potstickers (made with homemade potsticker skins) or a full meal. Eat on the side patio to savor the vigorous, up-and-coming ambience of San Pablo Avenue.

Shin Shin

1715 Solano Ave., 526-4970. Open Sun-Thurs 11:30 am-9:30 pm; Fri-Sat 11:30 am-10 pm. $ to $$. Shin Shin produces some of Berkeley's finest and most reasonably priced Chinese food. The potstickers, sweet garlic chicken, prawns with black bean sauce, and anything with fresh crab are all excellent. Expect good service in a decor of hanging lamps and black-painted mirrored walls.

Taiwan Restaurant

2071 University Ave., 845-1456. Open Sun 10:30 am-11:30 pm; Mon-Thurs 11:30 am-11:30 pm; Fri-Sat 10:30 am-2 am. $$. With some of the longest hours of any Berkeley restaurant and a wide choice of Taiwanese-style cooking, this is one of the most popular Chinese places in town. Service is always quick. Try the unusual Chinese brunch on weekends.

Tsing Tao

1767 Solano Ave., 526-6223. Open Sun-Thurs 11:30 am-9:30 pm; Fri-Sat 11:30 am-10 pm. $$. One of the best Chinese restaurants in Berkeley, Tsing Tao offers good prices and a variety of regional styles. Try their Kung-Pao chicken or their spinach with garlic.

EUROPEAN AND MEDITERRANEAN

Note: also see restaurants listed under California Cuisine and Pizza.

À la Carte

1453 Dwight Way, 548-2322. Open Sun-Thurs 6-9 pm; Fri-Sat 6-10 pm. $$$ to $$$$. One of the smallest and least known French restaurants in the East Bay, À la Carte is a charming neighborhood place with a menu that changes each month. The restaurant serves a wide variety of uncommon and delicious French dishes in an unpretentious romantic atmosphere.

Bertola's

4659 Telegraph Ave., Oakland, 547-9301. Open Sun 4-10 pm; Mon-Fri 11:30 am-2:15 pm; Sat 4-11 pm (bar open daily 11 am-10 pm). $ to $$. For more than half a century Bertola's has been dishing up family-style Italian meals and drinks at prices that can't be beat. The food isn't great (tolerable spaghetti and iceberg lettuce salad), and the interior is rather dingy, but you get massive quantities. Bertola's was a hangout for Mario Savio and others in the Free Speech Movement and is still popular with Cal students. It's friendly and loud, but you may have to wait awhile for a table.

Britt-Marie's

1369 Solano Ave., Albany, 527-1314. Open Tues-Sat 5:30-11:30 pm. $$ to $$$. While there are many good neighborhood cafes in the Berkeley area, Britt-Marie's ranks near the top of everyone's list. It has the friendly, informal atmosphere of a European cafe and fine food that includes a rich Hungarian goulash, outstanding roasted chicken, and luscious desserts. Regulars come to Britt-Marie's to taste appetizers while sampling wines at the bar.

Cafe Vin

1887 Solano Ave., 527-9313. Open daily 8 am-10 pm. $. Cafe Vin is one of Berkeley's lesser known gems. In a simple interior of checked plastic tablecloths, old posters, and a blackboard menu, you can have homemade calzones, fresh pasta, veal, or salads, served in generous portions for low prices. The coffee-shop atmosphere makes this a pleasant place to relax with friends. Cafe Vin's mocha (they call it a Piccadilly) is the best in town.

Caffe Giovanni

2420 Shattuck Ave., 843-6678. Open Sun-Thurs 11:30 am-11:30 pm; Fri-Sat 11:30 am-12:30 am. $$. One of the most popular Italian restaurants in Berkeley, Caffe Giovanni serves the old standbys along with a variety of salads, burgers, and mesquite-grilled meats. The pasta is freshly made on the premises. House specialties include cannelloni alla toscana and eggplant parmigiana. The restaurant has a dark interior and a homey, friendly feeling. The bar is a good place to relax while tasting wines or the many specialty drinks.

Caffe Venezia

1903 University Ave., 849-4681. Open Mon-Fri 11 am-2 pm, 5-10 pm; Sat-Sun 5-10 pm. $$ to $$$. No smoking. Caffe Venezia is a good place to sample fresh pastas with a variety of sauces. The interior is an amusing re-creation of an Italian village, complete with a central fountain and a clothesline that crosses the room. It is somewhat noisy, and you can expect a long wait on weekend evenings (they don't take reservations), but the food is excellent. Beat the queue by signing up in the Caffe and then heading across the street to Ristorante Venezia for a glass of wine. The Caffe will call when a table is ready.

Metropole

2271 Shattuck Ave., 848-3080. Open Mon-Thurs 11:30 am-4 pm, 5:30-10 pm; Fri 11:30 am-4 pm, 5-10:30 pm; Sat-Sun 5-10:30 pm. $$$$. Metropole is housed in one of the loveliest old buildings in downtown Berkeley, a vine-covered brick structure topped by a horn-blowing figure. Popular with the suit-and-tie crowd, the restaurant serves traditional French cuisine at Parisian prices. Downstairs is a popular cocktail lounge, **Cafe Bistro**, open daily 1 pm-1 am (see *Nightclubs and Bars*).

Nadine's

2400 San Pablo Ave., 549-2807. Open Sun 5:30-9 pm; Mon-Thurs 11 am-2 pm, 5-9 pm; Fri-Sat 11 am-2 pm, 5:30-9:30 pm. $$-$$$. One of the lesser known Berkeley restaurants, Nadine's is a large maroon building with an attractive California-modern decor and reasonably priced, delicious European cuisine. Nadine's also has a pleasant wine/espresso bar in front. The restaurant seems a bit out of place on San Pablo Avenue.

Oliveto Cafe & Restaurant

5655 College Ave., Oakland, 547-5356. Restaurant open Mon-Fri 11:30 am-2 pm, 6-10 pm; Sat 6-10 pm. Cafe open Sun 8 am-10 pm; Mon-Thurs 7 am-11 pm; Fri 7 am-midnight; Sat 8 am-midnight. $$ to $$$. This attractive Mediterranean-style restaurant specializes in Northern Italian cooking—owner Maggie Klein even wrote a book called *Feast of* *the Olive.* Downstairs a pleasant cafe/wine bar serves tapas and pizzas along with wine and espresso drinks. The upstairs restaurant serves creative Italian, French, and Spanish country cooking. The surrounding shops of "Market Hall" give this corner an upper-crust European flavor. This is a good place to hang out with university professors and other professionals.

Petrouchka

2930 College Ave., 848-7860. Open daily 11 am-10 pm. $$. Located in the heart of Elmwood, Petrouchka specializes in Russian food, offering both traditional meaty cooking and a variety of vegetarian dishes. The fresh borscht with homemade black bread is a real bargain if you want a light meal. For a taste of Eastern Europe, order the Romanian and Hungarian wines or Czechoslovakian and Polish beers. Petrouchka has live piano music most evenings. On weekends it is usually crowded.

Ristorante Venezia

1902 University Ave., 644-3093. Open Sun 5-9 pm; Tues-Thurs 5:30-9:30 pm; Fri-Sat 5:30-10:30 pm. $$$ to $$$$. No smoking. Compared to its cousin Caffe Venezia across the street, Ristorante Venezia has a more formal setting, a larger wine selection, more fish and meat dishes, and commensurately higher prices. Like its cousin, Ristorante Venezia has an interior that mimics an Italian street scene, with clothes hanging across the rear of the room. The food here is also consistently delicious. On Tuesday evenings you can listen to live opera performances while dining ($1 cover charge). On other nights, this is one of the few quiet, romantic restaurants in town.

INDIAN

Bombay Cuisine

2006 9th St., 843-9601. Open Tues-Thurs 11:30 am-2:30 pm, 5-9 pm; Fri-Sun 11:30 am-3 pm, 5-9:30 pm. $$. A pleasant small restaurant in Berkeley's "Little India," Bombay Cuisine offers vegetarian and non-vegetarian dinners for reasonable prices. The full dinners (served on compartmentalized trays) are cheaper than à la carte orders. The owners also operate the Indian grocery and spice store next door.

Indian Cafe

1810 University Ave., 548-4110. Open Mon-Sat 11:30 am-3 pm, 5-9 pm. $ to $$. You reach the Indian Cafe, one of Berkeley's least expensive North Indian restaurants, after trekking through aisles filled with cans of Indian vegetables, bins of spices, and racks of Indian cloth and up a flight of stairs. The cafe serves vegetarian and non-vegetarian dinners, and tasty mango custard or mango ice cream for dessert. It's rarely crowded.

Maharani

1025 University Ave., 848-7777. Open Sun-Thurs 11 am-9 pm; Fri-Sat 11 am-10 pm. $$. In the last several years lower University Ave. has attracted many Indian shops and restaurants, making this a major center for Indian culture in the Bay Area. One of the best of the restaurants, Maharani, serves superb, moderately priced North Indian dinners in an attractive, romantic setting. There is also an all-you-can-eat buffet lunch for only $5 on weekdays. The selection in the authentic Indian sweet shop is said to rival any in Bombay. Racks of pastries, colorful sweets, and mixed dry snacks (very spicy) fill a long counter.

If you haven't tasted Indian sweets, be forewarned that they exceed baklava on the sweetness scale.

New Delhi Junction

2556 Telegraph Ave., 486-0477. Open Tues-Thurs 11:30 am-2 pm, 5:30-9 pm; Fri-Sun 11:30 am-2 pm, 5:30-9:30 pm. $$ to $$$. Surrounded by several undistinguished Southside eateries, New Delhi Junction is a small but increasingly popular North Indian restaurant. The cooks prepare house specialties such as spicy eggplant or chicken in a traditional Tandoori oven. Lunch is a particularly good bargain.

Pasand Madras Cuisine

2286 Shattuck Ave., 549-2559. Open daily 11 am-10:30 pm. $$. The best-known Indian restaurant in Berkeley, Pasand serves consistently good South Indian food for a very reasonable price. If you're in a hurry, however, head elsewhere, since service can be slow at times. Pasand's tasty curries are not too spicy, and there's a sweets counter for desserts. Live Indian sitar music is played every evening from 6:30 to 9:30, and an adjacent lounge offers live jazz Monday through Saturday evenings (see *Nightclubs and Bars*).

Sujatha's

48 Shattuck Square (University and Shattuck Aves.), 549-1814. Open daily 11 am-10 pm. $$. This spacious restaurant includes a glass-enclosed side room, a large balcony, and a main room with a large sweets counter and a platform for live sitar performances. Sujatha's serves some of the best Indian food in Berkeley. Prices are reasonable, and the spices are used more sparingly than in other local Indian establishments.

JAPANESE

Daruma Teashop

1290 6th St., 528-3435. Open Mon-Fri 11 am-2 pm for lunches, followed by afternoon tea 2-6 pm. $$. A combination Japanese tea shop, cafe, and tea cake outlet, Daruma is the place to go for creative bento lunches served in a wooden box, or for a cup of fine Chinese tea and delicious tea cakes. Through a glass window you can watch the bakers make the tea cakes. Daruma's owner, David Vardy, spent several years in Taiwan and Japan, studying Tai Chi, Buddhism, and the traditional Japanese tea ceremony of Kaiseki. After returning to the U.S., he opened a tea cake bakery that eventually expanded into Daruma Teashop. The shop also sells a wide variety of bulk teas and several kinds of tea cakes to go.

Joshu-Ya

2441 Dwight Way, 848-5260. Open Mon-Sat 10:30 am-3 pm, 5-10 pm; Sun

David Vardy at Daruma Teashop. Photo by Don Pitcher.

5-10 pm. $$. Joshu-Ya offers a wide variety of Japanese foods in a setting that is serene in spite of its hectic Southside location. In addition to sushi, tempura, sukiyaki, and teriyaki, the menu includes a "hot rock" special (literally). Prices are lower than most Japanese restaurants, and the food is good (avoid the house tea, however). Joshu-Ya has an exterior patio as well as two low tables where you can dine in the traditional Japanese style.

Kirala

2100 Ward St., 549-3486. Open Tues-Fri 11:30 am-2 pm; 5:30-10 pm; Sat 5:30-10 pm; Sun 5-9 pm. $$. This popular restaurant has a pleasant ambience, excellent food, and courteous service. Housed in an industrial building, the interior is modern, white, and upscale. The huge tea mugs shaped to fit in your hand are a pleasure; the appetizers from the Robata bar grill are excellent.

Sushi-Ko

64 Shattuck Square, 845-6601. Open Mon-Thurs 5:30-9:30 pm; Fri-Sat 5:30-10 pm. $$ to $$$. A friendly and lovely downtown restaurant, Sushi-Ko offers both full Japanese fare and an outstanding sushi bar. The lunch specials are a good bargain.

Sushi Sho

1645 Solano Ave., 525-4551. Open Tues-Sun 5:30-10 pm. $$ to $$$. This Thousand Oaks restaurant serves some of the finest sushi in the East Bay, along with other Japanese specialties, in an attractive and spacious interior.

Yoshi's

6030 Claremont Ave., Oakland, 652-9200. Restaurant open daily 5:30-10 pm.

Sushi Bar open daily 5:30-midnight. $$$. Yoshi's is best known for its jazz club (see *Nightclubs and Bars*), but there is also a complete restaurant and sushi bar with a good selection of Japanese food. You can eat at low tables in their traditional Japanese dining room.

MEXICAN AND SOUTH AMERICAN

Amaru

2037 Shattuck Ave., 549-7075. Open Sun 5-9 pm; Tues-Sat 5:30-10 pm. $$ to $$$. If you're looking for something out of the ordinary, Amaru offers a wide variety of South American and Spanish dishes. Parilla (Argentinian barbecue) and Spanish paella are house specialties, and be sure to taste the South American beers and wines. Linen tablecloths and wine goblets at each table mark the pleasant decor. Amaru has live music on Friday and Saturday evenings.

¡Ay Caramba!

1901 University Ave., 843-1298. Open Sun-Fri 11:30 am-9 pm; Sat 11:30 am-10 pm. $. No smoking. Mexican fast food gets a holistic kick in the pants here. ¡Ay Caramba! uses lard-free beans, brown rice, and other fresh ingredients to pack gigantic burritos and tacos. Patrons waddle away happily filled. The cilantro-laced salsa atop each table is homemade and lively on the tongue. ¡Ay Caramba! is owned by the folks who bring you several other successful Berkeley establishments—Caffe Venezia (next door), Ristorante Venezia (across the street), and Westside Bakery and Cafe.

Cactus Taqueria

5940 College Ave., Oakland, 547-1305.

Outdoor Dining in Berkeley

The following Berkeley restaurants, cafes, and coffeehouses (described elsewhere, with addresses) have patios that provide a lovely setting for sunny lunches or summer evening meals.

- Augusta's
- Berkeley Thai House
- Cafe Strada
- Continental Garden Restaurant
- Gertie's Chesapeake Bay Cafe
- Gramma's
- Joshu-Ya

- La Méditerranée
- La Val's
- The Milvia
- Nadine's
- Panini
- Rich Potsticker House
- Santa Fe Bar & Grill
- The Swallow

The patio behind Augusta's restaurant. Photo by Don Pitcher.

Open Sun noon-9 pm; Mon-Sat 11 am-10 pm. $. Try lunch and dinner here in an amusing pseudo-desert environment of pastel colors and wooden cacti. California-style burritos, tacos, and tostadas are well prepared, and you can choose from nine different fillings such as chicken with smoked pork and ancho chilies or marinated roasted lamb and veal. Top them off with a choice of spicy salsas.

Cafe Violeta

3105 Shattuck Ave., 843-0662. Open Tues-Sun 5:30-9:30 pm. $. No smoking. Cafe Violeta is a part of La Peña, the long-time Latin American cultural center in Berkeley (see *Nightclubs and Bars*). Inside this brick-walled cafe you'll find a fine choice of south-of-the-border food, including the house specialty, Chilean empañada. There are also vegetarian dishes and à la carte bargains such as gazpacho or Cuban black bean soup with corn bread. Check the bulletin board for upcoming talks, films, protests, and other events dealing with Central and South American issues.

Casa de Eva

2826 Telegraph Ave., 540-9092. Open Tues-Fri 11 am-9:45 pm; Sat 3:30-9:45 pm. $$. Casa de Eva's interesting menu and consistent quality make it popular. This is authentic Mexican fare: chalupas (made with homemade chorizo sausage), flautas, homemade tamales, and even fresh fruit punch. The restaurant has an attractive interior of tiled walls and an open kitchen.

Guerrero's

2504 Shattuck Ave., 548-9830. Open Mon-Fri 11 am-8:50 pm; Sat 5-8:50 pm. $ to $$. One of the lesser-known Mexican restaurants in Berkeley, Guerrero's offers reasonable prices, huge portions, and fast service. The food in this tiny downtown eatery is on a par with places that charge considerably more.

Juan's Place

941 Carleton St., 845-6904. Open Mon-Fri 11 am-10 pm; Sat-Sun 1-10 pm. $ to $$. Hidden away in industrial West Berkeley, Juan's is not the kind of restaurant you accidentally stumble upon. Word of mouth brings folks here from all over the East Bay. The fast service and authentic Mexican food served in heaping portions make Juan's worth the long wait you can expect on weekends. Family-run Juan's is a Berkeley institution that everyone should visit.

Manuel's

2521 Durant Ave., 849-1529. Open Sun-Thurs 11 am-1 am; Fri-Sat 11 am-2 am. $. Durant Center is a cluster of grubby takeaway food joints oriented toward University students. Some aren't worth a passing glance, but Manuel's has huge tasty burritos and tostada salads along with cheap pitchers of cold beer. If you want food late at night this is the place to come, but be ready for a loud, hard-drinking fraternity crowd.

Mario's La Fiesta

2444 Telegraph Ave., 848-2588. Open daily 10:30 am-10:30 pm. $ to $$. Mario's is perpetually jammed with hungry folks. The Mexican food is good, portions are generous, prices are reasonable, and service is speedy. The budget-conscious order à la carte dishes and fill up for $4, including a beer! Ordering this way also lets you avoid Mario's tasteless soup.

Pepito's Mexican Deli

2200 San Pablo Ave., 845-0659. Open Mon-Fri 10 am-7 pm; Sat 10 am-6 pm. $. This busy corner shop serves authentic Mexican fast food in mass quantities—burritos, tacos, nachos, and other traditional fare. Pepito's also has Mexican pastries and spices, along with inexpensive packages of tortillas and taco shells.

Picante Taqueria and Cantina

1328 6th St., 525-3121. Open Sun noon-9 pm; Mon-Thurs 11 am-10 pm; Fri 11 am-12:30 am; Sat noon-midnight. $. For

Mario's La Fiesta. Photo by Don Pitcher.

cheap but substantial Mexican food in a noisy cantina atmosphere, head west to Picante Taqueria. A giant bar snakes around between two large dining rooms. Try their quesadillas or tortas with the excellent salsa. Picante has live jazz on Friday and Saturday nights (see *Nightclubs and Bars*).

Viva! Taqueria
2984 Russell St., 843-5565. Open Mon-Sat 11:30 am-9 pm. $. A popular Mexican-style shop near the Hotel Claremont, Viva! Taqueria creates gigantic tostadas, burritos, quesadillas, and tacos. They tend to be juicy and hard to manage, but will certainly fill you up. The black bean chili and nachos are both satisfying, and on sunny days you can enjoy the small patio outdoors (if you don't mind the exhaust fumes).

MIDDLE EASTERN

Cafe Mar-Mara

1730 Shattuck Ave., 644-1966. Open Sun 10 am-2:30 pm; Tues-Thurs 10 am-10 pm; Fri-Sat 10 am-11 pm. $$ to $$$. Probably the only Turkish restaurant in the Bay Area, Mar-Mara has simple finger food (stuffed grape leaves, lamb kebabs, and filo-wrapped boreks) as well as vegetarian specials. Eat inside the brick-walled cafe or out front on noisy Shattuck Avenue. There is live Turkish music on Thursday nights.

La Méditerranée

2936 College Ave., 540-7773. Open Mon-Thurs 10 am-10 pm; Fri-Sat 10 am-11 pm. $$. With a heated patio out front, this is a popular, relaxed place where you can expect consistently fine food and friendly service. For breakfast, try their steamed eggs (created with an espresso machine), or for dinner, one of the combination plates offering an assortment of kebab, dolma, hummus, tabbouleh, and other Middle Eastern foods.

Middle East Restaurant

2125 University Ave., 549-1926. Open Sun 5-9:30 pm; Tues-Thurs 11:30 am-2 pm, 5-9:30 pm; Fri 11:30 am-2 pm, 5-10:30 pm; Sat 5-10:30 pm. $$. This attractive restaurant run by a Lebanese family serves a good choice of delicious foods from the Middle East. You won't go wrong with the lamb kebab or the moussaka.

PIZZERIAS

As with most college towns, Berkeley has an abundance of pizza places, including most of the chains, many pizza-by-the-slice places, and a choice of sit-down restaurants serving pizzas and other Italian food. If you want something different in pizza, try Zachary's, but if you're in a hurry, head to Telegraph Ave. for Blondie's or Fat Slice. (See also Caffe Giovanni under "European and Mediterranean.")

Arinell Pizza

2109 Shattuck Ave., 841-4035. Open Mon-Thurs 11 am-8:30 pm; Fri 11 am-9 pm; Sat noon-9 pm. $. Berkeley's oldest pizza-by-the-slice place, Arinell serves both thin and thick crust versions from a downtown shop the size of a shower stall. The pizza gets mixed reviews—some love it, while others view it as cardboard topped with tomato sauce. The "Neopolitan" (thin crust) is the best bet and runs a little over a buck. Arinell's also has whole pies to go (free delivery).

Blondie's Pizza

2340 Telegraph Ave., 548-1129. Open Sun noon-midnight; Mon-Thurs 10:30 am-1 am; Fri 10:30 am-2 am; Sat 10:30 am-2 am. $. Anyone who has been on Telegraph Ave. knows about Blondie's. At its best it's a crowded joint with trash strewn everywhere, a queue going out the door, and a noise level that's off the scale. There is a reason for this insanity. The service is fast and for only a $1.25 ($1.75 for pepperoni) you get a hot-from-the-oven, dense slice of pizza. The quality is uneven, but it's hard to go wrong at these prices. For the full effect, you should eat Blondie's pizza standing up or while listening to a musician on nearby Sproul Plaza. For a real pig-out, order a whole pie (free delivery after 5 pm, but there may be long waits on weekends).

Blondie's Pizza on Telegraph Avenue. Photo by Mark Sarfati.

Fat Slice Pizza

2375 Telegraph Ave., 548-6479. Open Sun noon-midnight; Mon-Thurs 10 am-midnight; Fri 10 am-12:30 am; Sat 11 am-12:30 pm. $. Starting at just $1.25, Fat Slice sells pizza slices that are bigger than Blondie's and are made from a sourdough base. The atmosphere is similarly chaotic, but you can eat at tables in the back where things are sometimes tamer.

Kip's

2439 Durant Ave., 848-4340. Open Sun-Mon 11 am-11 pm; Tues-Wed 11 am-midnight; Thurs-Sat 11 am-1 am. $ to $$. Kip's upstairs is one of the most popular student hangouts on Southside for sport-watching and beer chugging. There are traditional pizzas

and all-American burgers. Things are much quieter downstairs where there is an attractive atrium in the back.

La Val's

1834 Euclid Ave., 843-5617. Open daily 11 am-11 pm. Also at 2516 B Durant Ave., 845-5353. Open daily 11 am-midnight. $. (See Nightclubs and Bars). The original La Val's is a noisy Northside watering hole that fills with students each evening. Large, reasonably priced pizzas and an outdoor patio draw the crowds, while the cheap beer keeps everyone happy. (Folks on the patio buy beer next door at **La Burrita** where prices are lower during Happy Hour.) Downstairs there is live music Thursday through Saturday evenings. Although the menu is similar at the Southside La Val's, the gloomy location (a basement with video games and a large screen TV) make it less appealing.

Lo Coco's Restaurant and Pizzeria

1400 Shattuck Ave., 843-3745. Open Sun 11:30 am-2 pm; Tues-Sat 11:30 am-2 pm, 5-10 pm. $$. This small North Berkeley restaurant serves thin-crust pizzas with uncommonly fine sauces. House specialties include such oddities as eggplant or salmon toppings. Also try the fresh linguini pasta with clams.

Zachary's Chicago Pizza

1853 Solano Ave., 525-5950. Also at 5801 College Ave., Oakland, 655-6385. Open Sun-Thurs 11 am-9:30 pm; Fri-Sat 11 am-10:30 pm on Solano Ave., and Sun-Thurs 11 am-10 pm; Fri-Sat 11 am-10:30 pm on College Ave. $ to $$. No smoking. The extremely popular (and noisy) Zachary's makes deep-dish pizza with a thin crust and fresh and rich fillings that make it seem more like lasagne. Opinions are mixed on these unusual pizzas, but try the daily specials.

SEAFOOD

Note: see also Augusta's in "California Cuisine."

Spenger's Fish Grotto

1919 4th St., 845-7771. Open Sun-Wed 6 am-11 pm; Thurs-Sat 6 am-midnight. $$ to $$$. The statistics are overwhelming—3500 lbs of fish, 250 gallons of clam chowder, 400 pounds of salmon, and 500 pounds of cooked crab—all served to more than 2500 customers each day. There are hour-long waits in the seven bars and seating for 700 people scattered through five large rooms. This is Spenger's, Berkeley's oldest restaurant, established in 1890, and at 24,000 square feet, the Bay Area's largest eating establishment. Spenger's has the tenth highest sales volume of any American restaurant—and does 10% of all the restaurant business in Berkeley! It is extremely popular with large groups and families.

The menu includes chopped iceberg lettuce salads and seafoods of all types, priced well below what you would pay elsewhere in town. If you aren't a fan of frozen fish, be sure to ask what's fresh on the menu. With its comfortable, gregarious setting, Spenger's is the sort of place you want to like, but the harried waiters and unexceptional quality tend to lessen its appeal. The seven bars are another matter, however. They are filled with all sorts of ship memorabilia—Japanese fishing floats, miniature ships, old photos, teak from the *USS Maryland*, gigantic mounted marlins, and old ship's wheels. The giant-screen TV makes Spenger's a good place to watch sporting events, but be ready for a lot of noise. There is also a well-stocked fish market.

Claremont Seafood Restaurant

2922 Domingo Ave., 540-8308. Open Sun 4:30-9:30 pm; Mon-Sat 11 am-3:30 pm, 4:30-9:30 pm. Fish market open daily 11 am-9:30 pm. $$$. Located across the street from the Claremont Hotel, this is one of a small collection of gourmet shops that have moved into the area. You'll find some of the freshest seafood in the East Bay at Claremont Seafood. Those who would rather cook at home can purchase fresh fish from the small market here.

Gertie's Chesapeake Bay Cafe

1919 Addison St., 841-2722. Open Sun 10:30 am-2 pm, 4:30-9:30 pm; Mon-Thurs 11:30 am-2:30 pm, 5:30-9:30 pm; Fri-Sat 11:30 am-2:30 pm, 5:30-10 pm. $$$. Gertie's, one of the area's top spots for seafood, is popular with the Berkeley Rep crowd and others looking for an evening out. The restaurant is a bit noisy, but has a snappy decor and an exceptionally friendly staff. Its menu changes frequently, covering regional seafood favorites, but there is always something from Chesapeake Bay. For an appetizer, try the crab cakes. You'll also enjoy the Maryland fried chicken or the Tuesday night clambake dinner. The small patio is a nice place for weekend brunches.

Yorkshire Fish & Chips

1984 Shattuck Av., 841-7743. Open Mon-Fri 11 am-8 pm; Sat noon-8 pm. $. This may be the place to find authentically greasy English fare. The fish and chips come with vinegar and a side of coleslaw (an American touch). Prices start around $2.

THAI

Outstanding Thai food has become a Berkeley specialty. There are now close to a dozen Thai restaurants, ranging from the bland to the sublime. Almost of them are artfully decorated, and are evidence of a pervasive and beautiful national aesthetic.

Berkeley Thai House

2511 Channing Way, 843-7352. Open daily 11 am-9:30 pm. $ to $$. Just a few feet from the bustle of Telegraph Ave. is one of the most reasonably priced Thai restaurants in Berkeley. Berkeley Thai House has outstanding lunchtime bargains (around $4) and a wide choice of spicy Thai dishes for dinner. For dessert try the fried banana. The front patio is a nice place on sunny afternoons.

Cha-Am

1543 Shattuck Ave., 848-9664. Open Sun-Thurs 5-9:30 pm; Fri-Sat 5-10 pm. $ to $$. When it comes to consistently fine Thai cooking, my vote goes to Cha-Am. Climb a flight of stairs to this small restaurant just down the block from Chez Panisse in North Berkeley. There is an enclosed patio out front. The friendly staff serves food that is wonderfully spicy and priced below many other Thai restaurants, making this one of the city's most delicious bargains. The word is out, however, and Cha-Am is jam-packed most evenings.

Plearn Thai Cuisine

2050 University Ave., 841-2148. Open Sun 5-10 pm; Mon-Sat 11:30 am-3 pm, 5-10 pm. $$. No smoking. As one of the best-known Thai restaurants in California, Plearn has long queues most evenings (reservations only for parties of six or more). The extensive menu includes spicy soups, salads, and entrees, all served in a setting of linen-covered tables and potted plants.

Siam Cafe

6706 San Pablo Ave., Oakland, 655-9799. Open Mon-Sat 11 am-9 pm. $. For cheap Thai food in a truck-stop atmosphere, head across the Berkeley border to Siam Cafe. Low prices and the authentic, grubby setting pull customers in the door. Siam Cafe has no liquor license, so people bring their own alcohol, knocking dinner costs down even more.

Siam Cuisine

1181 University Ave., 548-3278. Open Sun 5-11 pm; Mon-Thurs 11 am-3 pm, 5-11 pm; Fri-Sat 11 am-3 pm, 5 pm-midnight. $$-$$$. Don't confuse Siam Cuisine with Siam Cafe. Siam Cuisine is considered one of Berkeley's top Thai restaurants (and the competition is stiff), offering dishes that are both blazing-hot and deliciously exotic, including a good choice of vegetarian items. Prices are slightly higher than Plearn, but Siam Cuisine is less crowded.

Thai Bar-B-Q

1958 Shattuck Ave., 549-1958. Open Sun 3-9 pm; Tues-Sat 11:30 am-2:30 pm, 4:30-9:30 pm. $ to $$. This is Thai food with a difference. Instead of the dishes found in other Thai restaurants, you'll find a choice of barbecue specials such as pork spare ribs or frog legs. The lunch specials and à la carte dinners are outstanding bargains. Expect to get more than you can eat.

Won Thai Cuisine

2449 Sacramento St., 848-6483. Open Tues-Sun 5:30-9:30 pm. $ to $$. This is one of the secret Thai restaurants that locals discover through word of mouth. It sits just across the street from another of my favorites, the Homemade Cafe. Won Thai's heavy-

on-the-vinyl decor isn't much different from most greasy spoon restaurants, but the food is another story. This is home-style Thai cooking, priced very reasonably. For dessert, try the fresh coconut ice cream.

VEGETARIAN AND NATURAL FOODS

Although Berkeley is famous as a city of vegetarians and almost-vegetarians, it provides few places devoted to meatless cooking, and none with the gourmet standards of Green's in San Francisco. This is even more surprising given the fact that vegetarian dishes are considered high-profit menu items! Even restaurants such as Paloma or Chez Panisse that use natural foods and meats free of antibiotics have primarily non-vegetarian menus. Your best bets are the two Chinese restaurants listed below. Other good places for nutritious meals are Cafe Intermezzo and Soup Kitchen Heike described under "American Restaurants."

Amrit

1107 Stanford Ave., Oakland, 655-8677. Open Sun 9:30-10:15 am; Mon-Fri 8-8:45 am, noon-1:30 pm, 6:30-7:15 pm; Sat 8-8:45 am, 6:25-7:15 pm. $ to $$. Inside the Siddha meditation ashram is a large vegetarian cafeteria for the tofu and mantra set. The mellow crowd enjoys quesadillas, tofu burgers, and other light meals while large photos of Swamis Muktananda and Chidvialsananda watch from the walls. The food is not great, but does provide an alternative to the standard lunchtime fare. Note the hours, set around meditation schedules.

Good Earth

2175 Allston Way, 841-2555. Open Mon-Thurs 7 am-10 pm; Fri 7 am-11 pm; Sat-Sun 8 am-10 pm. $$. No smoking. One of a chain of Good Earth restaurants, this is Berkeley's best known vegetarian restaurant (it also serves non-vegetarian fare). Unfortunately you'll find bland and overpriced food in a Denny's-like setting. The restaurant's saving grace is its fine bakery.

Juice Bar Collective

2114 Vine St., 548-8473. Open Mon-Sat 10 am-4 pm. $. Open the door to this tiny shop and you may think you have stepped into a time warp. Founded in 1975 as an offshoot of the Cheese Board, Juice Bar Collective has the all-natural drinks, vegetarian sandwiches, and wholesome desserts that were once available in many Berkeley shops. It is particularly crowded at lunchtime.

Long Life Vegi House

2129 University Ave., 845-6072. Open Sun 11:30 am-9 pm; Mon-Sat 11:30 am-9:30 pm. $ to $$. One of the few places in Berkeley devoted to vegetarian cooking, Long Life has an ample selection of Chinese dishes for reasonable prices. The friendly staff, cheap lunch specials, gigantic portions, and absence of MSG make the place popular with both students and downtown workers. House specialties include Mu Shu vegetables, eggplant with spicy garlic sauce, and meatless sweet and sour "pork." The restaurant also has a special dim sum brunch on weekends.

Vegi Food

2085 Vine St., 548-5244. Open daily 11:30 am-3 pm, 5-9 pm. $. The simple decor (with prices to match) seems out of place in this Gourmet Ghetto Chinese restaurant. This is natural food—Vegi Food serves brown rice with the entrees and uses no animal fat, MSG, eggs, or garlic in their recipes. You'll enjoy the house specialty, sweet and sour fried walnuts.

Open Late

Sometimes it seems that the entire city of Berkeley shuts down at midnight, leaving only the bars open till 2 am. There are a few exceptions to this rule, most being take-out food places, particularly barbecue and pizza joints.

- **Au Coquelet** (coffeehouse) 2000 University Ave., 845-0433. Open daily to 1 am.
- **Blondie's Pizza** 2340 Telegraph Ave., 548-1129. Open Sun to midnight, Mon-Thurs to 1 am, Fri-Sat to 2 am.
- **Cafe Neutron** (fast food bakery) 2124 Center St., 540-7431. Open 24 hours a day.
- **Everett & Jones Barbeque** 1955 San Pablo Ave., 548-8261. Open Mon-Fri to 2 am, Sat-Sun to 3 am.
- **Flint's Bar B-Q** 6609 Shattuck Ave., Oakland, 653-0593 Open Sun-Thurs to 2 am, Fri-Sat to 4 am.
- **Giovanni's** (Italian) 2420 Shattuck Ave. 843-6678. Open Sun-Thurs to 11:30 pm, Fri-Sat to 12:30 am.
- **International House of Pancakes** 1598 University Ave., 644-2678. Open 24 hrs Fri and Sat, and Sun-Thurs to 8 pm.
- **King Pin Donuts** 2521-A Durant Ave., 843-6688. Open daily to 2 am.
- **Kip's** (pizza) 2439 Durant Ave., 848-4340. Open Sun-Mon to 11 pm, Tues-Wed to midnight, Thurs-Sat to 1 am.
- **La Val's** (pizza) 2516 B Durant Ave., 845-5353. Open daily till midnight.
- **Manuel's** (Mexican food) 2521 Durant Ave., 849-1529. Open Sun-Thurs to 1 am, Fri-Sat to 2 am.
- **Oscar's** (hamburgers) 1890 Shattuck Ave., 849-2164. Open Sun-Thurs to midnight, Fri-Sat to 2 am.
- **Siam Cuisine** (Thai food) 1181 University Ave., 548-3278. Open Fri-Sat to midnight, other days to 11 pm.
- **Taiwan Restaurant** (Chinese) 2071 University Ave., 845-1456. Open Sun-Thurs to midnight, Fri-Sat to 2 am.
- **Top Dog** (hot dogs) 2534 Durant Avenue. Open to 2 am Sun-Thurs, to 3 am Fri-Sat. 2503 Hearst Avenue. Open daily to midnight.

If everything else is closed, you can always head to the **Elmwood 7-11** (2887 College Ave., 841-6291), which is always open.

Coffeehouses, Bakeries, and Sweetshops

If the coffee-producing nations of the world ever organized an embargo such as OPEC's in 1973, the civil unrest that would result in Berkeley would make the 60s look like a pillow fight. Berkeley runs on coffee—not the flavored black water that passes for coffee in the rest of the nation, but the bone-jarring espresso that originated in the Mediterranean. One source recently estimated that Berkeley coffeehouses and retailers sell upwards of 830,000 pounds of coffee a year, equivalent to a cup a day for every man, woman, and child in the city. I suspect that this underestimates the fact. In a typical day, the most popular Berkeley coffeehouses serve upwards of 3500 cups of coffee a day, while the brewmaster of all coffeeholics, Peet's, sells more than 1000 pounds of roasted beans.

This addiction is nothing new. In 1884 the "ladies of the Congregational Church" published a *Berkeley Cook Book of Choice and Tested Recipes*, one of which is reproduced below.

Today the impact of coffee and the coffee culture go far beyond the caffeine jolt that jump-starts folks in the

morning. In many respects, the more than 70 coffeehouses in Berkeley serve the function that bars do in other cities: they provide a place to talk with

1884 Coffee Recipe

Berkeley resident, Mrs. Reid, provided the following coffee recipe for *Berkeley Cook Book of Choice and Tested Recipes,* published in 1884: Take one cup freshly ground coffee, equal parts Java and Mocha, three cups boiling water, one cup rich milk scalding hot, one cup cold cream. Soak the coffee several hours, or even overnight, in enough water to wet it well. Pour into it the boiling water. Set the coffee pot in a vessel of boiling water and steep twenty minutes over a hot fire. Drain off the liquid coffee and to each cup of this add one cup of rich milk scalding hot, and one cup of cold cream. To each cup as served add one teaspoonful of whipped cream. A double-boiler may be used instead of a coffee pot.

Opposite: Cafe Milano. Photo by Don Pitcher.

The Med

The Med is at the center of cafe culture in Berkeley. Sitting here, you wonder how many poems have been penned at its stained tables, how many people have fried their brains here, how many protests have been organized in this place. Although it's as clean as most other coffeehouses in town, the Med looks a mess—it's the old tables, the mismatched chairs, and the shabby over-30 crowd, most of whom look like they're still struggling with their dissertations. On the wall is a mural from 1958 (when the place was called Il Piccola Express), and just above the gum machine in the corner a sign warns, "No soliciting or dealing." But despite its general air of decay, the Med thrives as a place to discuss abstract theories, meet with old friends, and tackle the problems of the world.

The Med serves inexpensive food in the back during the day and coffees and hot chocolate at the counter. The big table at the front window seems perpetually filled with folks who probably arrived early in the morning and who won't leave till the Med closes. I have sometimes wondered if, when the doors are locked and the lights turned out, they crawl behind the counter and sleep here, breathing the aroma of coffee.

friends, to study, to check out the latest fashions, to write your dissertation, or to simply act cool. You won't get kicked out when the dishwasher picks up your empty cup. Some people seem to become permanent fixtures in the hallowed halls of places such as Caffe Med or on the sidewalks out front of Peet's.

Coffeehouses

The largest concentration of coffeehouses is just south of campus, where there are at least fifteen such places, each of which attracts a particular clientele. Half of these are new within the past few years, but as soon as they open, students, professors, and others pour in to fill the tables. The grand-daddy of all Berkeley coffeehouses (opened in 1957) is **Caffe Mediterra-neum** (2475 Telegraph Ave., 841-5634), known to most as the Med.

Other Southside coffeehouses differ markedly from the Med. The gleaming and architecturally award-winning **Cody's Cafe** (2460 Telegraph Ave., 841-6346) just across the street boasts bright lights, an arty decor, and dual-level seating. Light cafe food is served in addition to coffee. **Cafe Intermezzo** (2442 Telegraph Ave., 849-4592) also serves light meals. There is a front window counter for people-watching. The dozens of outdoor tables at **Cafe Strada** (2300 College Ave., 843-5282), just up from the Art Museum, are always filled with a hip crowd of art students, fraternity and sorority members, budding lawyers, and foreign graduate students. Formerly called Cafe Roma, this is one of the most financially successful espresso bars in the U.S.

Peet's

When Alfred Peet opened his North Berkeley coffee shop in 1966, it was the first local store to emphasize the high quality that has become a hallmark of "Gourmet Ghetto." Now retired, Peet came from a family whose history in the business reached back over 100 years to an Amsterdam coffee company. Each of the seven Peet's stores now offers 30 different kinds of coffee beans and teas, from aged Sulawesi to water-processed French Roast, along with all the necessary paraphernalia. One of Berkeley's quintessential institutions, Peet's loyal followers verge on fanaticism. I have watched Berkeley residents hoarding their last half-pound of Peet's coffee in the Alaskan wilderness, more concerned for its safety than their own. The store even does a strong mail order business with addicts who live as far away as Saudi Arabia and the Philippines, as well as with former Cal students now scattered around the country. One of the most authentic Berkeley sights is the scene outside Peet's on a sunny morning. The regulars (from psychologists to carpenters) sit sipping hot coffee, talking about computers, politics, and films–or just gossiping.

The scene outside Peet's Coffee at Walnut and Vine. Photo by Don Pitcher.

The French Hotel Cafe. Photo by Don Pitcher.

Sufficient Grounds (2431A Durant Ave., 841-3969) serves the biggest croissants I've ever seen, along with giant hot chocolates. The shop is packed with students every evening of the school year. **La Bottega** (2309 Telegraph Ave., 849-4099) has bakery goods and light meals to go with the coffee. The tables out front attract the punks and others who want to be seen; upstairs, La Bottega looks more like a study hall. Another split-level place, **Cafe Milano** (2522 Bancroft Way, 644-3299) is decorated like an art studio in a warehouse. For serenity, try the **Musical Offering Cafe**, a block down from Telegraph on Bancroft. In this record store/cafe you can listen to classical CD's while reading the paper or sipping coffee. It is quiet , a contrast to other Southside coffeehouses.

Other Berkeley neighborhoods also offer a wide choice of coffeehouses.

Along Solano Ave., **Cafe Vin** (1889 Solano Ave., 527-9313) serves excellent mochas, as well as full meals. Just a few doors away is the **Berkeley Bakery and Cafe** (1881 Solano Ave., 527-9616) with fresh, crisp pastries. North Berkeley has the **French Hotel Cafe** (1540 Shattuck Ave., 843-8958) in an old brick building that once housed a laundry. Now it is crowded with those in search of the perfect cappuccino. The best known place for coffee in North Berkeley, though you can't sit there, is of course **Peet's** (2124 Vine St., 841-0564).

In the downtown area, Berkeley's largest coffeehouse is **Au Coquelet** (2000 University Ave., 845-0433), which stays open later than any other in Berkeley (1 am). Au Coquelet is a popular hangout for high school students as well as for late-night theater and movie-goers. Breakfast and lunch are served in the quieter back room, while the smoky front room offers delicious gateau basque.

On Northside the Italian-styled **Caffe Espresso** (2481 Hearst Ave., 845-0050) has a covered patio in the front, marble tables, and a skylit interior. There are delicious bakery goods from nearby Pane e Cioccolata (owned by the same family) and inexpensive soups and sandwiches for lunch. Around the corner is **Coffee Connection** (1807 Euclid Ave., 540-8865), another pleasant place with freshly baked goods and coffees (but shorter hours).

Near the Claremont Hotel is a second **Peet's** store (2916 Domingo Ave., 843-1434) that, like its North Berkeley parent, attracts coffee drinkers of all types. The Rockridge area, which straddles the Berkeley/ Oakland border, has several popular coffeehouse/cafes, including **Edible Complex** (5600 College Ave., 658-2172). In addition to coffees and teas, the Edible Complex serves light meals, bagels from Brothers' Bagels, and desserts from Toot Sweets (the same people own all three places). **Oliveto Cafe** (5655 College Ave., Oakland, 547-5356), just across from the BART station, has a modern cafe downstairs with light meals and coffees and a pricey Mediterranean restaurant upstairs.

In West Berkeley you can watch the coffee roasting at **Uncommon Grounds** (2813 7th St., 644-4417) while sampling the chili con carne, sandwiches, pastries, and espresso.

Bakeries and Sweetshops

In much of America the only bakery is a Safeway shelf stocked with glazed donuts, gingerbread cookies, and rub-

Acme Bread. Photo by Don Pitcher.

bery croissants. Fortunately, this isn't true of Berkeley's many outstanding neighborhood bakeries. In the Thousand Oaks neighborhood, you'll find the tiny **Pring's Bakery** (1585 Solano Ave., 524-3107), specializing in pies, breads, muffins, and croissants. Closer to the center of action is the **Berkeley Bakery and Cafe** (1881 Solano Ave., 527-9616), which has a large assortment of cakes, cookies, pastries, and chocolate truffles. For more than 50 years, customers have patiently waited their turn at **McCallum's** (1825 Solano Ave., 525-3510), which serves over 100 flavors of ice cream.

Hopkins Street Bakery (1584 Hopkins St., 526-8188), just up the street from Monterey Foods, produces hearty breads, cookies, and cakes. In mellow Westbrae, **Brothers' Bagel Factory** (1281 Gilman St., 524-3104) offers all varieties of bagels, usually

Cocolat

Alice Medrich's résumé is the prototypical entrepreneurial success story. Having graduated from UC in Latin American history, she followed her husband when he landed a job in Paris. Bored, she began taking French cooking lessons. When they left Paris in 1973, they brought along her landlady's prize recipe for chocolate truffles—tiny, dense balls of rich chocolate rolled in cocoa. As the French ingredients were unavailable in the U.S., Medrich altered the truffles, making them golfball-sized and dipping them in dark chocolate. Selling through a local gourmet shop, the first day's production of 25 dozen sold out in three hours, and soon Alice and her husband were scouring supermarkets all over the Bay Area for semisweet baking chocolate. Medrich went back to Berkeley for her MBA just as the business was taking off. In 1976 she opened a shop in North Berkeley (1481 Shattuck Ave., 843-3265), offering the truffles and rich cakes that were already legendary.

Today the operation includes a 10,000-square-foot plant on 9th St. that produces 2.5-million truffles and 50,000 cakes a year. There are now seven Cocolat stores in the Bay Area, and their truffles are sold as far away as Zabar's, the famous Manhattan deli. Ironically, her method of truffle production is now even copied in France! (Cocolat will also ship by mail during winter months.) Be warned, however: the prices of these rich, addictive desserts make them an expensive habit.

Alice Medrich at Cocolat. Photo by Don Pitcher.

warm and waiting for fresh lox or cream cheese. Next door, **Toot Sweets Bakery** (1277 Gilman St., 526-0610) bakes mouth-watering whole-grain pastries, pies, cakes, and other treats.

Acme Bread (1601 San Pablo Ave., 524-1327) vies with the Cheese Board for the tastiest sourdough baguettes in the Bay Area: the bakers use a 24-hour fermentation to give the bread just the right amount of bite. The small bakery supplies many of the gourmet restaurants and markets in the area, including Chez Panisse, but its products are

Muli of Muliben Bakery Cafe. Photo by Don Pitcher.

better bought fresh at the source. The shop closes as soon as everything is sold out (generally between 2 and 4 pm), so get there early in the day. Farther to the west, **Bette's To Go** (1807 4th St., 548-9494) has a bakeshop and deli counter with delicious homemade pies, muffins, and other sweets. Another good West Berkeley bakery is the **Westside Bakery and Cafe** (2570 9th St., 845-4852).

Excellent bakeries and sweetshops flourish in North Berkeley's Gourmet Ghetto, including the **Cheese Board** (see "Cheese Shops" in *Groceries and Markets*). **Bel Fornaio** (1400 Shattuck Ave., 644-1601) has European pastries, pizza, and various pastas. **Sweet Temptations** (1600 Shattuck Ave., 845-2269) sells many sugary items, but if you love rich dark chocolate, try the chocolate-dipped candied orange peel. The **Virginia Bakery** (1640 Shattuck Ave., 848-6711), established in 1924, is one of Berkeley's oldest. It sells fresh pastries and breads, and is the place to order your child's traditional, gooey, decorated birthday cake. **Fatapple's** (1346 M.L. King Way, 526-2260) has a take-away bakery with fresh apple, berry, and chocolate pies, scones, cheese puffs, and other treats, as well as Peet's coffee.

In the downtown area, Francophiles should head for **La Tour Eiffel French Bakery** (2020 University Ave., 548-3354), an authentic French bakery. Try their deliciously flaky apple crisps. One of the nicest bakery/coffeehouses in Berkeley is the tiny, homey **Muliben Bakery Cafe** (1786 Shattuck Ave., 540-6103). Here, you can read the paper and sample the gigantic baked goods at two big tables behind the jungle of plants in the front window. For lunch, try their soups with fresh homemade bread. **Edy's of Berkeley** (2201 Shattuck Ave., 843-3096), established in 1932, has a loyal following of sweet-toothed old-timers and kids. The ice cream sundaes, milk shakes, and banana splits are served at orange vinyl booths.

Northside's **Pane e Cioccolata** (1878 Euclid Ave., 549-1277) is a wonderful Italian bakery with exceptionally buttery and flaky croissants. They also sell breads, fruit tortes, cookies, and other treats. Just up the street, **Swensen's Ice Cream** (1854 Euclid Ave., 841-6374) features a wall filled with paperbacks you can enjoy along with your ice cream.

On Southside, **Eclair Pastries** (2565 Telegraph Ave., 848-4221), established in 1946, is filled with dozens of Danish cookies, breads, and pastries. Check out their "hot secular buns" at Easter. You will also find large fresh croissants, muffins, and other baked goods in **Sufficient Grounds** (2431A Durant Ave., 841-3969). Next door is **Yogurt Park** (2433A Durant Ave., 549-0570) where you're likely to meet more Clairol blonds than in the rest of Berkeley combined. The low prices, late hours (to midnight), and proximity to nearby dorms, sororities, and frats make this a very popular frozen yogurt place.

Dream Fluff Donuts (2637 Ashby Ave., 540-9083) has old-fashioned all-American donuts and a dingy 40s interior. It provides an escape from the trendy Elmwood crowd. **Nabolom Bakery** (2708 Russell St., 845-2253) lies at the other end of the spectrum. Everything about Nabolom speaks Berkeley—the collective ownership, the leftist and feminist posters on the walls, and the mixture of students and professionals who come in for a morning fix of coffee. The huge Tollhouse cookies (three times the size of Mrs. Field's) are worth a try. Nabolom also bakes daily several types of bread, including those for people with allergies to wheat, eggs, or dairy products. There are a few seats inside and a bench out front for those who aren't in a hurry. For old-fashioned ice cream, visit **Botts** (2977 College Ave., 845-4545). The store makes its own ice cream, using high butterfat cream and other natural ingredients; specialties are fruit ices and dark chocolate flavors.

The **Bread Garden Bakery** (2912 Domingo Ave., 548-3122), directly across from the Claremont Hotel, produces more than a dozen different types of breads, ranging from Danish pumpernickel to German potato bread. You'll also find a variety of flaky pastries. In Rockridge, **La Farine** (6323 College Ave., Oakland, 654-0338) is a true French bakery, producing tortes, croissants, breads, and homemade jams. The single large table by the front window offers a pleasant place to read the morning paper over coffee and a pastry. Across the street is **Buttercup Bakery** (3201 College Ave., 652-6152), with tasty baked goods of all types. The popular (but undistinguished) Buttercup Restaurant is next door.

Groceries and Markets

Although large grocery stores account for much of the food sold in Berkeley, of increasing importance are the specialty markets that sell everything from sun-dried tomatoes to salted duck eggs. Shoppers in Berkeley have come to resemble European shoppers—people buy the best and freshest from the small markets while depending on the larger stores for staples.

Berkeley supermarkets include two **Safeways** (2020 Oregon St., 841-5212, and 1444 Shattuck Ave., 526-3086); and four **Andronico's Park & Shop** stores (1850 Solano Ave., 524-1673 and 2655 Telegraph Ave., 845-1062; as well as two stores once operated by the Berkeley Co-op at 1550 Shattuck and 1414 University—for these call 524-2696). There is also a discount place without fresh meats or produce, the **Canned Food Store** (1941 San Pablo Ave., 843-9903).

Cheese Shops

Many of Berkeley's delicatessens sell fresh cheeses along with other favorites, but a few are especially worth noting. **Country Cheese** (2101 San Pablo Ave., 841-0752) provides a good choice of pre-cut cheeses for low

Co-op: 1938-1988

One of Berkeley's best-known and longest-lasting institutions was the late, great Consumers Cooperative of Berkeley, once the largest urban-based cooperative in the nation. By 1975 it had eleven stores, including service stations, a hardware store, and a natural foods store.

Combining a commercial operation with membership education and political action, the Co-op introduced organic produce when other stores refused to do so (1970), established Berkeley's first recycling center (1970), fought for a bottle bill (1970-87), banned smoking in its stores (1971), refused to sell fluorocarbon-containing aerosols (1975), fought milk price fixing (1976), and boycotted Nestle's products (1983), Chilean produce (1984), and Coors beer (1985).

The increasing politicization of the Co-op paralleled its demise as a supermarket chain. Causes were multiple: its 1988 bankruptcy has been variously blamed on expansion into areas where the residents weren't interested, competition from the giant chains, inflexible unions, a senior staff that demanded high wages, and an inept and indecisive management.

Opposite: Farmers' Market. Photo by Don Pitcher.

The Cheese Board

Delicious aromas from fresh breads and cheeses waft forward from the door of the Cheese Board (1504 Shattuck Ave., 549-3183). Pick a card from the deck and wait with the crowd—you'll need time anyway to sort through the blackboard listing of more than 200 varieties of cheese, ranging from Ami Chambertin to Wensleydale. The Cheese Board also bakes a variety of unusual and delicious breads such as cheese-onion-curry or coriander-sunflower, in addition to wonderful sourdough baguettes. Pizzas made with sourdough crust and toppings such as goat cheese and eggplant are available two doors down, Tues-Thurs 11:30 am-1:30 pm.

Senior citizen discounts start at 10% for anyone over 60 and rise to "what you see is what you get" for those over 100! There is a 5% discount for "those who need it," and various customers through the years have heard Cheese Boarders say, to their astonishment, that they have a 20% discount because of this or that good deed. Surprising as it may seem, the Cheese Board is one of Berkeley's most influential commercial institutions. Established in 1967 as a collectively run venture, the Cheese Board brought the taste for gourmet provisions to North Berkeley, where other fine shops and restaurants now thrive. The Cheese Board's members helped fund several other Berkeley collectives, including the Swallow restaurant, the Juice Bar Collective, and Uprisings Bakery. Its activist membership financially supports leftist groups working on issues such as nuclear disarmament and U.S. involvement in Central America. Cheese Board breads are justly famous throughout the Bay Area, and you won't find a more knowledgeable staff. These folks know their cheese and will be happy to give you an advance taste of any variety.

prices in a rustic, narrow-aisled shop that also sells dried fruit, grains, nuts, beans, and other goods. **Cheese N' Stuff** (2442 Durant Ave., 843-9233), next to campus, has many kinds of cheeses, but is best known for its overstuffed, low-priced sandwiches. **Curds and Whey** (6311 College Ave., Oakland, 652-6311) is a gourmet wine and cheese shop in Rockridge. The best known Berkeley cheese store is the incomparable **Cheese Board** (1504 Shattuck Ave., 549-3183).

Fish, Meat, and Poultry Markets

A number of Berkeley markets offer high quality meats and fish. **Spenger's Fish Market** (1919 4th St., 548-2717) will celebrate its 100th birth-

Opposite: The Cheese Board. Photo by Don Pitcher.

day in 1990. Spanky Spenger, who has managed the market since he was sixteen, imports scallops from New Zealand, frog legs from India, prawns from Baja, and oysters from the East Coast. **Monterey Fish Market** (1582 Hopkins St., 525-5600) offers the highest quality fresh seafoods. Other good fish markets are **Tokyo Fish Market** (1220 San Pablo Ave., 524-7243), **Berkeley Bowl Seafood** (2777 Shattuck Ave., 548-7008), and **Claremont Seafood** (2922 Domingo Ave., 540-8306).

For meats, the long-time favorite is **Lenny's Meats** (1469 Shattuck Ave., 845-0751). Surrounded by elaborate Gourmet Ghetto shops, this is an old-fashioned butcher shop with high quality cuts and a friendly staff who will help you figure out what that mysterious foreign recipe means and cut your meat appropriately. The reasonably priced meats and cheeses at **Berkeley Bowl Meats** (2777 Shattuck Ave., 841-6346) make it a popular place. For fresh poultry that isn't chock-full of hormones, antibiotics, or preservatives, go to **Magnani Poultry** (1586 Hopkins St., 528-6370 and 6317 College Ave., Oakland, 428-9496), a local favorite since 1917. Magnani also sells fresh squab, pheasant, and other specialties. In North Berkeley, **Poulet** (1685 Shattuck Ave., 845-5932) is popular with discerning chefs for its organic, free-range chicken, available both in the deli and from the poultry shop next door. The deli sells a wide range of gourmet specialties such as pâtés, salads, and antipasto.

International Markets

Some of the most interesting markets in Berkeley are the international shops. Two stores that sell Thai spices, coconut milk, lemongrass, Thai eggplants, dried chrysanthemum flowers, and other foods unavailable elsewhere are **Erawan Trading** (1474 University Ave., 849-9707) and **Oy's Market** (2442 San Pablo Ave., 486-0515). For Chinese specialties such as dried seaweed, salted duck eggs, and sea cucumbers, head to **Lam Market** (1923 M.L. King Way, 268-8414) or **Happy Produce Market** (1240 Solano Ave., Albany, 525-1571). The **Tokyo Fish Market** (1220 San Pablo Ave., 524-7243) offers fresh fish, Japanese delicacies of all types, and Japanese cooking and eating utensils.

If you're looking for Indian food, University Ave. has three excellent grocery stores: **Bazaar of India** (1810 University Ave., 548-4110), **Bombay Bazaar** (1034 University Ave., 848-1671), and **Milan International Spices and Foods** (990 University Ave., 843-9600). You'll find green jackfruit, jars of chutney, dusty cans of lotus roots, and bins packed with lentils, spices, and dry goods. Milan, the largest of the shops, also stocks an extensive collection of Indian cookware, as well as Indian records and tapes.

My favorite international grocer is the **Middle East Market** (2054 San Pablo Ave., 548-2213). An overwhelming aroma of spices, mint teas, dried fruits, meats, and pastries fills the air. They sell Turkish figs, meat from animals slaughtered in accordance with the rules of the Koran, Iranian caviar, cans of Pakistani chili pickles, genuine Armenian string cheese, fresh yogurts, unusual pastries, and even Arabic-language newspapers. Just up the street another market, the Pakistani-owned **Indus Food Center** (1964 San Pablo Ave., 549-3663), offers Middle Eastern and South Asian foods.

Tom Fujimoto, owner of Monterey Foods. Photo by Don Pitcher.

Produce Markets

The most famous Berkeley produce market is **Monterey Market** (officially Monterey Foods, 1550 Hopkins St., 526-6042). Established in 1961, it has become the supplier for many local gourmet restaurants. Here you'll find Mexican jicama, taro root, elephant garlic, red bananas, many varieties of wild mushrooms, cactus leaves, and organically grown kumquats, as well as all the usual fruits and vegetables. Monterey Market is frequently crowded, particularly on Saturday mornings, when finding a parking spot can be an accomplishment. Another store offering a great selection of produce is **Berkeley Bowl Produce** (2777 Shattuck Ave., 843-6929). Established in 1977 within an old bowling alley, it offers an extensive selection of fresh fruits and vegetables, a fish market, a deli with good fresh meats and cheeses, and some other foods, primarily Asian specialty items.

Next door to the Cheese Board in North Berkeley, the **Produce Center** (1500 Shattuck Ave., 848-8100) has reasonable prices and high quality produce. **Burnaford's Produce** (2635 Ashby Ave., 548-0348) in Elmwood offers both organic and non-organic fruits and vegetables plus a limited stock of natural foods and juices. **Yasai Produce Market** (6301 College Ave., Oakland, 655-4880) in upscale Rockridge has a good selection of produce, but prices are a bit higher. The funkiest Berkeley market is the tiny **Sun's Produce** (2025 San Pablo Ave., 849-0505) in West Berkeley.

Berkeley's friendliest organic market is **Berkeley Natural Grocery** (1336 Gilman St., 526-2456), a modern store with reasonable prices. **Living Foods** (1581 University Ave., 549-1714), located in the old Co-op Natural Foods store, is the largest (and most over-priced) Berkeley natural foods market.

Every Tuesday from 2 pm-dusk the Ecology Center (548-2220) runs a **Farmers' Market** at Derby St. and M.L. King Way where fresh organic produce is available at bargain prices. Down on the corner of 4th and Hearst Sts., across from chic shops and the Spenger's parking lot, is Berkeley's most successful (and perhaps only) agricultural exporter, **Kona Kai** **Farms** (486-8334). It's easy to snicker at the half-acre of raised lettuce beds, but not at the $200,000 the tiny spread grosses each year. Using intensive organic growing techniques, workers at Kona Kai raise more than 20 varieties of lettuce and sell 35,000 heads a week to gourmet restaurants as far away as New York and Hong Kong. You can buy ultra-fresh lettuce, greens, and herbs straight from Kona Kai most days if things are not too busy.

Nightclubs and Bars

Berkeley citizens have fought a long battle over alcohol consumption. When the University was first built, it brought in hundreds of thirsty students, but state legislation quickly prohibited saloons within a mile of the campus. Just outside that limit lay the hard-drinking, blue collar settlement of Ocean View. By 1878, Ocean View had more retail liquor establishments than any other business except construction. To halt this, a complete prohibition ordinance was passed by the Town Trustees in 1899, but within a year the brewers and saloon-keepers managed to overturn the prohibition. Another anti-saloon ordinance passed in 1906 (the West Berkeley preacher who pushed for it was hung in effigy), and the law was strengthened in 1909 when temperance was added to the town charter. It was not until national prohibition ended in 1933 that drinking again became legal in Berkeley. Finally, in 1978 the legislature repealed the 102 year-old ban on liquor sales within a mile of campus.

The places listed below include several of Berkeley's most interesting drinking establishments. There are, of course, many other bars for major-league drinking and carousing.

Nightclubs

Berkeley nightclubs tend to be much more relaxed than those in other cities. Attire is less important, and it isn't uncommon to see folks dancing by themselves. In other words, don't expect the "meat market" atmosphere of a Honolulu disco at most of Berkeley's clubs. Listed below are some of the better drinking and dance establishments in town. Check the *Express* for a current schedule of nightclub action or listen to KALX's Entertainment Calendar at 7:30 am, 3:30 and 6:30 pm.

Ashkenaz
1317 San Pablo Ave., 525-5054. This is a spacious smoke-free club where you can take folk dance lessons or boogie the night away to world beat or Caribbean music. Weekend nights the dance floor becomes crowded, but everyone comes here for fun—this is not a place where people get drunk and rowdy. Ashkenaz's owner is unabashedly leftist, and the atmosphere is mellow enough that some parents bring along their kids (anyone under twelve gets in free). Light vegetarian meals are served. Cover charges are fairly steep.

Berkeley Square
1333 University Ave., 849-3374. This has become Berkeley's hip place for new music. It lets in anyone over eighteen, so the crowd tends to be young and trendy. The Berkeley Square attracts some of the best groups in the Bay Area and charges a stiff cover. The dance floor is tiny.

Eli's Mile High Club
3629 M.L. King Way, Oakland, 655-6661. The first-rate music here makes it worth the venture into seedy west Oakland. Eli's earns its title "home of the West Coast blues" with great live

blues action most nights, when a racially mixed clientele of ages eighteen and up and hot musicians crowd the small club. There is soul food in the kitchen. Cover charges are moderate.

Freight and Salvage

1111 Addison St., 548-1761. Northern California's oldest folk club attracts top performers of bluegrass, instrumental, and folk music. The atmosphere is from the 1960s—laid back and fun, with no age restrictions—but there is no dancing. The Freight is popular with couples who simply enjoy good tunes by great bands.

924 Gilman Street

525-9926. The location is remote, there is no sign out front, advertising is minimal, and you won't find any alcohol inside, but Gilman Street has become the *in* place for the post-punk crowd, including many young teen-

agers who cannot get into other local clubs. Located in an old warehouse, it consists of a large dingy room with graffiti-splattered walls, a concrete floor, a few beat up chairs, and a young chain-smoking audience with plenty of angst. Anyone who has spent time in Amsterdam's clubs will feel right at home here. Those who delight in sharp contrasts should drop by after a dinner at Chez Panisse.

La Peña

3105 Shattuck Ave., 849-2568. For a mega-dose of political correctness head to the collectively run La Peña Cultural Center. La Peña had its origins in local outrage over CIA involvement in the 1973 Chilean coup that overthrew Salvador Allende. Modeled after the *peñas* that sprang up in Chile and Argentina during that period, the center focuses on Latin and Central American culture. Events

924 Gilman Street. Photo by Don Pitcher.

include concerts by reggae bands, performances by Peruvian folk singers, films on Nicaragua, theater productions about American Indians, and discussions of U.S. policy in El Salvador. The moderately priced programs are held in a large auditorium (no age restrictions). Next door, a small shop sells books and other items from and about the other half of the Americas. Cafe Violetta, wedged between the auditorium and the Starry Plough Pub, serves moderately priced Latin meals (see *Restaurants and Cafes*), and is a pleasant place to talk between sets at the Starry Plough or after shows in La Peña. The center also has an extensive collection of information on Latin America, including video documentaries, publications, records, and tapes.

Larry Blake's Rathskeller

2367 Telegraph Ave., 848-0886. In town for almost half a century, Larry Blake's has become a local landmark. There's a cocktail lounge and a bland restaurant upstairs, but the main attraction is the Rathskeller in the basement, where street signs adorn the walls and students over 21 straddle the bar stools. Larry Blake's attracts some of the country's finest blues and R&B acts, and the place gets very crowded on weekends.

Picante Taqueria

1328 6th St., 525-3121. The Picante is an inexpensive Mexican restaurant with free jazz entertainment on weekend nights. The wrap-around bar and friendly, boisterous crowd of all ages make this an enjoyable place to drink with compatriots.

Pasand Lounge

2284 Shattuck Ave., 848-0260. The newest of several jazz venues in Berkeley,

Pasand is an offshoot of the adjacent Indian restaurant, for those 21 and over. No cover charge but a two-drink minimum per set.

Starry Plough Irish Pub

3101 Shattuck Ave., 841-2082. Here you'll find authentic Berkeley, in the leftist posters plastered over the brick walls and in the frumpy post-hippie crowd that jams the dance floor. This is one place where you don't need to dress up. The Plough serves pub grub, but most folks come to hear the music, dance, smoke cigarettes, and drink the Guinness on tap. Monday nights, starting at 7 pm, the Plough offers free Irish dancing lessons, with traditional Irish music beginning at 9 pm. Most other nights you'll hear rock music. There is also a board for dart enthusiasts. Customers under 21 are allowed in until 10 pm.

Yoshi's

6030 Claremont Ave., Oakland, 652-9200. In recent years the East Bay has become perhaps the primary center for jazz on the West Coast: in addition to such clubs as Kimball's East (Emeryville) and Pasand, there are numerous jazz concerts on campus and at the Maybeck Recital Hall. Just outside Berkeley's border is Yoshi's, one of the finest jazz clubs around. Yoshi's attracts the big name jazz acts and commands a stiff cover. The restaurant serves Japanese food (see *Restaurants and Cafes*) and admits customers of all ages.

Bars and Pubs

Albatross Pub

1822 San Pablo Ave., 849-4714. Behind the plain exterior of The Albatross is one of the few genuine pubs in Berkeley, open to those over 21. There are six dart lanes in the back room, a small fireplace, and all the free popcorn you can eat. Beer connoisseurs will enjoy the Anchor Steam and Guinness on tap, and graffitiologists will be amused by Berkeley's wittiest rest room scribblers.

Bison Brewing Co.
2598 Telegraph Ave., 841-7734.
Berkeley's newest brewpub has both stout and lager on tap, along with light meals, nachos, and espresso coffees available to all ages. There is a nice deck upstairs that overlooks the Avenue. Try to ignore the tasteless signs inside.

Brennan's
720 University Ave., 841-0960. West Berkeley's home to all-American food, Brennan's, is a big barn of a place with formica tables and pictures of prize bulls on the hospital-green walls. During the day, the cafeteria offers traditional American food at inexpensive prices. After 9 pm, Brennan's admits only those over 21. From the central horseshoe-shaped bar, bartenders serve great Irish coffees and other drinks to a boisterous clientele that includes all strata of the Bay Area population.

Cafe Bistro
2271 Shattuck Ave., 848-3081. This basement bar has jazz every night of the week and light meals served in a crowded, smoky atmosphere with a beatnik feel to it. Cafe Bistro is a popular hangout for those over 21 after an evening at one of the nearby movie houses.

Claremont Hotel Terrace Room
41 Tunnel Rd., 843-3000, ext. 210-211. The Terrace Room offers a quiet, romantic place for an evening in one of California's most spectacular hotels. There is live jazz most evenings, although only customers over 21 are admitted to the shows. Try to arrive early enough to get a window seat for a spectacular view of a Bay Area sunset.

Henry's Publick House and Grille
2600 Durant Ave., 845-8981. Leaded glass entrance doors, oak tables, and polished brass rails give Henry's an air of old-fashioned sophistication. Trendy appetizers, meals, and drinks are served up to a preppy crowd from nearby frats and sororities, although after 9 pm during the school year Henry's admits only customers 21 and over. The prim and proper Reverend Henry Durant, for whom this bar is named, would certainly not be amused.

Kip's
2439 Durant Ave., 848-4340. Southside's most popular student hangout, Kip's has a large-screen TV upstairs that packs them in for sporting events, pizza, burgers, and beer. This is the place to be seen if you're a dorm or frathouse resident, especially since those under 21 are admitted until 11 pm. Downstairs, things are quieter, and all ages are always welcome.

La Val's
1834 Euclid Ave., 843-5617 and 2516B Durant Ave., 845-5353. Another popular hangout for students of all ages seeking pizza, camaraderie, and serious beer drinking, La Val's can be found on both sides of campus. The

Skates on the Berkeley Marina. Photo by Don Pitcher.

dungeon-like Southside location has a large-screen TV for sports watching. On Northside you'll discover a pleasant patio and live music downstairs on weekends.

Pappy's

Lower Sproul Plaza, 843-0373. Pappy's big screen TV attracts all ages of the Monday night football gang as well as the soap opera afficionados. The grill has inexpensive pub grub, and you can choose from 99 different beers. When school is in session there are comedy shows and live music each week. Two dart boards are also available.

Raleigh's

2438 Telegraph Ave., 848-8652. Extremely popular with the college crowd, Raleigh's does restrict entrance for those under 21 at 9 pm during the school year. There are eight-

een imported and domestic beers on draft. To experience beer at its best, try St. Stans from Modesto or Germany's Spaten. There are hearty meals and you can try your hand at table shuffleboard in the back.

Schmidt's Tobacco & Trading Co.

1492 Solano Ave., 525-1900. This is one of Berkeley's least known but friendliest pubs, for those over 21. The interior looks like a shabby English sitting room, complete with puzzles to put together and card games to play. The English beer comes by the liter, and a pungent pipe tobacco smell permeates the place. There's a patio out front if the smoke gets too thick.

Shattuck Avenue Spats

1974 Shattuck Ave., 841-7225. The decor of Spats looks like it came from a taxidermist's back room, an antique shop, and a Goodwill store, and their gag drink menu is a bizarre assortment that includes a "Borneo Fogcutter" complete with dry ice. Overstuffed chairs and low lighting make this a popular place for socializing or hanging out after a movie. All ages are admitted.

Skates

100 Seawall Drive., 549-1900. Skates is an extremely popular place for couples and young singles, as it caters to an up-beat, ethnically mixed clientele. Sit at a window table and you'll find yourself facing the Golden Gate Bridge and San Francisco. Customers under 21 are admitted until 10:30 pm. Choose from many different wines and beers or a large selection of light meals. The adjacent restaurant serves up California Cuisine if you want something more substantial (see *Restaurants and Cafes*).

Triple Rock Brewery

1920 Shattuck Ave., 843-2739. Anyone who has been in an English tavern that brews its own beer knows the value of locally-made ale. Even after Prohibition it continued to be illegal in the U.S. to sell beer directly to the public, and brew pubs did not become legal in California until 1982. Triple Rock Brewery, a noisy, convivial place with excellent bar food, was an immediate hit when it opened in 1986. The beer comes in three strengths, all of which easily beat the watery, mass-produced brands. There is also a small patio upstairs and a shuffleboard table in the back. Age restrictions apply after 8 pm.

Spirits

Sure, you can always go to the giant Liquor Barn store in Albany for an

Triple Rock Brewery. Photo by Don Pitcher.

Takara Sake

Takara Sake (708 Addison St., 540-8250) is Berkeley's largest winery. Sake, the traditional wine of Japan, originated more than 2000 years ago. Originally, the fermentation process was begun by young virgins who chewed rice and spat the wad into a large wooden tub. Today the process is different. A special fermentation culture is added to the rice after it has gone through a mash. The product goes through a process of pressing, filtration, and pasteurization; is aged for five to six months; and is then blended before the final bottling.

Japan's largest distillery, Takara Shuzo Co., owns and operates the Berkeley plant, one of just three sake plants in the country. Its production of 100,000 cases per year makes up nearly a third of the sake consumed in the U.S. Most is sold in Japanese restaurants, but sake is one of the fastest growing segments of the alcohol market. Takara Sake produces five types of sake in Berkeley, all of which you can drink warmed or at room temperature. There are no plant tours, but a narrated slide presentation describes production. The tasting room is open daily noon-6 pm.

Sake making at Takara Sake. Photo by Don Pitcher.

impressive selection of wines and beers, but there are more pleasant alternatives. One of the best is the **North Berkeley Wine Co.** (1505 Shattuck Ave., 848-8910). In addition to wines you won't find elsewhere, North Berkeley always has four or five excellent wines at bargain prices in the front. **Enoteca Mastro** (933 San Pablo Ave., Albany, 524-4822) sells only Italian wines, and owner Mark Mastro really knows the business. Everything he offers, down to the $3 bottles of Chianti, is excellent. The

shop also has a tasting bar. If you are looking for fine French wines, **Kermit Lynch Wine Merchant** (1605 San Pablo Ave., 524-1524) imports and retails many vintages unavailable elsewhere. Kermit Lynch is considered one of the most influential wine merchants in the nation, buying from tiny European producers and then blending or importing directly. **Solano Cellars** (1580 Solano Ave., Albany, 525-0379) sells both European and domestic wines at moderate prices, and specializes in hard-to-find local wines. It also has daily wine tastings. **Trumpetvine Wines** (2115 Allston Way, 843-1311) in Trumpetvine Court, has a good selection of California wines, particularly zinfandels. **Alcatel Bottle Shop** (6363 Telegraph Ave., Oakland, 653-6418) has one of the largest choices of wines in the area. **Curds & Whey** (6311 College Ave., Oakland, 652-6311) is a wine merchant offering fine wines and daily tastings.

For those who would rather brew their own wine and beer, the informed staff at **Oak Barrel Winecraft** (1443 San Pablo Ave., 849-0400) will provide everything necessary—barrels, bottles, corks, testing equipment, and winepresses. They also offer books on wine and beer production.

Although the city of Berkeley is miles from any significant agricultural land, it has two wineries and a sake facility, in part because of the near perfect year-round fermentation temperatures and the proximity to Bay Area markets. **Audubon Cellars** (600 Addison St., 540-5384) has only been in existence since 1982, but produces 15,000 cases per year. This reasonably priced wine has garnered numerous awards at California's county fairs.

Audubon offers wine tasting daily from noon-6 pm, but tours should be arranged several days in advance. Their wines are also available under the name Sonoma Mission. A small percentage of the profit from Audubon Cellars wines goes to support the National Audubon Society. **Edmunds-St. Johns Winery** (805 Camelia St., 843-4737) is a tiny operation producing 1000 cases a year. Call for appointments to visit the winemaking operation. Their wines are available at Solano Cellars and Jay Vee Liquors. **Thousand Oaks Brewing Co.** (525-8801), a microbrewery in Berkeley, produces small quantities of Golden Bear beer, available at local stores.

In 1983, Berkeley Assemblyman Tom Bates pushed through the state legislature a bill legalizing brewpubs, and today there are more than a hundred in California. The difference between beer in brewpubs and the national brands is like that between a can of Chung King chop suey and authentic Chinese cooking. Berkeley's **Triple Rock Brewery** was the first brewpub in Berkeley and remains the most best known, but the **Bison Brewing Company** is also popular.

Hotels and Motels

Berkeley's accommodations cover the spectrum from fleabag flophouses to elaborate quarters that would make a prince feel at home. Although a youth hostel would seem appropriate in Berkeley, the young traveler on a tight budget will need to cross the Bay to the busy San Francisco hostel. Listed below are local lodging places, categorized into Bed and Breakfasts, Hotels, Motels, University Lodging, and Residence Hotels. Most of the cheaper places are along "motel row" in West Berkeley. Prices listed do not include the city of Berkeley's 11% hotel tax, the highest in the state. This tax is not imposed on stays longer than two weeks or on the private B&Bs. Note that during graduation time at the University (mid-May) all the better hotels fill up very early. If you need space during that time, it's a good idea to make reservations in January to be sure of getting a room. Because prices tend to change seasonally and to rise unexpectedly, it's best to call for current room rates.

Bed and Breakfast

Although popular in England, Bed and Breakfasts did not reach this country until 1978. When they finally did, Berkeley was the first American city to have one.

Bed and Breakfast International
1181-B Solano Ave., Albany, CA 94706, 525-4569, $30-$50 S, $35-$55 D. Bed and Breakfast International makes reservations for approximately 80 homes and apartments in the East Bay. Unlike commercial B&Bs, these are private homes offering pleasant accommodations and full breakfasts for a reasonable price. There is a two-night minimum stay. The homes are located throughout Berkeley; one has even been featured in *Architectural Digest*, and includes a swimming pool, hot tub, and panoramic views of the Golden Gate Bridge. (Most are not nearly this elaborate.) B&Bs provide a great introduction to both the city and its people, and it is even possible to make special reservations with people sharing similar interests or languages. Checkout times are flexible and many places allow you to use their phones, TV, kitchen, laundry, or iron. These homes are particularly good for single women travelers, visiting scholars, foreign visitors, and people who need to stay in a particular part of Berkeley.

Gramma's Inn
2740 Telegraph Ave., 549-2145, 29 rooms with TV and phones, $85-$175 S or D, government and corporate discounts, free parking. Built in 1900 by a Berkeley developer, this beautiful old Tudor-style house was converted into a B&B in 1980. Gramma's has since expanded to include three smaller houses behind the mansion. The Inn provides a complimentary light breakfast along with wine and cheese in the evening. The rooms have been beautifully redecorated with antique furnishings and many have separate balconies and fireplaces ("Duraflame logs," alas). There is a sunny courtyard behind the main building.

Gramma's is one of Berkeley's nicest and most comfortable places to stay. The pricey Sunday brunch ($19) here is a real treat.

Hotels

Durant Hotel

2600 Durant Ave., 845-8981, 140 rooms with TV and phones, $75 S, $85 D, government and corporate discounts, children free, parking $3/day. The recently remodeled Durant has an ideal close-to-campus location and free continental breakfasts Mon-Sat. The luxurious "Henry's Publick House and Grill" downstairs is popular both with guests and Berkeley's fraternity and sorority crowd. The Durant's Southside location can prove noisy, particularly on weekends, so it is best to select a room from the higher floors.

French Hotel

1538 Shattuck Ave., 548-9930, 18 rooms with TV and phones, $58-$95 S or D, government and corporate discounts, free parking. Once a French laundry, this building located near the center of Berkeley's Gourmet Ghetto is now a pleasant small hotel. The popular cafe downstairs serves cappuccinos in an arty atmosphere. Rooms are furnished in a European design, and most have separate balconies. If you're on a government or corporate expense account, rooms are $48.

Marriott Inn

Berkeley Marina, 548-7920, 325 rooms with TV and phones, $80-$155 S or D, government discounts, free parking. Built on the Berkeley Marina and offering magnificent views, the modern, attractively decorated Marriott is Berkeley's largest lodging place. It caters primarily to the business crowd, but its reduced weekend rates make it popular with other travelers as well. The Inn has a pleasant waterfront location, but is two miles from downtown Berkeley. Facilities include exercise equipment and two indoor pools. The Marriott also has a Swim and Fitness Club ($300/year) for the community.

Shattuck Hotel

2086 Allston Way, 845-7300, 110 rooms with TV and phones. $72 S, $82 D, government discounts, parking $3.50/day. When the Mission-style Shattuck Hotel was completed in 1914, it was one of the largest structures in the Bay Area. Recently remodelled, the centrally located hotel is now an enjoyable place with an outstanding (and expensive) restaurant, Sedona Grill, that offers southwestern-style cooking. Nearby, at 2105 Bancroft Way, the Shattuck operates a 23,000-square-foot Conference Center with ten meeting rooms accommodating up to 1200 guests.

UC Hotel

1040 University Ave., 540-9272, 78 rooms, no TV or phones, $20 S or D, bath down the hall, free parking, no visitors after 8 pm. The price is rock-bottom. This is not the sort of place that would get your mother's approval, unless she tolerates a rickety elevator, severely austere rooms, and a sleazy atmosphere.

Opposite: Gramma's Inn. Photo by Don Pitcher.

Victorian Hotel

2520 Durant Ave., 540-0700, 20 rooms with TV and phones, $52-$70 S or D, find-your-own parking. Located in the center of Southside action, the Victo-rian Hotel with its restaurant and cafe is a good place for visitors who want to be close to the University. Rooms are nicely furnished and well insulated from noise on Durant Avenue.

Claremont Hotel

41 Tunnel Rd., Oakland, 843-3000, 239 rooms with TV and phones, $109-$200 S or $155-$220 D, University and corporate discounts, parking $5/day. The Claremont Hotel is one of the Bay Area's best-loved buildings. Architect Frank Lloyd Wright once called it "one of the few hotels in the world with warmth, character, and charm." The huge, rambling masterpiece straddles the Berkeley-Oakland border, flowing over the contours of the site with a Victorian elegance.

In 1905 developer Frank Havens (responsible for planting many of the eucalyptus trees in the Berkeley hills), Francis "Borax" Smith (of Death Valley fame), and Berkeley developer John Spring proposed a major resort hotel for the East Bay. As the developers of the famous Key System of ferries and electric trains, these three men envisioned a palatial hotel at the end of the "E" line of trains, with the trains running directly to the hotel's subterranean entrance. A local architect, Charles W. Dickey, modelled the hotel on medieval half-timbered buildings, combining a Spanish-Renaissance tower with a flowing French Chateau design.

Construction began in 1906, but a financial panic and high taxes left the hotel an unfinished oddity for nearly a decade. Havens eventually took over complete ownership after winning two games of checkers with the other owners—the stakes being the hotel. In 1914, Erik Lindblom, a gold miner who struck it rich in the Klondike, became part owner, and the hotel was finally finished in time for San Francisco's 1915 Panama-Pacific Exposition. Key System train service, combined with ferries, took visitors to San Francisco in only 30 minutes, faster than most of today's traffic-jammed commutes.

After the Exposition ended, the hotel became less fashionable, in part because of a state law that prohibited alcohol from being sold within a mile of the University campus. This made the Claremont one of the few California hotels that did not have a bar, and probably contributed to its becoming a residential hotel. The fortunes of the hotel changed radically on the day a female student from the University (known for her fondness for alcohol) decided to see for herself if the hotel really was within a mile of the campus. With help from friends she laboriously measured the distance and found it to be a few feet over the one-mile radius. This discovery led to the opening of a new bar (now the Terrace Bar) in 1937, and transformed the

The Claremont Hotel. Photo by Don Pitcher.

hotel's image from that of a staid residential hotel to a major convention and entertainment center. Music from the big bands of Russ Morgan, Dick Jurgens, Tommy Dorsey, Woody Herman, Glenn Miller, and Lawrence Welk soon filled the air, drawing throngs to the Claremont. (Rumor has it that the woman was rewarded with free drinks at the bar for the rest of her life.)

For many years the 200-foot-long circular fire slides behind the Claremont were a major source of local entertainment. Many of Berkeley's residents can recall childhood adventures, avoiding the management while sneaking to the upper stories for a wild ride down. In later years the hotel went through changes in both ownership and condition, and by the 1960s the place had become rundown. The deteriorated hotel was beautifully restored in the 1970s at a cost of over $24 million, and today calls itself "the Bay Area's only resort hotel." Unfortunately, the fire escape slides were removed in 1979 as part of this renovation process.

The Claremont's present-day luxuries include laundry service, a lounge with nightly entertainment, an Olympic-sized outdoor pool, conference and banquet rooms, and a concierge. The spacious grounds are nicely landscaped, and those sitting at the Terrace Bar will enjoy the sunsets. If you really want to live it up, the Tower Suite for $650 a night should fill the bill. It rises three levels up the hotel's tower and even includes a private sauna at the top, with a spectacular view of the Bay Area. Guests to the Claremont are given free use of the swimming pool, tennis courts, and other facilities. Tennis lessons and a masseuse are extra. Locals can join the Claremont Hotel Pool and Tennis Club ($2200 a year) for access to these facilities.

Motels

Bel Air Motel
*1330 University Ave., 848-8061, 34
rooms with TV and phones, $36 S, $38 D,
free parking.* The Bel Air is clean, but
its furnishings are plain and barely
above Goodwill-grade. The roomy
suite ($56) includes a kitchenette.

Berkeley House Motor Hotel-Best Western
*920 University Ave., 849-1121, 111
rooms with TV and phones, $53 S, $64 D.
University and government discounts
available. Banquet and meeting rooms,
swimming pool, free parking.* Welcome
to middle America. At the Berkeley
House you get piped-in muzak, your
basic steak house complete with Ye
Olde Victorian decor, and a pool with
slightly more water than a waterbed.
The lounge has a piano bar and a
large-screen TV.

Berkeley Motel
*2001 Bancroft Way, 843-4043, 13 rooms
with TV but no phones, $37 S, $44 D,
free parking.* This very plain motel has
old furniture and a central Berkeley
location across from Berkeley High
School.

Berkeley Plaza Motel
*1175 University Ave., 843-9803, 60
rooms with TV and phones, $35 S or D,
University discounts, free parking.* The
Berkeley Plaza offers a large number
of kitchenettes ($55 S or D) and is one
of the few motels with weekly rates
($160 S, $200 D). Ask about special
rates for University employees. The
rooms are livable, but not at all fancy.
Although it is on busy University
Ave., the rooms are somewhat protected from street noise.

Berkeley Travelodge
*1820 University Ave., 843-4262, 30
rooms with TV and phones, $52 S, $58 D,
University discounts, free parking.* Central location.

Bonanza Motel
*1720 San Pablo Ave., 524-8778, 24
rooms with TV and phones, $31 S or D,
free parking.* The Bonanza, one of
Berkeley's cheapest lodging places, is
nothing fancy, but is in better condition than some of its more expensive
West Berkeley cousins.

California Motel
*1461 University Ave., 848-3840, 43
rooms with TV and phones, $35-$40 S or
D, free parking.* A fairly quiet motel in
spite of its location on busy University Avenue. The rooms are clean and
well-maintained.

Campus Motel
*1619 University Ave., 841-3844, 23
rooms with TV and phones, $50 S, $55 D,
free parking.* The Campus Motel is a
clean, well-kept motel that has had
the same friendly owner for over 30
years. Rates are a bit higher than other
motels on "motel row," but the quality is commensurate.

Capri Motel
*1512 University Ave., 845-7090, 26
rooms with TV but no phones, $35 S or
D, free parking.* This is the tawdriest
motel on University Ave., so be prepared for peeling paint, old furniture,
and worn carpets. When you select
the room with the king-sized bed you
get a free mirror on the ceiling.

Day's Inn Motel
*1603 Powell St., Emeryville, 547-7888,
154 rooms with TV and phones, $80 S,*

$90 D, government and corporate discounts, non-smoking rooms, handicap-accessible rooms, swimming pool, free parking. Located next to the freeway in "scenic" Emeryville.

Motel Flamingo

1761 University Ave., 841-4242, 29 rooms with TV and phones, $55 S or D, University and corporate discounts, free parking. The shocking-pink Motel Flamingo is relatively clean with typical budget motel decor, a fair level of street noise, and friendly owners. A must-visit for collectors of plastic flamingos.

Golden Bear Motel

1620 San Pablo Ave., 525-6770, 41 rooms with TV and phones, $35 S, $37 D, free parking. The Golden Bear's "No Vacancy" sign is usually the first one lit, and with good reason. The motel is exceptionally clean, has a very friendly management, and is nicely furnished. The motel is not as close to the center of town as others, and traffic on San Pablo Ave. can be noisy, but the rooms are well insulated. The Golden Bear is by far the best moderately-priced lodging in Berkeley.

Holiday Inn

1800 Powell St., Emeryville, 658-9300, 279 rooms with TV and phones, $85-$250 S, $95-$250 D, University and corporate discounts, outdoor swimming pool and conference rooms, free parking. According to the Emeryville Holiday Inn's publicity brochure, "this exciting Holiday Inn is located at the foot of the famous Bay Bridge." True. And also next to the other exciting Emeryville attractions: the towering Watergate complex and 50,000 cars a day hurtling by on the freeway.

Emeryville is the one town in the Bay Area which specializes in ruining one of the world's loveliest views by walling it in with joyless concrete rectangles. The rooms at the Holiday Inn are clean and well-maintained, and the bayside ones provide partially blocked sunset views of San Francisco.

Marina Lodge Motel

975 University Ave., 841-7410, 24 rooms with TV and phones, $60 S or D, free parking. Another of Berkeley's moderately priced motels on lower University Ave., Marina Lodge is fairly clean but suffers a bit from street noise.

San Francisco International Hostel

Building 240, Ft. Mason, San Francisco, 771-7277. 165 bunkbeds in separate-sex dorms at $10 each. (A few family or couples rooms are available by reservation at the same rate.) Baths down the hall, kitchen, pay phones, check-in 7 am-2 pm and 4:30-midnight, midnight curfew (2 am on weekends for $1 extra). Located near Ghiradelli Square with wonderful views of San Francisco Bay, this hostel is home each year to over 50,000 visitors from 90 nations (Bay Area residents cannot stay here, however). There are no age limitations, and you don't need to be a member, but stays are limited to three nights and reservations are recommended. To get to the hostel from Berkeley, take BART to the Powell Street Station and then catch the No. 30 bus to the corner of Van Ness and North Point. The hostel is an easy walk from there.

Villa Motel

1155 San Pablo Ave., Albany, 524-8234, 30 rooms with TV but no phones, $28 S *or D, free parking.* The location is a bit far from the campus and there is nothing fancy about the Villa Motel, but the price is hard to beat.

University Campus Lodging

Both men and women can stay in either faculty club. During the summer, students and University guests can stay at the **University Guest Residence** (2400 Durant in Ida Sproul Hall). Rooms are available between early June and mid-August each year for $30 S, $38 D. For information, call 642-5925 during the summer or 642-4444 during the school year. The lovely **Men's Faculty Club** (540-5678) near the center of campus has space for faculty or departmental guests on official University business. Rates are $46-$48 S, $54-$59 D (price including a continental breakfast). The nearby **Women's Faculty Club** (845-5084) has similar restrictions and charges, $59 S, $50-$60 D with continental breakfasts, plus $2 for dues.

Residence Hotels

Cal Hotel (2008 Shattuck Ave., 540-9475, 35 rooms, $43-$53/week), **Nash Hotel** (2045 University Ave., 841-1163, 46 rooms, $75/week), and **University Hotel** (2057 University Ave., 848-3133, 47 rooms, $50/week) all provide spartan furnishings with no cooking facilities, but they are centrally located, well maintained, and amazingly inexpensive. Unfortunately, they are almost always full and require a list of references before you can even be considered. The **Carlton Hotel** (2338 Telegraph Ave., 848-0481, 131 rooms, no cooking facilities, $201/month) on hectic Telegraph is used by both students and others, but don't expect peace and quiet. The **YMCA** (2001 Allston Way, 848-6800, 86 rooms, $20-$21 S) is a good place for males. The central location, low price, and excellent exercise facilities mean that it is often full. Farther afield, **Lake Merritt Lodge** (2332 Harrison, Oakland, 893-3130, 147 rooms, $165 S/week, $190 D/week, swimming pool) is the only nearby residence hotel with meals included in the price. Recent fires in the Berkeley Inn and Stark Hotel led to the loss of some of the cheapest rooms in the city, forcing many people onto the streets and exacerbating an already serious problem with homelessness. There are few options beyond the emergency shelters (see *On the Streets*) for many of these people.

Community Services

Not surprisingly, Berkeley has a far wider variety of assistance programs, referral agencies, consumer help-lines, support groups, adult classes, and guided hikes than most similarly-sized cities. The best source of up-to-date information on local services, events, and programs is one of the free local papers, particularly the *Express*. This chapter details a potpourri of other community resources, ranging from radio stations to recycling centers.

Children's Services

Berkeley provides an amazing variety of ways to keep kids entertained, some of which are of equal interest to adults (see *City Parks, Recreation*, and *Arts and Entertainment* for a sampling). For current information on raising kids in the Bay Area—health, child-care services, clothes, family adventures, entertainment, books, classes, and activities—pick up a copy of the free monthly newspaper, *Parents Press*, available in local libraries and in many shops.

Bananas
6501 Telegraph Ave., Oakland, 658-7101. When the women's movement flowered in the early 70s, its members tended to focus on discrimination, abortion, and equal employment issues rather than on issues related to childcare. To fill the gap, three feminist mothers got together in 1972 to form children's play groups. After getting a desk and a phone in the Berkeley Women's Center, they put up flyers announcing a new organization with an unforgettable name—"Bananas"—as in "going bananas." They produced a simple ten-page guide listing free or inexpensive places to take kids in the Bay Area that proved an immediate hit. It grew into today's comprehensive *Bananas' Guide for Parents and Children*, which contains descriptions of local children's activities, museums, family support services, health care, and more.

One of the first childcare referral agencies in the nation, Bananas continues to offer its services to a diverse clientele from welfare mothers to well-to-do couples. The group receives funding from the United Way, the State of California, and bingo games at San Pablo Ave. and Gilman Street.

The racks at the Bananas office are filled with dozens of free pamphlets on every facet of raising children, from breast-feeding to head lice. There's a pre-crisis "warmline" for parents (658-6046) and inexpensive workshops on such topics as choosing infant care or dealing with the "terrible twos." The bulletin boards at Bananas are crowded with training programs, childcare job openings, adoption information, and listings of childcare providers. A *Bananas Newsletter* published five times a year ($5/yr) provides current information on childcare issues, workshops, and other events.

Twinline

Anyone expecting twins should call Twinline (2131 University Ave., 644-0861), a valuable source of information, mutual support, and technical assistance. The first such organization in the nation, Twinline now serves more than 2000 Bay Area families. Classes are free or low cost.

The Disabled

Bay Area Outreach and Recreation Program (BORP)

605 Eshleman Hall, 849-4663. Located on campus, BORP offers classes for disabled individuals in swimming, scuba diving, tennis, and basketball, and sponsors sports tournaments,

Phil Draper and Michael Winters at Center for Independent Living. Photo by Don Pitcher.

rafting trips, and theater productions. BORP membership ($15/yr or $12/yr for students) provides trip discounts and a bimonthly newsletter.

Center for Independent Living

2539 Telegraph Ave., 841-4776. Many newcomers to Berkeley are struck by the abundance of people in wheelchairs and their almost complete integration into society. Before the 1970s, most of America's disabled individuals lived in nursing homes and institutions, but opportunities have changed radically since then, due largely to the work of Berkeley's Center for Independent Living, or CIL. The center started in 1972 when several wheelchair-bound individuals wrangled a $250 grant from the Berkeley Rotary Club to study the local disabled population. Led by Ed Roberts and Phil Draper, the group soon pulled in a major federal grant and used it to form the nation's first center run by and for the disabled community. (See *The People of Berkeley* for more on Ed Roberts.)

In addition to providing a focal point for people tired of being kept in institutions, CIL's activism helped to make Berkeley a mecca for the disabled. Under pressure from CIL, the city instituted a comprehensive program of curb cuts for wheelchairs, not just downtown (as in other cities), but also on all the back streets. CIL lobbied for full access to BART and AC Transit, for "mainstreaming" disabled children into regular school programs, and for full implementation of the Rehabilitation Act of 1973, which said that people had a right to live independently, no matter how severe their disability. In winning all three of these battles—the latter only after a three-week vigil in the San Francisco Federal Building—the center became a model for more than 300 similar groups across the country. In addition to these changes, the city's mild weather, University support, and progressive community and government earned Berkeley such a reputation as a haven for the disabled that by the late 70s disabled people were arriving at local airports, calling up CIL and stating: "I want to live here." In recent years, Proposition 13 and Reagan-Era funding cuts forced CIL to scale back some of its services and to turn increasingly to private funding sources, but with a staff of 40 (half of them disabled), CIL remains one of the largest disability organizations in the nation.

Today CIL works to dispel myths and stereotypes about disabled people, and to remove physical and psychological barriers in order to enable people to live independent lives. Free services include attendant referral, counseling on jobs and benefits, and independent living skills classes. One of the major accomplishments of CIL becomes apparent when you step through the sliding doors of the center or when you walk down a typical street in Berkeley—those who don't have disabilities are forced to meet those who do as equals. You can join the **Friends of CIL** for $50/year (tax-deductible).

Disabled Students Program
2515 Channing Way, 642-0518. The Disabled Students Program provides services to more than 350 disabled Cal students each year, making the University a national leader in such assistance. Services include housing, career planning, financing, learning disabilities assistance, sign language transla-

tors for the deaf, wheelchair repair, assistance in developing independent living skills, and a special recreation program (CalSTAR).

World Institute on Disability
1720 Oregon St., 486-8314. Established by Ed Roberts and Judith Heumann, two severely disabled individuals, this public policy center was set up to combat "handicappism"—viewing people with disabilities as pitiable or unable to live independent lives. The group works to promote independent living centers around the world, to educate the public and other disabled people, and to make society more accessible.

Information Services

Berkeley Chamber of Commerce
1834 University Ave., 549-7000. This local office is of limited help to the traveler or new Berkeley resident, but it does have a few city brochures. Their detailed Berkeley map is well worth getting.

Berkeley Historical Society
1325 Grant St., 524-9880. For historical information and a substantial collection of old photos, newspapers, and books on the city and its buildings, check out the Berkeley Historical Society.

Berkeley Information Network
540-0666. The public library's unique telephone referral service is available to answer almost any question. Invaluable for serious research, it's also great for trivial pursuits of all types: want to know how whales procreate? When the next Giants home game

Finding Work

Adelante (830 Bancroft Way, 549-0232) has a bilingual job training program teaching secretarial, computer, and janitorial skills as well as classes for amnesty applicants. The center also assists with GED and employment exams.

Asians for Job Opportunities in Berkeley (AJOB) (1222 University Ave., 548-6700) provides job training and placement services for Asian immigrants, particularly those from Vietnam, Laos, and Cambodia. They also teach English and assist with cultural adjustments.

ASUC Personnel Office (400 Eshleman Hall, 642-1117) has information and applications for 500 part-time or 80 full-time positions with the ASUC.

The Bay Area Urban League (2198 6th St., 644-3796) offers job search workshops, vocational counseling and referral, job placement services, and other counseling programs.

Berkeley Adult School Career Center (1222 University Ave., 848-6730) has job training and placement for a variety of areas. It also has a job board and employment hotline, teaches job search skills, and provides other information for continuing students.

Berkeley High School Career Center (2246 Milvia St., 644-6209), open to Berkeley students during the school year, helps kids locate summer, part- or full-time jobs, and has information on colleges, financial aid, résumé writing, volunteer internships, and work-study programs. Kids under eighteen can get work permits here. During the summer, the staff and the Employment Development Department run a Summer Jobs for Youth Program that is open to the community.

Berkeley Youth Alternatives (BYA) (2141 Bonar St., 849-1402) helps low income youths find summer jobs or park maintenance work during the school year. Youth and family counseling services are also available. In the same building you'll also find a recreation area with ping-pong and pool tables, a youth boxing ring and weight room run by the Police Department.

Career Planning and Placement Center (2200 Bancroft Way, 642-0440) lists part-time, temporary, and summer jobs, as well as career positions, student internships, classes in job search skills, and career workshops for University students and recent graduates.

Employment Development Department (EDD) (1375 University Ave., 540-2833) is the place to go for unemployment claims. It also has employment listings and can direct you to job training programs.

Temporary Assistance Program (TAP) (2539 Channing Way, 642-1013) advertises short-term positions (maximum ten weeks) at the University. Most are secretarial and word processing jobs, but there are also occasional openings in delivery, custodial, and mail processing

University Personnel Office (2539 Channing Way, 642-1011) lists permanent jobs with the University. If you apply diligently for months and get nowhere, don't flagellate your ego too severely. Rumor has it that while most jobs appear to be open listings, they are often sewn up by insiders.

The Women's Employment Resources Corporation (1810 6th St., 549-1421) helps women with low income to find employment by providing extensive job listings, career workshops, résumé assistance, and special recruitment programs.

Work Ability Program (644-6046 for young people, or 1222 University Ave., 549-9132 for adults) assists physically, mentally, and emotionally disabled people by offering job training and evaluation, skills counseling, résumé assistance, and other help. Young people work through the high school's Special Education Program while adults use the Work Ability Program at the Adult School.

Youth Employment Services (YES) (1730 Oregon St., 644-6031) is a place for young people to start looking for work. YES has classroom and on-the-job training, job search, employment counseling, and summer employment programs for youths aged 14-21. YES aims primarily at low income youths, but lists summer jobs for anyone. Apply early (March) for summer employment.

comes up? Berkeley Information Network has all the answers, or can at least steer you in the right direction. The line is open Mon-Thurs 10 am-9 pm; Fri-Sat 10 am to midnight; Sun 1 pm to midnight. Frequently, the line is connected directly to the reference desk at the Main Library, so you may also call 644-6648.

University Information

Although primarily oriented toward the campus, the **University Visitor Center** in the main lobby of the Student Union Building at Bancroft and Telegraph (642-5215) is a good source of local information, ranging from AC Transit schedules to lists of campus events. **Student Activities and Services** (102 Sproul Hall, 642-5171) puts out a helpful reference guide for new Berkeley students called *Resource*.

Libraries/Public

Berkeley's first public library, a collection of 54 books, opened in 1882, just four years after the city's incorporation. It lasted only six months, however, and another decade was to pass before a more permanent library opened. In 1892, two new University graduates, Dr. John Kelsey and William Waste (later Chief Justice of the California Supreme Court) began a campaign to bring a library/recreation hall to Berkeley. The impetus was, in Kelsey's words, a "great sensation when it became known that a number of [University] boys were frequenting a billiard parlor where gambling and drinking were indulged in." Businessman Francis Shattuck supplied two downtown rooms, and with money raised by Kelsey and Waste, a librarian was hired at a $50/month salary (including janitorial duties). The new Holmes Public Library (named for Oliver Wendell Holmes) had a front room filled with 264 books, nearly all of them donated by the Women's Christian Temperance Union. Behind a set of swinging doors lay an entertainment room filled with tables, games, and a piano.

Initially, patrons had to pay a dollar a year for a library card, but to open the library up to everyone, the Board of Town Trustees voted to take over the library in 1895 and establish the Berkeley Free Public Library. The new (district-elected) library trustees decided at their very first meeting to open branch libraries in South and West Berkeley. Even so, the expanding city soon overwhelmed its library facilities, and in 1903 Berkeley received a $40,000 grant from Andrew Carnegie to build the new Main Library at Shattuck and Kittredge. Despite the creation of six branch libraries—two in South Berkeley, two in West Berkeley, a North branch, and a Claremont branch—Berkeley's booming population made a new main library necessary. In 1931, it was rebuilt on the same site with funds from a library building fund tax.

In an era when many California cities have seen library hours axed as a result of Proposition 13, the people of Berkeley have continued to support their libraries strongly. In 1980, local voters overwhelmingly passed Measure E, a tax on residential and commercial buildings to support the library system; when this proved insufficient eight years later, voters supported Measure H, which provides a more permanent financial base for the library and allows it to remain open seven days a week. On a per capita basis, Berkeley is now one of America's top five cities in terms of library spending, number of books held, and number of books loaned. The system has more than 515,000 books, 850 magazine subscriptions, 20,000 records, tapes, and CD's, 15,000 slides, 7000 maps, and 500 art prints. The **Friends of the Berkeley Public Library** (644-6100) holds an annual book sale each June to raise funds for the library. You can donate books for them at the Main Library.

The three-story **Main Library** in downtown Berkeley (2090 Kittredge St., 644-6100) is crowded most afternoons and evenings with a combination of bookworms, high school students, housewives, researchers, and a

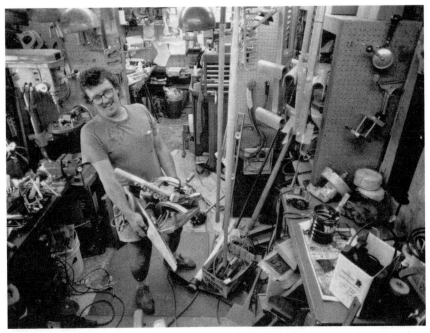

Pete McElligott at the Tool Lending Library. Photo by Don Pitcher.

few patrons who aren't playing with a full deck. The art and music room is particularly strong, and provides a pleasant place to listen to records before borrowing them. The Main Library is open Mon-Thurs 10 am-9 pm, Fri-Sat 10 am-6 pm and Sun 1 pm-5 pm.

Berkeley's four branch libraries are: **South Branch**, opened in 1896 (1901 Russell St., 644-6860), **West Branch**, opened in 1896 (1125 University Ave., 644-6870), **Claremont Branch**, opened in 1909 (2940 Benvenue Ave., 644-6880), and **North Branch**, opened in 1910 (1170 The Alameda, 644-6860). The nicest is the Claremont Branch, a quiet and comfortable place to read or study. Branch libraries are open Mon-Thurs 10 am-9 pm, Fri-Sat 10 am-6 pm. The Main Library and all the branches also offer weekly story times for children from six months to five years old. Call the library for specifics. The Berkeley Information Network (540-0666; see "Information Sources" in this chapter) is another very helpful public library service.

Berkeley's most unusual library is the **Tool Lending Project** (644-6101), located in a trailer next to the South Branch. It lends everything from screwdrivers to cement mixers for a fee of 50¢ to $3. Items may be borrowed for up to three days by Berkeley residents. Tool Lending Project hours are Tues and Wed noon-4 pm, 5 pm-7:30 pm, Thurs and Fri 1 pm-5:30 pm, and Sat 10 am-2 pm, 3-5:30 pm.

Libraries/University

The University's 25 libraries range from small specialized collections with restricted access to all-encompassing, multi-story collections. With more than seven million volumes and 100,000 periodicals and serials, Berkeley's library is the third largest academic library in the nation (after Harvard and Yale). Its manuscript collection of nearly 50 million makes it one of the world's largest. A complete listing of University libraries and their locations is available at the reference desks of the Main (Doe) and Undergraduate (Moffitt) libraries.

Although campus libraries are primarily for University students, faculty, and staff, others may borrow books by obtaining special cards. The basic fee is $50/year for California residents, or $12/6 months for students from other colleges. The "Library Lending Rules," available from the circulation desk of the Main Library (642-3403), give complete details. Be aware that the University library system charges very stiff fines for overdue or lost books. For information on the ever-changing library hours, see brochures in the various campus libraries. Studious types will be sad to learn that most University libraries are closed Fri and Sat nights.

Finding books in the University's huge collection can be an adventure. The traditional card catalog has now been replaced by two computerized systems, GLADIS and MELVYL. For newer books and other publications, the computers are a cinch, but if you're searching for something published before 1977, you may need to visit several campus libraries. Eventually the old system will be replaced by the computerized database.

Bancroft Library

642-6481. The Bancroft has an astounding treasure trove of historical lore and specializes in rare books and western U.S. history. Items in the collection include the original letters and diaries of Father Junipero Serra and Don Gaspar de Pertolá, documents from the ill-fated Donner party, and Gertrude Stein's letters, while among the selection of magnificent rare books are a Bible printed in 1466 and a 4000-year-old papyrus. Hundreds of old maps, photos, newspapers, and microfilmed documents make up the archival material. The library is also home to **University Archives** and the **Regional Oral History Office**, the former containing nearly 400,000 books and pamphlets, two million photographs, and more than 47 million manuscripts. One of the Bancroft's most interesting sections is the **Mark Twain Papers**, a collection of Samuel Clemens' journals, manuscripts, and letters. From this collection, UC Press is publishing what will eventually become a 70 volume edition of all his writings. To prevent damage to its valuable historical manuscripts, you cannot borrow anything from the Bancroft, but copy services are available. No pens—only pencils, typewriters, and computers—are allowed in the library.

East Asiatic Library

642-2556. Located in Durant Hall, the East Asiatic Library has an extraordinary collection of nearly 500,000 bound volumes from China, Japan, Korea, Manchuria, Mongolia, and Tibet, as well as some English-language volumes. The material includes early printed works, scrolls, woodblocks, engraved maps, and stone rubbings. This is the only U.S. depository for

Japanese Government publications outside Washington, D.C.

Eshleman Hall Library

642-2892. Eshleman, another popular place to study, houses the ASUC archives. Patrons may be distracted by the great views from its seventh floor location or the music of bongo players in the plaza below. Eshleman is open very late during the school year (Mon-Thurs 8 am-1 am, Fri 8 am-midnight, Sat and Sun 10 am-midnight), and is perhaps the only library that lets you drink coffee—it's even sold here.

Main (Doe) Library

643-9999. Designed by John Galen Howard, Doe has stacks open only to graduate students, faculty, or those with signed statements. Other patrons (including undergraduates) must write down the requested book and wait for employees to get the volume.

Access to most other campus libraries is not as restricted. Map enthusiasts will love Doe Library's **Map Room** (642-4940), with a collection of maps, some hundreds of years old, from all over the world. For great bargains on discarded library books (including some real gems), check out the **Book Sale Shop** (642-3318), open Mon and Thurs 11 am-2 pm, in room 105 of the Doe Library.

Moffitt Undergraduate Library

642-5070. This modernistic library has a cross-section of most popular books, over 550 periodicals on open stacks, and reserve readings for many undergraduate classes. The library becomes a huge, rather noisy study-hall during the school year.

Morrison Library

Located near the north entrance to the Main Library, Morrison is everyone's favorite campus library. The room is

UC's Morrison Library. Photo by Don Pitcher.

for recreational reading and for listening to recorded music (with headphones), not for study. Its overstuffed chairs give it the air of an exclusive club at an Ivy League college. Morrison Library has travel guides and general-interest books to borrow, along with a non-circulating collection of records, books, and magazines.

Local Events

Berkeley Bay Festival

644-6530. Booths, exhibits, music, children's programs, boat tours, free sailing rides, environmental walks and more at the Marina. Held each April. Call for details, and don't miss the crab races.

Berkeley Farmers' Market

Derby St. and M.L. King Way, 548-2220. Fresh organic produce, eggs, and honey are available Tuesday afternoons 2 pm-dusk. For details call the Ecology Center.

Botanical Garden Spring Plant Sale

642-3343. Every May the University Botanical Garden has a special sale of unusual vines, trees, orchids, native plants, and more. Call for the specific dates, and get there early—there's always a crush at the gates.

Cinco de Mayo

549-0232. This is a time for Mariachi bands, salsa and rock music, dancing, and dozens of booths offering food, craftwork, and trinkets—all at Provo (M.L. King Jr.) Park on the weekend nearest May 5th each year. This is one of the most popular yearly festivals in Berkeley. Contact Adelante for details.

National Condom Day on the UC campus. Photo by Don Pitcher.

Christmas Trees

642-3765. Students from the UC Forestry Department sell the highest quality fresh-cut trees anywhere in Berkeley. The trees are reasonably priced, but generally sell out quickly. Call for details.

Flea Market

Ashby BART Plaza. On weekends the plaza becomes one of the East Bay's finest flea markets. Proceeds from rental of space go to help a variety of non-profit community groups (see *Economy and Business*).

Himalayan Fair

843-1907. Held each May at Live Oak Park, this festival re-creates a Himalayan bazaar. In addition to various craftworks, you'll find music, dancers, Asian food, and environmental groups. Call for details.

Holiday Pottery Sale

Each December, usually the first, second, and third weekends, the fifteen or so West Berkeley pottery studios open their doors to the public with special sales of hand-crafted pieces. The largest shops are **Berkeley Potters' Guild** (731 Jones St., 524-7031), **Earthworks** (2547 Eighth St., 540-9267), **The Mug Shop** (1659 San Pablo Ave., 527-9353), and **The Potter's Studio** (2397 San Pablo Ave., 845-7471). For more information call any of the studios listed above.

Juneteen

655-8008. On the Sunday nearest June 19, South Berkeley celebrates the memory of the 1865 proclamation by Union General Granger of freedom for the slaves of Texas. Juneteen brings a parade, entertainment, arts and crafts booths, and other activities to Adeline St. between Woolsey and Alcatraz.

KPFA Holiday Crafts Fair

848-6767. Arguably the finest crafts fair in the San Francisco area, the KPFA fair includes exhibitors of jewelry, ceramics, weaving, and much more. It is held on two weekends in late November and early December in the ASUC Student Union Building. Benefits go to radio station KPFA, which broadcasts live from the fair while it goes on.

Live Oak Park Arts and Crafts Fair

526-7363. Art exhibitions, music, puppet shows, and other entertainment each June in Live Oak Park. Call for specific dates.

Multi-Cultural Arts Festival

644-6084. Put on by the Civic Arts Commission every October, this is a week-long series of exhibitions, events, concerts, and even a parade. The grand finale is a weekend of music, ethnic foods, and hanging out in Provo Park. Call for details and dates.

National Condom Week

Sproul Plaza. Helium-filled condoms, "dik-athalon," water-filled condom toss, pregnant man pageant, and other humorous events publicize condom use. Held on the week nearest Valentine's Day.

Nutcracker Suite

841-8913. Each December, students of the Berkeley Conservatory Ballet perform this holiday classic at Zellerbach Auditorium. Call for specifics.

Pickle Family Circus

826-0747. Every year on Mother's Day

Face painting at a street fair. Photos by Don Pitcher.

weekend the Pickle Family Circus puts on an outstanding exhibition of clowns, acrobats, jugglers, trapeze artists, and music at Cedar-Rose Park. Kids love this event, sponsored by Bananas. Call for specific dates.

Solano Avenue Stroll
527-5358. First held in 1974, the Solano Avenue Stroll attracts 10,000-15,000 people to the street each September. Sponsored by the Solano Avenue Merchants Association, the fair includes clowns, music, dancing, food, and conspicuous consumption.

Sproul Plaza Music
You'll find free concerts of all types here—from big band jazz to heavy metal—most weekday noon hours during the school year. On weekend afternoons when the weather is warm, Lower Sproul attracts a rag-tag collection of bongo players, bottle-bangers, sax players, and whatever else fits the rhythm.

Telegraph Avenue Street Fair
Each December the city closes Telegraph Avenue for a weekend of holiday crafts, shopping, eating, listening to music, and hanging out, that draws thousands of people.

Pets

Berkeley has an estimated 15,000 dogs, and who knows how many cats, hamsters, birds, snakes, turtles, and fish. The city maintains a unique **Dog Park** within Ohlone Park (Hearst Ave. and Grant St.) where dogs can play in a large fenced-in area. Most early evenings find the park crowded with owners of all breeds and dispositions, eagerly discussing their dogs' socialization, house training, and grooming problems.

Berkeley Animal Shelter
2013 2nd St., 644-6755. Berkeley's first dog tax ordinance was passed in 1891, and licenses have been required ever since. Dog licenses ($8.50/yr or $4.25/yr for spayed or neutered dogs) are available from the Berkeley Animal Shelter, or by mail from the Department of Public Health (2180 Milvia Street, 644-6510). If you've lost a pet you'll be told that Berkeley strays are brought to the Animal Shelter and that you should not call the Humane Society. What they don't tell you is that if your Berkeley pet has strayed into Albany, it *will* be at the Berkeley Humane Society. If you're interested in adopting a pet, both dogs ($15) and

cats ($10) are available from the shelter. A refundable deposit of $15-$30 is added to this fee to ensure the adopted pet is spayed or neutered. The best time to get a kitten is during "kitten season"—May through October. Stray animals brought to the shelter are held for five days before being put up for adoption. Of the 3000 strays brought in each year, approximately 60% are adopted out; the rest are euthanized. The shelter is open Mon-Sat 9 am-4 pm (closed 1 pm-2 pm) and has "night deposit boxes" out front for after-hours donations of animals.

Berkeley-East Bay Humane Society

2700 9th Street, 845-7735. The Humane Society has services similar to those of the Berkeley Animal Shelter. Adopt vaccinated dogs here for $35 and cats for $22. The Humane society houses approximately 2500 animals each year (no strays), finding homes for nearly all of them. There is no limit on how long animals may stay here. The Humane Society is open Mon-Fri 9 am-5 pm and Sat 9 am-1 pm and offers a low-cost pet clinic, obedience training classes, and even a "Behavior Hotline" (845-7735). They also have "Teacher's Pets"—Candice the pet chicken, Sunshine Rabbit, and Artie, the world's mellowest dog. The pets are taken to schools and retirement homes to delight all ages. Membership in the Humane Society costs $15/year.

Contact the society to report stray dogs, to enforce city laws on dogs, and to find out about veterinary facilities.

Pet Alternatives

Call Berkeley Police (644-6743) to report dog bites or problems with animals when the shelter is closed. If you find an injured wild bird, take it to the shelter, or on evenings and weekends, drop it off at the **Pet Emergency Treatment Service** (1048 University Ave., 548-6684). Both the shelter and Pet Emergency transport the birds to the **Alexander Lindsey Center** (935-1978) in Walnut Creek for treatment. The **International Bird Rescue Research Center** on Aquatic Park (841-9086) cares for injured seabirds, par-

Farms in Berkeley?

Berkeley animal ordinances still on the books:

10.12.150 "It is unlawful for any person within the limits of the city to allow any stallion, bull or jackass to be kept in the same enclosure with a mare, cow or jenny, except in an enclosure sufficient to obstruct the view of all persons outside such enclosure."

10.12.220 "It is unlawful for any person, firm or corporation to stake out, or to cause or allow to be staked out, any animal or animals during inclement weather."

Nancy Frensley at the Berkeley Humane Society. Photo by Don Pitcher.

ticularly during Bay Area oil spills. For other injured wildlife (and some exotic pets) contact the Humane Society or a local vet.

Radio Free Berkeley

Sure, your radio will pull in those stations full of the latest hits and "forty minutes of commercial-free modern rock," but Berkeley has two stations that will shake you out of mainstream complacency: on "the left end of your radio dial" are listener-sponsored KPFA (FM 94.1) and student-run KALX (FM 90.7).

KALX

The UC student radio station, KALX (642-1111), began in 1961 when a group of engineering students started broadcasting AM signals through dormitory wiring systems; listeners literally had to plug in to hear the station. KALX reached the FM airwaves in 1967 as a 10-watt microstation for the University community, but with an antenna high in the Berkeley hills, the tiny station can be heard in many parts of the Bay Area. To the chagrin of University administrators, instead of broadcasting Cal Band concerts and straight-laced commentaries, KALX became known as a rebel station that dished up psychedelic sounds and controversial programs. In 1974, the theft of equipment and battles between various ethnic factions on the staff forced a shutdown of the station, but it reappeared the following year.

In addition to Cal sports and news, you'll hear unknown rock bands, punk, reggae, heavy metal, and other music that will make you sit up and listen. Listeners love KALX's willingness to play almost anything—from Barry Manilow to the Surf Nazis. But with 500 watts of power, KALX is now an even bigger thorn in the side of the University. Detractors call it uneven, obscene, degrading, discordant, chaotic, and anarchistic. Fans would probably agree. For all its brashness and creative programming it has repeatedly been voted the nation's best college radio station. KALX is also a good place for volunteers to get started in broadcasting.

KPFA

For many people living in the Sierra foothills or in Sonoma County, Berkeley is not so much a city as it is 94.1 on their FM dial. KPFA is thoroughly "Berkeley": it not only reflects the political passions and musical tastes of the city, but over the years it has played a major role in shaping them. And as the nation's first publicly sponsored station, KPFA can take credit for revolutionizing American radio.

The station originated in 1946 when former White House correspondent and pacifist Lewis Hill established the Pacifica Foundation to develop an alternative to commercial radio. Three years later, on April 15, 1949, "This is KPFA, listener-sponsored radio in Berkeley" was heard for the first time. The initial station lasted until 1951. (Ironically, a State Department official chose this time to show several Eastern European visitors that U.S. citizens were interested in more than just money. As proof, he brought them to Berkeley's non-commercial KPFA. It must have been a rude awakening when he found the station had closed for a lack of money.) Fortunately, less than a year after it closed, a core of supporters attracted a thousand new members and won a $150,000 grant from the Ford Foundation.

KPFA was back on the air, but it quickly came under attack for its diverse programming. KPFA was not content to dish out the same stories as commercial stations, instead giving air time to communists and marijuana advocates while championing First Amendment rights with other controversial guests. The Pacifica network eventually grew to include stations in New York, Los Angeles, Houston, Fresno, and Washington, D.C. During the early 60s Pacifica's commentators were called before the House Un-American Activities Committee and the Senate Internal Security Subcommittee and charged with "subversion." Subsequently, numerous attempts have been made by right-wing groups to silence the station through the FCC and the courts. In 1974, both KPFA and KPFK (Los Angeles) came under strong criticism when they became centers for communiques from the Symbionese Liberation Army (SLA) (see *Touring Revolutionary Berkeley*). But through all the harassment and criticism, KPFA has continued to provide invaluable services for the community. Many of the journalists on National Public Radio came from Pacifica stations, and KPFA directs the most comprehensive broadcast training program for minorities in the nation.

Today KPFA is a 59,000-watt station with a broad mix of programming: music of all types (from Irish jigs to classical fugues); readings by writers and poets; special programs for gays, women, Latinos, Native Americans, and other minorities; and discussions on almost any subject imaginable. The station is probably best known for its public affairs and news programming, particularly the hour-long evening news. A 150-watt sister station (KPFB, FM 89.3) airs the Berkeley City Council meetings in addition to KPFA's regular programming. While some people find the tone of the station strident at times—the newscasters revel in protests, no matter how small the group or obscure the cause—KPFA provides listeners one of the only alternatives to the pre-packaged stories dished out from Washington or New York, and offers many groups their sole access to the airwaves.

In spite of a tight budget, cramped aging studios, and a largely volunteer staff, KPFA has produced a remarkable legacy of programming, winning most of the top awards in radio, including one for its gavel-to-gavel coverage of the Iran-Contra Hearing in 1988. It was home to the first phone-in talk show and the first live debate. Its broadcast staff has included such diverse personalities as Angela Davis and Caspar Weinberger.

Three times a year KPFA's announcers plead, cajole, and threaten suicide to persuade listeners to call in subscriptions that will keep the station on the air. Members ($45/year or $25 student/low income rate) receive the monthly *Folio* newspaper with detailed program listings, and gain the satisfaction of supporting one of America's most unusual radio stations. Call 848-6767 for details. Profits from the popular annual KPFA Holiday Crafts Fair in December also help support the radio station.

Recycling

The people of Berkeley produce nearly 300 tons of garbage a day, an average of six pounds for each man, woman, and child in the city. Waste disposal has always been a problem—the stench from garbage wagons en route to the shoreline led to Albany's "secession" from Berkeley in 1908. In later years the stench came from garbage incineration in West Berkeley, before the burning was replaced by bay fill. Shoreline dumping continued into the 1980s, when the dump finally reached capacity and was closed. The city then graded the old landfill into small hills, covered it with topsoil, and planted grass, producing the still-incomplete 90-acre North Waterfront Park. One alternative to the shoreline dumping initially considered was a garbage incineration plant that would produce energy from the waste, but citizens concerned about air pollution fought the plant. In 1982 voters approved a five-year moratorium on garbage burning, and today Berkeley's garbage is hauled more than 40 miles to a huge Livermore

Recycling at the Community Conservation Center, Dwight at M.L. King Way. Photo by Don Pitcher.

Where to Recycle

A recent state law has finally brought a watered-down version of the bottle bill to California, and most major grocery stores now have recycling centers where you get a lowly penny each for glass or plastic bottles and aluminum cans. The city has several other options for recycling various materials:

Curbside Pickup of newspaper, glass bottles, wine bottles, aluminum, and tin cans is available for free on a weekly basis, on the same day as garbage pickup. Call the Ecology Center (548-2220) for details.

Community Conservation Center, Dwight and M. L. King Ways (524-0113) is open daily 8 am-dusk. The center takes newspapers, paper bags, cardboard, mixed paper, glass, aluminum, and tin cans.

Berkeley Recycling Center, 2nd and Gilman St. (524-0113) is open Tues-Sun 9 am-4 pm. Here you can sell used newspaper, glass, aluminum, cardboard, wine bottles, glass, and scrap. The center also takes donations of paper bags, mixed paper, magazines, tin cans, scrap metal, and used motor oil.

Urban Ore Flea Market, 2nd and Gilman St. (526-9467) is open daily 8 am-4:30 pm. Urban Ore accepts old furniture, clothing, building materials, scrap metal, glass of any kind, appliances, and household goods. You can donate items or buy inexpensive used goods.

Recycled Items for Sale

Berkeley Architectural Salvage, 2741 10th St. (849-2025) sells used plumbing, lighting, marble, architectural detailing, and doors in a covered warehouse.

The Sink Factory, 2140 San Pablo Ave. (540-8193) has used ceramic sinks and bathroom accessories.

Sunrise Salvage, 2204 San Pablo Ave. (845-4751) has recycled Victorian-style plumbing fixtures, pedestal sinks, clawfoot tubs, marble, and doors.

Urban Ore Building Materials, 6th and Gilman Sts. (526-7080) sells recycled building materials of all types—doors, windows, lumber, pipes tubs, sinks, toilets, and cabinets. Also available are appliances, furniture, and various other household items.

landfill operation. To lessen this wasteful and expensive dumping, in 1984 Berkeley voters enacted the most comprehensive recycling law of any American city, requiring the recycling of half the city's garbage by 1991, a goal that almost nobody believes can be reached. Still, Berkeley recycles more than the national average—12% of the total garbage produced. In 1989 the city passed an ordinance banning dangerous CFC styrofoam. After January 1990 all styrofoam will be banned and some of this non-biode-gradable waste may be avoided.

Schools

A national center for education at the collegiate level, Berkeley has also long been a leader in elementary and secondary school innovations. The city produced California's first accredited high school (1884) as well as one of the earliest junior highs in America (1910). Berkeley was the first large city both to integrate its schools (1964) and to establish a program of two-way busing (1968).

Early History
In 1864, Patrick Rooney donated an acre of land and Captain William Bowen supplied the wood for the community-built, two-room **Ocean View School**, the first public building in what later became Berkeley. Since it was the only school for an area that now encompasses Berkeley, Albany, El Cerrito, San Pablo, and northern Oakland, many students walked long distances each morning, following cowpaths across the open fields. In 1903 the school was replaced by the **Franklin School** (still standing, but now closed) at Virginia St. and San Pablo Avenue. The original Ocean View School buildings were eventually lost to fire and the wrecking ball.

Controversies over where to locate the city's schools precipitated long-running political battles between East and West Berkeley. Given the distance to the West Berkeley school, many residents from the eastern half of the city chose to send their children to private but secular schools. One of the primary reasons Berkeley incorporated in 1878 was to resolve these problems. After incorporation, the new school board immediately rented rooms in Clapp's Hall at Shattuck and University Aves., where it opened the first East Berkeley public school. With financial help from downtown businessmen, the more permanent **Kellogg Grammar School** opened on Center and Oxford Streets in 1880. It soon began to offer high school classes, and in 1884 it became the first University-accredited high school in California, a move that ensured its graduates admission to the University upon recommendation from the principal.

Boomtimes in the Schools
Berkeley's rapid growth during the late 1800s caused serious overcrowding in its schools. By 1885 Berkeley had 817 children between ages five and seventeen, but space for only 494 in its public schools. Some attended private schools, while others attended classes in crowded rented rooms and used vacant lots and streets for playgrounds. Without blackboards, some teachers were forced to use thick manila paper coated with liquid slating for their lessons. One teacher simultaneously taught four rooms filled with children, positioning her desk to command a partial view into each room.

Sanitary conditions (outhouses) for these rented schools were termed "fierce."

The **Rose Street School** helped to alleviate some of these problems. Opened in 1886, it was the first public school in rapidly-expanding North Berkeley. (The school was later turned into an apartment building at 1329 Milvia Street. Although considerably altered, it is Berkeley's oldest remaining public school building. Look closely and you'll even see the old outhouse, now a storage shed.) Another early Berkeley school that still stands is the **7th Street School** (1814 7th St.), built in 1887 and now a private residence. In 1891 voters passed new school bonds to buy several lots for future school buildings, and within a year three new grade schools had opened: **Whittier**, **Columbus**, and **LeConte**.

Berkeley High School

Berkeley High grew rapidly during the first years of its existence, and by 1896 the school had 300 pupils overflowing its 200 seats. In 1900 voters passed a bond to fund construction for the new high school at Milvia St. and Allston Way. The building was completed in time for fall classes in 1901. Most of the present high school buildings were added in the late 30s and early 40s.

Crowding in Berkeley's schools only got worse after the 1906 San Francisco earthquake and fire, which drove many of that city's residents into Berkeley. To lessen crowding in the high school, two schools established a special "Introductory High School" program (grades 7, 8, and 9), thereby creating one of the first junior high programs in the nation. Berkeley opened its first kindergarten in 1914,

parent nurseries in 1934, and full daycare centers in 1944. By the 1940s the city had 20 different public schools and had completed most of its present high school buildings.

A Changing Student Body

Conflicts between East and West Berkeley over schools re-emerged in the 1950s and 60s, this time over racial issues. The arrival of many black workers during World War II dramatically altered the racial makeup of West Berkeley, and as in many other cities, a schism developed between the predominantly black schools in one part of the city and the mainly white schools in the other. Parents and students in West Berkeley protested the paucity of minority teachers, discriminatory counseling, and the unfair grouping of black students into lower "tracks" based on achievement levels. Berkeley's conservative school board dragged its feet on racial issues. (In 1953, a liberal school board member had lost an election to a conservative former Cal football player who ran on the slogan,"It takes an All-American to beat an un-American." The liberal's un-American behavior consisted of his vote to let well-known socialist Paul Robeson sing in the Berkeley Community Theater.) A highly critical 1958 committee report finally brought attention to the problems, but it took a different issue to galvanize the city into action.

In 1960, the California Senate Fact Finding Committee on Un-American Activities cited two Berkeley teachers as unfit to teach because of their leftist beliefs. The issue of firing the teachers split the school board between conservatives and liberals, and led to a wild series of hearings that brought out almost 1000 stomping, shouting citizens. Angered by the witch hunt, voters threw the conservatives out of office and elected a liberal majority. The new school board promptly acted to address problems in many areas, approving a plan in 1964 to turn predominantly black **Burbank Junior High** (now **East Campus**) into a 9th grade school while splitting the 7th and 8th graders between the two other junior highs. Opponents of the decision mounted a virulent campaign to oust its supporters—headlines such as "Five Willful People Act Against the Rights of Thousands," and "The Board is Destroying a City to Test a Theory" ran in the conservative *Berkeley Daily Gazette*—but voters rejected the recall effort and the desegregation policy remained intact.

Other changes followed. In 1966, the city instituted a voluntary busing program to carry black elementary school children from West Berkeley to other less-crowded schools. (Some schools in the hills had been 98% white while others in South Berkeley were 90% black.) "Tracking" of students was made less important, black history classes were introduced at all age levels, and more minority teachers were hired. In 1968, after years of public forums, committee reports, and proposals, the board of education finally voted to begin complete elementary school desegregation. Full-scale busing arrived that fall, making Berkeley the first major racially-mixed American city to completely integrate its schools—years before federal courts forced the rest of America to follow suit.

A Shrinking School System

Enrollment in the Berkeley public schools reached a peak in the 1960s as the generation of baby boomers attained school age, but it has since dropped precipitously. Today total enrollment stands just over 8000, half the level of twenty years ago. Controversy over closures of schools has divided and continues to divide both the school board and the voters.

In 1986, the combination of dropping enrollments, cuts in funding, and alleged mismanagement left the school district deeply in debt, forcing it to borrow $3 million from the state. Berkeley voters came to the rescue of the schools in 1986, approving a tax levy that raises $5 million a year to help reduce class size, provide instructional material, and improve maintenance and enrichment programs. By 1988—two years ahead of schedule—the school district was able to repay the state loan. The people of Berkeley have continued to support public schools with one of the highest per pupil spending rates in the state. When Governor Deukmejian in 1988 ordered money that had previously gone to schools returned to California taxpayers, the Berkeley schools received $103,000 in voluntary contributions!

Public Schools Today

Berkeley now has twelve primary schools, two junior highs, Berkeley High School, and an East Campus for students needing special attention. Class sizes average 26 students (28 in the high school). Berkeley students score above statewide norms at all levels. By sixth grade, the average Berkeley student shows scores equivalent to those for students in the eighth and ninth grades elsewhere. Berkeley ranks in the top 10% of all high schools in the state, achieving the "exemplary high school" listing

Berkeley High seniors, 1988. Photo by Amy Cook.

from California. At Berkeley High School 80% of grads go on to college, and the dropout rate is 10%. Parents find that teenagers who don't like school tend to fall through the cracks at BHS, but those who like to learn and have a positive attitude can get an excellent academic education. Fortunately, most students graduate from Berkeley High with a firm sense of reality, and many later excel at both public and private colleges.

Problems reported in the Berkeley public schools include gang violence, drug dealing, rampant absenteeism, graffiti, and vandalism—problems common to many large urban schools. In 1988 a new school superintendent and high school principal introduced more stringent rules and constructed a fence around the high school campus, dramatically reducing problems.

Some people point to the declining enrollment in Berkeley's public schools as evidence of woeful inadequacy. It is estimated that 20%-30% of elementary age students now attend private schools. Some parents of private school children say this is because of the academic superiority of such schools; others believe the disciplined atmosphere allows both slow and fast learners a chance to succeed.

The racial makeup of Berkeley's public schools is 43% black, 40% white, 7% Hispanic, and 10% Asian. The city's desegregation plan ensures that students from East and West Berkeley are bused to create a racial balance and to allow children to stay together with their classmates as they progress. The city also spends twice

Students at Berkeley High School. Courtesy of Berkeley High School Yearbook.

the amount other districts do on "mainstreaming" disabled children in the schools.

The Berkeley Unified School District is run by a board of education consisting of five members elected for four-year terms. Meetings are held on the first and third Wednesday of each month at 2134 M.L. King Way (the old City Hall) at 7:30 pm.

For more information on the correct school for your child, contact the School District at 644-6315. You may also call the school superintendent's hotline at 843-0228 for information on any school-related issue or problem. For a much more detailed description of each school and its pluses and minuses, as well as an overview of the entire school system, be sure to get a copy of the excellent annual book produced by the League of Women Voters, *Berkeley Public Schools: A Guide for Parents*. For a comprehensive description of local private schools, see **Private Schools of the East Bay** by Dixie M. Jordan.

Berkeley Adult School

1222 University Ave., 644-6130. Here you'll find classes in such practical fields as computers, business, and fashion design, as well as Shiatsu, Polynesian dance, and auto mechanics. Classes are offered in a variety of locations around Berkeley for fees of $15-$60 per quarter. Pick up class schedules from the Berkeley Adult School.

Language Studies International

2015 Center St., 841-4695. Many foreign visitors to the Bay Area choose Language Studies in Berkeley, which for ten years has offered intensive courses in the English language. It further provides students the opportunity to learn about American culture by living in student housing at the University or with an American family. The many Berkeley families who have been hosts to these students often find themselves with lifelong friends and with an equally intimate view of foreign habits and personalities.

UC Extension

2223 Fulton St., 642-4124. The continuing education branch of the University of California, the UC Extension, offers the general public more than 750 courses each semester in almost any field imaginable, from computer programming and self-hypnosis to more traditional academic subjects. Most are evening or weekend classes. Since the Extension must support itself without state funds, the fees tend to be high: one-day classes start around $60, and multiple-session evening classes run from $160-$220. At the Extension office you can pick up a copy of the free general catalogue published three times a year, or one of the specialized catalogues in correspondence study, engineering, or business.

Vista College

2020 Milvia St., 841-8431. A part of the Peralta Community College District, Vista College was founded in 1974 as a college without a campus. Classes are held at more than 250 different locations around town, from University classrooms to senior centers. Vista students are older than those at most colleges—the average age is 40—and come not so much for a degree as to learn a specific skill or advance a career. The classes are split between academic subjects such as history and languages and practical skills such as business, tax preparation, and health education. For more information, pick up a class schedule from the admissions office (2020 Milvia St., 841-8431). Enrollment fees for academic classes are minimal—only $5 per semester unit ($50 total for more than six units). Community education classes range from $15-$125 each.

Senior Citizens

You might not realize it from walking on campus, but not everyone in Berkeley is young—14% of the residents are over the age of 60 (compared to 10% nationally). Berkeley takes care of its elderly, spending more per capita on senior citizens than any other East Bay city.

Berkeley Gray Panthers

Continuing the activist tradition of the city, the Gray Panthers (527-3790) promotes issues affecting the elderly, such as health care, housing, and death with dignity. Membership costs $15/year.

Senior Citizens Centers

The city of Berkeley operates three large senior centers: **North Berkeley**, 1901 Hearst St. (644-6107), **South Berkeley**, 2939 Ellis St. (644-6109), and **West Berkeley**, 1900 6th St. (644-6036). Activities range from classes in French art to discussions of current events, from trips into the country to consciousness-raising workshops. Members may join poetry groups, dance classes, bingo games, and les-

sons in Tai Chi. The centers also provide listings of nurses, aides, masseuses, gardeners, cooks, and other assistants. The most active center, North Berkeley, sees a constant stream of people attending more than 50 classes and workshops each week, or just using the center as a place to talk to long-time friends. The West Berkeley Senior Center's bilingual staff provides assistance for Spanish-speaking citizens. For a complete listing of current classes and events, pick up the monthly newsletter at any senior center. See the *Berkeley and Albany Guide for Seniors* (also available at senior centers) for a complete list of local services.

Other senior centers in Berkeley include the **New Light Senior Center**, located in the South Berkeley YMCA (2901 California St., 549-2666), the **Berkeley-Richmond Jewish Community Center** (1414 Walnut St., 848-0237), **Berkeley Nikkei (Japanese) Senior Center**, (1901 Hearst Ave., 524-7639), and **St. John's Senior Center** (2727 College Ave., 845-6830).

Most of these senior centers have noon-time meals available weekdays for $1-$2. Homebound people who are unable to cook for themselves can get a hot lunch ($2.25) delivered to their homes on weekdays by contacting the **Portable Meals Program** (644-8590). The **Blue and Gold Market** (2257 Shattuck Ave., 843-3028) is the only Berkeley grocer that delivers groceries to the home (for a service charge). Elderly Berkeley residents may use the city's free minibus to get around town (call 644-6107).

Health Care

In addition to Alta Bates Hospital and a variety of other medical facilities, the City of Berkeley has a number of unusual health-related programs. It operates the only city-run health department in California, and is home to the California State Department of Public Health, one of Berkeley's largest employers (650 workers). Those with little or no money can use the Berkeley Free Clinic (see *On the Street*), the William Byron Rumford, Sr. Medical Clinic, or the Berkeley Women's Health Collective, while the adventurous can take advantage of alternative health care providers not accepted by the medical establishment, such as practitioners of rolfing, homeopathy, and psychic healing.

The city has long been responsive to the health concerns of its residents. In 1880, just two years after Berkeley was officially chartered, the town appointed a Chief Health Officer, Dr. Frank H. Payne. Although much of his time was spent trying to clean up sanitation problems from outhouses along Strawberry Creek, he also had to attend to outbreaks of smallpox, cholera, and yellow fever. The 1895 city charter passed 27 new health ordinances, ranging from prohibiting the common practice of spitting on the floor in public buildings to regulating the number of cows per acre. Though World War I spawned the creation of a venereal disease clinic and a health clinic for babies, it wasn't until a major outbreak of influenza in 1918, which forced 3000 people into a makeshift hospital, that the city was forced to take a more prominent role in public health and enact a variety of health ordinances.

Today, most health departments in California are run by county governments. By keeping Berkeley's program at the city level, the Berkeley Health and Human Services Department has managed to pull in funding from the county, state, and federal government to maintain a much larger health program than other cities. The department provides public health nurses, over-the-phone advice (644-6500), plus programs that include an immunization clinic, blood-pressure screening clinics, health education, and HIV testing. There is also a special center for **Women and Children's Services** at 830 University Avenue. For a complete listing of local health care options, pick up a copy of the **Health and Human Services Directory** from the office in City Hall (2180 Milvia St., 644-6459).

"Santa Claus" Bill collecting for the Free Clinic on Shattuck Avenue. Photo by Don Pitcher.

Clinics and Support Services

AIDS

Berkeley has the third highest per capita rate of AIDS in California (after San Francisco and Long Beach). For free testing for the virus, call the **Health and Human Services Department** (830 University Ave., 644-8569). Free testing is also available through Planned Parenthood (526-1103) and at several other sites run by the Alameda County Community Health Services Department (268-2639). The **AIDS Project of the East Bay** (400 4th St., Oakland, 420-8181) maintains a variety of AIDS support services, including counseling, education, and limited emergency medical treatment. The San Francisco-based **Bay Area AIDS Hotline** (863-2437) provides education, counseling, and a chance for AIDS sufferers to talk. Alta Bates runs the **East Bay AIDS Center**, a for-fee outpatient clinic at 2640 Telegraph Ave., 540-1870.

Alcohol and Drug Addiction

For help with alcohol addiction call **Alcoholics Anonymous** day or night at 653-4300. Also ask for information about their Narcotics Anonymous and Cocaine Anonymous programs, which use the AA twelve-step method. **Berkeley Addiction Treatment Services** includes methadone treatment (2975 Sacramento, 644-0200, open 5:30 am-2 pm). The Herrick Hospital **Center for Chemical Dependency** (3001 Colby, 549-3544) sponsors both inpatient and outpatient programs.

American Red Cross

2116 Allston Way (845-1430). Berkeley's Red Cross office offers classes in first aid, CPR, earthquake safety, and many other areas, and provides temporary lodging and support for victims of home fires, earthquakes, storms, and other emergencies. Free blood pressure screenings are available Fridays at noon at The Red Cross, which also assists mentally disabled adults through its Creative Living Center (540-9065).

Berkeley Free Clinic

2339 Durant Ave., 548-2570. Open to anyone free of charge and staffed by volunteers, the Berkeley Free Clinic offers basic medical care and counseling. (For more information about the Free Clinic, see *On the Street*, following.)

Berkeley Women's Health Collective

2908 Ellsworth St., 843-6194. This program grew out of the counterculture and the women's liberation movements. In 1970, feminist medics at the Berkeley Free Clinic began to hold organizational meetings to establish a separate clinic. With a grant from Alameda County, the newly formed Berkeley Women's Health Collective purchased a building and began offering a variety of low-cost services. A lesbian clinic opened in 1979, and three years later a clinic specifically for minority women opened in **South Berkeley** (1802 Fairview St., 843-6204). (To ensure that the staff was not predominantly straight and white, in 1976 the members decided on a quota system for hirings—50% Third World and 50% lesbian women.)

The Health Collective emphasizes preventative and holistic medicine, along with health education, in an effort to take medicine out of the hands of medical experts and place it in the hands of women themselves. Fees are on a sliding scale, and many of the 5000 women who visit each year would be unable to afford treatment at other clinics in the Bay Area. Services include pregnancy and mental health counseling, health information and referral, a speakers bureau, plus community health and counseling training.

Eye Care

The School of Optometry at the University (Minor Hall, 642-5761) operates an excellent **Optometry Clinic** where faculty-supervised interns give thorough (and lengthy) eye checkups. There are also specialty clinics for contact lenses, eye diseases, low vision, and other eye problems. Fees are reasonable, and the clinics tend to book up well in advance.

In the Third World few people can afford such amenities as eye glasses. To provide for this need, the local Kiwanis Club and the physicians' group Direct Relief work together to collect, check the prescription, and send out used eyeglasses. The program is called **Share Old Spectacles**. To donate an old pair, take them to Dr. P. Harold Woodring (1621 Solano Ave., 526-3937).

Over 60 Health Clinic

1850 Alcatraz Ave., 644-6060. This was the nation's first consumer-controlled health clinic, specializing in preventive health care for the elderly. Established by the Gray Panthers, it now treats more than 2000 patients at any given time, with fees on a sliding scale.

William Byron Rumford, Sr. Medical Clinic

2960 Sacramento St., 549-3166. Named

for California's first black legislator, the non-profit Rumford Medical Clinic serves primarily low-income and Medi-Cal patients, operating from a building that for 30 years housed a pharmacy operated by Rumford. Inside the clinic are facilities for immunizations, physical exams, and other non-emergency medical problems.

Hospitals

For many years, two hospitals—Alta Bates and Herrick—competed in Berkeley, but in 1984 the Alta Bates Corporation bought out its weaker sister and has gradually gutted services, despite promises to the contrary. The Alta Bates Corporation, one of California's largest non-profit medical corporations, operates a variety of hospitals and related services (such as nursing homes and sports care clinics) around the Bay Area.

Alta Bates Hospital

3001 Colby St., 540-0337. Founded in 1905, the hospital has continued to grow to its present size of 317 beds, a process that has caused neighbors to complain about serious traffic problems as well as the replacement of homes by hospital additions. Today, Alta Bates has a reputation as the East Bay's luxury hospital—the obstetrics birthing rooms resemble a plush hotel, and the cafeteria even attracts non-patients. The hospital specializes in bone marrow transplants and runs one of the most successful in vitro fertilization programs in California.

Herrick Hospital

2001 Dwight Way, 845-0130. Berkeley's "other hospital," Herrick, has a very

Alta Bates. Courtesy of Alta Bates Hospital.

different heritage from that of Alta Bates. It was founded by Francis Herrick, who became interested in medicine when his wife died suddenly and he was forced to work as a hospital orderly to care for his young child. The experience inspired Herrick (once a gold miner) to get a degree in medicine. He practiced in South Africa for several years before returning to California in 1904. Sensing the need for a hospital in the rapidly growing city, Herrick converted an ornate Victorian mansion in downtown Berkeley into the twenty-bed Roosevelt Hospital (later renamed for Herrick). After his death in 1932, the hospital continued to grow, reaching nearly 250 beds.

Herrick Hospital was the first in California to offer psychiatric counseling and treatment, and was also an early leader in providing equal care for minorities and in employing black doctors. Unlike Alta Bates Hospital, the traditional focus of Herrick's care has been on helping lower or moderate income people. Ironically, the death knell for the hospital sounded in 1982 when Alta Bates outbid Herrick for the contract to serve Medi-Cal patients, thus depriving Herrick of its biggest source of funding (77% of its

Alta Bates—the Person

She was a real person, a 23-year-old registered nurse who opened her parents' home as a medical facility in 1904. The following year, with $114 in cash, a building designed by her contractor father, and the credit of local merchants, she opened an eight-bed sanatorium for women and children. Soon after it opened, the place was overflowing with injured from the 1906 San Francisco earthquake. After moving the hospital in 1908 to a new building at its present location, Bates established a nurse training program, while working simultaneously as chief anesthesiologist. She was widely respected for her kindly concern. Until her retirement in 1949, she made it a point to visit each hospital patient every evening.

patients had come from Medi-Cal rolls). Two years later, the hospital was forced to merge with Alta Bates. Today, Herrick has a psychiatric ward, a rehabilitation center for stroke patients, and a drug treatment center (see "Alcohol and Drug Addiction" in this chapter), but it no longer offers traditional hospital care. Its emergency room was axed in 1988, and even its limited "Urgent Care Center" faces extinction. The official explanation is the hospital's severe financial problems, but critics charge the Alta Bates Corporation with mismanagement and a desire to monopolize local medical services at the expense of the community.

The **Herrick Hall of Health** at (2484 Shattuck Ave., 549-1569) is popular with children. Hands-on exhibits include an exercycle to measure calories burned, a model of the lungs that shows the effects of cigarette smoke, a microscope to see what blood cells look like, and an explanation of the birth process. At the same location is the **Vintage Health Library and Resource Center**, offering free blood pressure and hearing testing, plus a collection of health publications for older people.

UC's Cowell Hospital

642-7660. Built to provide medical care for all UC students, Cowell is located on the eastern edge of campus. The Student Health Service operates the hospital, in addition to a variety of medical, dental, and health care services. Most services are free to students. The Student Health Service also operates acute care, specialty clinics, and a variety of health programs in contraception, stress management, nutrition, AIDS prevention, eating disorders, and other areas. The University plans to demolish Cowell to make room for a new Business School, and the future size and location of the Student Health Service remains uncertain. Rumors abound that students with emergency problems will be sent to Alta Bates.

Other Concerns and Options

Alternative Health Care

Berkeley is a major center for the alternative health care movement in this country. The city has dozens of holistic health practitioners, psychic massage instructors, channelers, and others who fall outside the medical mainstream. The most complete source for the hundreds of Bay Area groups in the broad area of "new age personal transformation" is *Common Ground*, a free quarterly published in Marin County and available in many Berkeley shops. It provides an exhaustive listing of classes, businesses, and practitioners offering masque rituals, conga drumming, holistic color consulting, brain wave synchrony, colonics, astrology, firewalking, and other ways to transform your life and empty your wallet. The **Berkeley Holistic Health Center** (3099 Telegraph Ave., 845-4430), is a private clinic with practitioners in medicine, rolfing, psychotherapy, biofeedback, homeopathy, Shiatsu, and other fields. The **Berkeley Psychic Institute/Church of Divine Man** (2436 Haste St., 548-8020) has been around since 1974, offering a blend of spirituality and healing. It offers six-week classes in meditation and healing and a year-long program in clairvoyance. Also available are free healing clinics and psychic ability demonstrations, as well as Sunday church services. The Institute produces a supplement to the *Psychic Reader* (called "The Voice Within"), a free monthly newspaper. Both contain articles about and ads for various psychic services. In the same vein is **Heartsong** (1412 Solano Ave., Albany, 527-1245), a store which offers books, tapes, psychic healing, religious services, etc.

Smoking

Berkeley's **Smoking Pollution Control Ordinance** prohibits smoking in retail stores, banks, schools, theaters, museums, libraries, and other public buildings. An area of controversy, however, has been restaurants and coffeehouses, where the ordinance requires a 50% nonsmoking section. Owners have responded by grudgingly setting aside tables in the back and upstairs for non-smokers, but they often fail to post the legally-required signs or to set aside adequate space. Enforcement of the ordinance has been almost nonexistent. To initiate a complaint against an offending establishment, contact the **Berkeley Department of Health and Human Services** (644-6459). Copies of the ordinance are available from the city or from **Americans for Nonsmokers Rights**, an influential national group based in Berkeley (2054 University Ave., Suite 500, 841-3032).

Funerals

The **Bay Area Funeral Society** (1744 University Ave., Room 209, 841-6653) is a non-profit consumer organization founded in 1955 by members of the Berkeley Co-op. The group provides education for members and helps arrange simple, economical mortuary service to lessen the emotional and economic trauma that often accompany death. It is one of fourteen such societies in California and has over 20,000 members. Lifetime membership is $20. Berkeley's only cemetery—a tiny one—is at Presentation Convent, 2116 Jefferson Avenue.

Finding Rental Housing

With vacancy rates for rental housing hovering at less than 1%, finding a place to live in Berkeley is a major headache. There are many reasons for this: a University that attracts 30,000 students every year while only providing housing for 8000; renters reluctant to move from rent-controlled apartments; a lack of undeveloped land on which to build; and the fact that Berkeley is so desirable a place to live that few want to leave it. Finding an apartment frequently requires many days or even weeks and a willingness to suffer through dozens of phone calls and interviews. It isn't unusual to see flyers posted everywhere offering from several hundred to a thousand dollars for leads to a Berkeley apartment, and when apartments do become available, queues of folks all vie for the same spot. For many people the hassles of finding a place in Berkeley are not worth it, and they eventually settle into neighboring communities.

The cost and availability of rental housing in Berkeley varies depending upon the location and type of unit. Expect to pay considerably more for, and have a harder time finding, a place in the desirable neighborhoods of the Berkeley hills, North Berkeley, Northside, or Elmwood (see *Neighborhoods*). The cheapest rents are in South and West Berkeley. If you're willing to share a room in a house or apartment, your options improve and monthly rents drop. Although most multi-unit dwellings are rent-controlled, many landlords require a stiff initial deposit of first and last month's rent plus a security deposit, so moving in may still prove very expensive. Berkeley's few "boarding" houses usually cost less than rentals, but they generally do not allow cooking, rarely have vacancies, and can be rather seedy (see *Hotels and Motels*).

When to Look

The University's schedule dramatically affects rental unit availability. Mid-semester months (October-December and February-May) are the best times to look, and as spring semester ends (mid-May) hundreds of places come open, although many of these are only summer sublets. By June and July, the hordes start to pour over the Berkeley hills in search of fall housing. You're better off avoiding late summer if possible.

How to Look

The local grapevine carries the freshest news on the Berkeley housing situation; a recent study by the city found that two-thirds of Berkeley tenants found places by word of mouth. New graduate students should speak with professors or others in their department for leads. If you show flexibility, your chances of finding a place are better.

The standard ads are also helpful—check bulletin boards, classified ads in East Bay or San Francisco newspapers, and local property management companies (listed in the yellow pages under "Real Estate Management"). Other less-productive options are to take a long bike ride through Berkeley looking for apartments with vacancy signs or talking to the managers of large apartments to get on their waiting lists.

Rental Services

Project Share (3102 Telegraph Ave., 845-9030) is a city-run referral program which matches people looking for housing with people who have extra space available. There is no charge, but the office works by appointment only. Every month Project Share has an open meeting for anyone interested, offering an informal way to meet potential housemates.

The following rental listing service companies charge (approximately $50 for two months), with no guarantee of finding you a place to live. Be sure to ask questions about their services, such as what cities the rentals are from (often they have few Berkeley listings) and how often the database is updated. If you don't find a place through the service, you are legally entitled to a refund of $25 or half of the fee you paid, whichever is less. **Berkeley Connection** (2840 College Ave., 845-1111) provides rental listings and shared housing listings. Coverage includes the entire East Bay with daily updates. **Homefinders** (2158 University Ave., 549-6450) has similar services with daily updates and free call-in services, and also includes San Francisco listings. **Bay Area Space Finders** (1600 Shattuck Ave., 849-1800) limits its coverage to rentals and shares in Berkeley, El Cerrito, Albany, and the less crime-ridden parts of Oakland. There is no phone-in service, and the listings are updated twice a week, but you can see new daily listings at their office.

Students and Staff Only

If you are a new or continuing student at the University, the excellent **Community Living Office** (2401 Bowditch St., 642-3642) provides hundreds of listings in the Berkeley area and counselors to help you in your search. They also produce a detailed guide to off-campus living called *On Your Own*, as well as a *Housing* publication that details all the options available for students—residence halls, student co-ops, I-House, theme houses, fraternities, and sororities. Since there are twice as many applicants as spaces in the residence halls, residents are selected by a lottery.

Don't wait too long before you start looking for housing because the market is very tight and acceptance to the University does not mean that you will have a place to live. A University Guest Residence is available for those looking during the late summer months (see *Hotels and Motels*). Students should also consider living in adjacent cities, especially Albany and El Cerrito, where the competition for housing is less intense.

Faculty, staff, and Alumni Association members may use the Community Living Office in a different way. Their separate housing service includes individual computer printouts of rental housing, home purchase counseling, and mortgage loan information. The office provides lists of furnished sabbatical houses for visiting faculty, and offers relocation counseling for newcomers. Call 642-0667 for more information.

The University has over a thousand apartments specifically reserved for married or single-parent students. Most of these are located in aging World War II-vintage Army and

Navy barracks in Albany. These apartments are very popular because of their have hard-to-beat rates (starting around $200 a month) and Albany's excellent public school system. There are long waiting lists for the apartments (up to eighteen months!), so incoming married students should sign up even before they know if they will be accepted at the University. For details, contact the Department of Housing and Food Services (2401 Bowditch St., 642-4109).

Rent Control

Few issues have proven so divisive in Berkeley as rent control. Berkeley had federal rent ceilings in the 1940s, due to skyrocketing rents during the housing shortage caused by the influx of wartime factory workers. When these federal laws expired in 1949, a temporary state law came into effect. City rent control was finally voted out in 1951, after the largest public hearing ever held up to that time. (The mayor, Lawrence Cross, voted in favor of continuing the controls, noting their supposed value in controlling communism.)

More recently, supporters of rent control have become an important constituency within Berkeley Citizens Action (BCA) group, while detractors frequently dominate the rival Berkeley Democratic Club (BDC). After years of political squabbling, Berkeley voters finally passed a rent control law (Measure D) in 1980. The act was strengthened in 1982 with passage of Measure G, the Rent Stabilization Ordinance, and is now considered one of the strongest rent control laws in the nation. The law includes stringent

eviction provisions, registration of all apartments, and control over rent increases through an "Annual General Adjustment" process. The law was upheld by the U. S. Supreme Court and appears to be here to stay, unless real estate interests succeed in convincing the state legislature to kill all rent control in California. (Berkeley's innovative but short-lived commercial rent control law was thrown out by the state legislature in 1987.)

Rent control has proven financially beneficial to tenants, and some have even speculated that the resulting discretionary income is one of the primary reasons for the success of Berkeley's many gourmet restaurants. In sharp contrast to surrounding cities without rent control laws, Berkeley's rates have risen less than 9% per year.

On the negative side, rent control has exacerbated an already serious housing shortage by encouraging students, who might otherwise leave after graduation, to stay in Berkeley. It acts as a magnet to people in surrounding areas and reduces the incentive to build new rental units. The University claims a 40% drop in city rental housing since 1980, although tenant advocates dispute this. Some landlords have retaliated by reducing maintenance on their buildings, accepting "finder's fees," and getting low-income (federally subsidized) tenants, whose rent bills are not controlled by rent control. Others have taken their apartments off the market or operate them outside the law, with tenants who are not aware of rent control or who are desperate for a place to live.

Rent control covers most, but not all, permanent multi-unit housing facilities in Berkeley. A nine-member elected Rent Stabilization Board sets the annual rate of rent increase, informs tenants of their rights, and enforces the law (at least in theory). The Rent Board gets mixed reviews, with tenant rights groups calling it a patsy and property owners viewing it as an intrusion into their affairs. It has generally been dominated by members of the tenant-supported BCA, but Rent Board elections have divided the city, with BCA supporters winning the swing seat in the 1988 election by just a single vote out of 40,000 cast.

For more information on rent control, get *Everyone's Guide to Rent Stabilization in Berkeley* from the Rent Board (2100 Milvia St., 644-6128). The Board will check to see if your landlord is legally registered and if your rent is what it should be. They can also provide mediation of some rent disputes. Rent Board meetings are held at 7:30 pm on the first and third Monday of each month at a rotating location. The meetings are broadcast live over KPFB (89.3 FM).

The **Tenants Action Project** (2022 Blake St., 843-6601), gives free tenants' rights classes on Tuesday evenings and distributes a handbook describing the rent control law and other housing issues. The group actively tries to stop the gentrification of low-income areas and organize tenants. One of the most helpful local groups is the **Renters' Assistance Project for Students (RAPS)** at 304 Eshleman Hall on campus (642-1755). RAPS has dozens of pamphlets on all aspects of renting in Berkeley and publishes a free *Tenant Guide to Rent Control in Berkeley*. Officially, RAPS is only for University students, but they are often willing to help others as well.

On the Street

Berkeley has long been a gathering place for people who could not fit in elsewhere. Hippies and other free spirits flocked to the city in the 1960s, dropping acid, doing odd jobs, and crashing out in the parks or in communal houses. They helped establish a network of support that included free meal programs, a free store, a free clinic, and a hostel. Today, much of the counterculture is gone, and the infrastructure of support that sprang up is used primarily by a more desperate group. While some are still attracted by the freedom of living "on the road," most of those who live on the streets do not do so through choice.

Berkeley has a reputation as a city with a heart, but its facilities are being stretched by escalating numbers of people in need who are drawn to the city's social tolerance and array of services. Telegraph Ave., and particularly People's Park, are the traditional places to hang out, but homeless people can be found in many other sections of Berkeley. The figures are astounding—an estimated 1200-2000 people now live on Berkeley's streets, perhaps twice the per capita rate for San Francisco. Many of these people are on the streets because of gaping holes in the governmental "safety net" for the poor. Estimates as to the percent of alcohol and drug addiction problems among the homeless vary from 25% to 75%; some have just been released from prison; and many more have watched their lives spiral downwards due to a series of unfortunate events. The numbers have also been swollen by people released from mental hospitals since the 1970s—on the theory that they can live more normal lives in the community while using specialized services. Unfortunately, the live-in mental health facilities that do exist are underfunded and grossly overcrowded, and Highland Hospital's psychiatric wing is so packed that patients brought in are held for only twelve hours instead of the legal maximum of 72 hours. The patients are soon back out on the streets, where living is difficult even for the sane. Even in open-minded Berkeley where it is impossible to avoid the homeless, many people find themselves so overwhelmed by panhandlers, the people sleeping in doorways, and the mentally ill who hobble down the streets in rags, that they simply choose to turn away.

From a distance, the abundance of services in Berkeley—the Free Clinic, the meals for a quarter provided by the Emergency Food Project, the temporary shelters—might seem to offer an easy ride. Such is not the case. Not only are the facilities overcrowded and underfunded, they are scattered throughout Berkeley, making for a long walk from the West Berkeley shelter, to the Catholic Workers' breakfast in People's Park, to the free lunch in South Berkeley, on to an evening meal on Southside, before the hike back across town for a bed. Living on the street, you are also vulnerable to weather and crime. These difficulties take their toll, making it even harder to find work for those willing and able to make the effort.

Street People

Street people are being hyped
as the new seals to be saved
and that's silly.
Everything bad ever said
    about us
is true:
the crime, the grime, the de-
    spair,
the mocking laughter that sees
    too much—
why deny it?
Everything good ever said
    about us
is true too:
the starving geniuses, the
    wandering wise men,
the dancing fools, the free-
    dom.
And they're both lies as well
because the streets are like
    that.
Street people are sometimes
    killer sharks
and sometimes singing dol-
    phins
and usually it's the same
    people
being both at different times,

depending.
But not seals.
The ordered world assumes
that if street people work
    hard
at 9-5 jobs nobody would
    give us
on a bet
we could rise to poverty level
and wouldn't that be nice
to get what we need?
but how about what the or-
    dered world
needs from us?
People need dreams and dis-
    content
and the darkness we hide in,
the null and void before
    creation,
the cancelled cornucopia
where we're hunted by cops
and hunting each other
and giving to anyone passing
    by
a soul worth selling.
    Yes, dreaming's a dirty job
    but somebody's got to do
    it.

—*Julia Vinograd*

In her more than 25 years in Berkeley, street poet and "bubble lady" Julia Vinograd has published hundreds of poems about life on the Avenue. "Street People" is from *Holding up the Wall*, 1987.

Food for Survival

There are several places in Berkeley where people without resources can find meals. The following list should be of help to those with no alternatives.

Berkeley Food Pantry

The Friends Church, 1600 Sacramento St., 525-2280. This group provides groceries to those who are without income, but who do have a place to cook. It is open Mon, Wed, and Fri from 2 to 5 pm. The Food Pantry

Julia Vinograd, Telegraph Avenue poet. Photo by Don Pitcher.

gladly accepts donations of canned or dried foods.

Daily Bread Project
848-3522. The Project also provides groceries to those in need. Every day volunteers pick up extra food from dozens of restaurants, bakeries, dormitories, and churches. (The Cheese Board bakes 30 loaves of bread each week specifically for them.) The food is delivered directly to the hungry, particularly mothers with young children and the elderly.

Emergency Food Project
2425 College Ave., 841-2789. Located in the basement of the University Lutheran Chapel, the Emergency Food Project is a long-time Berkeley program to help the poor and homeless. Volunteers from the Project shaking their yellow boxes for donations are a common sight on the streets of Berkeley. Every evening at 4:45 pm the food line forms outside the church basement, with folks buying tickets for a quarter or trading a meal for a small task. Many queue up early, talk-ing to buddies and smoking cigarettes out front as they wait for their number to be called. Most are men, though a few women and children can be spotted among the nearly 200 people who gather for the "quarter meal."

McGee Avenue Food Program
McGee Avenue Baptist Church,1640 Stuart St., 843-1774. This program offers free lunches for upwards of 150 people on Mon, Wed, and Fri from noon-1 pm.

People's Cafe
People's Park. In May 1989, members of the Berkeley Catholic Worker, a small activist organization, rolled a trailer onto People's Park and cut off the wheels, thus creating an instant "People's Cafe." Immediately challenged by the University as trespassers, the cafe began serving free breakfasts from 8-9:30 each morning, with coffee from 7 am to noon. (Previously, they had provided breakfast at People's Park from a truck.) The University then offered them space on Dwight Way near Telegraph.

Shelters

Only a small percentage of the homeless people in Berkeley find space in local shelters. The **Emergency Shelter** in West Berkeley (711 Harrison St., 526-9963), run by Berkeley/Oakland Support Services, fills quickly most evenings, particularly during the winter. After 5 pm the shelter opens its simple dorms to 65 men, women, and families. It serves a light dinner and breakfast and provides hot showers and laundry facilities. The shelter is not really a place to live, particularly with a 7:30 am checkout time, but for $4 a night (negotiable), it provides a chance to get off the streets for a while.

Every evening the Emergency Food Project operates two **church shelters** that rotate among several Southside Berkeley churches, each holding a total of 125 people. They're free and open from 10 pm to 7 am, but because of the high demand, there is often a waiting list. The Food Project also operates a **drop-in recreation center** for homeless people on Mon, Tues and Thur evenings between 7 and 9:30 pm in Southside churches. This gives people a chance to watch TV, play dominoes and card games, or get some hot coffee, fresh bread, peanut butter, and jam.

Women's Refuge
Twenty-four hour hotline, 547-4663. Established in 1971 by the Berkeley YWCA, the Women's Refuge offers a safe shelter for women in crisis. Many of the women who stay here do so because they are either without a home or are being violently abused. Many also arrive with their children and with next-to-nothing of their own. The Women's Shelter provides a roof over their heads, safety, bunkbeds, and meals for up to a month, housing up to 20 women and their children each day.

Support Services

Berkeley/Oakland Support Services
2100 M.L. King Way, 848-3378. The primary agency for those living on the streets (especially the mentally ill) is the Berkeley/Oakland Support Services. Established in 1971, when the word "homeless" had not yet crept into the vocabulary, the project was originally set up for de-institutionalized patients, and in 1975 opened California's first hostel for the chronically mentally disabled. Today Berkeley/Oakland Support Services is a county-wide organization with a million dollar budget. In Berkeley it operates a temporary (one to two months) shelter to help people put their lives back together, a house for up to eight families on a longer term, as well as a drop-in center. Many of the clients lack basic skills and education, and would fall through the cracks of traditional programs. On weekday mornings 200-300 people visit the drop-in center to pick up assistance checks, or to get job counseling or medical care advice. The center holds mail for more than 800 people.

Berkeley Community Law Center
3130 Shattuck, 548-4040. During President Reagan's years in office, legal aid for the poor took a beating. The Berkeley office of the Legal Aid Society was closed and the Alameda County staff was slashed from 54 to thirteen attorneys. Until 1988, the only source of help in Berkeley was one

Reverend Alicia Bowley of the Berkeley Chaplaincy to the Homeless with Reverend Dick York of the Berkeley Free Church. Photo by Don Pitcher.

lawyer coming in for four hours a week to staff the Legal Aid office. Simultaneously, the problems of the poor and homeless were becoming more apparent each day. Since the University's law school at Boalt Hall wasn't helping either—it is the only one of the nation's top twenty law schools that does not offer a clinical education to its students—several Boalt law students went out and raised $200,000 in grants from foundations, law firms, and the federal government to establish the Berkeley Community Law Center in 1988. In a building that once housed the Black Panther Party, two attorneys and a rotating group of Boalt students deal primarily with housing and public benefits problems. They also sponsor classes in poverty law at Boalt Hall. Services are offered free, but since the staff has been flooded with people in need of legal help, its services are limited.

Berkeley Ecumenical Chaplaincy to the Homeless

2345 Channing Way, 548-0551. This remarkable group, funded by contributions from eight local churches, in 1988 appointed Reverend Alexia Bowley to work with homeless people (following in the footsteps of Reverend Dick York's Free Church of the 60s). Reverend Bowley, a Lutheran pastor, trains and organizes core groups of street people, making them "peer-chaplains" to help build a sense of self-worth and hope. The program has been successful in helping many find work, in moving people into transitional housing, and in lessening tensions between merchants and the homeless. Homeless Press, run by street people, even produces and sells Christmas cards.

Berkeley Free Clinic

After the devastating 1906 San Francisco Earthquake, hundreds of people fled to the East Bay seeking temporary shelter and medical treatment. To care for them, a temporary free clinic was set up in Berkeley. Sixty-three years later another flood of new arrivals caused the creation of a more permanent service. Today's Free Clinic had its roots in the 1969 fight over People's Park, when it became apparent that alternative care was needed for the injured who did not have insurance policies. Through the combined efforts of church groups, street people, medics, and community leaders such as Fred Cody, a "People's Blue Shield," the Berkeley Free Clinic, was formed. Unlike most medical facilities, the Free Clinic was built on the premise of health care as a right, not a privilege. Anyone can use the facilities free of charge. The Clinic operates almost entirely with volunteer workers, including a staff of approximately 150 professionals and lay health workers. Each of its five sections—medical, peer counseling, gay men's, dental, and switchboard (community referrals, crisis counseling, etc.)—operates as a semi-autonomous collective. Nearly half of the Free Clinic's income comes from donations to street solicitors, and although it receives heavy government funding, the Clinic refuses contracts that might endanger client confidentiality. To volunteer at the Free Clinic, or to receive any of its services, call 548-2570. The Clinic is located at 2339 Durant Ave. and is open Sun-Thurs evenings and Sat mornings.

Collecting for the Free Clinic. Photo by Don Pitcher.

Earthquake Country

Underlying the daily life of Berkeley, buried deeply in everyone's mind, is the knowledge that Berkeley lies in the heart of Earthquake Country. The Hayward Fault, a major branch of the San Andreas Fault system, runs through the city, more or less where the hills meet the flatlands. For those untrained in geology—unable to read the eloquent language of escarpments and creek offsets—its power lies hidden. Yet twice in the last century, in 1836 and 1868, the Hayward Fault produced earthquakes estimated at 6.8 on the Richter scale. The quake of October 21, 1868 caused major destruction in much of the then sparsely-populated area. Until 1906 this was known as "the great earthquake." A crack 12-20 inches wide opened all along the southern half of the faultline, from the Santa Clara County line to Mills College. Hayward was leveled, and in San Leandro only two chimneys were left standing. Sacramento felt the quake, and a two-foot-high wave of water rushed up the Sacramento River. Residents of the East Bay reported mountains bobbing up and down, freight trains gyrating like snakes.

Every few years an earthquake along the San Andreas or some other neighboring fault—such as the cataclysm that hit the Bay Area on October 17, 1989, severing the Bay Bridge and causing the collapse of a freeway in Oakland—shakes people into a keen and terrified awareness of their vulnerability. The violent rattling of buildings brings everyone into the street to form ad hoc pacts of mutual aid and mutual concern. For the next few days, as electricity is restored and glaziers race through the city to replace windows, people swap tales of shaking walls, broken vases, panicked pets. During the next few weeks virtually everyone resolves to hire a contractor to bolt the house to its foundations, tie down the water heater, stock up on water and batteries, buy first-aid kits for home, work, and automobile, and take a Red Cross course. A few do. But within a month or so earthquake amnesia sets in once again, life goes back to normal, and conversations return to the mundane affairs of work, school, the sports field, or the movie theater.

Yet the stubborn fact remains that each year the chances of the "big one" increase, and the potential for damage and destruction is enormous. No one knows, of course, when the next earthquake along the Hayward Fault will occur. But scientists estimate that the fault has a 20% chance of producing a quake of 7.0 magnitude in the next 30 years. If it should happen, the destruction will be immense—especially in Berkeley's older high-rises and among buildings and factories constructed on landfill in West Berkeley. Landslides, if they occur, will crumple buildings in the hills, and subsequent fires have the potential of creating a nightmarish scenario.

If you live in Berkeley, you owe it to yourself and your family to be prepared for the worst. A first-aid kit and knowledge of its use should be at least as mandatory as automobile insurance. The most accessible and clearest guide, for residents and visitors alike, on what what to do before (or after) an earthquake, can be found in the front matter of Pacific Bell's white pages—the phone book. Read it now and act on its recommendations quickly.

Transportation

It doesn't take a genius to see that the Bay Area suffers from ever-increasing traffic congestion. Rush-hour commuters tune their radios to constant traffic reports warning of stalls in the fast lane, overturned big rigs, spilled chemicals, demented pedestrians wandering across the meridian, and hour-long delays at the toll plazas. Add to this picture a rapid transit system with trains filled beyond capacity during rush hour and a bus system on the verge of financial collapse, and it's easy to see why polls consistently rate traffic one of the most serious problems in the Bay Area.

Transportation Patterns

Berkeley is no stranger to the Bay Area traffic morass. The California Department of Transportation ranks the Eastshore Freeway from Gilman St. to the Bay Bridge as having the worst delays of any highway in the area, while Highway 24 near the Caldecott tunnel is ranked fourth worst. It isn't just the highways, either. Shattuck and Ashby Aves. now carry over 30,000 vehicles a day, while lower University Ave. is jammed with more than 53,000 cars a day, reflecting a 40% increase in traffic between 1977 and 1987.

Traffic on Highway 80 from University Avenue. Photo by Don Pitcher.

There are many reasons for this congestion: regional population and business growth that outstrip local transportation systems, suburban commuters who use highway corridors through Berkeley to reach San Francisco and the Southbay cities, the growth of the University and its research facilities, industrial and commercial ventures in West Berkeley, and gourmet shops and restaurants in North Berkeley. All this has led to more commuters and shoppers within Berkeley itself.

This influx has created enormous parking headaches, particularly downtown and near the University campus. Pressure from residents has led the city to zone many areas to allow longterm parking only for residents, forcing non-residents into parking garages, meter feeding frenzies, or even (heaven forbid) public transit. University parking on or near campus is also difficult, particularly after 8 am. (Rumor has it that when Chancellor Heyman asked Czelaw Milosz how the University could honor him for winning the Nobel Prize, Milosz asked if he could be provided with a parking space.) There are four times as many fee-lot permits sold as the number of spaces available, and the 75¢ student or staff parking permit is really only a "hunting license" to search for parking within a lot. (These lots are open to the general public only on weekends and weekday evenings.)

The people of Berkeley could reduce many of the traffic problems by simply using other means of transportation. Even though half of those who work downtown and at the University live within walking or biking distance, most drive alone, and the average number of passengers per car in Berkeley is 1.13. It seems a bit hypocritical for people who complain about squandered world resources, air pollution, and parking problems to drive half-a-mile to work each day by themselves.

Fortunately, a variety of transportation choices are available in and around Berkeley. The simplest options are walking and bike riding, but several public transit systems exist. The BART system is relatively simple (albeit expensive), but its connections to AC and other public bus systems can be confusing. AC Transit alone has over 50 different rate structures. (Example: Zone 2 express fares with an unlimited pass, or an off-peak pass, except in commute hours, are $1, unless you are a youth, senior, or disabled person, in which case there are no zone changes.) Maybe one day all the Bay Area's transit systems will come up with a common card offering a flat rate and unified service—don't hold your breath.

Building the BART System

Although the idea of a "submarine railway" first appeared in 1872, it was the Bay Area's rapid growth during World War II and the resulting congestion on the Bay Bridge that forced people to look seriously for options to automobiles. In 1947 a joint Army-Navy study recommended construction of a transit tube beneath San Francisco Bay. Unlike the early days when an entire transit system could be built in fifteen months, it took another 27 years before the first BART train finally rolled through a transbay tube.

After the Army-Navy study was released, business boosters compelled the state legislature to set up a Bay Area Rapid Transit Commission (BARTC) composed of representatives from nine Bay Area counties. The Commission's final report in 1957 led to the legislature's creation of the BART District (BARTD) to design a new transit system for the region. A property tax supplied initial support for the plan, but once the engineering groundwork had been laid, voters had to decide on how to fund the construction. By this time BART's nine counties had shrunk to just three: San Francisco, Alameda, and Contra Costa. The biggest loss was San Mateo County (home to San Francisco Airport), whose supervisors rejected BART, claiming it would duplicate existing train service. (The supervisors were influenced on the matter by a local shopping mall developer who was concerned that BART would make it too easy to shop in San Francisco.) Napa, Solano, and Santa Clara counties were viewed as too far away to benefit from the service. Marin and Sonoma counties wanted to join, but the Golden Gate Bridge District refused to allow BART trains to run under the bridge deck, and a tunnel was considered too expensive. When the $792 million bond measure was finally put to the voters of the three remaining counties in 1962, it surprised everyone by eking out a 1% margin of victory.

The 71-mile BART system was to reflect a new national emphasis upon high technology. Sleekly modern trains—computer controlled, with no need for operators—would arrive every 90 seconds and travel at 70 mph between stations. Construction began in 1964, but another eight years passed before a train carried its first passenger. In the meantime, the state legislature approved a "temporary" half-cent sales tax to complete funding of the construction (and made it permanent in 1977).

Unlike several other East Bay cities, Berkeley refused to allow the new system to divide the city with towering elevated tracks. Voters in 1966 passed a $12-million bond measure to pay for the extra cost of underground construction. This led to the demolition of many homes along the route, but the resulting open space became Ohlone and Cedar/Rose Parks.

Shortly after it opened on September 11, 1972, the system's general manager and all-round BART booster, B. R. Stokes, was showing off the space-age control room to the head of the New York subway system. "Watch," he told his visitor, "There is a train headed for the Fremont station." As they stood by, the light suddenly went out, and a few minutes later a call came from the train operator, "I've just landed in the parking lot!" The train had plowed through a dirt embankment and off the end of the track. No one was seriously hurt, but the BART system has never quite lived down that moment.

In spite of planners' high expectations, BART carries just two-thirds of its anticipated daily passenger load (200,000 vs 300,000 a day) and has never come even close to profitability. The system has shaken off much of the uneven service that dogged it for years, but its sky-high fares (nearly $2 to San Francisco) discourage ridership. Because of computer problems, trains operate at an average of 35 mph, rather than the 70 mph envisioned. Critics like to compare BART to the Key System of the 1920s: with an affordable transbay crossing that took just a few more minutes than the space-age BART system, the Key System attracted almost as many passengers (nearly 30 million across the Bay each year), even though the East Bay's population then was only a quarter of what it is today.

Traffic Management

Berkeley's streets were laid out in an era of pedestrians and street cars, when there were only 10,000 cars in all of California. Today there are an estimated 74,000 vehicles in Berkeley alone. As traffic problems became more severe in the early 1960s, city traffic consultants recommended the widening of 50 local streets. The Elmwood shopping district and other homes along the route were to be destroyed as Ashby Ave. would become a six-lane expressway. The resulting public outcry led to an alternative tack: limiting traffic. One of the main strategies of the new focus was to force traffic onto a few main thoroughfares by placing barricades on the side streets. Twenty-six traffic diverters were put up from 1964 to 1974. In 1975 the city approved a new Traffic Management Plan to add another 44 diverters, 21 traffic circles, 310 stop signs, and eleven traffic lights. Anti-diverter forces fought back both in elections and in court, charging the barriers created safety hazards, were unsightly, and illegal. The diverters won majority support in both 1976 and 1977 city elections, but lost in the California Supreme Court. In 1983 the issue was laid to rest by passage of a state law (AB 366) that allowed cities to establish street barriers.

Getting Around Town

BART Service (the Subway)

BART trains run Sun 9 am-midnight, Sat 6 am-midnight, and Mon-Fri 5 am-midnight at 5-20 minute intervals. There is direct service to Richmond and Fremont everyday, and service to San Francisco Mon-Sat 6 am-6 pm, but for other destinations and times you should transfer at the MacArthur Station. Train schedules are available in the stations, but cannot always be counted upon. BART allows bikes on board the last car of its trains during non-commute hours and with a special pass. Bike lockers are also available at some BART stations. Call 464-7133 for details. For general BART information call 465-BART (465-2278).

Bus Service on AC Transit

At one time Alameda-Contra Costa County (AC) Transit was the paragon of public transit systems, offering dependable bus service, friendly drivers, reasonable rates, and healthy finances. That era is unfortunately long past. The double whammy of Proposition 13 tax slashes (which forced higher fares to offset lost revenue) and low gas prices put many folks back in their cars. Add alleged administrative mismanagement in the mid-80s and you end up with a ridership largely of those without options: the aged, the handicapped, those too poor to own a car, and those too young to drive one. Even on their popular Bay Bridge routes, AC Transit has been losing out, ironically, to "casual carpoolers" who pick up riders at the bus stops and then sail past other vehicles in the carpool lane.

Despite its problems, AC Transit provides relatively complete coverage of Berkeley, the East Bay, and across the Bay Bridge to San Francisco. After decades of stagnation the system is presently undergoing a complete overhaul, with new routes and schedules to be phased in over several years. Most bus service in Berkeley starts around 6 am and ends at midnight, but a few operate through the night. Buses run anywhere from 10-60 minutes apart. Bus route schedules are available in the Student Union Building on campus, the main public library, and the TRiP office (see below) or call 839-2882 for more specific AC Transit information. Discounts are offered to handicapped persons (AC Transit has special "kneeling" buses), the elderly, and youths. Bus transfers are good for an hour in any direction; BART-to-bus transfers can be obtained as you exit the BART stations. During the summer, there are special bicycle-carrying buses into Tilden Park ($.25 per bike).

Lawrence Berkeley Lab Shuttles
LBL operates a free shuttle bus to the Lab from the campus. Officially these buses are for LBL employees and visitors only, but this policy is not strictly enforced. The shuttles circle the campus in a clockwise direction and make a detour through downtown on a route that varies with the time of day. Be sure to get off before the bus enters LBL's restricted perimeter. LBL buses operate at 10-20 minute intervals Mon-Fri 6:40 am-6:50 pm. Phone 486-4165 for details.

TRiP Commute Store
TRiP (as in Transit/Rides/Parking) provides information on AC Transit, BART, bikes, carpools, vanpools, parking discounts, Park and Ride Lots, and other alternatives to the All-American commute. Call 644-Pool (644-7665) for free information on any of these subjects, or stop by the TRiP office at 2033 Center Street. Berkeley vanpools include those from most surrounding cities, and the computerized carpool list has over 13,000 names of fellow commuters. The TRiP office also sells discounted BART cards and special AC/BART passes.

University Campus Shuttles
The University operates a number of excellent free campus shuttle buses. Although meant for students, anyone can ride. The **downtown shuttle** runs from the Bank of America building in downtown Berkeley (Center and Shattuck) to the campus. Buses leave every 8-15 minutes Mon-Fri 7 am-7 pm with stops at West Circle, the Main Library, and Hearst Mining Circle. A **hill shuttle** continues on from Hearst Mining Circle to Lawrence Hall of Science with intermediate stops at Strawberry Canyon, the Botanical Garden, and Lawrence Berkeley Lab's South Gate. These buses leave every half hour Mon-Fri 7:45 am-6:45 pm. Call 642-4834 for details.

The following schedules might change, so be sure to check them to ensure your safety. Buses at night take students safely off campus during the school year. The **night services** operate on Northside Sun-Thurs 7:30-10 pm, and on Southside nightly 9-10 pm. Between 10 pm and 1:30 am the fixed route is replaced by door-to-door service within nearby areas. For specific shuttle bus schedules see postings in Moffitt Library or call 642-5149. In addition, the Campus Police provide an **escort service** across campus at night and will wait with you at the bus stops. Call 642-WALK (642-9255) to get an escort.

Getting Out of Town

The Bay Area has two international airports, Oakland and San Francisco, along with bus and train service to most cities. In addition, the Bay Area has a range of alternative means of travel such as rideboards, private bus services, and driveaway cars.

Airports

Oakland International Airport. Oakland Airport is easily accessible by public transit. **The Oakland-Air BART Shuttle Bus** (444-4200) takes you between the Oakland Coliseum BART Station and the airport for $1. It operates Mon-Sat 6 am-midnight, Sun 9 am-midnight, and arrives every fifteen minutes. To reach Oakland Airport directly by bus, take AC Transit bus No. 51 to MacArthur and Broadway, and then transfer to No. 57. Carry-on luggage is allowed.

The **Bay Area Shuttle** has service between five Berkeley hotels (Claremont, Durant, Shattuck, Berkeley House, and Marriott Inn) and Oakland Airport for $10/adult, $8/children (ages 5-15), and free for children under five. Residents of the Claremont Hotel and Marriott Inn are not charged for this service. Advance reservations are required (873-7771) or (800-345-8687), but you don't need to be a hotel resident to use the shuttle. The shuttle operates daily 5 am-10:30 pm. If you have a late night flight, your only real option is to get a taxi, for a hefty $25-$30. **BayPorter Express** offers direct service from your home to either Oakland or San Francisco Airport for $15 between 5:30 am and 8:40 pm. Make reservations several days in advance by calling (800) 548-8811.

San Francisco International Airport. The cheapest way to reach SFO is by taking BART to the Daly City station ($2.05) and then catching **SamTrans** bus 3B to the airport (50¢). Buses run Mon-Fri 6:20 am-7:20 pm, Sat and Sun 9:20 am-6:20 pm. There are other options, but this is the only SamTrans bus that allows carry-on luggage (although the rules are sometimes overlooked on other buses). Call SamTrans (761-7000) for details.

The Airport Connection (841-0150) provides van service between SFO and the Durant, Marriott, and Claremont Hotels in Berkeley for $13/person while kids under five years old ride free. They also offer door-to-door service for $26/person ($10 each additional person). The service operates 24 hours every day. Make reservations 24 hours in advance. You need not be a resident of the hotels to ride the shuttle. **Bay Area Super Shuttle** is an excellent choice for those taking late-night flights from SFO (558-8500). Super Shuttle will pick you up from any San Francisco address for $8. Getting to San Francisco is another story, however. After midnight when BART shuts down it is still possible to reach San Francisco via AC Transit, but the buses are infrequent and follow an excruciating routing through parts of Oakland you may not want to visit after dark. Call AC Transit for the gruesome details. Another late-night option, a taxi, will set you back $40 to $45 from Berkeley, but if there are three or four people to share the fare it may actually prove somewhat of a bargain. Also try **BayPorter Express** (see "Oakland International Airport").

Buses

Greyhound and Trailways. Located in downtown Oakland, the two major longhaul bus systems have combined their schedules and service and are a tolerable way to see the country, particularly towns inaccessible by other means. Recently, however, buses have struggled to stay in business. As cutthroat competition between the airlines has brought their prices close to, and sometimes below, what the buses have been charging and more people ride the faster and more comfortable planes, the bus system becomes even more tenuous. The bus terminal at 2103 San Pablo Ave. in Oakland, (834-3070) is open daily 5:30 am-1 am and has routes throughout the US and Canada. They often offer special discount fares for extended trips or cross-country travel.

Green Tortoise. Bus trips bring to mind endless road-miles clocked inside lumbering Greyhound buses, interspersed with brief stops at dreadful restaurants. Green Tortoise offers an alternative kind of ride. Spawned in the hippie era (circa 1973), Green Tortoise is the funky outgrowth of founder Gardner Kent's personal love for old buses (the service uses aging GM diesel coaches). Relying for business on word of mouth and ads stapled to telephone poles, Green Tortoise provides communal meals for its American and international travellers with a friendliness you wouldn't expect from a bus company. The drivers are combination cooks/social directors/mechanics, and the buses all have couches and tables up front and bunkbeds hanging from the ceiling. They cover a route up and down the Pacific coast twice a week, and make excursions to a variety of other destinations, from Alaska to the Yucatan. The routes don't always follow freeways—expect a detour to hot springs

where the "clothing optional" crowd goes into action. Bring your guitar for sing-alongs or your tapes for the onboard stereos.

Green Tortoise has direct overnight service from Berkeley to Seattle ($49), while LA, at $30, is cheaper than the taxi fare from Berkeley to SFO. Seattle-bound buses leave Berkeley from Park and Shop (1414 University), while other buses leave from the San Francisco Transbay Terminal at First St. and Natoma. In addition to these direct trips, Green Tortoise has cross-country trips to everywhere from Mardi Gras in New Orleans to Alaskan glaciers. You'll need to make reservations (confirmed within 48 hours of the date) for most trips. For an additional $5-$10 you can get off the bus and back on a later one. Call 821-0803 for more details.

Buses to Other Universities. Several student buses operate between UC Berkeley and nearby universities. The **UC Davis Intercampus Bus** (916-752-8287) costs $1.50 each way, while the **Gutenberg Express** (642-5149) operates between Stanford and Berkeley for $5 each way. The UC **Santa Cruz Intercampus Bus** (408-429-2803) is $4 each way, and the **UC San Francisco Intercampus Bus** (476-1511) runs $1.25 each way. A free **Richmond Field Station Bus** departs from Hearst Mining Circle (642-5149). All other intercampus buses leave from the West Campus Entrance. The UC Santa Cruz bus operates Mon-Sat while the others run only Mon-Fri. The UCSF bus takes the general public (lowest priority), but other intercampus buses are only for UC students, faculty, and staff. The Main (Doe) Library has a phone for inquiries or reservations.

Cars

Carpool Transit Systems. On bulletin boards around Berkeley you'll often see crudely-printed notices for riders wanted. The source of these is the oddly-named Half-Cost Carpool Transit Systems (2720 MLK Way, 845-1769), a tiny operation that provides connections for commuters and those looking to share a ride. Half-Cost also arranges connections with drive-away companies and even advertises "cheap heaps"—old cars in fair condition for under $500. All requests for rides or riders are listed free, but access to the listings costs $10 for a six-month membership.

Cars to Drive Cross-country. One of the cheapest ways to cross the country is by delivering a vehicle for a drive-away company. As a driver you are given a free tank of gas and several days to deliver the car. (Three of us once drove a new Cadillac to Seattle for a grand total of $7 each!) For more information, check the yellow pages under "Automobile Transporters," or the *Chronicle* classified ads. The latter is also a good place to look for discounted airline tickets and courier companies.

Rental Cars. In Berkeley, **Avis Rent-A-Car** (548-7363) rents cars at 1900 Oxford St., near the corner of Hearst, and the address is convenient to campus. **Enterprise Rent-A-Car** (841-8300) at 3001 Shattuck Ave., near the Ashby intersection, is generally reliable, friendly, and economical, as is the **Lincoln-Mercury dealership** (845-7010) at 2352 Shattuck Ave., near Shattuck and Durant. For other rental car agencies, look in the *Yellow Pages*.

Rideboards. The ASUC operates a rideboard in lower Sproul Plaza, across the hall from the electronics store. Here you'll find rides or riders for your destination, be it Orinda or Ottawa. The student radio station, KALX (FM 90.7), has a twice-daily (10 am and 10 pm) Ridefinder program with more listings. Call 642-KALX (642-5259) to put your name on the rides-wanted or rides-offered listings.

Railroad Passenger Service

Competition from airlines, limited routes, and a slashed budget continue to threaten railroad passenger service, so ride Amtrak now while you still can. Travelling by train is not for those in a hurry—it takes two days just to reach Chicago—but the reward is an opportunity to see the towering mountains, majestic deserts, and expansive plains of this country up close. Amtrak is easily accessible from Berkeley. For trains to most destinations simply take BART to the Richmond Station. Amtrak trains stop just outside the station, leaving daily for the East Coast, Seattle, or Los Angeles. Amtrak is a great way to reach the ski slopes of Truckee or the gambling tables of Reno. Daily trains to the Central Valley depart from Berkeley next to the China Station Restaurant at University Ave. and 3rd Street. Call 982-8512 for Amtrak fare and schedule information.

Travel Service

If you are under age 31, Council Travel (2511 Channing Way, 848-8604) has the cheapest airline tickets to be found. The company is a member of the Council on International Educational Exchange (CIEE), a non-profit organization that emphasizes international education and student travel. Non-students may use their travel services, but students get special discounts on transportation, accommodations, and admission fees. One major advantage of using Council is the ease in changing your travel schedule without penalties on extended, multi-stop trips.

Berkeley Trivia

Total city acreage: 11,568 (18 square miles)
Miles of streets: 231; of unpaved streets: 6.7
Number of footpaths: 120
Number of public swimming pools: 12
Number of traffic diverters: 64
Number of boat slips: 975
Number of motor vehicles: 74,000; persons of driving age: 87,439
Percent of workers who ride public transportation to work: 20;
    who drive alone to work: 43
Time to reach San Francisco via public transit in 1920: 36 minutes;
    in 1989: 23 minutes
Number of dogs: 15,000; of dog parks: 1
Number of churches, temples, and ashrams: 200
Number of books in UC Berkeley library system (1989): 7 million
Number of city parks: 50. Percentage of land in city parks: 3
Largest structure in North America built with volunteer labor: Finnish Hall
National rank of Berkeley in total population: 167
National rank of Berkeley in population density: 10
Number of small press publishers in Berkeley: 55; in Arkansas, Delaware,
    Kansas, Kentucky, Mississippi, North Dakota, Rhode Island, South
    Carolina, South Dakota, West Virginia, and Wyoming combined: 53
Number of books about Berkeley in the public library: 189
Kinds of lettuce grown by Kona Kai Gardens: 20
Price of a meal (excluding wine, tip, and tax) at Chez Panisse: $55;
    at the Berkeley Food Project: 25¢
Gallons of clam chowder consumed per day at Spenger's Fish Grotto: 250
Number of chocolate truffles sold by Cocolat each year: 2.5 million
Number of tons of coffee sold in Berkeley each year: 415
Number of tons of garbage produced each day: 300
Median 1980 household income in Southside: $4,426; in Claremont:
    $42,063
Percent of persons over 24 with four or more years of college: 52;
    without a high school diploma: 14
Number of people living on Berkeley streets: about 1500
Percent of Berkeleyans born in California: 41; foreign born: 13
Percent who do not speak English at home: 14
Number of streets named for presidents: 9; for writers: 8; for a horse: 1
City where more copies of *Dell's Horoscope* are sold than any other: Berkeley
University with largest number of Peace Corps volunteers: UC Berkeley
Only element named for a city: Berkelium
Number of Nobel Prize winners from the USSR: 15; from UC Berkeley: 15

Sources: Primarily the Census Bureau (1980) and Berkeley City Auditor Annual Report (1988).

Index

References to photos and graphics are printed in italic.

À La Carte, 265
AC Transit, 356, 358-359
Addison Annex, 255
Adventure Playground, 216, *216*
AIDS, 338
Airports, Bay Area, 360
Airport shuttles, 360
Albatross Pub, 239, 299-300
Alcoholics Anonymous, 338
Alta Bates Hospital, 104, 339-340
Alvarez, Luis W., 64
Amaru, 269
American Red Cross, 338
Americans for Nonsmokers Rights, 342
Amrit, 277
Amtrack, 362
Angulo, Jaime de, 38
Animal Shelter, Berkeley, 324
Anza, Juan Bautista de, 10, 11
April Coalition, 122-123
Aquatic Park, 206, 210-211
Architectural styles, 165-171
Arinell Pizza, 273
Art galleries, 191-193
Arts and Crafts Coop (ACCI), 191
Artworks Foundry and Gallery,192
Ashkenaz, 196, 297
ASUC, 61, 104
ASUC Art Studio 191-192
Au Coquelet, 284
Augusta's, 260, *270*
Avakian, Bob, 148
¡Ay Caramba!, 269

Bach, Leo, 119
Bachenheimer, Richard, 155
Bade, Dr. William, 191
Baez, Joan, 142
Bailey, D'Army, 122, 128
Bakeries, 285-289
Bananas, 113, 313
Bancroft Library, 79, 320
Barrington Hall, 112, 140
BART. *See* Bay Area Rapid Transit District
Bates, Ms. Alta, 340, *340*
Bay Area Funeral Society, 342
Bay Area Outreach and Recreation Program
  (BORP), 314
Bay Area Rapid Transit District (BART), 356-358

Bay Conservation & Development Commission
  (BCDC), 220
Bay Warehouse, 113
Bechtel, Steven D., Sr., 65
Bed and Breakfast International, 305
Bénard, Henry Jean Emile, 69
Berkeley Addiction Treatment Services, 338
Berkeley Adult School, 335
Berkeley Architectural Heritage Association,
  165, 168
Berkeley Area Interfaith Council, 161
Berkeley Art Center, 192, 199
Berkeley Ballet Theater School, 196
Berkeley Barb, 144-145, 149
Berkeley Bay Festival, 322
Berkeley Chamber of Commerce, 315
Berkeley Citizen's Action (BCA), 119, 123-124,
  159, 345
Berkeley Civic Arts Commission, 187
Berkeley Community Law Center, 159, 350
Berkeley Conservatory Ballet, 196
Berkeley Daily Gazette, 103, 120
Berkeley Day Nursery, 174
Berkeley Democratic Club (BDC), 119, 123, 345
Berkeley Department of Health and Human
  Services, 342
Berkeley Ecumenical Chaplaincy to the
  Homeless, 351
Berkeley fire of 1923, 31, *31*, 181, 183-184
Berkeley Food Pantry, 348
Berkeley, Bishop George, 18, 81
Berkeley Higashi Honganji, 163
Berkeley High School, 25, 171, 242, 331-333,
  333-334
Berkeley Historical Society, 315
Berkeley Holistic Health Center, 341
Berkeley House Motor Hotel, 310
Berkeley Information Network, 315-317
Berkeley/Oakland Support Services, 350
Berkeley Opera, 199
Berkeley Psychic Institute, 341
Berkeley Public Library, 318-319
Berkeley Recycling Center, 329
Berkeley Repertory Theater, 193-194, *193*
Berkeley Shakespeare Festival, 194
Berkeley Square, 297
Berkeley Symphony, 197
Berkeley Tenants' Union, 114, 155
Berkeley Thai House, 276

Berkeley Unified School District, 335
Berkeley Zen Center, 163
Bertola's, 265
Bette's Oceanview Diner, 258
Bette's To Go, 287
Bhutto, Zulfikar Ali, 65
Big C, 77
Big Game, 246-247, *247*
Bingo, 237, *237*
Biondi, Matt, 65
Bicycling, 235-236, *236*
Billiards, 238
Bison Brewing Co., 300, 304
Black Oak Books, 109, 200, *201*
Black Panthers, 35, 121, 134, 147-149, 159
Black Pine Circle School, 174
Black Power, 35, 146-148
Black Repertory Group, 194, *194*
Blake, George M., 51-52
Blake Street Hawkeyes, 93, 114, 195
Blondie's Pizza, 273, *274*
Blue Nile, 254, *254*
Bluet (John J.) House, 176
B'nai B'rith Hillel Foundation, 162
Boalt Hall School of Law, 84
Body Shop, 116
Bombay Bazaar, 294
Bombay Cuisine, 267
Bonanza Motel, 310
Bookpeople, 109, 159
Bookstores, 109-111
Botanic Garden, Tilden, 225-226
Botanical Garden, University, *231*, 232, 322
Boudrow (Capt.) House, 166
Bowen's Inn, 15-16, 176
Bowen, William, 15, 176
Bowley, Rev. Alexia, 146, 351, *351*
Bowling, 238
Boynton, Ira and Florence, 185
Brazilian Room, 226
Brennan Family, 16
Brennan's, 5, 255, 300
Brick Hut Cafe, 258
Britt-Marie's, 265
Broderick, Tracey, 62, *62*
Brower, David, 89-90, *89*
Brown, Arthur, Jr., 69
Brown (Charles R.) House, 177
Brown, Jerry, Jr., 65, 99
Buddhist Temple of Berkeley, 163
Budge, Don, 90
Burke, Stoney, *76*, 77
Buses, 360-361
Buses to other universities, 361
Businesses, Berkeley's oldest, 106-107

Cactus Taqueria, 269-270

Cafe at Chez Panisse, 261
Cafe Bistro, 300
Cafe Fanny, 260
Cafe Intermezzo, 282
Cafe Mar-Mara, 273
Cafe Milano, *280*, 284
Cafe Pastoral, 261
Cafe Strada, 238, 282
Cafe Vin, 266, 284
Cafe Violeta, 270
Caffe Espresso, 285
Caffe Giovanni, 266
Caffe Med, 282
Caffe Venezia, 266
Cal Adventures, 244, *244*
Cal Hotel, 312
Cal Performances, 197
Cal Sports Clubs, 243-244
CalSTAR, 245
California Senate Fact Finding Committee on Un-American Activities, 331-332
Calso, 61
Calvin, Melvin, 64
Cambodiana, The, 264
Camejo, Peter, 146
Campanile, 77, 78, *78*
Car Rentals, 362
Carlton Hotel, 312
Carousel, Tilden Park, 228, *228*
Casa de Eva, 271
Casbah, 254
Castro, Francisco, 12, 15, 51
Cedar-Rose Park, 207
Center for Independent Living (CIL), 99, 314-315
Cha-Am, 276
Chamber of Commerce, Berkeley, 315
Chamberlain, Owen, 64
Cheese Board, 113, 114, 159, 287, 292, *293*
Cheese shops, 291-292
Chess, 238-239
Chez Panisse, *252*, 261, 263
Chicago Seven, 147, 149, 157
Children's Services, 313-312
China Station Restaurant, 178
Chinese for Christ Church, 161
Chochenyo Language, 8, 9
Christopher's Cafe, 261
Church of the Good Shepherd, 161, 175, *175*
Cinco de Mayo, 322
City Council, 117-125, 127, *131*, 132, 143, 147
City Hall, *126*, 171
Claremont Canyon Regional Preserve, 229
Claremont Hotel, 308-309, *309*
Claremont (neighborhood), 42, *44*
Claremont Seafood Restaurant, 276
Clark (Estelle) House, 182
Cleaver, Eldridge, 90-91, *90*, *90*, 147-148

Clinics, 338-339
Cocolat, 286, *286*
Codornices Creek, 8, 13
Codornices Park, 181, *184*, 207
Cody's Books, 5, 109, 154
Cody's Cafe, 282
Cody, Fred, 91, 152-155
Cody, Pat, 153-155
Coffee Connection, 285
Coffee Renaissance, 255
Cohelan, Jeffrey, 120-121
Collectives, 113-114
College Homestead Association, 17-18
Communal Living, 155-158
Community Conservation Center, 329
Congregation Beth El, 161
Congregation Beth Israel, 161
Congress on Racial Equality (CORE), *36*, 140
Continental Garden Restaurant, 259
Co-op (Consumers Cooperative of Berkeley), 112
291
Council on International Educational Exchange,
362-363
Council of Neighborhood Assoc., 41
Cowell Hospital, 341
Cox, Rev., 161
Coxhead, Ernest, 170, 174
Cragmont, 42
Creative Arts Press, 109
Crespi, Juan, 10, 161
Crime statistics, 132-135

Daily Bread Project, 349
Daily Californian, 61, 188
Dance, 195-197
Darts, 239
Daruma Teashop, 268, *268*
Dave's Smoke Shop, 115
Deakins, Alfred, 44
DeBonis, John, 143
Debreu, Gerard, 65
Delacour, Michael, 149
Delaware St. Historic District, 49, 176-177
Dellums, Ron, 91-92, 120-121, 123
Demographics, Berkeley, 87-89
Dempster House, 181
Design Associates Working with Nature, 217
Dickey, Charles W., 308
Didion, Joan, 65-66
Disabled, services for, 314-315
Disabled Students Program, 315
Doe (Main) Library, 79, 321
Dominoes, 239
Dog Park, *207*, 324
Downtown (neighborhood), 47
Draper, Phil, 314, *314*
Duncan, Robert, 38, 140

Durant, Rev. Henry, 17, 19, 23, 52
Durant Hotel, 307
Dwinelle Hall, 57, 76-77, 148
Dwinelle, John W., 24, 76

Earthquakes, 29, 340, 354
East Bay Metropolitan Park Assoc., 223
East Bay Municipal Utilities District, 29, 223, 230
East Bay Regional Park District, 223-225
East Campus, Berkeley High, 332
Ecology Center, 114, 159, 233
Edible Complex, 285
Edwards, Harry, 92, *92*
Ehret (Anatole) House, 177
El Cerrito Creek, 8-11
Eli's Mile High Club, 297
Elmwood (neighborhood), 44, 343
Elmwood Pharmacy, 44, 256, *256*
Emergency Food Project, 146, 159, 164, 349
Employers, Berkeley's largest, 104
Employment, 316-317
Environmental Education Center, 226
Environmental organizations, 233
Eshleman Hall Library, 321
Eu, March Fong, 66
Everding, John, 15
Everett & Jones Barbeque, 255
Express, 187

Faculty Club (Men's), 83, 312
Faculty Club, Women's, 83, 312
Faculty Glade, 83
Fages, Pedro, 10
Fair Housing Ordinance, 120
Fantasy Records, 111
Farmers' Market, *290*, 296, 322
Farquharson, David, 68, 77
Farr, Albert, 170
Fat Slice Pizza, 274
Fatapple's, 255, 288
Finnish community, 175-176
Finnish Hall, 175-176, *176*
First Church of Christ Scientist, 180, *180*
First Congregational Church, 162
Fish markets, 292-294
Flagg-Wright House, 166
Flatlands (neighborhood), 47
Flea Market, 115, 323
Flint's Bar-B-Q, 256
Fonda, Jane, 145, 157
Fort Soap, 185
Founders Rock, 81
Fourth Street Grill, 261
Free Church, 145-146, *146*, 163
Free Clinic, 113, 146, 153-154, 159, 338, 353
Free Library, 153
Free Speech Movement, 141-142, *141*

Free Store, 153
Freight and Salvage, 298
French Hotel, 307
French Hotel Cafe, 238, *238*, 284
Frey House, 174
Friends of Center for Independent Living, 315
Friends of the Berkeley Public Library, 318
Friends of the Botanical Garden, 232
Fujimoto, Tom, *295*

Galbraith, John Kenneth, 66
Galvez, Daniel, 201, 202, 204
Games, 238-239
Games of Berkeley, 115
Gannon House, 185
Gardening, 241
Gayley, Charles, 52
Geirrine (Charles) House, 174
Gertie's Chesapeake Bay Cafe, 276
Giauque, William F., 63
Gilbreth, Lillian Moler, 66
Gilman, Daniel, 19, 27
Ginsberg, Allen, 38, 140
Glaser, Donald A., 64
Go, 239
Goines, David Lance, 92-93, *93*
Goldberg, Rube, 66
Goldberg, Whoopi, 93, *93*, 195
Golden Bear Clubs, 245
Goldfarb, Alan, 131
Golf, 288-289
Good Earth, 278
Gorman & Son, 106, *106*
Gramma's Inn, 259, 305-307, *306*
Gravy, Wavy, 93-94, *94*
Graduate Theological Union, 164
Grey Panthers, 336
Green Tortoise, 361
Greyhound Bus Co., 360-361
Guardian, The, 192, *192*
Guerrero's, 271
Gutterson, Henry, 42

Haas, Walter, Jr., 66
Habib, Philip, 66
Hackey Sack, 239
Half-Cost Carpool Transit Systems, 362
Hall, Camilla, 158
Hancock, Loni, 122, *122*, 124, *131*
Hare Krishnas, 163, *163*
Harmon Gym, 76
Hass, Walter, Jr., 66
Havens, Frank, 308
Hayden, Tom, 145, 157
Health and Human Services Dept.,
    City of Berkeley, 338
Hearst, George, 82

Hearst Greek Theatre, 81
Hearst Gymnasium, 85
Hearst Mining Building, 80, *81*
Hearst, Patty, 158
Hearst, Phoebe Apperson, 29, 69, 81, 82, *82*, 85,
    174-175
Hearst, William Randolph, 82, 97
Hearst, William Randolph, Jr., 66
Heartsong, 342
Heller Gallery, 191
Heller, Lenny, 144
Hells Angels, 144
Henry's Publick House and Grille, 300
Herrick, Francis, 340
Herrick Hall of Health, 341
Herrick Hospital, 104, 339-341
Hershey Bar, General, *144*
Hertz Music Building, 83
Heyday Books, 109
Heyman, Chancellor Ira, 356
Heyns, Chancellor Roger, 149
Heywood (Charles W.) House, 178
Heywood, Samuel, 221
Heywood (Walter)/Ghego House, 178
Heywood, Zimri B., 16, 178
Hill, Lewis, 326-327
Hillegass, William, 51-52
Hillside Club, 168, 181
Himalayan Fair, 232
Ho Chi Minh Park, 153
Hoffman, Abbie, 66
Holiday Inn, 311
Holy Hill, 164
Home Missionary Society, 17
Homeless, help for, 347-353
Homemade Cafe, 259
Hong Fu, 264
Hong Kong Villa, 264
Honig, Bill, 66
Hospitals, 339-341
Hostel, 311
House Un-American Activities Committee, 120,
    139, 327
Howard, John Galen, 42, 70, 76, 78-79, 81-83, 182
Howard (John Galen) House, 182
Huchiun Indians, *6*, 7-11
Hughes, Bonnie, 260, *260*
Humane Society, Berkeley, 324-326, *326*
Hume Cloister, 186, *186*
Hutton, Bobby, 148

Iceland, 240, *240*
Ice-skating, 240
Incorporation of Berkeley, 23-25
Indian Cafe, 267
Indian Rock Park, 208
Indians, California, *6*, 7-10, 153, 209

International Bird Rescue Research Center, 325
International House, 84, 196
International House Cafe, 257
International Markets, 294

Jacobs, Helen, 97
Jacobs, Capt. James, 15, 178
Jacob's Landing, 15-16, 21, 219
Jewel Lake, 222, 223
Jewish Community Center, 336
Johnson, Lyndon B., 120
Joshu-Ya, 268-269
Juan's Place, 27
Juice Bar Collective, 114, 158, 278
Julia Morgan Center for the Arts, 168, 195
Juneteen, 323

Kala Institute, 192
KALX, 188, 326, 362
Karkin Indians, 8
Keach, Stacy, 66
Keeler, Charles, 38, 134, 168, 180
Keeler House, 181
Keeler, Leonard, 134
Keith, William, 38
Kelham, George W., 69
Kelsey, John, 318
Kerouac, Jack, 140
Kerr, Chancellor Clark, 37, 69
Kesey, Ken, 143
Key Line, 28, 32
King, Martin Luther, Jr., 128, 146-147
King, Martin Luther, Jr. Park, 128, 207, 209
Kip's, 274, 300
Kirala, 269
Kona Kai Farms, 296
KPFA, 114, 139, 158, 188, 326-328
KPFA Holiday Crafts Fair, 323, 328
Krishna Temple, 163
Kragen, Ken, 94
Kroeber, Alfred, 36, 77, 181

La Bottega, 284
LaLanne, Jack, 95
La Méditerranée, 273
La Peña, 114, 159, 298
La Val's, 274, 300
Lake Anza, 227
Lake Merritt Lodge, 312
Lalime's, 262
Landmark Preservation Ordinance, 165
Lange, Dorothea, 95
Language Studies International, 335
Laotian Handicraft Center, 114-115, 114
Lappe, Francis Moore, 95, 95
Larry Blake's Rathskeller, 299
Lawn Bowling, 239, 239

Lawrence Berkeley Lab, 71-72, 104, 359
Lawrence Hall of Science, 4, 64, 188, 242
Lawrence, Ernest O., 63, 72
Lawson (Andrew) House, 182
League of Women Voters, 130
Leary, Timothy, 95-96
Lee, Yuan Tseh, 65, 65
Leonard, James, 51-52
Libraries, University, 79, 79, 320-322, 322
Library, Berkeley Public, 171, 318-319
Liebert, Michael, 193
Lilly's, 264
Lindblom, Erik, 308
Little Farm, 227
Little India, 50
Little Trains, 227-228, 227
Live Oak Park Fair, 323
Livingston, M. Stanley, 72
Lo Coco's Restaurant and Pizzaria, 275
Lois the Pie Queen, 259
Long Life Vegie House, 278
Lowie Museum of Anthropology, 189
Lower Sproul Plaza, 74
LSD, 95-96, 142
Ludwig's Fountain, 74

Ma Revolution, 153-154
Magnes (Judah L.) Museum, 189
Maharani, 267
Mama's Royal Cafe, 259
Mandel, William, 96, 96, 139
Manuel's, 271
Mark Twain Papers, 320
Marina Sports Center, 218
Marina Environmental Education Program, 215
Mario's La Fiesta, 271, 272
Marriott Inn, 307
Martin, Billy, 96-97
Mason, Joseph, 26
Mason-McDuffie Co., 27, 106
Mather, Stephen T., 66-67
Mathewson House, 182
Maybeck, Bernard, 42, 69, 83, 85, 168, 179-185, 179, 184
Maybeck Recital Hall, 182, 199
McCreary House, 168
McDonald, Country Joe, 97
McDougall, Walter, 60
McDuffie, Duncan, 26-27, 42
McGee Ave. Baptist Church, 160, 162
McGee Ave. Food Program, 349
McMillan, Edwin M., 63
McNamara, Robert S., 67
McVey (Joseph B.) House, 174
Meade, Ken, 121
Meal Ticket, 259
Meat markets, 292-294

Medrich, Alice, 286, *286*
Meese, Edwin, III, 67, 152
Metropole, 266
Middle East Restaurant, 273
Miller, Joaquin, 26
Milosz, Czeslaw, 64-65, 356
Milvia, The, 264
Misrach, Robert, 67
Mission Dolores, 10-11, 13
Moe's Books, *108*, 109, 153-154
Moen, Kevin 247
Moffitt Library, 79, *79*, 321
Monroe, A. Randolf, 185
Monterey Market, 295, *295*
Monthly, The, 253
Moody, Helen Wills, 97
Moon Unification Church, 162
Moran, John Paul, 166
Morgan, Julia, 42, 44, 81, 85, 97-98, 168, 174,
    181- 182
Mork (Walter) Metal Works Co., 174
Morrison Library, 79, 321-322, *321*
Morton, Craig, 67
Moskowitz, Moe, *108*, 153
Motels, 310-312
Motivity Center, 197
Muliben Bakery Cafe, *287*, 288
Multi-Cultural Arts Festival, 323
Murals, 200-204
Museums, 189-191
Museum of Paleontology, 191
Music, 197-199
MusicSource, 199

Nadine's, 266
Nagano, Kent, 198, *199*
Nash Hotel, 312
National Condom Day, *322*
National Condom Week, 323
National Guard, 143-144, 152
Neighborhood Preservation Ordinance, 41, 165
Neumann, Osha, 201-202, *203*, 204
New Delhi Junction, 268
New El Salvador Today (NEST)
New Light Senior Center, 336
New Pieces, 193
Newman Hall, 162
Newport, Gus, 123
Newton, Huey, 147, *147*
Niehaus, Edward F., 172, 174
Niehaus Villa, 172, *172*
Nikkei Senior Center, 336
Nimitz Way, 226, 236   —
Nine-Twenty-Four Gilman St., 298, *298*
Nobel laureates, 63-65
Nolo Press, 109
Noonan, Allen, 157

Noriega, Father, 10
North Berkeley (neighborhood), 46, 343
North Berkeley Hills (neighborhood), *40*, 42,
North Berkeley Senior Center, 336
North Waterfront Park, 218
Northbrae, 42
Northbrae Community Church, 161
North Cragmont, 42
North Face, The, *102*, 104-105
North Point Press, 109
Northrop, John H., 63
Northside (neighborhood), 46, 343
Nutcracker Suite, 323
Nyingma Institute, 162

Oakland International Airport, 360
Ocean View, 14-16, 20-25, 31-32, 49, 172-179, *173*
O'Hanlon, Richard, 189
Ohlone Indians, 6, 7-11, 153, 209
Ohlone Park, 153, 207-209, *207-208*
O'Keefe (John) Saloon, 177
Oliveto Cafe & Restaurant, 266, 285
Olmsted, Frederick Law, 18, 27, 68-69
Olympic Circle Sailing Club, 218
Omnivore, 262
One World Family, 157
Opera. *See* Berkeley Opera
Oppenheimer, J. Robert, 71, 98
Optometry Clinic, 339
Oriental Food to Go, 264
Ortega, Sergeant, 7,
Osborne, "Ozzie", 44, 256, *256*
Over 60 Health Clinic, 339

Pacific Film Archives, 191
Pacific Jewish Theater, 195
Pacific School of Religion, 164
Pacific School of Religion Museum, 164, 191
Packard, Emmy Lou, 74
Panini, 262
Pappy's, 239, 301
Park Hills Homeowner's Assoc., 41
Pasand Lounge, 299
Pasand Madras Cuisine, 268
Paschold (Carl) House, 177
Payne, Rev. Edward, 23
Payne, Frank H., 337
Peace and Freedom Party, *90*, 91, 148
Peck, Gregory, 67
Peet, Alfred, 283
Peet's Coffee, 283, *283*, 285
People's Cafe, 349
People's Food System, 153
People's History of Telegraph Avenue , 201-202, *203*
People's Park, 149-153, *150*
People's Park Annex, 153
Pepito's Mexican Deli, 271

Peralta, José Domingo, 12-14, 47, 51
Peralta, Luis Maria, 11-14, 51
Peralta, Vicente, 11-12
Pets, 324-326
Petrouchka, 267
Picante Taqueria and Cantina, 271, 299
Pickle Family Circus, 323-324
Pioneer Starch and Grist Mill, 15-16
Plearn Thai Cuisine, 276
Poetry, 200
Police, 30-31, 132-135, 141-152 passim
Police Review Commission, 128, 134-135
Portable Meals Program, 336
Portolá, Gaspar de, 7, 10
Pottery, 115, 323
Produce Markets, 295-296
Provo Park, 153, 207
Putzker, Otto, 23

Quakers, 155
Quitzlow, Sülgwynn, 195

Raleigh's, 241, 301
Rancho San Antonio, 11-14, 11
Ratcliff, Walter, 174
Reagan, Ronald, 92, 121, 123, 142, 148-149, 152, 155
Recreational Equipment Inc. (REI), 105, 112
Recreational Sports Facility, 76, 248
Rector, James, 152, 201-202
Recycled materials, 329
Recycling, 328-330
Red Family, 157
Red Mountain Tribe, 155
Redwood Railway, 227
Regional Oral History Office, 320
Rehabilitation Act of 1973, 314
Rental Housing, 343-346
Rental Services, 344
Republican Party, 120
Reynolds, Malvina, 98, 98, 202
Rich Potsticker House, 265
Ridefinder, 362
Ristorante Venezia, 199, 267
Roberts, Ed, 99, 99, 314
Robeson, Paul, 331
Role-Playing Games, 239
Romney, Hugh. See Wavy Gravy
Rose Garden, 186, 205, 206-207, 210-211
Rowell, Galen, 99-100
Rowell House, 186, 186
Rubin, Jerry, 100, 100, 142-143
Rumford, William, Jr., 122
Rumford, William, Sr. Medical Clinic, 339
Running trails, 241
Rusk, Dean, 67

Sack House, 185
Saclan Indians, 8
Sailing, 217-219, 244
Saint Heironymous Press, 93
Saint John's Presbyterian Church, 161, 168
Saint John's Senior Center, 336
Saint Joseph the Worker, 164
Saint Mark's Episcopal Church, 162, 170
Saint Mary Magdalen Church, 161, 162
Saint Procopius Latin Rite Church, 175
San Francisco Bay, 7-8, 219-221
San Francisco International Airport, 360
Sandwiches A-Go-Go, 257
Santa Fe Corporation, 220
Santa Fe Station, 143, 170
Sather, Jane K., 76, 78
Sather Gate, 60, 73, 76, 151
Saul's Deli, 257
Save San Francisco Bay Association, 220
Savio, Mario, 67, 142, 143, 201
Scheer, Robert, 120, 142, 157
Scherr, Max, 144
Schindff House, 182
Schmidt-Kennedy House, 182
Schmidt's Tobacco & Trading Co., 301
Schneider-Kroeber House, 181, 181
Schools, 16, 25, 330-336
Schoolhouse Creek, 177
Schultz, Gus, 164
Schuster (Gustavus) House, 174
Scott, Jack, 158
Seaborg, Glenn T., 63-64, 63, 71
Seale, Bobby, 147
Sedona Grill & Bar, 262
Seeger (Charles) House, 182
Segrè, Emilio, 64
Sellander House, 171
Senger House, 181
Senior citizens, 336
Serra, Junipero, 10
Share Old Spectacles, 339
Shattuck Ave. Spats, 301
Shattuck, Francis. K., 21, 25, 47, 51-52
Shattuck Hotel, 307
Shawl-Anderson Dance Center, 196, 197
Shelters, 350
Shin Shin, 265
Shorebird Park, 219
Shuffleboard, 241
Shuttles, 359-360
Siam Cafe, 277
Siam Cuisine, 277
Sibley, Robert, 223
Sidewalk Astronomers, 189
Siegel, Dan, 152
Sikh Dharma Brotherhood, 163
Sister Cities, 130-132

Skates, 262, 301
Ski Hut, The, 105
Smale, Stephen, 142
Small Press Distribution, 109
Smoking Pollution Control Ordinance, 342
Snyder, Gary, 38, 140
Solano Ave. Stroll, 324
Soliah, Steven, 158
Soltysik, Patricia "Mizmoon," 158
Soup Kitchen Heike, 257
South Berkeley (neighborhood), 49, 343
South Berkeley Senior Center, 336
Southside (neighborhood), 45
Spectator, The, 145
Spenger, Johann, 178
Spenger's Fish Grotto, 9, 104, 178, 275
Spenger's Fish Market, 292-293
Spicer, Jack, 38
Spring, John Hopkins 46, 51, 308
Sproul Plaza, 4, 55-56, 56, 74, 141, 324
Sproul, Robert Gordon, 32, 74
Stanford University, 245, 246-247
Stanley, Augustus Owlsley III, 142
Stanley, William M., 63
Starr, Rick, 56-57
Starry Plough, 196, 299
Steinberg, Leigh, 100
Steppenwolf Bar, 144
Stewart, Rev. James, 160, 162
Stone, Irving F., 67, 143
Strawberry Creek Park, 209
Strawberry Creek, 8, 10, 15, 20, 76, 221, 337
Straw into Gold, 115
Street names, 50-53
Strellinger, Maurice B., 53
Students Activities and Services, 61, 317
Stuffed Inn, 257
Sujatha's, 268
Summer camps, 241-242
Sushi-Ko, 269
Sushi Sho, 269
Swallow, The, 257
Sweeney, Wilmont, 35, 122
Swimming, 242-243
Symbionese Liberation Army (SLA), 158, 327

Tail of the Yak Trading Co., 115
Taiwan Restaurant, 265
Takara Sake Plant, 178, 303, 303
Tarthang Tulku Rinpoche, 162
Tattoo Archive, 115, 116
Taxi Unlimited, 113,154, 159
Telegraph Ave., 4, 27, 45, 45, 73, 135, 153
Telegraph Ave. Street Fair, 324
Temple of the Wings, 185, 196
Ten Speed Press, 109
Thai Buddhist Temple Mongkolratanaram, 163

Thai Bar-B-Q, 277
Theater, 193-195
Theater of the Blue Rose, 195
Thiele, O'Brian, 201, 204
Third World Liberation Front, 148-149
Third World Strike, 148-149
Thomas, John Hudson, 42, 168, 170, 171
Thomas, Capt. Richard, 185
Thousand Oaks (neighborhood), 46-47
Tilden Park, 4, 224-229, 224
Tilden, Charles Lee, 225
Tilden, Douglas, 100-101
Titus, Louis, 42
Tolman, Edward Chace, 80
Tool Lending Project, 319, 319
Top Dog, 257
Totland Park, 209, 213
Townes, Charles H., 64
Trailways Bus System, 360-361
Trinity Methodist Church, 164
Treaty of Guadalupe Hidalgo, 13
TRiP, 359
Triple Rock Brewery, 302, 304
Tufts House, 185
Tsing Tao, 265
Twinline, 314

UC Campus Tour, 74-85, 75
UC Extension, 335
UC Hotel, 307
UC Press, 109
UC Theater, 199
Uncommon Grounds, 285
University Archives, 320
University Art Museum, 84, 84, 189-190, 190
University of California, 17-21, 29, 30-31, 36-37, 54-85
University Guest Residence, 312
University House, 79
University Hotel, 312
University Lutheran Chapel, 164
University Police Department, 135
University Research Expeditions Program, 249
University Visitor Center, 74, 317
Urban Sculpture Garden, 193

Valasca (Juan) House, 174
Vegi Food, 278
Victorian Hotel, 308
Video Games, 241
Vietnam Day Committee (VDC), 142-143
Viet Nam Village, 264
Vinograd, Julia, 201, 348, 349
Vintage Health Library and Resource Center, 341
Vista College, 335-336
Viva! Taqueria, 272
Vollmer, August, 30, 133-134

Ward, Jay T., 101
Warren, Earl, 67
Warren, Robert Penn, 67
Waste, William, 318
Waste-More-Land, General, *144*
Waters, Alice, 113, *252*, 263
Weekes, Fred, 131
Weills, Anne, 157
Weinberg, Jack, 141
West Berkeley (neighborhood), 49-50, 343
West Berkeley Senior Center, 336
Westbrae (neighborhood), 47
Wheeler, Benjamin Ide, 28, 77, *82*
Whole Earth Access, 113, 115-116
Widener, Warren, 35, 122
Wildcat Canyon Regional Park, 229
Wilkes (Frederick and George) houses, 176
Willey, Rev. Samuel, 17, 19
Wilson, J. Stitt, 33, 119
Wilson, Lionel, 120, 123
Wilson, Pete, 67
Wine and Spirits Shops, 302-304
Winters, Michael, *314*
Women and Children's Services, 337
Women's Faculty Club. *See* Faculty Club,
  Women's

Women's Health Collective, Berkeley, 338
Women's Refuge, 350
Won Thai Cuisine, 277
Workingman's Party, 119
World Institute on Disability, 99, 315
Worth Ryder Art Gallery, 191
Wozniak, Steve, 67
Wrubel Gallery, 193

Yelland, William R., 170
YMCA, 250, 312
York, Dick, 145, 146, *146*, 149, 157, *351*
Yorkshire Fish and Chips, 276
Yoshimura, Wendy, 158
Yoshi's, 269, 299
Young Socialist Alliance, 146
Yrgin Indians, 8
YWCA, 250

Zachary's Chicago Pizza, 277
Zaentz, Saul, 101
Zellerbach Playhouse, 195
Zellerbach Hall, 76, *198*